Memories of RUDOLF NUREYEV

Nancy Sifton

ARNICA PRESS

Published by ARNICA PRESS

www.ArnicaPress.com

Copyright © 2021 Nancy Sifton

Cover photo by William J. Reilly

www.NancySiftonAuthor.com

This work is a memoir. It reflects the author's present recollections of her experiences over a period of years. Certain names, locations, and identifying characteristics may have been changed, and certain individuals are composites. Dialogue and events have been recreated from memory and, in some cases, have been compressed to convey the substance of what was said or what occurred. This work is also designed to provide information and historical record.

Printed in the United States of America.

ISBN: 978-1-955354-06-6

All rights reserved.

No part of this book may be reproduced or transmitted in any form or by any means, electronic or mechanical, including photocopying, recording, or by any information storage and retrieval system, without the prior written permission.

To Noreen who said I should….

To Dorothy who said I must…

And to all Nureyev fans – you know who you are!

*Nureyev curtain call, Metropolitan Opera House, 1974, NYC
Photo: William J. Reilly*

ACKNOWLEDGEMENTS

Writing this book has been a labor of love for decades. After combing through my diaries and numerous letters, I interviewed fellow Nureyev enthusiasts who shared their personal stories with me. Many of their stories are incorporated here, for they all reveal different aspects of Nureyev's character. For many years, Madeleine Nichols, former Curator of the Dance Division at Lincoln Center's Performing Arts Library in New York City, encouraged me to write. She ultimately led me to my publisher and expert editor, Sabrina Mesko, of Arnica Press.

Along the way I owe a wealth of gratitude to Sue Wells, whose writing workshop pushed me into the book's final stages. To my long-time friend, Susan Schwarz, whose crack proof reading was remarkable when I could no longer look at the text. I say "bravo!"to Linda Maybarduk, who read an initial draft and inspired me to continue whenever I became discouraged.

Yelena Demikovsky's support, technology assistance, and friendship has been a blessing since we first met while organizing the Nureyev Symposium in 1997. To Helene Ciolkovitch, whose writing for the Circle of Friends Newsletter inspired me, and whose friendship made it possible for me to attend the grand opening of the CNCS Museum (Centre National du Costume de Scene) in Moulins, France, where Nureyev's costumes are on display.

I owe my deep thanks to Barbara Cauterucci for providing me with numerous photographs taken by her late uncle, William Reilly. I always told Bill that if my book ever got published, I'd include many of his photos. To those who took their own photographs and shared them with me, I am deeply grateful.

A huge round of applause to all the fans, some scattered around the world and others who are no longer with us. You have enriched my life with your friendship and encouraged me along the way to the final product.

Lastly my great appreciation to Dr. Claude Blum, Irene Pozzi and Rosalind Bentley of the Rudolf Nureyev Foundation for their permission and interest in my unique account of what it was like to witness the genius of Nureyev.

For further information about the Rudolf Nureyev Foundation and their work to perpetuate his memory, visit their website. There you will find biographical information, news and events, books, DVDs, interviews, and other useful information about the life of this remarkable dancer.

Rudolf Nureyev Foundation
www.nureyev.org

TABLE OF CONTENTS

Acknowledgments 7
Introduction... 11

PART ONE
The Auction - Preview.. 19
Celebrity 27
Resourceful Fans 37
Waiting for Rudolf 57
Big George.. 85
Autographs 99
Photographs 115
Banners and Flowers 127
Anniversaries and Birthdays.. 157
23 Quai Voltaire 173
Rehearsals... 185
Randolf Neveroff 215
Dr. Nureyev 257
On the Road 265
The Petition 287
Other Performances... 311
Conductors and Conducting.. 321
Reflections 337

PART TWO
Anecdotes Introduction.. 355
The Show Must Go On 359
Missteps.. 373
Strikes 385
Pranks 399
Production Bloopers 405
The Auction - Final sale.. 427

PHOTO ALBUM 434
About the Author.. 439

"It is not man who chooses art. Art chooses man, and man must not escape. Man who escapes regrets it all his life."
~Rudolf Nureyev, Redbook Magazine, 1970~

INTRODUCTION

It all began with a photograph that changed my life. On a cold November day in 1964, I was leafing through a copy of *Life Magazine* and was suddenly mesmerized by a photo of Russian dancer Rudolf Nureyev in mid-flight, as if hanging on a trapeze. The caption said "This Mastery Won 89 Curtain Calls." Several pages of stunning photos followed, captured by the renowned photographer Lord Snowdon, who was documenting the premiere of Nureyev's *Swan Lake* production in Vienna. I decided anyone who received 89 curtain calls was worth seeing. I asked myself how could I possibly accomplish this, since I had never been out of the Midwest, except to visit relatives in Boston.

I had read about Nureyev's widely publicized defection from the Soviet Union in 1961 and even saw him in his early television appearances. But as of that November day, I wanted to see him in person, which at that time just seemed like a crazy dream.

I lived in a residential neighborhood in Detroit, Michigan, with my parents, two brothers and two sisters. My middle-class family had little interest in the arts, because we were too busy trying to make ends meet. Despite our modest means, my childhood was a happy one. My mother read me bedtime stories and fairy tales and I quickly developed a vivid imagination. When I was three years old, one of my uncles introduced me to classical music. I remember listening to Rossini or Tchaikovsky for hours, repeatedly pleading with him to "play the record again." Later, when one of my cousins took dance classes at school, I attended her ballet recitals. I loved what I saw.

Combining my love for music and dance, I began "putting on shows" for neighborhood friends. They were the "stars" and I was the all-round "backstage" person, organizing the program, directing, creating the publicity flyers and programs, providing the records for the music, and everything else.

Once I even choreographed a simple waltz to the music of Tchaikovsky's *Nutcracker*.

Our family huddled around the TV to watch numerous variety shows, including *The Ed Sullivan Show* that featured everything from circus acts to ballet. I was awestruck by all the beautiful people moving to gorgeous music. They created magic that seemed far away from my everyday neighborhood and life.

When I was in my teens, my aunt treated me, her daughter who studied ballet and another cousin, to a weekend trip to New York. We literally walked everywhere and spent the evening soaking our aching feet in the hotel tub. The highlight of the trip was attending my first Broadway show, *West Side Story*. It was captivating and after that, New York was all I could think about.

The local library became a source of information and a refuge, where I could read about things happening outside of working-class Detroit. I soon figured out that by reading weekly copies of *Variety*, I could keep up to date with what was going on in New York and elsewhere, even if the possibility of seeing a ballet performance was remote.

In April 1965, Nureyev appeared on the covers of both *Newsweek* and *Time* in the same week, to promote the London Royal Ballet's performances in the States. One of the stops on their cross-country tour was Detroit. Immediately I began plotting how I could see him. I managed to save a bit of babysitting money and realized I could afford to buy one or two tickets to the ballet. I took the bus to the Masonic Auditorium and sat way up "in the gods" for my first *Swan Lake* performance, which featured Rudolf Nureyev and Margot Fonteyn. I didn't even know the story, but everything "spoke" to me. The combination of the gorgeous scenery and costumes, the grandeur of Tchaikovsky's music, and the magic the two dancers created moved me to tears. Crazy as it sounds, it became an almost transcendental experience and I was hooked. People weren't indifferent to Rudolf Nureyev – you either loved or loathed him. I felt I was "called" somehow to witness his genius.

I decided then and there that I had to see them again and promptly returned the next night. The performance wasn't the same, but why? The answer was simple: the cast had changed. In those days, casting was not announced, so people took their chances on buying tickets hoping to see Fonteyn and Nureyev. I lucked out with that first performance, but noticed the difference with another cast. Somehow I expected everyone to perform like those two did. It was then that I realized how special they were.

After high school graduation, I worked at a university in order to attend evening classes. Many visiting artists appeared on campus, but unfortunately not the ballet. Auto-based Detroit, known as the "Motor City," morphed into Motown and ballet was not on the radar.

When the opportunity to travel arose, I joined one of those "six countries in six days" tours. The travel bug bit hard and I asked myself, "How can I see more of the world that also includes the ballet?" I considered becoming a flight attendant but, because I was a fraction of an inch under five feet tall, I didn't meet the height requirement.

A like-minded friend asked me if I'd like to move to San Francisco. I jumped at the chance, despite my mother's question, "Why so far away?" There I made new friends and explored the numerous things to do. The city was a cultural hub and I saw many visiting theatrical and ballet companies. The more I saw, the more I learned and when Nureyev brought to the city his own production of *Don Quixote* with the Australian Ballet, I made sure I was in the audience.

I felt somewhat restless, despite all that I learned and experienced. I had already taken that tour to Europe, but longed to return and my new friends were similarly inclined. Was it by chance that we all linked up? For months we plotted, budgeted, scrimped, saved, then when the time came, we quit our jobs and hit the road. The plan was to drive across country to New York and then travel throughout Europe for a year. In other words, it was our version of "The Grand Tour."

Before reaching New York, we stopped in Ottawa where the National Ballet of Canada was premiering Nureyev's new production of *Sleeping Beauty*. It was a gala performance and everyone was dressed to the nines. Without sufficient time to change, we arrived at the theatre in our travel clothes. It didn't matter to me. When the curtain went up, I felt somehow "at home."

The sumptuous production dazzled me and I vividly recall Nureyev's entrance in the Hunting Scene. He strode onto the stage in a fur-trimmed jacket and plumed hat. After removing it with a flourish, he was handed a dart, tossed it at a target, and, with a bit of stage magic, hit the center. He had the entire audience, including my fellow travelers, in the palm of his hand without dancing a single step.

We continued our adventures in Europe and North Africa. It was the early 70s when it really WAS possible to travel on $5 a day. We bought bread and cheese for sandwiches, stayed with host families and got to know the people and the places more personally than on an organized tour. After eleven months of nonstop travel, I longed to return to an English-speaking country again. We parted company and on arrival in London I began to ponder what my future would be. I knew I didn't want to return to Detroit and had no job waiting for me in San Francisco. My bank account was depleted and I couldn't think of borrowing money from anyone. "What now?" I asked myself with a mixture of fear and exhilaration.

I got a room in a London hostel and met a fellow American, who said that London Transport needed workers to hand out surveys in the various subway stations throughout the city. She also said she was looking for a roommate. Could that be me? For someone from the Midwest, raised by a family that worked hard just to get by, I did the unthinkable: I sold my return plane ticket in order to remain in London.

Despite living in a bedsitter in Earl's Court, I was incredibly happy. Every day I was assigned to a new section of London and on our frequent shifts from handing out passenger surveys, I explored each area, thus getting to know the city. When the survey finished, I was asked to work in the office to compile the results. The salary wasn't much, but it paid my weekly rent.

Then I registered with a part-time agency that placed me in various office jobs. My weekly pay barely allowed for "extras." Sometimes I asked myself, "Do I buy soap this week or spend 50p on a standing room ticket for the ballet?" I worked by day and spent my evenings at the Royal Opera House.

The 1970s was a wonderful time to be in London. Many of the greatest names in the performing arts were seen on the city's stages: Pavarotti, Sutherland, Domingo at the opera; Olivier, Scofield, Guinness, Richardson, O'Toole, Finney, Redgrave in the theatre; Fonteyn and Nureyev, Sibley and Dowell at the Royal Ballet; and visiting companies like the Bolshoi with Maximova and Vasiliev, the Stuttgart with Haydee and Cragun and other companies like Bejart, the Netherlands and the Danes – it was a cultural feast. London became my classroom as I attended lectures at the National Gallery, visited historic houses and museums, and above all, made new friends, for I soon discovered I was not alone in my enthusiasm for the arts and especially the ballet.

Tickets for Fonteyn and Nureyev's performances were always sold out and huge queues filled Floral Street at the side of the Royal Opera House, all hoping to get in. After queuing for numerous performances, I began to recognize familiar faces in line and we became friends. I learned a great deal from them in our countless enthusiastic discussions.

This was the very first time I got to meet Fonteyn and Nureyev face to face. It was a rare occasion when both of them graciously signed autographs after the performance. I found myself in front of those two larger than life figures. I was transfixed.

When Nureyev began his peripatetic schedule, while performing with other companies, groups of us made plans to travel in order to see him. We built friendships with many of the dancers as well as with Nureyev's agent, so we could keep abreast of performance dates.

A small core of us followed Nureyev's career to the very end. His passion, commitment and galvanizing personality made us curious to see him in everything he challenged himself to do, whether classical or modern dance, television, films, a stage musical or conducting engagement. We knew instinctively that we would not see such a phenomenon again in our lifetime. We began exchanging letters in all parts of the world, giving our report of performances others were unable to see.

Rudolf Nureyev changed my life because he awakened in me an intrinsic desire to be more adventurous, resourceful, resilient, and grateful. He inspired me to envision to "be more" and "do more." He enriched my life in so many ways. His sense of curiosity and desire to never stop learning helped me develop mine. Motivated by Nureyev, I have traveled, experienced other cultures, and made lasting friendships far beyond what my childhood imagination could have envisioned. It is this inspiration that motivated me to write this book and share it with those who might not have seen Rudolf Nureyev perform, and to resurrect memories from those who have had the great fortune to witness the otherworldly presence that he exuded.

Part One

Nureyev curtain call, Metropolitan Opera House, NYC, 1976
Photo: Nancy Sifton

"I just love seeing and doing things. Beautiful things. They please me."
~Rudolf Nureyev, Classical Music, Spring, 1983~

THE AUCTION ~ PREVIEW

Le Spectre de la Rose, Joffey Ballet's Diaghilev Season, NYC, 1979. Photo: William J. Reilly

"**H**ave you seen today's paper?" exclaimed my friend who phoned me at work. "Not yet," I replied, somewhat puzzled by the urgency in her voice. "There's a full-page ad in *The Times* about the Nureyev Auction at Christie's." It was January 6, 1995, exactly two years since the death of Rudolf Nureyev. "Look in the first section, Page A-18."

The first portion of *The New York Times* is generally reserved for news, rather than arts coverage. We were surprised that such an ad, which must have cost a fortune, appeared in the front section. A stunning photo of Nureyev in one of his signature roles, *Le Corsaire*, captivated the reader's gaze. Beneath it, emblazoned in bold letters were the words, "Dance home with something

Nureyev loved!" The text continued: "For every balletomane, for each dedicated collector, for all who thrill to the touch of genius; here on display and for auction, is the never-before-seen Rudolf Nureyev Collection."

I was beginning to get a sinking feeling in the pit of my stomach, as my friend continued reading over the phone:

"Now you can own, forever, the objects he chose and loved and lived with. Ancient sculpture he couldn't live without. Neo-Classical furniture he reclined on. A carpet he strode on, Old Masters he gazed on. Costumes he twirled in; capes he swirled. Slippers he leapt with; outfits he kept. Jewelry that adorned him; those caps he adored. It's a once-in-a-genius opportunity!"

The text was truly embarrassing. Immediately after discovering this advertisement, we phoned Christie's Press Department to register a complaint. We felt that the ad was rather tasteless and unworthy of both Nureyev's memory and Christie's reputation. A very professional staff member said the message would be relayed to the proper person and mentioned that others had called with the same complaint.

The fans knew that Nureyev's belongings were being sold at auction to benefit the Rudolf Nureyev Dance Foundation. However, the sale was postponed after his sister and niece contested the dancer's will, and the contents of Nureyev's apartment were frozen by court order. Nevertheless, we put our names on Christie's mailing list in order to be informed when the Auction would take place. In December of 1994, we received letters from Christopher Burge, Chairman of North and South America's division at Christie's New York, announcing "with great pride" that "the long-awaited sale of the Rudolf Nureyev Collection" would take place on January 12th and 13th, with a pre-sale exhibition open to the public from January 7th through January 12th, 1995.

Christie's catalogs were ordered, but mine never arrived. I stopped at the auction house located at Park Avenue and 59th Street to complain that my catalog went astray, so they gave me another in a large black shopping bag with NUREYEV in bright red letters printed on the side. I heard frantic hammering as workers were preparing for the pre-auction viewing the following morning, while hanging some of the enormous paintings that adorned the walls of Rudolf's New York apartment. Christie's wanted to recreate the feeling of his apartment, by placing the objects as they were in the Dakota when Nureyev lived there. An array of mannequin torsos displayed many of Nureyev's costumes. Attendants stuffed tissue paper into the shoulders to make them more form fitting, because the dancer had broad shoulders tapering into a small waist.

The thought of all his costumes, ballet shoes and possessions being sold at Auction made me feel terribly depressed. There had been talk of a museum, but it never materialized and once everything was sold piecemeal and scattered everywhere, the physical evidence of Nureyev's legacy would be lost.

Publicity surrounding Nureyev's death in 1993 was quite unprecedented - front-page news in most newspapers, as was his defection from the Soviet Union in 1961. Similarly, the media frenzy leading up to the Auction was also remarkable. A full-page ad about the Auction even appeared in the New York City Ballet Playbill. So it came as no surprise, when attendance during Christie's six-day viewing period of the Nureyev Collection set a new record.

That first day of the viewing on Saturday, January 7th, left me with very mixed emotions. I was eager to see his costumes up close and admire his possessions, but I knew it would be difficult, because we would never see them all in one place again. A friend I met at a Nureyev performance many years ago, came with me for moral support. We went through the revolving doors and immediately saw the costumes displayed in the window. As we headed to the second floor, we heard the music from *Swan Lake* accompanied by the crowd's laughter. It was then I realized they were showing the footage from *Swine Lake*, where Nureyev danced with Miss Piggy on *The Muppets Show* in 1977.

Christie's had prepared a twenty minute introductory video in a waiting area on the second floor. Narrated by Nureyev's friend and former Royal Ballet dancer Lynn Seymour, the video contained interviews with Lord Snowdon, many of Nureyev's dance colleagues from the Royal Ballet, as well as Christopher Burge of Christie's. They all discussed Nureyev's passion for collecting and how he wanted to be surrounded by beautiful things. In between the interviews were film clips from *Le Corsaire, Marguerite and Armand, Sleeping Beauty* and his many other roles. People sat on sofas and chairs around the screen and seemed transfixed. We could tell that even visitors who had never had the privilege to see Rudolf Nureyev dance, were equally mesmerized. The video gave a very good picture of Nureyev the artist, as well as Nureyev the collector.

In a short time, crowds gathered three or four rows deep around the video. Others went to the Christie's information counter asking if the video could be purchased. The staff explained that it was made specifically for Christie's and was not for sale. There were numerous auction leaflets, as well as pens and notepads everywhere to write down lot numbers. We decided to register so we could bid on some items, especially Nureyev's dance shoes that were being sold in various lots, starting at $40.

Adjacent to the video display were glass cases containing some of Nureyev's hats from various ballets, such as his plumed hat from *Sleeping Beauty*, his turban from *La Bayadere* and another hat from *Bach Suite*.

Once we found ourselves in the main gallery, we became truly overwhelmed. The contents of Nureyev's New York apartment were on display for all to see. The walls were lined with paintings, and his voluminous collection of colorful kilims and textiles were draped everywhere – on sofas, on the Jacobean canopy bed, rolled up under the table, displayed on sideboards – the place was ablaze with exotic colors. Over the dining room table was the elaborate Venetian chandelier and on the back wall some of the Chinese wallpaper. Attendees walked in, stopped in their tracks, and exclaimed, "He LIVED like this? It looks like a museum."

Crammed into any spare space were more costumes, including Margot Fonteyn's *Swan Lake* tutu, which she apparently gave to Nureyev for his collection. Right next to it was Rudolf's costume from *Giselle*. "How can they sell these?" people asked. Just as many remarked about how small Nureyev's costumes seemed. "But he looked so big on stage – look at that tiny waist. It's the same size as Fonteyn's!" I spotted a New York City Ballet corps dancer staring at both costumes in a daze. Suddenly he became overwhelmed, his eyes filled with tears and he had to walk away.

By this time there were so many people viewing the Collection that we actually had to queue to see each object. There was such a crush I thought the crowd size and force must have surely been against fire regulations.

I slowly made my way past the hundreds of people and thousands of textiles to a large bookcase containing many of Nureyev's books. There were several sets of them in Russian, French and English including the complete works of Byron, Pushkin, Tolstoy and quite a few on Stanislavski. Nureyev's unquenchable curiosity was reflected in the type of books he accumulated. Dance books abounded - some personally autographed - but so did other genres such as theatre, architecture, poetry, history, art, several auction catalogs, psychology and a few surprises such as yoga or fly-fishing. Mixed in were murder mysteries, a few best sellers, novels and humor books, probably given to him from fans or friends.

Also on display were some of the musical instruments the dancer collected, including a mandolin, his harpsichord, and a large barrel organ that, when cranked by an obliging staff member, played *Adeste Fidelis,* which could be heard periodically throughout the day.

We bumped into fellow Nureyev fans and one asked if we had seen the items in the back room. She had done her homework and had written down the lot numbers of everything she specifically wanted to see. We followed her directions to a room in one corner of the gallery with a "Staff Only" sign in front of it and in smaller letters, "For more Nureyev items backstage, please see a staff member." I asked if we might go back and the staff member showed us what looked like a storage room, with rows and rows of Nureyev shopping bags on shelves behind a caged area. An attendant stood behind a long table, asked us for the specific lot number we wanted to see, fetched the proper shopping bag and placed it on the table for our inspection. Most of the items in this "Back Stage" area were memorabilia that the Christie's staff had undoubtedly no time to catalog. Consequently the lot number we requested was merely described as "a bag of hats."

In this bag I spotted a red Stetson cowboy hat complete with a red ostrich feather. Some friends and I gave it to Nureyev in 1984, when he danced in Texas and flew mid-week to Philadelphia for a gala in which he performed *Bach Suite* in a Baroque plumed hat. I was so touched to see that he had kept it all those years.

Also in the bag was his sable hat that he had been photographed in numerous times as well as a sailor hat, straw hats, baseball caps, berets, knitted caps, peaked caps – everything he wore off stage. There must have been two-dozen hats in the bag and I made a note of the lot number with the idea of buying back the plumed red Stetson hat as a souvenir.

In another lot were miscellaneous items including the script from the film *Exposed*. I looked for some sort of margin notes that Nureyev might have made, but there were none. Except for some signed contracts when he appeared in *The King and I* and had to join the Actor's Union, the only thing in writing was Nureyev's signature.

Our friend discovered a book of photographs and when she opened it exclaimed, "Oh! These are the ones I gave him." She had taken photos at the curtain calls of his 50th birthday gala at the Metropolitan Opera House in New York, as well as a collection of various stage door pictures. In another album were photos given to him by one of his fans, when Nureyev was presented with an Honorary Doctorate degree in Philadelphia. Each of us rediscovered something we had given him over the years. The Christie's attendant was quite excited and exclaimed to her colleague, "These people actually gave him these things!"

After about an hour of exploring various lots, we were asked to make room for other people who wanted to look at things, so we reluctantly returned to the main gallery. By this time the crowds were so thick we could barely move. Determined to see as much as possible before closing time, we queued to see the contents of some glass cases that housed more memorabilia. One case included evidence of Nureyev's eclectic taste including precious rocks, seashells, ceramic statues, a crystal, swords, walking sticks, a stuffed Snoopy dog no doubt given to him by a fan – Nureyev obviously kept everything.

We finally came to the shoes - loads and loads of them - all in shopping bags and within easy reach of anyone to slip a pair into their own bag. It was truly tempting, but we also noticed security cameras everywhere.

As we admired Nureyev's collection of lithographs and antique maps on one wall, I heard someone calling my name. It was my colleague from the Performing Arts Library at Lincoln Center. She introduced me to a Russian gentleman from Radio Moscow and asked if he could interview me. He shoved a microphone in my face and asked, "So what do you think of all of this?" I replied that it was difficult to take it all in, because there was so much of it. I told him that I had followed Nureyev's career since 1965 and thought it was a crime that many of his costumes were being auctioned off to the highest bidder. Seizing the opportunity, I added, "I only hope that someone listening to this with the financial means will buy those costumes and put them in a museum where they belong."

My colleague nodded her head in approval and signaled me to "keep going." Realizing that most people in Russia had never seen Nureyev dance, I added, "Unless you had been there and had seen him dance, you can't imagine the impact he had on so many people's lives. The power he generated on stage was unimaginable. The energy in the theatre shifted when he stepped on stage, much like the energy in this room surrounded by all his things has now shifted. You can actually feel it."

Following the interview I bumped into more friends and one of them mentioned to be sure and see the photographs "up front." I noted the lot numbers and asked to see them. An attendant showed us into a room at the front that had a large table with several chairs. After retrieving the specific box we requested, she placed it on the table. The box was enormous – about three feet wide – and contained at least 500 photographs in no particular order. There were portraits by Lord Snowdon, Richard Avedon and Cecil Beaton, various performance and rehearsal shots, as well as snapshots taken from vacations or given to Nureyev by fans. Our impression was that when Nureyev's apartment was cleaned out, all the photographs were scooped up into a box and listed as a "lot" to be bid on "as is." None of the photos were labeled or dated, but since we were familiar with most of them, we knew the exact ballet, date, and so on. The attendant was impressed and said to us, "If I were to bid on one, I'd choose this one," and fished out a photo of the dancer putting on his make-up for *Petrushka*. But, of course, single photographs couldn't be purchased.

We managed to look through the entire box and even found snapshots of ourselves in the enormous Stage Door crowds that surrounded Nureyev wherever he went. It was a strange feeling seeing ourselves in his photo collection. The attendants got very animated watching us sort through the photos and remarked to one another, "They actually knew Rudolf Nureyev. Some of them are in photos with him!"

I noticed someone standing in the doorway watching the fans sharing their enthusiasm and discussing the photos. "Oh, that was when we went to Paris to see him perform," and so on. The woman joined us at the table saying, "You seem to know a lot about him. I'm writing a book on Nureyev."

"You must be Diane Solway," I replied. I had recently read that she had signed a book contract. She gave me her card and for the next few years I helped Diane with research, transcribed numerous interviews and provided photos for her book, *Nureyev, His Life*.

Rudolf's spirit was in the room that day, bringing everyone together. Long after his death, Rudolf Nureyev remained a strong presence, continually changing my life.

"I think of myself as a dancer, first and last, who happened to become a star."
~Good Morning America interview with Nancy Dussalt, July 1976~

CELEBRITY

*Closing night at the Metropolitan Opera House, NYC, July 26, 1980.
Photo: William J. Reilly*

Sometimes it is truly difficult to realize the scope of Rudolf Nureyev's "celebrity." His much-publicized defection made worldwide headlines and the press couldn't get enough of him. He became the most photographed dancer in history, graced international magazine covers, newspapers, society pages, and television - all without really trying. Rudolf never actively sought publicity, but nevertheless the journalists flocked to him. The interviews all usually included the same question, "When will you stop dancing?" He had been asked that as early as the 1960s. Nureyev became a master at fielding questions, once teasing a reporter, "Don't you love these journalist intrigues?" However, if the subject was dance, he could speak eloquently – often in English, Italian or French.

His name became a household word, synonymous with the best in his field. A sportswriter once profiled hockey player Wayne Gretzky, by saying he was "The Rudolf Nureyev of ice hockey." On another occasion, Vladimir Horowitz gave a concert at New York's Lincoln Center on the same day Nureyev was performing across the plaza at the Metropolitan Opera House. The enormous crowds queuing to buy tickets made the plaza look like a mass gathering. After mentioning the crowds, the press stated, "Horowitz is the Nureyev of pianists."

Even if people didn't know how to pronounce his name, they knew who Rudolf Nureyev was. In an interview with *Paris Metro* in March 1977 he explained, "My name is pronounced Noo-Ray-Yev or Nooree. The Tartars used many Arab words. It means sun, ray or halo."

The *New York Times* even used both Fonteyn and Nureyev in a 1973 crossword puzzle. The clues were "Well-known Dame" and "Well-Known Ex-Russian."

Agatha, a British comic strip, ran for some time. It depicted the young Agatha inviting Rudolf Nureyev for dinner or tea and even tried out his name, when she told her mother she would marry him.

In Francois Truffaut's 1970 film, *Bed and Board*, the heroine is seen in bed reading Nureyev's autobiography while a poster of the dancer is above the bed.

New York's Russian Tea Room, one of Nureyev's favorite hangouts, named a drink in his honor.

There was even a racehorse named after him. This didn't please Nureyev who remarked that if something happened to the horse, headlines would read, "Nureyev Breaks Leg."

One day while waiting for the elevator at work, I overheard a young woman complaining to a co-worker about someone. "He thinks he's God's gift to women. Really, who does he think he is, anyway?" Her co-worker agreed. "Yeah. After all, he's no Rudolf Nureyev."

During a 1970s broaD.C.ast of the Leningrad Ice Show, one of the commentators was the American TV actress Sally Struthers. She was ad-libbing about a current tune that everyone danced to, whether they could dance or not. She ad-libbed, "We can't all be great dancers like Rudolf Nureyev." Her Russian co-host immediately tried covering up by commenting on the skaters, but the entire stadium was buzzing when they heard the name she uttered. Both Nureyev's image and name were banned in the Soviet Union after his defection, but the people still remembered him.

Rudolf Nureyev popularized ballet in the West and was largely responsible for the great "Ballet Boom" in the 1970s. By 1975, ballet became so popular that even free tickets to performances in Central Park were difficult to obtain. He revolutionized the image of the male dancer, giving him equal status with the ballerina. His influence was felt for generations and I know several friends who became dancers due to his inspiration.

Rudolf also adorned the pages of fashion magazines with his trademark caps or woolen hats, and his stylish boots, jackets, and fancy coats. Many copied his style, including his haircut.

He was the darling of the jet set, not because he sought these people out, but because they wanted to be seen with one of the most popular, charismatic figures of the era. Nureyev was photographed dancing with Liz Taylor in a disco, doing a tango dip with ballerina Natalia Makarova at a party at Maxim's, yachting with shipping magnates Aristotle Onassis or Stravos Niarchos in Greece, weekending in the country with Lee Radziwill and Jacqueline Kennedy, attending receptions with Prince Charles and Princess Diana, giving ballet lessons to Princess Margaret, dining with King Hussein of Jordan or Princess Grace of Monaco, spending weekends in the Manila palace of Ferdinand and Amelda Marcos, seeking advice from neighbors John Lennon, Yoko Ono, Leonard Bernstein and Lauren Bacall, and cavorting on television with the Muppets, Jimmy Durante, Fred Astaire, and Julie Andrews.

Deep down, Rudolf Nureyev was incredibly shy, and being photographed was easier than carrying on conversations. Rudolf's method of expression was the dance and people were often disappointed that he could be quite abrupt or ill at ease in conversation. While in a crowded elevator someone once asked Nureyev, "Say, aren't you that great dancer. . .?" Rudolf blushed and looked down, then cracked a wry smile and replied, "Well, sometimes." Someone else thought he was one of the Beatles.

Despite his fame, he was quite down to earth. In England, Nigel Gosling, Nureyev's "adopted father" and mentor, once told me that there was a scarcity of mirrors in the dancer's Richmond house. Yet they surrounded him in the dance studio, where it really mattered.

Nureyev was a keen observer of human behavior. Curiosity drove him throughout his life but given his background, he seemed more comfortable with the common people, and it was this side of him that he revealed to us, his fans. I recall this story told by a London friend in 1978:

She was giving a dinner party and one of the invitees asked if they could bring somebody along. That "somebody" was Rudolf Nureyev. He arrived with a cold and used endless tissues; even borrowing some when his supply ran out. He didn't quite know what to say and wasn't in a talkative mood with the dinner guests. The party hosts had two dogs that had been shut out of the dining area and Rudolf asked if he could go and see them. He disappeared and some time later the guests went to find him. There was Rudolf, sitting on the kitchen floor with one of the dogs on his knee. He probably sensed he was making the atmosphere strained by his presence and felt more comfortable with the dogs.

Another example came from a London taxi driver named Steve, who shared a cup of tea with Nureyev. The story appeared in London's *Sunday Observer* on February 27, 1977 and related by TV host Russell Harty, two years after Nureyev did an interview with him. The busy dancer was reluctant about fixing a date or time for the interview. When he finally agreed, Harty proposed a light lunch and an amble to the television studio. He went to collect Nureyev at Covent Garden where he was rehearsing. Rudolf emerged, smiled warmly, said he didn't want any lunch and intended to go home. He bid farewell to Harty, thus ending the carefully prepared TV interview. "Would you like to take my taxi?" Harty offered. Nureyev said no, he had his car. The nervous host inquired, "What time will you be back?" Rudolf just smiled and left. Harty told his taxi driver to follow Nureyev and use his East End initiative to get Rudolf back as soon as possible.

The taxi driver followed Nureyev to Richmond, parked behind him, rolled down the taxi window and offered to take him back to the studio. Harty said later that he had little reason to disbelieve the taxi-driver's account of what happened next.

Taxi driver: "Well, 'e's a right charmer, that Rudolf. 'E says 'e might as well come back with me 'cos it'll save 'im the petrol! So I says I'll wait. So 'e says 'you'd better come in and 'ave a cuppa tea while you're waitin' Steve' -- 'cause that's me name, see. So Randolf makes this cuppa tea and says is there any 'urry and I say not as far as I'm concerned, mate, there isn't. So 'e sits down and I says when did you start all this ballet dancin' lark, then? An 'e starts to tell me so I lets 'im 'ave his say, right? An' it's all comin' out, Russia and everything an' like there's no stoppin' 'im. Course I watched 'im on the program, didn't I? Well, I tell you, I got more out of that Randolf Nureyev in a quarter of an hour than that bleeder got out of 'im in an hour on telly."

Photographs of blocked traffic captured the enormous Stage Door crowds that gathered just for a glimpse of Nureyev. His performances were attended by the Royal Family in England, especially Princess Margaret and Princess Diana, who were particularly fond of the ballet. Hollywood celebrities like Elizabeth Taylor, Paul Newman, Joanne Woodward, and Lauren Bacall were very much in evidence in New York audiences, along with Jacqueline Kennedy Onassis and her family. In France, we saw Maria Callas, Catherine Deneuve and Sofia Loren attending his performances.

Fonteyn and Nureyev, often billed as "the hottest item in show business," caused enormous lines at the Box Office. In order to guarantee full houses, casting was not announced, but of course the fans knew "from the horse's mouth" by asking him about his dates at the Stage Door. As Rudolf told us, "If I don't know when I'm dancing, then nobody knows!"

I distinctly recall two police cars pulling up in front of Lincoln Center where we queued for tickets. We thought they were there for crowd control but instead they asked us, "Do you know which nights Nureyev is dancing?" After providing them with the dates, the officers sat in the patrol car studying the schedule so they could buy tickets to Nureyev's performances.

During those Royal Ballet tours at the Met, "hawkers" in the Opera House lobby sold souvenir programs. Rudolf used to do a great imitation of their thick "New Yawk" accents. These men would shout, "Get yaw programs heah, stories and photographs." One enterprising seller even announced, "Nureyev will sign posters for you – only $3." Of course Rudolf knew nothing about this sales pitch, but autographed them anyway.

Tickets for Nureyev's performance sold out in the first few hours they went on sale. For his Broadway *Nureyev and Friends* programs, the frazzled Box Office staff told me they sold over $200,000 worth of tickets in the first two hours. For his historic Diaghilev Program with the Joffrey Ballet in which Nureyev performed roles made famous by the legendary Vaslav Nijinsky, a full-page ad in the *New York Times* billed the performances as "the most exciting dance event of 1979." The entire season was sold out and scalpers bought tickets for all forty standing room places for opening night. When irate fans rang the Nederlander Organization and complained to the producers, the next day the Box Office put a two-ticket per person limit on all standing room. Despite this, standing room was often three rows deep. By the final performance, people were simply desperate to attend and I noticed even Lee Radziwill was in standing room.

Because this Broadway engagement was the talk of the town, comics Steve Martin and Gilda Radner did a spoof of *Spectre de la Rose* for television's *Saturday Night Live*. Clad in tights, Martin parodied Nureyev, including the famous leap out the window, while Radner flitted around in her long tulle dress. At its conclusion, gun-toting KGB agents presented the couple with floral bouquets.

In addition to his innate sense of movement, Nureyev had a quick ear for voices and did great impressions, particularly of those with unique accents. This ability to "digest" words served him well, learning English, French, Italian, and some German during his long career.

When he appeared with Martha Graham's dance company in 1975, the theatre had 75,000 mail order applications for tickets. Prior to this time period, ballet and modern dance remained separate, but because of Nureyev's immense curiosity to learn all kinds of dance, he helped bridge the gulf between the two dance styles. The press once quoted Nureyev as an "international corporation" for introducing audiences to many worldwide dance companies, who wouldn't otherwise be able to fill the theatres without the name of Rudolf Nureyev.

Of course the critics felt differently. Most believed he was "finished" even as early as the 1960s, but the public continued to come to his performances. In one of the long lines waiting to buy tickets, I overheard someone remark, "If Nureyev isn't good anymore, why are all these people in line to buy tickets?" Some twenty years after he arrived in the West, Rudolf Nureyev still sold out 50,000 seats in huge arenas and amphitheatres.

Following the defections of Natalia Makarova and Mikhail Baryshnikov in the early 70s, several Jewish musicians were allowed out of the Soviet Union in 1979 and gave a concert at Carnegie Hall. These same musicians ended up playing for Nureyev's "encore" Diaghilev season at Lincoln Center and Rudolf acknowledged them nightly with a bow.

After Nureyev completed his performances, the Bolshoi Ballet moved into the same theatre. Security was very tight. The Russian presenters insisted that a photo of Nureyev in the Playbill be removed as well as any posters, since Rudolf was still considered "persona non grata" in the Soviet Union. It was curious, however, that many of the Bolshoi dancers asked their fans in hushed tones, "How is Nureyev doing?"

Shortly afterward, Alexander Godunov defected followed by Valentina and Leonid Kozlov, as well as the skating couple the Protopopovs. A cartoon appeared in one of the papers, depicting several defectors dropping in by balloon and helicopter, captioned: "But comrade, can Lincoln Center take them all?"

The Moscow Symphony was scheduled to appear in New York but was suddenly cancelled. One journalist wrote, "The authorities were probably afraid they'd return as the Moscow String Quartet!"

The National Ballet of Cuba appeared at Lincoln Center opposite Nureyev with the National Ballet of Canada. On his free nights, Nureyev went to see the Cuban company. The Cuban dancers along with their director, Alicia Alonso, also went to see Nureyev perform – a case of art trumps politics.

Whenever Rudolf attended other performances, the audience knew it. Usually arriving at the last minute to avoid attention, Nureyev slipped into an aisle seat. Somehow the electricity he generated soon had the audience buzzing and people in the upper regions of the theatre stared at him through their opera glasses. At the intervals, he was bombarded by well-wishers or autograph hounds and there were always throngs of people gathered around him, often just staring as if transfixed.

Arriving at one performance, the crowds were so thick around him that an usher announced, "Clear the aisle, HE is here." Nureyev entered and smiled at everyone as he headed for his seat.

Since I attended quite a few other performances myself, I often spotted him but always respected his privacy. If by chance he saw me, as happened one day when I nearly bumped into him on the staircase – he was going up and I was coming down – we said a brief hello and that was it. But wherever he went people remarked, "I sense Rudolf's in the audience," and sure enough, he was.

He literally changed the temperature, or perhaps it was his way of "transmitting" subtle energy that the public felt.

During one of his Broadway *Nureyev and Friends* seasons, a photographer friend tacked a sign on the Stage Door that read, "Rudolf Nureyev Avenue." After the closing matinee, it took Rudolf ten minutes to get from the Stage Door to his waiting car, a mere few feet away. For every three steps forward, he was pushed four steps back due to the crush of people trying to shake his hand or get an autograph. When he finally reached his vehicle, he turned to the crowd in a mock "I made it!" gesture and collapsed in the back seat.

That same evening, I had a ticket for a performance of the Joffrey Ballet. Nureyev also attended. His appearance caused a sensation as crowds of dancers and well-wishers flocked around him. When he got up at the interval, a parade followed him from one side of the theatre to the other. Ushers tried to control the crowds that were blocking the lobby doors in a desperate effort to catch just a glimpse of the famous dancer. Rudolf was talking to the young Ron Reagan, Jr., who had just joined the Joffrey Ballet, and appeared to be giving him some advice. Only when the lights blinked on and off for people to return to their seats, did the crowds finally disburse.

In 1979 Nureyev created his original production of *Manfred*, based on Lord Byron. There seemed to be a Byron Boom, because I couldn't find any books on Byron in my local library.

Rudolf was injured for the Paris premiere of *Manfred,* yet wanted the production to be seen in New York, but that never materialized. In 1981 *Manfred* was revised for the Zurich Ballet and later performed in Washington and Chicago, but was never performed in New York. However, the city was decorated with life-sized posters of Rudolf Nureyev at the bus stops and other areas advertising Santori Vodka. The posters showed a smiling Nureyev posing next to the bottle with the quote, "Is very good vodka." He said he did the ad, because it helped pay to bring *Manfred* to America.

After he performed *Manfred* in Chicago, Rudolf could barely get out of the alleyway Stage Door to the relative safety of his car due to the crush of people waiting for him. Just as the car reached the street, a tour group of about fifty teenagers passed by. They asked who was in the car that caused such crowds. We told them, "Rudolf Nureyev." "I've always wanted to meet him," one girl exclaimed, and with that she dashed over to his car, now caught in street traffic, and knocked on the window. Rudolf rolled the window down and the teenager stuck her entire head and shoulders inside, shook his hand and gushed, "I've always wanted to meet you!" She pulled back and rejoined her friends, while Rudolf couldn't stop laughing. Still waiting for the traffic to move, he turned in my direction and asked, "Who was THAT?" I shrugged, having no idea, but he found the whole incident very amusing.

When Rudolf was joined by the Boston Ballet in their production of *La Sylphide* on Broadway, we spotted dancers and other celebrities in the audience at every performance. On opening night, half of the New York City Ballet was present, along with George Balanchine. Also spotted were Anton Dolin, Valery and Galina Panov, and numerous others including impresarios Hochhauser and Edgerton. Spotting me at the interval, Mr. Hochhauser asked, "Do you think this program will go down well in London?" I assured him it would. Later at the Stage Door, Rudolf told one of the fans, "I just love dancing this ballet." "Yes, we can tell," we chimed in unison.

Emerging from the depths of the Metropolitan Opera Stage Door one afternoon, Rudolf, as usual, had dozens of people following him. He crossed Broadway to eat at a nearby restaurant. Since Broadway is a wide street, many of the stragglers were stuck at the curb waiting for the traffic light to change. Rudolf, by now well ahead and across the street, glanced back to make sure the "kiddie poos" were safe. That was the endearing way he called us sometimes. Once at his destination, he turned, waved and the crowd disbursed.

After a matinee, Rudolf left the Met and, like the Pied Piper, had a throng of people following him. He carried a small bouquet given to him by a young girl. When he got to the corner, he turned to everyone, waved the bouquet as a signal that it was far enough to follow, and crossed the street. He strolled towards his Dakota apartment on 72nd Street, occasionally looking in shop windows and enjoying the warm sunshine. Dressed for winter, people stared at him, exclaiming after he passed, "That was Rudolf Nureyev!" When he reached 72nd Street, an Italian sweater shop caught his eye so he disappeared into the store. A few of us were meeting friends for dinner on the same street and as we passed the shop, we observed Rudolf looking at long-sleeved woolen sweaters. It was a curious thing having this private glimpse of the dancer who, just minutes before, had over 3,000 people at his feet, hordes of them clamoring for his signature, and suddenly walking almost anonymously through the streets of Manhattan.

In 1981, Nureyev appeared with the Vienna Ballet at the amphitheatre by the Acropolis in Greece. The Viennese press reported "Nureyev Delirium" because the demand for tickets was so great – 30,000 tickets on the first day. The unnumbered seats at the Herod Atticus were more than sold out, with numerous extra people squeezing in on the stone benches. Those who attended reported they were disappointed, because while they waited after the performance, they never saw Rudolf. Apparently he was flown in from one of the islands via helicopter, and on subsequent evenings was provided with such police protection, that they could not catch even a glimpse of him afterwards. Even in his 40s, Rudolf Nureyev was a true celebrity.

*"Being a slave means you do something without pleasure.
Here there is always some exchange, some kind of give and take."*
~Rudolf Nureyev, Vanity Fair, July, 1986~

RESOURCEFUL FANS

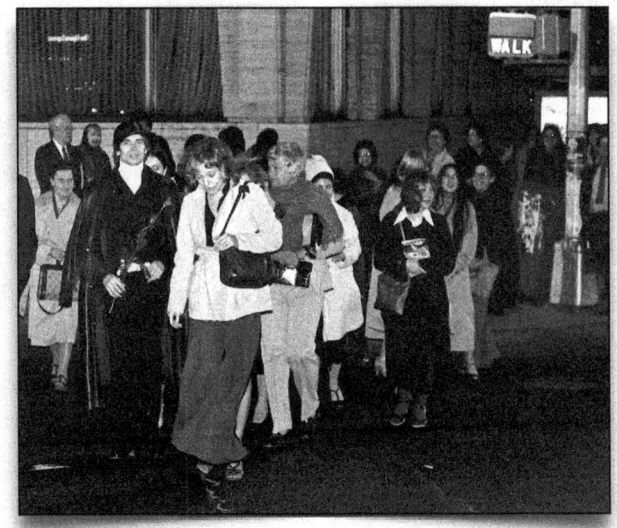

*Crossing Broadway with fans, NYC, April 22, 1980
Photo: William J. Reilly*

Who were these people who followed Nureyev's career? Like in any field of interest, whether sports, music, art, dance or theatre, like-minded people often became friends. They may have discussed the same things and even followed some of the people they admired.

I was not married to a wealthy businessman or an airline pilot. But I was determined to live a life that included travel, the arts and continuing education. Watching classical ballet, I, like so many others, experienced deep emotions of both beauty and "drama without words."

So how did average people like us, become so deeply involved in following the career of Rudolf Nureyev? It required a lot of organizing, planning, many sacrifices, and much enthusiasm. Everything we did was prior to the Internet. We relied on each other through corresponding by "snail mail," mailing checks or money orders for tickets, and buying train or plane tickets by telephone or through travel agencies. Circumstances forced us to be self-reliant. Eventually, our relationship as Rudolf Nureyev's fans grew into a resourceful and dependable support system.

Rudolf Nureyev had a truly unique relationship with his fans. In the early years following his defection, the enormous crowds of people waiting for his autograph whenever he left the theatre, made him very cautious. At times he looked like a caged animal. He was wary or suspicious of which people he could trust. He had a valid fear that he was being followed and could be kidnapped and forced to return to Russia. If that happened, Nureyev would face a seven-year prison sentence as a "traitor" for defecting from the Soviet Union. Nureyev was polite and soft spoken, but somewhat uncomfortable with all the attention his fame brought him. "We had nothing like that in Russia," he once remarked about the hordes of autograph seekers or journalists, constantly clamoring for interviews or photographs.

Even though Nureyev seldom sought out publicity, he realized that being in the public eye could protect him. As the years passed, he began to recognize familiar faces in the crowds and acknowledged us with a smile. After seeing the same admirers in different cities, he may not have known our names, but eventually came to rely on us for support.

For most of his career, Nureyev never wore a watch or used a calendar. His photographic memory meant that he easily memorized steps – not just his own part, but all the parts of the entire ballet – as well as different versions of the same ballet. He truly mastered the astounding ability to remember very complex information. It also meant that he kept his entire performance schedule in his head. However, once he became the Director of the Paris Opera in the mid-80s and had a very efficient secretary, he no longer needed to memorize schedules and often told us, "Check with Marie-Suzanne" if we asked when he was performing. Keeping track of Nureyev's performance schedule was never easy, but we managed. It made us very resourceful.

Sometimes we needed clarification of his dates. One inventive fan went backstage with three questions written on a clipboard with a pen attached. The questions were:

1. Where are you going now?

2. Who are you going with? (Meaning, the company he was performing with)

3. When will you be back?

After laughing at the second question, Nureyev rattled off future performance dates so fast that the fan could barely write them down. "What about this one?" she asked and Rudolf grabbed the clipboard and pointed, "There, November 4th in Berlin." By the time she left the dressing room, she had his schedule for fifteen months – all from Nureyev's memory!

At most European theatres, ballet performances alternated with the opera. In his early years, Nureyev performed primarily with the London Royal Ballet and the company toured the United States for several weeks. Under impresario Sol Hurok, casting was seldom announced in advance and ads often appeared the day the Box Office opened. Usually we had Nureyev's dates in advance, but I recall one time when casting kept changing and we only learned of Nureyev's performance dates at midnight the day before tickets went on sale. We scrambled to inform each other and were in the Box Office line the next morning, to be sure of getting our tickets.

When Hurok died in 1974, there was a large shake-up in the offices and Nureyev wondered if his future performances were in jeopardy. However, he reassured his fans, "No matter what happens, I'll be here."

When Nureyev's schedule expanded by making guest appearances with numerous companies, we doubled our efforts to keep each other informed. His performances were always sold out, whenever and wherever he danced. Tickets went on sale months in advance and many of his fans had to settle for standing room or last-minute returns, if we couldn't afford to purchase tickets earlier.

Letters flew back and forth across the Atlantic. "Rudolf told us he's dancing two performances in Vienna," I related to my Viennese friend, who responded, "I've booked you a ticket in case you can come." The fans knew how difficult it was obtaining tickets and many of us who traveled abroad often did so without any tickets at all.

One of my friends was married to an airline pilot and therefore had flight privileges. She, more than many others, was able to see Nureyev perform in far-away places such as the Herod Atticus in Athens or in Jerusalem. Sometimes she hopped on a plane at the last minute, obtaining a hotel room and tickets once she reached her destination. Being resourceful, she always managed to get a ticket or some nice person would sneak her in, even when nothing was available. It was nerve-wracking to say the least, but well worth the risk. Many times Rudolf saw her after a performance and quipped, "Oh, I see you got in."

I usually got a return ticket minutes before curtain time or opted for standing room, providing it wasn't sold out as well. But more often than not, our vast network of Nureyev fans around the world helped each other obtain tickets.

In times of desperation, we resorted to the old trick of stubbing each other in. Once inside the theatre, we borrowed a friend's ticket stub, used some excuse to go outside, and gave the stub to the person without a ticket. It was up to them to find an empty seat or standing place once they got inside. I recall a few Nureyev performances hiding behind a pillar or sitting on the steps to watch, because nothing was available. We often remembered the words of impresario Sol Hurok who said, "No theatre is impenetrable to the true balletomane."

Because Nureyev danced so frequently and tickets were difficult to get, often our only option was to get standing room. It used to be extremely affordable, usually less than $3 a ticket. The fans organized the standing room lines in New York and everyone put their names on a sign-up sheet the night before the Box Office opened. You were issued a number based on the order you signed in. If you missed signing up, you could do it in the morning, but by then you had a much higher number and the chances of getting a ticket were not as great.

Since the Met Box Office didn't open until 10 a.m. and crowds began arriving at dawn, we often congregated in the park across from Lincoln Center, to check ourselves in and receive the number corresponding with our place on the list. We were free to go to breakfast, but had to return for periodic "roll calls." The system was orderly and monitored so latecomers couldn't cut in line. Newcomers learned very quickly and made sure they were on "the list." The best part about the Metropolitan Opera is the fact that the 275 standing room places are numbered, so you always know "where you stand." With that detail sorted out and tickets in hand, we were free to resume our daily schedules until the performance.

Standing room in London was a different matter altogether, especially for the Fonteyn and Nureyev performances. At that time standing room was in the back of the orchestra stalls. For me, it was impossible to see over the heads directly in front of me so I usually tried my luck with return tickets. The Box Office didn't release these tickets until just prior to curtain time on the day of the performance. Yet huge queues formed along Floral Street the night before. Not too many people could sleep due to all the activity from the Covent Garden Market or the cold wind howling through the street. Those who camped out in sleeping bags or someone's car fared slightly better. If you had a thermos of something hot to share, you made friends immediately.

As the day wore on, the queue snaked back and forth, making it difficult to find the end of the line. The excitement mounted and as the queue inched ever so slowly toward the Box Office, shouts of joy by the lucky ticket holders echoed along the street. The rest of us remaining in line continued to wait with endless patience and steadfast determination. There were many close calls when an inexpensive ticket was returned at 7:29 p.m. for a 7:30 curtain. Consequently many of us raced up all those stairs to the Amphitheatre or Upper Slips, just like the fans did in *The Red Shoes* film. We were dirty from sleeping in the street the night before, and hungry from skipping dinner, but filled with adrenalin throughout the performance. Magic was happening on that stage and we certainly didn't want to miss it. The sheer euphoria of the event filled us with an inexplicable charge.

Standing Room in Vienna involved hard work. The queue started the night before the performance and everyone camped out around the magnificent Opera House. Unlike in New York, we were not permitted to leave the line, but they did open the Opera House the next morning and allowed the hordes to wait inside, which was most welcome during the winter months. This meant that we needed to bring provisions such as food or a book to read, because we were camped out all day until 6 p.m. when the standing room tickets were made available. Once we were issued our tickets, we waited at the appropriate entrance corresponding with our standing place or stehplatz.

Imagine my horror during my first visit to Vienna when an usher at the top of the balcony stairs yelled out "Stehplatz" and hordes of people literally ran all the way up those stairs. I was nearly trampled in the crush and by the time I reached the balcony, all places were taken and I was relegated to the second row unable to see over anyone's head. One learns quickly not to let that happen a second time.

Another friend, also going through the standing room routine in Vienna, was literally carried up to the balcony, her feet never touching the stairs, by two strapping young music students, thus securing her a decent spot. Someone lost a shoe in the stampede. None of the places are numbered, and I was amused that everyone "secured" their spot by tying a scarf or placing a program over the railing where they chose to stand.

The ten years of *Nureyev Festivals* at the London Coliseum proved challenging, because of the ever-changing Box Office policy. Standing room or returned tickets were sometimes released in the morning, disappointing those of us who arrived just prior to curtain time. Other times tickets weren't released until after 6 p.m. or later. We just never knew and therefore hanging around the theatre was necessary since few tickets were seldom available. I often resorted to buying a balcony ticket and then, if standing room became available, sold my balcony ticket for the cheaper standing room place.

Sometimes standing room just wasn't available. In these instances I resorted to sneaking in with the crowd. I recall performances of *Sleeping Beauty* when several of us rushed to the balcony and the friendly usher who had seen us nightly instructed, "Please take your seats – if you have them." We searched for empty seats and found ways of moving from the upper balcony to lower levels. One night during a long season, we all congregated near the main entrance at the interval when choreographer Murray Louis recognized us and asked, "Are there any empty seats?" He watched the first part of the performance from the wings, but wanted to watch the rest from "out front." We immediately replied, "Third row, fourth seat from the left," and he was most amused.

When Russian dancers Valery and Galina Panov made their London debut at Sadler's Wells Theatre, ticket demand was high. Of course Rudolf attended. One of his eager fans approached him in the theatre lobby and asked if he might have an extra ticket. He did not. Seeing the disappointed expression on his fan's face, he added, "I can't very well tear my ticket in half, can I?" I hung around the lobby but didn't have any luck, other than a sympathetic smile from Rudolf. However, another fan did manage to get in and went backstage afterwards to chat with the Panovs. This time it was Nureyev who waited outside their dressing room until invited in.

Most of us earned a modest living, but with so many performances to see, money was always tight. Occasionally small miracles occurred, such as the night one fan waited outside the Metropolitan Opera House wondering how she would get in. At the last minute a woman approached asking if she'd like to use an extra orchestra ticket since her husband couldn't make it. Best of all, it was free. Another friend contemplated how she would afford five performances in one weekend when she found a $20 bill on the sidewalk. That paid for all five standing room tickets with money left over to eat.

In 1975, I borrowed money to pay for my move from London to New York. Almost as soon as I arrived, there were numerous tickets to buy, including a Broadway *Nureyev and Friends* season, Nureyev's performances with the Martha Graham Company, as well as with the American Ballet Theatre. I had also signed up for my first trip to Russia at the end of that year in addition to Fonteyn and Nureyev performances with the Royal Ballet in London. It seemed I was always working to pay for tickets and rent. Even when I traveled for those annual marathon *Nureyev Festivals*, I had to work in London to pay for tickets as well as rent on my New York apartment. It was always a juggling act, but I became a prudent budgeter.

One resourceful fan temporarily rectified a dismal financial situation by going on a television game show, winning $8,000. When she told Rudolf of her good fortune, he asked, "Did you have to pay taxes on it?"

Most of the time when we traveled to see Nureyev's performances, we planned months in advance in order to get a cheaper airfare or queue at the airport on our departure date for the "bargain" airlines that existed then. Nureyev was made aware of this one evening, when one of my friends from London made his first trip to New York. As we chatted near the Stage Door before a performance, Rudolf's assistant spotted the British fan and said, "Rudolf wants to see you. Come with me." Nureyev was in his dressing room putting on his make up and insisted, "Come in and sit down. Talk." He asked how the fan was enjoying his visit to New York. My friend admitted he would be glad to return to London, since he had a lengthy stay and had "seen enough." Nureyev laughed and quipped, "Inverted Englishman!" When the fan explained the standing room procedures and how expensive the trip was,

Rudolf surprised him by asking, "Did you fly Laker? Did you have to queue?" Nureyev was curious to learn the procedure, since he normally flew overseas on the Concorde.

Nureyev was also aware that the fans often had more information than he did. He gave us all the dates of his future performances so we could plan, but added that he was keeping his options open in case things changed. Nureyev had hoped to mount his *Swan Lake* production on London Festival Ballet, but at that time company director Beryl Grey had just submitted her resignation. "Do you have any news on her?" Rudolf inquired. The British fan explained that the situation was unresolved and eventually the new director declined to acquire Nureyev's production.

On another occasion, Rudolf asked if we knew what repertory he was dancing on an upcoming tour. We were able to give him the information we just learned that very morning from the company's press office.

Once we called Nureyev's agent, Sandor Gorlinsky, to confirm performances in Paris since there were posters advertising it all over the city. Gorlinsky was surprised and asked, "Oh, is he dancing there?" It turned out the posters advertised a different production and not Nureyev's.

Fans attending a concert in Vienna spotted Nureyev and asked if he was dancing in a new ballet called *John The Baptist*, which they read in the newspaper. "Where do you hear those things?" he questioned. He dismissed it with, "I choose my own choreographers – *John* can wait!"

The fans also heard that Nureyev would mount one of his own productions for New York City Ballet. When asked, Rudolf stopped dead in his tracks, wondering how we knew about it before it was finalized, but replied with twinkling eyes, "There's a very good possibility." As it turned out, he was in discussions with George Balanchine about staging his production of *Manfred* as part of the company's 1981 Tchaikovsky Festival, but it never materialized.

In London for a Royal Ballet Gala, Nureyev asked us, "Is it sold out?" The Gala was so overbooked and overpriced, that the public petitioned the director to open a dress rehearsal for all those whose ticket orders were refused.

While Nureyev was the highest paid dancer at the time, all he wanted to do was dance and often did so for free. When an article appeared about the higher salaries charged for opera singers as well as higher ticket prices, Rudolf supposedly told the directors not to charge too much, saying "Don't soak the public!"

In the summer of 1978, Nureyev's production of *Romeo and Juliet* with the London Festival Ballet was presented at the Met, after its successful London premiere the previous year. At the same time, the National Ballet of Canada performed at the State Theatre without Nureyev. On the final day of *Romeo and Juliet*, with all the standing room sold out and a line of over 550 people waiting for returns, the Box Office staff was inundated and advised ticket buyers to cross the plaza to see the Canadians. When the Canadians dancers came to see Nureyev, some had to stand, despite the critics reporting that Nureyev was old and had lost his popularity.

For the historic 1979 Diaghilev program in New York, when Nureyev joined the Joffrey Ballet to perform roles made famous by the legendary Vaslav Nijinsky, the mad scramble for tickets was simply unbelievable. I recall when buying tickets, the Box Office staff member told me, "It's the same program every night, you know." The ballet was booked at the Mark Hellinger Theatre, a Broadway venue, and they were unaccustomed to people buying tickets for multiple performances.

For another *Nureyev and Friends* season on Broadway, I ordered tickets for all performances, except a Wednesday matinee. The gentleman at the Box Office told me, "You missed one!" I explained I needed to work that day to pay for the rest of the tickets.

There are any number of things that can disturb your enjoyment of a performance, particularly the flash cameras from the audience. Most of the professional photographers found ways of silencing their cameras, but many tourists continued to snap away, causing Nureyev to glare at them from the stage. At the intermission, fans dashed to the house manager and reported some of the offenders. The cameras were confiscated and the offender got a tongue-lashing from management. Tourists seldom realized how disturbing it was to the performance when they took photos. It is also dangerous for the dancer, who is momentarily blinded by the flash and risking a fall. Despite the ban on photographs, a barrage of flashes occurred during curtain calls, but at least by then the performance was finished and Rudolf didn't mind as much.

Equally disturbing were the conversations taking place during a performance with some audience members feeling obliged to "explain" the plot to the person beside them.

The orchestra playing at one *Giselle* performance was simply appalling. Every time the players hit a wrong note, members of the orchestra began laughing, and at other times even singing. Some orchestras simply dislike playing for the ballet, but on this occasion, an irate fan lashed out at them when the performance finished. "You are very unprofessional and if you think it sounds nice to hear false notes, laughing and singing, you're crazy. If you don't respect the dancers, you could at least show respect for the paying audience!"

Following the incident in New York when an overly enthusiastic audience member bolted onstage during the curtain calls, nearly crushing Nureyev in a bear hug and swinging him precariously over the orchestra pit, the fans bombarded the Hurok Organization with phone calls. "How can you risk the safety of your top Box Office star?" At subsequent performances at the Met, ushers and security staff stood on either side of the stage, preventing anyone from repeating such antics.

The fans welcomed the chance to assist Nureyev whenever possible, even providing "crowd control" at some of the Stage Doors. In New York, the fans frequently hailed a taxi for Rudolf. Sometimes, despite our best efforts, it was impossible since most Broadway theatres finished at the same time and taxi drivers didn't like waiting while Nureyev signed autographs. Rudolf, followed by long lines of people, sometimes walked to the corner to find a cab. The fans tried flagging down every passing taxi, but to no avail. Finally, Nureyev decided to walk to his destination, looking rather like the Pied Piper with dozens of fans trailing behind him. After walking about four blocks, a taxi finally stopped and Rudolf jumped in as the astonished taxi driver saw the crowd disappear.

Another night Rudolf left the Stage Door and there was the usual, "Taxi, taxi, where's the taxi?" routine as he made his way to the corner. No taxis could be found, so he signed autographs at the nearby bus stop. Several buses stopped while an embarrassed Luigi, Rudolf's masseur and personal assistant explained, "No, no, we want a taxi" to the confused bus drivers. Three policemen on horseback completed the chaotic picture, not to mention various photographers jostling to get their photos. The fans pulled together and vowed to have a taxi "on call" for future performances.

The Martha Graham season proved equally chaotic. After the opening night's performance, Rudolf and his entourage exited the theatre and got into a cab. His fans pointed out that there was a limousine waiting to take him to a party. "Hey, this time they got us a limousine!" Nureyev informed his friends. They piled out of the taxi and into the limo, much to the disgust of the waiting taxi driver.

During his annual *Nureyev Festivals* in London, Rudolf used to drive his brown TR7 sports car. When leaving after a performance, he found it difficult to navigate due to the throngs of people surrounding the vehicle. There were those dedicated fans that always watchfully stood by the car, making room for him to get in and receiving a goodnight kiss or handshake from him. However, if Rudolf himself was driving, his passenger always looked extremely skeptical. I still recall the look of apprehension on Margot Fonteyn's face when she sat in the front seat next to him, as they battled their way through the throngs of people and finally drove off to a restaurant. Nureyev may have had total command on stage but in a car, he was not one of the best drivers.

At one point Rudolf drove a green Volkswagen, which was easy to park. Still, if he was dining or doing business following a performance, it was amusing to watch his passengers cram into this little bug, often sitting on Rudolf's lap while he joked, "We'll have to play kneesies." Fortunately he wasn't driving those nights!

As several of us left the Opera House in London after a matinee, we saw Sir Frederick Ashton and Margot Fonteyn leaving the Stage Door at the same time that Nureyev arrived for a rehearsal. He smiled and casually walked inside. We noticed his car was peculiarly parked and he left on the headlights. We informed the Stage Door attendant, who phoned Nureyev's dressing room to tell him. Rudolf never emerged to turn off the lights, but no doubt designating someone else to do it for him.

Nureyev once handed over a ten pence piece and asked one of his British fans if he could put two five-pence coins in the parking meter, because he didn't have exact change. The fan replied, "Of course I'll take care of it," and Rudolf went inside the theatre to warm up for the performance. The fan paid the meter and decided to keep the ten-pence coin as a souvenir!

Over the years Rudolf loved to tease us, especially when he saw the same fans in different cities where he performed. When he saw a contingent of fans that were in Paris, he grinned and jokingly said, "Please get out of my way. You have been in my way in New York, Washington, London, Amsterdam and you are STILL in my way!" While continuing to his car, he recited a litany of cities where his fans traveled to see him, but then finally turned around and playfully waved to us all as he drove off.

As he approached the London Coliseum Stage Door one evening, Rudolf asked the waiting fans, "Why don't you make yourselves useful and find me a parking spot?" One fan retorted, "So you want us to toss our bags and personal belongings in the street so nobody will park there and hope they don't get run over?" Embarrassed, Rudolf said nothing and quietly entered the theatre.

He invited some of the fans to a special film preview of *Don Quixote* in Paris. Later when one of the fans told him how much she enjoyed it, he replied, "Yes, I heard!" He was in the audience ardently observing the public's reactions.

Another fan was a great admirer of Erik Bruhn and Nureyev teased her, "I suppose you'll be going to Copenhagen to see your beloved Erik?" When she replied, "No, I'm staying in London to watch YOU," he beamed.

In 1979, when I presented Nureyev with the second volume of his performing chronology, I teased him that he would soon be in the Guinness Book of World Records for the most performances by a ballet dancer. The book was presented on the eighteenth anniversary of Rudolf's arrival in the West. My friend asked him, "You know what eighteen means, don't you? It means you've come of age legally." Rudolf roared with laughter and contentedly used the volume as a writing surface to sign autographs.

Even Luigi began teasing us. A woman named Dora sent flowers to Rudolf when he had pneumonia, so Luigi called her "Interdora" rather than Interflora. Another time when he saw Rudolf's British fans in France, he asked in mock confusion, "Is this London or Paris?"

On a few occasions, some of Nureyev's fans went to the airport, either to welcome him or to chat with him briefly before his departure. When Nureyev was released from the hospital in 1976, following his bout of pneumonia, fans went to New York's Kennedy Airport where he was to meet with Hurok Management before his connecting flight to Morocco. During this layover, Rudolf mentioned he would love some of those "brown cookies."

Nothing more. This resulted in a few fans rushing throughout the airport searching for "brown cookies" and tea before Nureyev's overseas departure.

Having traveled to Europe to see Nureyev perform, two British fans waited for their return flight to London when they spotted the man himself. Despite knowing them, Rudolf made no sign of approaching and remained where he was. Finally one fan went up to him and said, "Don't stand there like that. Come and talk to us!" Rudolf looked sheepish but then said "All right." As one friend wrote later, "Rudolf frightens everyone except dogs and children. As a famous artist, he obviously must keep a certain distance, but he shouldn't be surprised if people sense that."

Sometimes Nureyev relied on his fans for special requests. One fan worked at a music publishing company and managed to secure copies of a score Rudolf wanted to consider for a new ballet he was creating. Other fans obtained books he was interested in. Still others provided him with hand-made legwarmers or a special brand of toothpaste he preferred; the more gifted ones made him cheesecakes or other goodies. When one fan gave Nureyev some kind of vitamins, he quipped, "You want me to get diarrhea before performance?"

Even though he claimed he didn't care about reviews, we knew otherwise. We often handed him copies of reviews and he usually read them immediately. If he liked them, he beamed, but he was more often bothered by what a critic didn't review. After one glowing report about a series of different ballets he performed, Rudolf remarked to us, "But they didn't say a word about my *Swan Lake.*" When one New York critic wrote of Nureyev in *La Spectre de la Rose*, "I fail to see the light," the next night a fan handed this critic a flashlight.

In London, Nureyev attended a concert performance at the Festival Hall and as the interval ended, he got into a crowded elevator to return to his seat. One of his fans happened to be in the same elevator. When people recognized Rudolf, they began to applaud. He seemed shy and slightly embarrassed by this, as he was merely attending the performance and not dancing that evening. Recognizing his discomfort, his fan piped up, "Oh, is that applause for me?" Everyone laughed and Rudolf turned to the fan and smiled gratefully.

A couple of the dancer's fans worked for the airlines and they, in turn, proved useful to Rudolf in booking various flights for him. They often told him which airlines were available or booked him on the Concorde. Sometimes he was vague because he didn't know himself when he was catching a return flight, so they double or triple-booked him on various airlines on different days until his plans were confirmed. Often they didn't even know his final destination.

Once he asked, "What time is my flight tomorrow?" The fan teased, "You didn't say where you were headed, so I booked you on a flight to Istanbul." She even reminded him to change his clock to daylight savings for the next day's matinee. Nureyev responded, "I'll be there for 2 o'clock." "That's what you say NOW," she countered.

After Nureyev's bout with pneumonia, his practice clothes were "abandoned" when he left the hospital. One fan with flight privileges offered to return them to him in London.

Nureyev began asking the fans for help in carrying his costumes from one city to another. One fan took an extra suitcase to the airport, since Rudolf had 124 pounds in excess weight, because most of his costumes were in his suitcase. How he managed to keep track of the different costumes needed for various productions of *Swan Lake* or *Sleeping Beauty* was amazing, but his team of supporters willingly provided assistance when needed.

Once Nureyev asked a fan to carry his enormous Albrecht cape from one city to another. The cape was extremely heavy, but was such an integral part of Rudolf's entrance in the second act of *Giselle*, that the performance would be simply ruined without it. The cape was successfully delivered, but its weight made his fan truly appreciate how Rudolf manipulated it so effortlessly on stage.

A European fan was given his *La Sylphide* kilt, jacket and cap to carry to another city in Europe. Prior to returning it to Rudolf, she freshened it up and ironed it for him. When many of Nureyev's costumes were auctioned off after his death, this same fan was able to obtain the very costume she had ironed for him years earlier.

On another occasion, Nureyev entrusted a fan to bring two suitcases full of costumes from New York to London. The cases were brought to the Opera House with instructions not to leave them unattended, but delivered straight to his dressing room. Thus, the fan delivered them directly to Rudolf and as a result, was entrusted with other challenges.

He once asked to have a very long tripod returned to New York. It was in an unsealed box and the fan had to painstakingly search for tape strong enough to secure it, before taking it on the plane.

Rudolf acquired an exercise machine that he used following one of his injuries. He wanted to use it in New York and asked a fan to get it there. After a lot of effort and logistics, the machine was duly transported from London and delivered across the Atlantic.

As this relationship with his fans deepened, Rudolf entrusted them with one of his most prized possessions: his Blackgama fur coat. In 1975, Nureyev, Fonteyn and Martha Graham donned the furs and posed for the "What Becomes a Legend Most?" ads. They all got to keep their furs. Rudolf wore his fur hat and coat to most major social events, primarily because they kept him warm. He even wore his fur coat to an exhibition benefiting Animal Rights and was told, "You shouldn't be wearing that HERE." "But it's dead already," he explained.

After performing in New York, he wanted his prized fur coat with him in London, but couldn't carry it, so he entrusted it to a fan with flight privileges. Since she was flying to London to see the performance anyway, she agreed. The coat was in a sealed garment bag and stitched along all sides so she wasn't able to see it. "Don't leave it alone in your hotel room" and "keep it with you all the time" were Rudolf's precise instructions. Since she arrived just prior to his London performance, she delivered it immediately to his dressing room. "Ah, my coat!" Rudolf exclaimed. He immediately cut the garment bag stitches and unzipped it to inspect the marvelous coat and she finally got to see it up close.

During one New York season, a large framed portrait was given to Rudolf and he wanted to take it back to his house in Richmond, just outside of London. He asked one of the British fans who was staying with me, to collect it at his hotel. When the fan saw it, he exclaimed, "I thought you said it was a SMALL painting!" The nearly life-size painting of Nureyev was brought to my apartment, where it remained for several days.

The following day, my friend spotted Luigi entering the theatre while merely shouting, "We'll talk later," to which the fan replied, "We certainly will!" After the performance, he explained his concerns to Nureyev about getting the cumbersome painting to London. It was too big to take on the plane, unless it was removed from its frame and rolled up. "Rudolf, it's your painting – what if it gets damaged?" Tossing up his hands in a carefree manner, the dancer responded, "You figure it out."

Everyone made calls to airlines about how to get it on board the plane without paying for an extra seat. After exhausting all of our contacts, the painting was returned to Luigi. He eventually found a way of getting it back to Rudolf, who by this time had returned to England. We later agreed that the dancer didn't care as much for the painting as he did to challenge us.

When Nureyev returned to England after filming *Valentino*, his luggage was lost. When it was finally located, one of his fans returned it to him in the Concorde lounge, before his overseas departure.

Another one of Rudolf's fans made a visit to India, a place that - up to that time - Nureyev had never visited. She asked him if he needed anything. "I'd love a maharajah costume!" he exclaimed excitedly. The fan researched old Indian prints and spent half of the vacation in India trying to find such a costume. She traveled to several places and finally came back with a magnificently colored costume, complete with pearled turban and white satin pants. Nureyev was in New York filming *Exposed* and the ever-resourceful fan found out the location of that day's filming. She just missed Rudolf, however, who dashed off to take a class when filming finished. She managed to catch up with him later and handed over the costume. He was thoroughly delighted.

Some fans even got involved in making costumes. Aside from the admirers who knitted legwarmers and scarves for him, a small cadre of fans assisted with the *Petrushka* costumes during the Joffrey Ballet's season with Nureyev in 1979. Robert Joffrey wanted to restore the costumes to match the original Bakst designs and because the production is of such magnitude, the costume department needed outside assistance to complete the task in time for the first performance. Once the production was up and running, these same fans had the satisfaction of knowing that they made the aprons for the Nursemaids or the hats for dancers in the crowd scenes.

I got my own direct "assignment" from Rudolf some time after he debuted in *Clytemnestra* with the Martha Graham Company. In London at the time, he spotted me after a performance and asked, "Do you know if anybody filmed me?" Puzzled, I asked, "Tonight?" "No, in *Clytemnestra*." I didn't think so but told him, "I'll find out for you." I thought one of the fans might have secretly videotaped it. I inquired through all my sources and we found out that to the best of my knowledge *Clytemnestra* was not filmed.

When some fans went to Russia, they met Nureyev's sister and were able to bring back some of the dancer's record albums he bought before his defection. In addition to some Russian folk music, the collection included music of Mozart and Rachmaninoff.

In the later years when Nureyev's schedule became less known, we relied on the dancer's close friend, Nigel Gosling, for information. The London fans either called him or slipped a note in his mailbox. One fan had to give something to Gosling en route to a party nearby to celebrate Rudolf's birthday. The fan explained to Gosling, "I'm going to a party, but the main participant is missing!"

In 1980, Nigel Gosling rang one of the London fans to take some of Rudolf's costumes to Italy, but was told that the fan was studying for exams. "Of course," replied Gosling. "I should have remembered this after Rudolf told us all about your studies."

Gosling later recalled how Rudolf rang him at 3:30 one morning and talked for an hour about the Salvador Dali exhibit he had seen in Paris. Nigel asked him, "What if Dali designed your *Manfred* production for you?" Rudolf replied that it would be "mind-shattering." The original *Manfred* designs were not Nureyev's choice, but since the Paris Opera ran short of funds for the production, they had to improvise with what they could find on hand. When the production was mounted in 1981 for the Zurich Ballet, Rudolf wanted it redesigned. He called upon his trusted designer, Nicholas Georgiadis, to conceptualize a new design for his revised production.

Once when trying to determine which dates Nureyev was performing abroad, I resorted to writing a letter to the Goslings. I asked specific questions and dates and provided a box where they could check "Yes" or "No" concerning Nureyev's schedule. They immediately filled it out and sent it back so I could plan.

Nigel Gosling became the "mediator" between Nureyev and some of the most trusted fans. One of them stopped by the Gosling's home to collect costumes to bring to Nureyev for his next performances. While Nigel was on the phone with Rudolf, the fan assumed from their conversation, that they were making rude jokes with each other. Later when this fan moved out of London, the Goslings said, "Phone us any time."

During one Christmas season, Maude and Nigel Gosling invited me and another fan to their home for a holiday drink. We had a long and enthusiastic conversation about dance and explained we were en route to Paris the next day to see Nureyev perform *Swan Lake* with Natalia Makarova. Upon leaving, they asked, "Give Rudolf a kiss for us."

When Rudolf performed *Miss Julie* with the Cullberg Ballet in Stockholm, one of his ardent British fans couldn't get tickets. She rang Mrs. Gosling to see if Rudolf could arrange a ticket for her. A few days later, Mrs. Gosling phoned to say that Rudolf would leave her a ticket at the Box Office. Arriving in Sweden, the Box Office staff knew exactly who she was and provided her with a very good seat. At the interval, a friend of Nureyev's approached and asked for her ticket stub, because Rudolf insisted that the fan didn't have to pay for it.

Nigel Gosling was hospitalized in early 1982 with cancer and because Rudolf was on tour and couldn't be there, he asked a friend to stay with Maude Gosling. Many of the fans phoned for updates and to show their support. We decided to send Nigel a Snoopy card that said, "You're wanted back by popular demand." Despite his illness, Nigel wrote back immediately and thanked all the signees with an added message, "It won't be long until RN is here for his Coli season – perhaps you, too?"

Gosling was hospitalized again a few months later. Rudolf's schedule was very complicated due to touring, but he thoughtfully phoned Gosling every day. He promptly made a stopover en route to a Paris engagement to visit Nigel for one hour. Sadly, his "adopted father" died just days before the 1982 *Nureyev Festival* and Rudolf dedicated his entire Coliseum Season to his close friend and mentor. During that season, any flowers he received, he took "for Maude."

At further performances, Maude Gosling often took time to speak to the fans, letting us know how supportive we had been, adding, "Rudolf has taken especially good care of me." He invited her everywhere, hoping to cheer her up.

Later in his career, Rudolf relied on some of his fans to advise him about dancers they were aware of, that he might team up with for various *Friends* programs. For one performance of Nijinsky's *L'Apres midi d'une Faune*, he called one of his loyal supporters to recommend a dancer. The fan cast his leading lady and it worked out very well.

As he got to know the fans throughout the years, some of them acted as chauffeurs and picked him up at various airports – often on very short notice – or drove him around the city on shopping sprees. Rudolf loved to collect antiques and textiles. One friend saw him heading into a New York antique shop where he inquired about a large armoire. After ascertaining the price, Rudolf said to the shop owner, "I need two," and when the antique dealer informed him there was only one, Rudolf departed.

In 1980, on the advice of his neighbors, John Lennon and Yoko Ono, Rudolf purchased the Woodburn Farm in Leesburg, Virginia. The property seemed to stretch for miles, with dairy cows, a huge barn, trees and streams, and a large Federal style house. Rudolf was seldom able to enjoy it due to his peripatetic existence. His dream was to convert the barn into a dance studio and conduct teaching seminars to pass on his vast knowledge of the art of dance. In the meantime, the large house was used as storage for the overflow of his many antique purchases, including an enormous pipe organ that filled the entire dining room.

Following a triumphant season at the Kennedy Center with the Paris Opera in 1986, Nureyev arranged to take the entire company to his farm. His friend Douce had come from Paris for the season and she arranged an outdoor picnic for the dancers. Tablecloths were spread on the ground and multiple steaks were grilled. Following the meal, dancers piled into a hay-filled cart as Rudolf gave them a guided tour of the extensive land and farm property. The dancers were amazed when Rudolf said, "I own all those trees!" He was obviously very proud of it.

When one of Nureyev's trusted fans informed him she was leaving New York, he offered her the position of caretaker for his farm. After wrestling with her decision, she agreed to take his offer and moved to Virginia. Her life experience organizing things for Rudolf paid off and she remained on the farm for quite some time.

We paid a brief visit to Woodburn when Nureyev was away on tour. The farm was indeed a haven of tranquility and we enjoyed taking long walks on the grounds. However, the inside of the main house was another matter. The pipe organ indeed filled the entire dining room. The living room overflowed with hundreds of books. On one shelf, prominently displayed, was a model train, a gift from Jacqueline Kennedy Onassis. Since Rudolf was born on a train, he had a lifelong fascination with them.

Rudolf checked in with the farm's new caretaker and made occasional visits, but his primary residence at that point in his career was his Quai Voltaire apartment in Paris. He also paid brief visits to La Galli, an island he purchased off the Italian coast. When in the process of decorating his island home, one of his fans researched decorative tiles for him and some were eventually used on the walls. As with most of his homes, they became storage places for his massive collections.

Probably the most resourceful and determined of his fans was a woman from Vienna. In 1991, Nureyev was suddenly invited to dance *La Sylphide* at his alma mater, the Kirov Ballet, in St. Petersburg. The last time he danced there was in 1961 and the Viennese fan wanted to be there for this historic occasion. Tickets were impossible to get since his performances sold out immediately. Visas and plane tickets to Russia had to be obtained on very short notice and there were numerous challenges to get into the theatre.

Undeterred, she arrived at the theatre and announced herself as a friend of Rudolf's from the ballet company in Vienna. Functionaries in charge were embarrassed that her name was not on the reserved ticket list. After bluffing her way in, she managed to get a very good seat. She even went backstage following the performance and saw Nureyev giving an interview for American television about his return to Russia.

Rudolf Nureyev challenged his fans as much as he challenged himself. His thirst for new dance roles took him all over the world, while learning a variety of dance styles. His fans could barely keep up with him. But he taught us to be resourceful and we discovered we were capable of doing more than we ever dreamed possible. The ultimate test of our resourcefulness came, when we started a campaign to get his mother out of the Soviet Union for a brief visit. But that is a whole other complicated story I will gladly share with you later on.

"I can see nothing wrong with being recognized and liked…
I enjoy the contact with people."
~Rudolf Nureyev, Montreal Star, September 22, 1977~

WAITING FOR RUDOLF

At the Uris Theatre Stage Door, NYC, January, 1983
Photo by William J. Reilly

The closing shots of the film *I Am A Dancer*, depict Rudolf Nureyev waving off the Stage Door crowds with a single red rose. While neophytes soon learned that his Tartar temper could be formidable and unpredictable, I seldom witnessed such scenes, at least at the Stage Door.

No matter where Nureyev was dancing, whether in a glittering opera house or a sports palace, the easiest place to meet up with friends was at the Stage Door, usually before a performance. We would sell extra tickets to new arrivals, exchange hotel information, and finalize sightseeing plans. Gathering before a performance provided us with a meeting place in which to catch up with news and see who was there, because once inside, we were scattered throughout the theatre.

Whenever I traveled to see him, the first order of business was to collect my tickets and find the Stage Door. If I arrived late, friends would buy my ticket and meet me there before the performance. Rudolf generally arrived about ninety minutes before curtain time, but occasionally we missed him if he wasn't in the first act or the first ballet of a triple bill.

For one London matinee performance, a very sleepy Nureyev arrived with his head wrapped turban style in a bright yellow towel. As he emerged from the car, the former London Festival Ballet director John Field greeted him by saying, "Hello Rudi, how are you, sunshine?"

During the ten annual summer *Nureyev Festivals* held at the London Coliseum, it seemed that the entire stage crew gathered outside the corner pub next door, while trying to cool off. We knew it was hot when Nureyev arrived wearing shorts. All the stagehands whistled at him. A couple of nights later, some of us were delayed at dinner. When we arrived at the Stage Door, the stagehands informed us, "Rudi's in already."

Rudolf had a love-hate relationship with the stage crew and could curse with the best of them. While the stagehands had very lucrative summers thanks to those long *Nureyev Festival* seasons, it didn't prevent them from teasing him. They often greeted him while waiting outside, beer pints in hand, "Hey Roodi, how are ya, luv?" On one occasion, the stagehands told Rudolf that they had saved him a parking space – in front of a pile of garbage. By closing night, even the stagehands and Stage Door Attendant asked Rudolf to sign a program for them. He willingly obliged and the Attendant remarked, "There goes a swell chap!" After one long Coliseum season, Nureyev asked the stage crew to join him for drinks in his dressing room. They happily obliged. When they emerged, one showed off the shirt that Nureyev had signed for him, quipping, "Oi'm a valuable property now, Oi am!"

Cast parties were the norm after most of the opening or closing nights. This meant a long wait for the fans, depending on how long Rudolf remained at the party. Not wanting to go home right after an exciting performance, we often went to a coffee shop or café and returned to the Stage Door in time to see the party guests leaving. Sometimes we simply remained talking at the Stage Door and, by the time we realized it, Nureyev was leaving the reception.

Some theatres were better than others for observing the cast parties. The glass-fronted Metropolitan Opera House in New York usually afforded us a view of the Grand Tier festivities. We always knew where Rudolf was by the camera flashes from the press photographers as they followed him from the orchestra, up the grand staircase, and on to the Grand Tier. The next day's society pages were filled with photos of Rudolf and whoever happened to be near him.

During one post-performance party, a group of us peered through the glass on the London Coliseum's doors to watch the festivities. The company dancers performed balletic grand jetés followed by a tango or the Twist and even formed a conga line that snaked through the lobby. Rudolf, dressed all in white, was energetically dancing to music by Mick Jagger and the Rolling Stones after just having danced a full-length *Giselle*.

After one performance of *La Bayadere* at Covent Garden, the crowds outside began to disappear when it became evident that a cast party was taking place. Some of us felt so elated that we began "dancing" sections of the performance. We formed a chain of "Shades" - corps de ballet dancers from the ballet's vision scene - and executed endless arabesques along Floral Street. Suddenly Nureyev emerged from the Stage Door, looking at us with an amused grin. Giddy from champagne, he walked down the middle of the street, with a long line of people trailing after him. "Rudolf, where are you taking us?" one of them asked. "I'm looking for my car, if I can find it!" As we turned the corner, someone from the Bow Street police station across from the theatre jokingly asked Rudolf if he had a parade permit. He quipped, "My flag has a hammer and sickle on it!"

Over the course of the annual seasons at the Coliseum, we became friendly with the ushers. During one hot summer, while perched atop my last-row balcony seat, I heard a voice behind me whispering, "Your drinks are here." Our friendly usher handed me a nice cold glass of lemonade. The Coliseum ushers were very helpful when performances were sold out. We walked up the back stairs, were greeted, and then either found a vacant seat or else stood at the back.

If we were having a street party following a closing night performance, we brought champagne and one of the ushers provided sandwiches. One usher had Stage Door duty by directing traffic when people lined up to get Nureyev's autograph. The usher told us that it was fascinating to hear the things people asked Rudolf and what he replied.

When Nureyev performed *Brighton Venus* in 1979 with the Murray Louis Dance Company, we had another closing night celebration in the street. We toasted each other with champagne served in paper cups and wore our replicas of Rudolf's *Venus* sailor hat and white gloves, that were part of his performance.

In May 1983, Nureyev brought his original production of *Manfred* to Washington, D.C. There was a reception on the Kennedy Center's rooftop terrace following the closing night performance. En route, Rudolf momentarily left his escorts and did a little dance for us in the corridor before getting into the elevator. We had a champagne party in the street and when Nureyev appeared two hours later, he feigned astonishment at seeing us still waiting for him. We formed a receiving line while he greeted and spoke to each of us. Most of us were returning to New York on a 2 a.m. bus, so we went to the nearby Howard Johnson's Hotel for our "after-after party." We spotted conductor Andre Presser alone at an adjacent table, so he joined us until it was time to depart for the bus station.

One of the longest wait times for fans occurred early in Nureyev's career. At one Covent Garden performance of *Giselle*, he fell on stage. Always seeking perfection, he was so upset that he didn't stop at the Stage Door. His fans were disappointed because, despite the fall, they enjoyed the performance and wanted to see him before traveling home. Some took the subway to Richmond where Nureyev had a house. After waiting for some time, the young fans found an unlocked parked van adjacent to Nureyev's home. Because the weather had turned bitterly cold, they huddled inside the vehicle for warmth. Soon the police on patrol spotted them and asked what they were doing. "We're waiting for Rudolf Nureyev," they explained. The fans asked if they could wait in the police car, which was not permitted. But the British police offered to get them some hot coffee and kept an eye on them for the duration of the night.

After waiting all night in the unheated van, they were about to give up when Nureyev arrived at his home about 7 a.m. The fans jumped out of the van to greet him. As they approached his car, and he saw their familiar faces waiting in the predawn hours, he rolled down the window and said softly, "I thought I was dreaming! How are you?" he inquired, to which one answered quite honestly, "So cold!" "I'm sorry," he replied sincerely. After a brief conversation, they explained they had to catch their ferry to Europe. Nureyev wished them a good journey, adding, "The sea will be rough."

Rudolf Nureyev as weatherman? It seemed so. When a British friend made his first trip to New York, Nureyev asked him, "How do you like it here?" The fan responded, "It's cold." "Wait till tomorrow. It will be warmer." was Rudolf's prediction. And indeed it was.

Waiting for Rudolf sometimes proved logistically challenging. In London, especially on closing nights, we had to steer clear of the stagehands striking the sets and carrying large pieces of scenery to load into trucks. Occasionally we could see through the loading dock into the theatre. Sometimes Nureyev remained on the stage, still in costume, greeting people or going over certain steps with one of the dancers.

After one performance where it was impossible to get near the Stage Door due to stagehands hauling scenery, I spotted Luigi driving Rudolf's TR7, so I knew he would be out momentarily. The other fans were engrossed in conversation and never noticed that Nureyev walked past them en route to the car. He decided to get their attention, waved, and said "Hi." Before any of those waiting realized, Nureyev swiftly made his escape in the "getaway car," as we often called it.

Sometimes the crowds were so enormous, even friends visiting Nureyev after the performance had difficulty exiting the Stage Door. Margot Fonteyn came out one evening and the crowds parted for her like the Red Sea. King Constantine of Greece, who also attended the performance, didn't get this treatment when he departed rather unnoticed. When Nureyev emerged, screaming ballet school students surged forward while Rudolf slowly made his way to the waiting car. The Stage Door attendant tried to separate him from the excited crowd. One thoughtful fan supported the dancer's arm, cautioning, "Mind the step, Rudolf," because he couldn't see the curb for the hysterical mob pushing at him. The teenagers ran after him, dodging in front of the car to driver Luigi's great annoyance.

In London, there was a ritual that always amused us. It seemed that the garbage trucks managed to make their rounds just as Nureyev emerged from the Coliseum Stage Door. The huge crowds had to clear the street to let the sanitation trucks pass. Sometimes Rudolf was stranded near the Stage Door because the trucks blocked the space where his car was parked. At other times, he waited in his car, stuck behind the truck. Since it was a one-way street, there wasn't much he could do, but if he was in an impatient mood, he backed up the car and drove around the block. The garbage trucks became such a fixture on Bedfordbury Street, that we joked with the sanitation workers, "Would you mind coming a bit earlier tomorrow night?" It seemed that everyone, stagehands included, stood around and saluted the first to leave – whether it was the garbage truck or Rudolf Nureyev.

During a series of performances in Boston, the Stage Door area was being renovated. Wooden planks were strewn over a huge expanse of mud to form a rather precarious pathway to the Stage Door. Waiting in the muck wasn't exactly what we had anticipated, so we gingerly navigated the boards and huddled inside the Stage Door, or, alternatively, waited in the street. If navigating was difficult for us, it was equally difficult for Rudolf, who came out each night more or less tiptoeing from plank to plank, until he safely reached the street.

During one London season, renovations were going on at the corner near the Stage Door and the building was encased in scaffolding. As we walked with Rudolf to the nearby restaurant, he spotted a workman's ladder and suddenly veered away from it and into the street, saying, "We go here." Superstitious or not, we dutifully followed.

Usually waiting for Rudolf was an enjoyable experience. But when Rudolf performed at the *San Antonio Festival* in Texas, gun-toting security guards prohibited anyone from gathering near the Stage Door. Fans were forced to wait across the street.

The Stage Door presented the ideal place for an opportunity to exchange a few words with Nureyev. One evening when Nureyev left the theatre, he was still conversing with his backstage visitors. After he departed, I overheard them say, "I had to listen very carefully to what he said." Nureyev's "shorthand" method of communicating was often amusing. He never wasted a single word and if, as was frequently the case, you asked him something during his dash from the theatre to the waiting car, his answers were brief and to the point. In London, a wealthy socialite invited Nureyev to a dinner party and he responded, "Friday? No. Finish." Translation: his last performance finished on Friday and he wouldn't be able to attend her party. Another time one of my friends asked him when he would dance in *Raymonda* again, to which his response was a brisk, "No *Raymonda*. Disposal." The production had been dropped from the company's repertory. "Well, at least we can look forward to seeing your production of *Nutcracker* later this year." "That's cancelled, too," came his sharp reply. One fan who spoke rather broken English asked him, "How long can we miss you?" Rudolf understood instantly and promptly stated, "July."

Some of Nureyev's performances in Venice were cancelled due to opera scheduling conflicts. One fan asked Rudolf what his next performance would be. "Holiday," he replied. A new ballet called "Holiday" sounded intriguing so the fan asked, "Where will it be performed?" Nureyev laughingly responded, "No, no, vacation!"

His abbreviated way of speaking sometimes confused his fans. One of them stopped by to see him at the Stage Door and Rudolf looked at her in surprise and asked, "Where did you go?" She didn't "go" anywhere so replied, "I've been right here." "No, no, where did YOU go?" he repeated, this time indicating with his hands that her size had dramatically changed since he last saw her. Indeed, she lost quite a bit of weight and dropped to a size four, after taking up ballet classes.

Whenever he was tired, especially after long afternoons of rehearsing, Rudolf would announce, "I want my bedski!" He then repeated one of our favorite quotes that his bed was "the most loyal and tender of lovers."

Nureyev loved watching old movies and often picked up slang expressions of the era. He found phrases such as "23 Skidoo" or "cat's pajamas" highly amusing. This quirk sometimes carried over into nicknames he had for both fans and colleagues. Two sisters at the Stage Door were unofficially dubbed "Poopsy" and "Woopsy." He teasingly addressed us by our home country or city with "Howdy, New York" or "Hello, London" or "How are you, Japan?"

His Viennese colleagues Gisela Cech and Gabriela Haslinger were affectionately called "Gizzy" and "Gabby." London Festival Ballet dancer Andria Hall was from a town called Grimsby. Rudolf called her Grimsby because it amused him. Designer Rouben Ter-Arutunian, who recreated the Bakst backdrop and set for *L'Apres Midi d'un Faune*, met Rudolf at the Stage Door one evening. When Rudolf spotted him, he called out, "Ruby-Booby!"

In rehearsals he was known to instruct the corps dancers to "Point those galoshkis" or "tootsies" instead of toes. Exiting the Stage Door to a huge crowd, he often said, "Howdy-doody, everyone" or when asked how he was, might reply, "Hunky dory." He seemed to pick up expressions from his current surroundings, once responding to a British fan asking how he was with, "Jolly good, sport."

Nureyev had a photographic mind that enabled him to remember all of the steps in all the ballets he learned when in Russia. This gift served him well when he restaged many productions in the West. It also meant he could absorb choreography as soon as it was taught to him.

We often joked that with his phenomenal memory, he knew which one of us came to particular performances. "He's got some giant board at home where he keeps track of us," I joked. Others scoffed at this, but his frequent remarks such as, "I didn't see you last night" or "You missed my performances in Paris" only reinforced this theory.

After one London performance, Rudolf reproached one of his faithful fans by asking, "Why didn't you see me in Florence?" His assistant, Luigi, confirmed that Nureyev's performance there had been "a triumph." The Italian audiences slept in the street for three nights in order to get tickets and enormous crowds greeted him there. Never mind that this fan had flown to Zurich to see him perform shortly afterward. Nureyev remembered the fan missed the specific performance in Florence.

It was like déjà vu when this same fan, unable to see him perform in Manchester, sent him a good-luck telegram. As they walked together after a Paris performance, Nureyev teased, "But you didn't come to Manchester!" When this fan commented that his production of *Romeo and Juliet* looked better on the Paris stage than in London, Rudolf responded, "You should have been in Sydney; there it worked even better because the stage was bigger." After the fan countered that traveling to performances had become too expensive and time-consuming, Rudolf genially replied, "Don't torture yourself."

In the spring of 1974, I was still in London and especially arranged my vacation in order to see Rudolf's production of *The Sleeping Beauty* for the National Ballet of Canada at the New York's Metropolitan Opera House. I worked until the last possible moment, and then took a flight to New York the next morning. The flight left twenty minutes late. Due to turbulence, we lost another fifteen minutes crossing the Atlantic. Luck was with me, however, for I was one of the first travelers off the plane and cleared customs in less than two minutes. After collecting my luggage, I was delighted to find a bus waiting to take passengers straight into Manhattan. Good subway connections allowed me to pick up my ticket at the Box Office, check my luggage, and race upstairs to the Dress Circle, just as the lights went down where my friends were waiting for me. They exclaimed, "We can't believe you made it in time!" Nureyev spotted me at the Stage Door and amusingly asked, "Back here now?"

One night during one of his long London seasons, many of us were really tired and decided to skip the Stage Door routine in favor of a good night's sleep. The next night it was Luigi who asked, "Where WERE you last night? We didn't see you."

After the premiere of his *Romeo and Juliet* production in 1977, one of his fans asked about the symbols that appeared over Juliet's tomb in the last act. "I haven't had time to look!" Rudolf replied, adding "Ask Frigerio," the designer. A full week later, he passed the same fan and swiftly said, "Alpha and Omega – the beginning and the end," continuing their discussion in mid-sentence.

It took a lot of advance planning to keep up with Nureyev's schedule. As one French fan reminded him, "We have to plan our holidays for next year, so is your schedule finalized yet?" He rattled off his performance schedule for all those who asked. When asked about performances in France, he replied, "It's not signed yet, so I cannot say and things are always very difficult with the Paris Opera." Rudolf was truthful, but since contracts were still pending, he could not respond to our questions. However, we assumed something was in the works whenever we saw a mysterious twinkle in his eye when he responded. He often gave fans his dates even before his agent learned of them.

In 1975, the Royal Ballet instituted a "no Guest Artist" policy and Nureyev's contract was not renewed. Even though Rudolf felt the Royal was his "home company," he decided he had to "become my own impresario" and began to create his many *Nureyev and Friends* or *Nureyev Festival* seasons. One fan asked, "So you won't be dancing with the Royal Ballet anymore?" to which the dancer retorted, "Do you see me crying? I have to work." It was a sore spot with him for some time.

Nureyev's unquenchable thirst for dancing meant he often danced nightly for a six-week London season, then boarded a plane for another season elsewhere. Living in London afforded me the wonderful opportunity to head across the Channel for a weekend, to see him perform in Paris or Amsterdam. Unfortunately, time, finances, and work prevented me from attending every single performance, as I would gladly have done. Once I moved to New York in 1975, I certainly logged many frequent flyer miles going back and forth across the Atlantic whenever possible.

Whenever fans traveled to see him, he usually asked questions like, "Here for the weekend?" or "Back to work tomorrow?" When Nureyev performed at the *Edinburgh Festival*, one of his British fans went backstage to greet him. Rudolf said, "I thought that was you!" after spotting him during curtain calls.

After a wintery night's *Nureyev Festival* performance in Paris, Rudolf came out of the Palais des Sports to find a line of fans waiting for him in the falling snow. He made his way down the "receiving line" shaking hands and saying "Hi" to each person. When he got to me, he did a double take since most of the fans were French or British and he knew I came a long way to see him. He greeted me with an especially warm smile and asked, "How are you?"

For one of Nureyev's performances in Washington, D.C., I joined a busload of New Yorkers to make the trip. When Rudolf emerged from the Stage Door, he looked momentarily confused as to where he was, since he saw so many New York fans gathered outside the Kennedy Center. "But this is Washington!" he exclaimed.

Over the years, we watched Nureyev change from tolerating his fans to genuinely caring about us. He became familiar with our names and knew which ones he could trust, tease, or seek advice from. His 1974 appearance on the *Dick Cavett Show* in New York marked a turning point, in which he pointed to the very enthusiastic balcony crowd and proudly announced, "Those are my fans!" Cavett remarked in amazement "You've gotten more applause than Mick Jagger got."

Nureyev had a genuine curiosity about his fans and was interested to know about our lives outside of dance. One fan introduced Nureyev to her husband who said, "I've always wanted to meet the man who's spending all my money." Laughing, Rudolf suggested, "Maybe it's tax deductible?" Not surprisingly, given his memory, the next time Rudolf saw the same fan, he humorously inquired, "Still spending your husband's money?" One of

Nureyev's fans took up ballet at the age of fifty because she was so inspired by him. When Rudolf heard this, he was truly pleased for her and wished her good luck. She ended up becoming a respected teacher and staff member of a ballet company. When a young fan informed Rudolf she was studying for her exams, he wished her good luck. Several nights later, he thoughtfully inquired, "How did you do on your exams?" Another fan moved away from London, and Rudolf kindly wished her well. He then asked, if she would be working for a company that she told him about several YEARS before, a testament to his amazing memory.

Maude and Nigel Gosling, Rudolf's unofficial "adopted parents," frequently chatted with us at performances and obviously shared any news with Rudolf. When one fan that studied law had a successful career, Maude told us, "WE are all so proud of him," meaning Rudolf as well.

This personal approach with his public was a unique quality of Nureyev. When a student presented him with champagne and caviar, he heartily exclaimed, "You're mad!" Rudolf knew that she had little money. "You noticed?" she quipped, to which he laughed but immediately added, "You shouldn't spend all your money on me."

In Paris, two elderly sisters waited for Rudolf at the Stage Door whenever possible. Later only one sister was there. Rudolf greeted her and inquired politely where was her sister. "She died," the woman answered sadly. Rudolf tenderly took both of her hands in his and squeezed them, saying gently, "Hold on." Several years later, this same woman, then in her 80s, made the trip from Paris to Vienna during the winter, to see Nureyev's production of *Swan Lake*. He was so touched at seeing her. He held her hands for a while, remarking how cold they were. He then invited her to attend the rehearsal.

Luigi got to know the usual fans and often engaged in conversation. One night a woman waited for Rudolf at the Stage Door, while her husband chatted with a waiting taxi driver who asked, "How long has your wife been watching Rudi dance?" Before he had a chance to reply, Luigi, who stood nearby waiting for Rudolf to finish signing autographs, piped up, "Fifteen years!" Luigi's own daughter, Alessandra, sometimes came from Italy with her mother during long seasons. In 1977, when Nureyev danced an unprecedented seven-week London season, performing every night, it was necessary to keep his body in top form, so Luigi was needed as his masseur. After one performance, we noticed Rudolf bouncing a baby on his lap and playing with her prior to signing autographs and we realized it was Luigi's daughter. Years later, Luigi related one instance when he took Alessandra to see a performance of another company on his night off and after some time she turned to him and said, "Daddy, let's go. Rudi's not dancing."

After an exhilarating matinee performance of *Nutcracker*, a small child was clutching a program outside the Stage Door with tears streaming down her face. Rudolf called her over to him, bent down, embraced her and gently dried her tears. When she quickly calmed down, he inquired, "Did you enjoy the performance?"

On a New York television interview, Rudolf compared his American public with those in other countries. "People are cheerful here and they're not uptight. Anybody can come to you and talk to you…and leave you alone. People are relaxed in America, also in France and Italy. Not in Britain. They would be very polite by their upbringing, but they would leave you alone too long." That *Good Morning America* program was aired on July 4, 1979, the day one of his British fans arrived to see him perform in New York. After the performance, he went backstage, gave Rudolf a huge hug, and said, "I'm here to dispel the rumor that the British are unfriendly." Rudolf laughed uproariously, and quipped, "It's taken eighteen years!"

In Amsterdam, one sunny afternoon in the late 70s, I waited at the Stage Door with several European friends, prior to a matinee performance with the Dutch National Ballet. It was my first visit to Amsterdam, and, since many fans had arrived from other parts of the world, we were busy catching up on the latest news. We formed a semi-circle around the Stage Door, with an opening at one end facing the street, expecting Nureyev to arrive by car or taxi. After much animated discussion, we saw a familiar figure strolling toward the theatre on foot, enjoying the warm sunshine. As Nureyev approached the Stage Door, and the ever-familiar crowd, he remarked somewhat sarcastically, "Same old faces." One of the fans objected to his remark, saying, "And thank God for that, Rudolf, or you wouldn't have anyone to greet you." He grinned sheepishly and disappeared into the theatre. The next day, seeing the "same old faces," he changed his tactics. "How are the guards?" he inquired, to which we replied, "Just fine, thank you," and playfully saluted him.

Similar salutes became a standing joke over the years. Outside of the Kennedy Center in Washington, several fans formed two rows of "guards" when we raised our umbrellas in place of swords as he passed under them. He always merited applause as he made his Stage Door entrance or exit.

Over time, Nureyev began having fun with us and his witty sense of humor was always in evidence. One December season in New York, Nureyev exited the theatre wrapped in his fur coat. In a teasing mood, he hesitated between the Stage Door and his car as though wanting to speak with the fans, but seemed reluctant to do so. Instead he began talking into thin air with a mock New York accent, "Really? Fantastic! Incredible!" When he got into a waiting car, the driver said, "I almost didn't recognize you; is that a new coat?" "No," Nureyev explained, "it's the same furry coat I had all season." "Oh, somebody else must have one just like yours," the driver suggested, to which Rudolf retorted imperiously, "Somebody ELSE?"

Rudolf Nureyev made a historic "crossover" from classical ballet to modern dance by performing as a guest artist with the Martha Graham Company. Up until that time, the two styles of dance had remained separate. He studied diligently with Graham herself and she created several works for him. By the summer of 1975, I had returned to New York and was able to see Rudolf in many of his modern dance roles. He debuted in Graham's *Night Journey* on a Wednesday matinee and quite a few us had an imaginary "dentist appointment" that afternoon, so we could leave work in order to see Nureyev's debut.

There were many Graham enthusiasts in the audience, ready to evaluate Nureyev's performance. Dramatically, Nureyev was wonderful, but he hadn't yet perfectly mastered the Graham style. At the curtain calls, the Graham devotees roundly booed him. Rudolf was mortified and looked as if he wanted the floor to swallow him up. When Graham came out to take a bow with him, she squeezed his hand and gave him an understanding smile. When they emerged from the Stage Door, an unhappy-looking Rudolf headed directly towards a waiting car. Graham then told him, "Don't worry, doll, it will be better tonight." And it was.

While waiting at various Stage Doors, we often had conversations with some of Nureyev's colleagues. Once they got to know us, they sometimes provided bits of private or exclusive information, such as "Rudolf is tired tonight," or "Did you know he's going to be on TV tomorrow?"

At his 1978 *Nureyev and Friends* season on Broadway, several of us engaged in a lengthy discussion with choreographer Murray Louis, whose works Rudolf was performing. Louis gave us his analysis of Nureyev in modern works. He reported that Rudolf was becoming very fluid in his choreographic style and that such modern movement could prolong Nureyev's dance career "by another ten years." "But then," Louis continued, "He's going off to dance *Swan Lake* again next week and he'll have to start all over again" when returning to the modern style.

Despite Nureyev's superstar celebrity and charismatic stage persona, we often witnessed a different side of him at the Stage Door. His good friend, Douce Francoise, came from Paris to see one of Rudolf's London seasons during the early 80s. After signing numerous autographs, he and Douce headed for the car to go out to dinner. As Rudolf fumbled to unlock the car, he became self-conscious due to the staring crowds and couldn't open the door. Suddenly he grew impatient and tossed the car keys over the top of the car toward Douce, saying, "YOU open it." Douce wasn't about to be intimidated by Nureyev or the crowds, so she tossed the keys back to him and retorted, "It's your car – you open it!" Before our very eyes, this exploding powerhouse suddenly turned into a cowering puppy dog as he tried – and eventually succeeded – in opening the car door. He quickly got into the car and looked sheepishly at Douce beside him and at the crowd on the sidewalk. He was thoroughly embarrassed as they drove off into the night.

Another late evening in London, Rudolf became flustered at not being able to start his new car. He couldn't find the ignition, flashed the retractable headlights, and honked the horn. The car lurched forward in a burst of speed, only to come to a screeching halt at the corner traffic light. When the car careened around the corner and disappeared, I remarked, "It's a good thing he's a better dancer than a driver."

Nureyev was a master of practical advice. One of his fans jokingly complained that because of escalating ticket prices, she would have to cut back on seeing him perform. "I can't keep doing this, Rudi. I'm living on bread, butter and cheese as it is." Without missing a beat, he offered, "Why don't you skip the butter?" Rudolf consoled another fan who complained about being unable to travel to see all the foreign companies. He explained, "But you live in New York City – you just stay in one place and see everybody pass by!"

Several fans crowded around Nureyev after a Broadway performance and tried to guess what he would dance in his next upcoming season. The advance publicity merely said Nureyev would perform in "other works" or "to be announced." In a playful and teasing mood, Rudolf commented, "It's not listed? That's funny." Then, putting on his "Now listen carefully, children" tone of voice, he advised, "Look, you come to theatre, you buy ticket, you sit in seat, and you wait for curtain to go up. Then you be surprised!"

One of Nureyev's fans was an artist and wanted to show Rudolf the portrait he had painted of the dancer. He brought the painting backstage one night and patiently waited for Jacqueline Kennedy Onassis and other visitors to leave the dressing room. Rudolf studied the fan's painting and remarked, "My eyes are more twinkling than that." The painter agreed to go home and put more sparkle in the eyes. The next night, Rudolf studied it again and teased, "My lower lip is fuller than that." The fan teased him right back and said, "Is it? Let's have a close look." Rudolf gave a hearty laugh.

Another friend of mine was an outstanding painter and really managed to capture Rudolf on canvas. She showed him a painting she had created from a photograph of Nureyev performing in a modern work. He took one look at it, pointed to a muscle where the shoulder meets the neck and muttered, "Hmmm, big muscle." "Too much?" the fan inquired. "A bit," he replied, quickly adding, "There's my haystack hair." It was very unkempt in the photo and she had merely copied it.

While much of our Stage Door conversations with Rudolf centered on dates for future performances, he also offered good travel advice, such as what to see or how to get to a certain destination. The advice was often reciprocal. When a fan remarked, "Tonight's performance was different," Rudolf asked "How is it different?"

After Nureyev's unusually long absence from New York, several fans flew to Miami to see him perform there. When Rudolf emerged from the theatre, the crowd burst into enthusiastic applause and he teasingly cocked one hand to his ear as if to say, "What? I can't hear you!" As he went through the crowd greeting everyone, one of his long-time fans threw her arms around his neck and exclaimed, "Rudolf, I haven't seen you in over nine months. I could have had a baby by now!" Nureyev gave an uproarious laugh. His comeback was, "Or a false pregnancy?"

While Rudolf seemed to relish the attention he received at the Stage Door, occasionally it proved challenging. London had its share of eccentric characters including one elderly lady who cackled like a witch whenever she laughed. She walked Rudolf to his car, arm in arm, causing one fan to remark, "How come SHE's so lucky?" Rudolf patted the woman on the head and she cackled with delight. "Wait, dearie," she babbled to him. "Let me give you my address in case you come to see me."

One young girl invited him for coffee. "I will come to dinner with you," Rudolf replied, "But I don't drink coffee." She ran to her mother, exclaiming, "Mother, he said he would come to dinner but not coffee!" This was most amusing because at that time a local British comic strip called *Agatha* ran a continuing series about a young fan inviting Rudolf Nureyev for afternoon tea and all the fuss she made in preparing for his visit.

A rather down-and-out British woman with a shopping cart used to jabber excitedly whenever she saw Rudolf, but was basically harmless. We called her "Granny." Nureyev always seemed slightly amused by her whenever she babbled, "You were lovely, dear, just lovely tonight," in a motherly fashion. One evening she was gushing endlessly about Nureyev's performance and the Stage Door attendant turned and joked, "Hey Rudi, are you writing her a script?" Another night she walked Rudolf to his car, telling him, "Take care. See you soon, bye-bye, luv," and the likes, while Rudolf tried getting into his car. Finally he put his arm around her shoulder and teased her, "I'm being raped!"

Usually the crowds surrounding Nureyev at the Stage Door were respectful, but sometimes there was an individual who could cause trouble. One woman in New York tried to close the car door on Rudolf's foot as he got in his car. One fast-acting protective fan pulled her away and the two got into a scuffle. Some of the fans formed a barrier between the ruckus and Nureyev's car so he could get away safely and we knew that police protection was necessary. For the remainder of that Broadway season, police were assigned to "Door duty" to monitor the crowds and ensure Rudolf's safety.

Another incident occurred when a large, rather strange man waited outside the London Coliseum. Nureyev exited the theatre so quickly that the waiting crowd didn't even notice him. Luigi, thinking Rudolf was inside signing autographs, returned to the theatre to get Rudolf's bags. Rudolf strolled over to the TR7, parked behind the permanent garbage bin, only to find the car was locked. Suddenly the large man headed directly for Nureyev, pointed his finger and yelled, "You, Russian boy!" He threw both arms around him, nearly squashing Rudolf against his car. He winched in discomfort and pulled away from the man trying to humor him. When Luigi appeared, Rudi asked him in Italian, "Were you sleeping?" and gently bopped him on the head with his bouquet of flowers. The large man began sobbing uncontrollably so Rudolf told him, "Go cry to him. He's a good listener," pointing to Luigi who had by now unlocked the car. Once inside, Rudolf relaxed, especially since the guy was leaning on the car, but thankfully the window was closed. The car safely departed, leaving the rest of us somewhat relieved.

Rudolf usually managed to pacify these characters with humor and grace. The year of 1977 marked Queen Elizabeth's Silver Jubilee and Rudolf was sipping tea from a new Jubilee commemorative mug while signing autographs in his car. One overly enthusiastic fan thrust herself at him through the open window and Rudolf promptly instructed, "Don't break my cup!"

A young man outside the Stage Door one night was waxing rhapsodic about this "great dancer" Nureyev. Rudolf paused while signing autographs, looked up with a grin and exclaimed, "Ah, the voice of the people!"

Once while signing autographs, a strange woman planted herself next to him. She kept whispering in his ear. "I'm a Pisces, too – we're both flighty, you know." She asked him to kiss her. He replied mockingly, "If I did I'd probably faint dead away." When the woman refused to move from Rudolf's side, he finally said to her, "Aren't you tired of being a pest?" The crowd around him applauded heartily.

In 1981, Rudolf Nureyev and Mikhail Baryshnikov joined forces to perform in Paul Taylor's *From Sea to Shining Sea* for a fund-raising gala. Despite the media hype concerning the two dancers performing "together for the first time on stage," some in the gala audience loathed this spoof about episodes from American history. When Taylor appeared on stage for a curtain call, there were some audible boos, so Rudolf pulled him forward, insisting the audience applaud him. The crush to see Nureyev at the Stage Door was so large that Baryshnikov was able to slip out unnoticed. When Nureyev emerged, he "conducted" the applause, joking, "It was nothing, really."

Ballerina Natalia Makarova joined Nureyev in *The Lesson* in London. I very much wanted my program signed by these two former Kirov stars. Just as I was about to hand my program to Rudolf, Makarova came out, dressed in a long gown and carrying masses of flowers. Rudolf quickly asked her, "Are you ready?" He put his pen down and escorted Makarova to his two-seat TR7. He placed all her bouquets on the ledge behind the seat. Then he crawled in and sat on the tape deck while Makarova sat on his lap. With Luigi in the driver's seat, they glamorously headed to dinner.

If Rudolf was in particularly good spirits, we were often treated to an extra "performance" at these Stage Door gatherings. During a freezing New York winter season, he signed half a dozen autographs in the cold, when some of his fans yelled "Bravo!" hoping that would signal him to get into his waiting and warm car. He gave us a mock bow, did a little pirouette, and elegantly backed into the car.

After traveling to Toronto to see his production of *The Sleeping Beauty,* several fans from New York applauded him vigorously when he emerged from the Stage Door. He stopped still in his tracks and began conducting the applause, even swaying his body and waving his arms as if to force more crescendo or fortissimo out of his "orchestra." Then he put one hand on the Stage Door, and pretended to fall out of it, grinning and waving. He finished with a Groucho Marx flash of the eyebrows and an old vaudeville routine. He went back inside, then poked his head out as if to say "That's all, folks!"

Arriving one night at the Stage Door, he discovered musicians dressed as troubadours gathered around while arranging their sheet music to serenade him. Rudolf sang out, "One, two three let's go" and they began playing while he did a little dance for everyone, hiking up the edges of his coat. As he turned to enter the elevator, he tossed his head back and kicked one leg behind him.

It was in Washington that we first saw Nureyev emerging from the Stage Door wearing shorts. The temperature was extremely hot that 1980 summer season. After a matinee, he left the theatre wearing a sweater, his cap, clogs, and very short shorts. A camera crew was filming Rudolf for TV as he left the Kennedy Center. The fans all cheered and the crew remarked, "It's the same fans we saw in New York." Rudolf walked from the theatre to the nearby Watergate Hotel, waving a single red rose at the cheering crowd. Hordes of fans followed him at a respectful distance. As he headed into the hotel, Rudolf turned and bowed to us. The film crew was amazed and amused, not just by the attention Nureyev commanded, but by the fact that his fans respectfully stopped at the hotel and refused to follow him any further.

After another matinee in Washington, Rudolf walked across the road and sat on the edge of the nearby fountain, removed his clogs, and soaked his feet in the cool water.

Some of the fans shared rooms at the Watergate Hotel that season. After the last performance, they went to have a late-night meal at the hotel's restaurant and discovered Valery and Galina Panov and most of the Berlin Ballet Company sitting with Nureyev for a cast party. The fans were seated at an adjacent table and did their best not to stare. In a celebratory mood, Rudolf entertained everyone with an aria from *La Traviata*. When finished, he glanced to his fans at their table to see their reaction. One jokingly gave him a "so-so" gesture, hoping he wouldn't give up his "day job."

During a freezing cold Broadway season in 1983, one of his fans gave Rudolf a battery-operated rose that lit up. Rudolf clutched this tacky thing as if it were a new toy. When he left the theatre, he sat in the back seat of the waiting limo and waved it back and forth, passing it to everyone in the car. Because of traffic, it took the driver a while to depart, so we observed this world-famous dancer, who could buy anything he wanted, playing with a silly $3 rose. Following the performance, a couple of fans went for a drink at the Russian Tea Room. Shortly after they arrived, Rudolf entered, wrapped in his glamorous Blackgama fur coat. He waved his battery rose as if blessing one and all. Everyone in the restaurant burst into applause.

Nureyev always made a fashion statement with his wide assortment of stylish hats, boots, sweaters, scarves, and distinctive attire. After one performance at the Met, I noticed him sporting a new outfit. He wore a white sailor suit with his fur coat and cap. When he sat in the back seat of the waiting taxi, he stuck his foot on the back of the front seat, pulled up one pant leg and asked us with a self-satisfied smile, "Did you see the shoes?"

When not performing, Rudolf could be ambivalent about crowds of people surrounding him. He expected an "audience" at the Stage Door, and proved amusing if people didn't notice him. With his teasing sense of humor, he sometimes played tricks on his fans. Occasionally, the fans turned the tables on him.

Behind the London Coliseum was a block of flats on Bedfordbury Street, directly opposite the Stage Door. A short wall with a wide ledge divided the street from the property, which provided a perfect meeting place on which to sit while waiting for Rudolf. Sometimes we were so busy talking that we didn't notice him arrive for the performance. When that happened, he would exit his car, pause in the Stage Door entrance, clear his throat, and practically announce, "I'm here!" More often than not, however, we were attentive, and even opened the door for him when he was laden with things to carry. When the suitcases on wheels became popular, Rudolf went everywhere with one, calling it "my dog" as he pulled it behind him.

Following one New York performance with the National Ballet of Canada, some of the fans gathered near Rudolf's waiting limousine to escape the huge crowds huddled by the Stage Door. Just when Nureyev approached, he made a sudden decision to get into the car parked behind the limo. One of his loyal fans quipped, "First time I've been this near the car and what happens – he goes to another one." Obviously overhearing this remark, Rudolf laughed, turned to us and said, "Fooled you!"

On another occasion in London, Rudolf and fans tried outsmarting each other. After a company party, Luigi brought Rudolf's car around to the Coliseum's front entrance, informing us that Rudolf would be quite late due to the party. Most fans waited at the Stage Door while one decided to check out the front. At the corner, the fan bumped into Rudolf. With his Cheshire cat grin, he merely said, "Hi!"

I recall the time when two of his British fans were walking away from the Stage Door after a performance. They talked animatedly and didn't notice that Rudolf was just behind them en route to a nearby restaurant. "Hello" he said, as he was about to pass them. They assumed it was another friend trying to catch up with them so they matter-of-factly said "Hello." Both did a double take when they saw it was Nureyev, who was highly amused by their reaction.

In 1975 there was an intense campaign, primarily supported by the London public, to allow dancers Valery and Galina Panov out of the Soviet Union. At that time they were under house arrest for trying to emigrate and both of their dancing careers were in jeopardy. When they were finally granted visas, Galina was scheduled to dance with Rudolf in his production of *The Sleeping Beauty*. The British public enthusiastically looked forward to seeing her perform with him. When Galina arrived, she had just eight days to learn the role. Whether due to nerves or an eagerness to please, Galina changed the choreography in several places, adding multiple pirouettes and surprising Nureyev with many unrehearsed moments. In addition, the performance finished a full quarter of an hour earlier than usual, due to a much faster orchestra tempo.

Nureyev, whose car had been stopped earlier that evening for speeding en route to the theatre, was not in the best of moods. He "behaved badly" towards his ballerina by pulling faces on stage whenever he was displeased with something. In his quest for perfection, he grew impatient with himself and with others over musical tempi, incorrect lighting cues, or mistakes with the dancing – especially in his own production. Nureyev made no attempt to hide his irritation, and with the consequential lack of applause the British public showed that they were not amused.

At the Stage Door, we discussed how appallingly he had behaved. Someone suggested we forget about waiting for him and go directly home. It suddenly began to rain, so we ducked into a nearby alleyway adjacent to the theatre for shelter. The conversation about the evening's performance continued. Just as we peered around the corner, Nureyev emerged from the theatre. We watched his reaction at not seeing anyone waiting for him. Not a soul was in sight, which was most unusual. Nureyev's car was fairly close by, so he wouldn't have to walk far in the rain. Before he reached the protection of his car, he halted and glanced left and right for someone – anyone – to interact with. He looked so disheartened that we couldn't resist hiding any longer and popped out from the alleyway, unable to contain our laughter. He broke into a huge laugh, enjoyed our prank, and drove off into the night in considerably better spirits.

Sometimes when Nureyev left the Stage Door quickly, he delighted in slipping through the crowds to see if he would be recognized. Standing next to the locked car sipping the last of his tea, he and I exchanged glances but I wasn't about to spoil his moment of fun. He enjoyed a few minutes of anonymity before someone shouted, "Oh look, there's Rudi" and he was instantly surrounded. He was in a marvelously relaxed mood, greeting old friends with a handshake and large grin. A helpful fan took his arm, explaining, "The car is this way," to which Rudolf teased, "Are you my driver?"

A small group of fans went backstage to see Rudolf and their brief visit stretched to an hour. As Nureyev and the others were about to exit the stage door, Luigi handed Rudolf a pen to sign autographs. Given the hour that had elapsed since the performance finished, Rudolf stated, "Nobody will be waiting." But, of course, once he opened the stage door, an enormous crowd greeted him.

One friend was backstage just before Nureyev danced *Spectre de la Rose* with the Joffrey Ballet. Beatriz Rodriguez, debuting in the role of the Young Girl, entered his dressing room in full stage makeup. Nureyev reminded her, "Be sure to keep your eyes closed or you'll give the whole game away." The audience had to see that she was "dreaming" of the rose's spirit, but dancing with one's eyes closed cannot be easy.

After a gala in honor of Martha Graham, a couple of friends who paid extra money to attend the post-performance party related, that everyone stood around gawking at Nureyev. One of my friends approached him and asked how he was being treated, since he took over the Directorship of the Paris Opera. He merely replied, "It's more important what you do." Later in the evening, Rudolf said to the fans, "Why don't you guys come backstage with me?" Once in the dressing room, Rudolf seemed more relaxed and my friend presented him with a box of cookies. His eyes lit up as they were a particular favorite of his. He also enjoyed the new coffee mug imprinted with the words, "Damn, I'm good!"

The only time I ever went backstage was when a friend invited me to visit Eva Evdokimova, after opening night of the 1984 Broadway *Friends* season. The corridor was jammed with dancers from various dance companies, including recent Russian émigrés Valentina and Leonid Kozlov, and Alexander Godunov. We visited briefly with Eva and after the crowd disbursed, crossed the stage to Rudolf's dressing room. Lillian Libman, the producer of the season, ushered us in, a few at a time. Rudolf was dressed in a three-piece suit, his "administrative look" for important Paris Opera events. He had just washed his hair but hadn't combed it yet. With the dressing table lights shining in my eyes, all I could see was this dapper man with porcupine hair sticking up every which way. Nureyev greeted everyone warmly and with a smile.

While waiting for the elevator to street level, Rudolf and his entourage came up behind us and insisted that we join them. To "entertain" us, Libman and dancer Jean Guizerix did a little chorus kick for designer Rouben Ter-Arutunian, who was also present. Rudolf placed his foot next to Jean's to compare shoe sizes and asked, "Where did you get those sandals? We could use them next time I dance in *Faune*. Do you know how much we paid for mine? Too much!" When we followed Rudolf out the Stage Door, I got a sense of what he experienced when he left theatres: a barrage of flashbulbs, tumultuous applause, and multiple hands reaching out with programs and pens for autographs. Rudolf usually obliged, even if it meant being late for the cast party.

As Nureyev matured, he began confiding with his fans, often at the Stage Door. In 1974, Mikhail Baryshnikov was about to make his American Ballet Theatre debut on the same night that Nureyev was performing his *Sleeping Beauty* at the Met. Rudolf remarked to the fans, "I hear there's a new boy in town." I went to see Baryshnikov perform in *Giselle*, but felt conflicted about missing Nureyev's performance. *Giselle* finished before *Sleeping Beauty*, so I raced across the Lincoln Center plaza in time for Nureyev's curtain calls, which were so generous and filled with pride, that I got enough from those few minutes to make up for missing the entire performance. The next night after Nureyev's performance, one of the fans remarked, "I know all about the new boy, but I still like the old boy." Rudolf beamed.

In the privacy of his dressing room, he frequently opened up. One fan went backstage and found Rudolf in a very low mood. He had danced through many injuries that season and was in pain. He confided that the producers "just want me to dance. I could kill myself on that stage and they wouldn't care. I'm a dance machine, that's all. They don't care about me as a person." Yet when he emerged from the theatre to see us waiting, his mood definitely brightened and he paused to chat. As my friend remarked, "Sometimes the worse he is, the more he fusses with the public." He said that he worried if his fans didn't turn up for his performances. "Am I really finished? Maybe the fans no longer like me?" While it was true that some no longer came to his performances, I was part of the loyal core group that watched him to the end.

Rudolf continued to work, often in increasingly smaller cities and venues. One of his fans spotted him at London's Euston Station waiting for the train to Manchester, where he was performing as a guest. She bought him a cup of tea and found him in a melancholy but talkative mood. Rudolf complained about the Royal Ballet and said "they don't want me anymore." They offered him a paltry four performances for the year. He confided, "That's hardly worth flying the Atlantic for." When he did return to dance a previously scheduled *Petrushka*, Founder and former Director Dame Ninette de Valois was spotted in the company box, applauding wildly long after the houselights came up. It was de Valois who first saw Rudolf Nureyev in the early 60s and thought he would be a good partner for Margot Fonteyn. When she left as Director of the Royal Ballet, a bust of de Valois was placed inside the Opera House. She once joked with Rudolf to cut his hair, because people thought the statue was of Nureyev!

When Nureyev became Director of the Paris Opera in 1983, his schedule grew increasingly more complicated. In addition to creating productions and coaching the dancers, he continued dancing with other companies or with a group of French dancers for his *Friends* programs. Sometimes these programs were organized rather hastily, so several fans became "Pen Pals" with Rudolf's assistant, Marie-Suzanne Sourbie, who usually notified us whenever possible about his performances. Taking a group of his French dancers on tour provided them with amazing opportunities to perform on all kinds of stages and under different circumstances. It enabled some of the younger dancers to take on leading roles, prior to their Paris Opera debuts.

At the age of 48, Rudolf performed the role of Franz in *Coppelia* with London Festival Ballet, taking a few days off from his directorial duties in Paris. He later stated that he loved dancing with them, because "the company respects me." "You must understand," he confided, "that the French dancers are very capricious. Some nights they just don't turn up for the performance, so I have to put in other dancers who don't know the ballet. They eat me inside out, but they deliver." By 1988, when asked how things were going, Rudolf confided, "I won't dance in Paris any more. There are too many claques and I've had enough."

One night in London, Luigi confided to us that Rudolf wanted to give a party for his fans to show his appreciation. He wasn't sure how to organize it, because we all lived in different countries and he didn't have our contact information. To save him the trouble, we invited Rudolf to a picnic we planned on a Sunday when he wasn't performing. Even though he didn't turn up because he went to an opera at Glyndbourne that afternoon, we still had a good time walking along Sussex Downs and drinking to Nureyev's health.

After the fall of the Berlin Wall in 1989, Nureyev was invited to Russia to make guest appearances with the Kirov. Even though he only danced with his former ballet company for three years before his defection, many of his Russian fans never forgot him and were eagerly waiting at the airport to greet him. Shortly after returning, he performed a *Friends* program in Washington, D.C. His loyal fans waited at the Kennedy Center's Stage Door and when Rudolf appeared, he genuinely commented, "How cheerful your faces are compared to those in Leningrad."

Nureyev continued performing, even accelerating his schedule, dancing anything and everything that was offered to him. When the Cleveland Ballet asked him to perform Dr. Coppelius in their production of *Coppelia*, he willingly accepted, but quipped to one of his fans, "Come for the second night. I might know the choreography by then!" It was the first time he performed the character role, rather than the leading role of Franz.

Disappointed that none of the New York critics had gone to Cleveland to see his debut in *The Overcoat*, a work created for Nureyev in 1991 by Flemming Flindt, Rudolf openly expressed this letdown to his fans. One mischievously said, "Next time we see this person, we'll dump a bucket of shit over the critic's head." As he was driven away from the Stage Door, Rudolf rolled down the car window and quipped, "Make sure it's fresh!"

One of his longest artist-fan relationships was with Katherine Healy. From the age of four, when her parents first brought her to Nureyev's performances at the Met, she was one of his greatest admirers. Every evening, she waited at the Stage Door with her bouquets to greet him. In the early years, Rudolf seemed puzzled by this, and even said to her, "You should be home in bed." What he didn't realize was that Kathy had the same passion for dance that he did. Once he saw how serious she was, he befriended her. Spotting Kathy as he approached the theatre, he frequently took her hand and walked with her as far as the Stage Door. Katherine studied dance at the School of American Ballet and was chosen by George Balanchine to dance in *The Nutcracker* at the age of eight. She went on to win the Gold Medal at the Varna Competition in 1983 and became a ballerina with London Festival Ballet at the age of fifteen. The following year, at the age of sixteen, Sir Frederick Ashton personally coached her in the title role of his revived production of *Romeo and Juliet*.

It was a pity that Rudolf was busy with his own London season at the same time that Kathy was performing Juliet and he never had the chance to see her. On her nights off, Kathy came to see Nureyev dance Albrecht, during his Coliseum season. She went backstage to visit him one night and he exclaimed, "It's Kathy 'Seven Pirouettes' Healy," acknowledging her natural turning ability. Nureyev finally saw her dance years later, when they both appeared at a gala. Kathy performed the *Flames of Paris* pas de deux, a very bravura Russian ballet, while Rudolf watched in the wings. The applause was so enthusiastic that he signaled Kathy to do an encore.

Kathy had a brief but remarkable career as a dancer, even performing in some of Nureyev's ballets, before returning to skating, her first love. She became a respected teacher and coach of both skating and dancing, successfully choreographing her own routines.

At his last performance at the Met with the Paris Opera in 1988, Nureyev was overwhelmed by the Stage Door crowds, who all carried roses to give him one last send-off. As he made his way through the multitudes of people, he seemed to look at each face, trying to commit it to memory. One little girl, wearing a long white dress, obviously conjured up earlier memories for him, because he paused in front of her and then turned to some of his longtime fans and said, "Remember Kathy?"

Certainly one of our more adventurous experiences occurred following a *Friends* program in August of 1985. Nureyev appeared with some Paris Opera dancers at the Garden State Arts Center in Holmdel, New Jersey. This was an open-air theatre with a covered stage in the middle of a huge park. Two of Rudolf's loyal fans went backstage after the performance, because they had arranged to take some of his costumes back to his Dakota apartment for him. The rest of us tried to figure out where the Stage Door was. We tried entering from the stage area, but three burly security guards, feet firmly planted and arms crossed, prevented anyone from entering. We walked around to the back of the theatre, in the dark, and saw – to our amazement – barbed wire fences. It seems this venue was used for rock concerts and they were very concerned about security.

We walked through the parking lot and ended up on a road leading to the back of the stage area. Immediately a young guard stopped us and asked, "Do you have a pass?" We said no, we merely wanted to wait for Rudolf. "You can't wait here; it's a restricted area," he said. "Restricted? It's a street," we protested. "I'm going to get my supervisor," the young man threatened. "There's no people allowed here – EVER!" We laughed and thought the whole thing was a joke. Soon the two loyal supporters came out with Rudolf's luggage and piled it into the nearby car. We gathered around the car and another guard came out shouting, "If you don't leave, you'll be arrested." We defended our right to wait, while one enthusiastic fan remarked that it was just like the 60s again, getting arrested for passive resistance. A police car arrived, expecting trouble. Someone else emerged from the Stage Door, only to return again to tell Rudolf what was going on outside. Another policeman got on his radio and called for reinforcements and still another police car pulled up, practically surrounding us.

At this point, Nureyev emerged with one of his fans. She pointed to all of the police and to the rest of us cowering around his getaway car. Rudolf nearly collapsed with laughter. Instead of applauding him, we shouted, "Rudolf, they're going to arrest us!" To break the tension, Rudolf began doing a little dance for us – a pirouette, a soft shoe – followed by a deep bow. The cops looked on in amazement as we applauded him. Rudolf got into his waiting car, rolled down the window and then asked one of the policemen, "How do I get to the expressway from here?" They couldn't do enough for him and eagerly began giving him specific directions. "Thank you," Rudolf said matter-of-factly, waved to us, and drove off. As we quietly departed, the cops looked at us and mimed to each other, "That's it?" They had anticipated a riot, but we always respected Nureyev for the artist that he was and certainly didn't want to cause trouble. We laughed about what had happened all the way home, picturing the headlines: "Fans arrested and thrown in jail, because they were waiting for Rudolf!"

"Friendship isn't something you get by looking for it. It is something that happens. You have an instinct for knowing who is sincere and who is just trying to use you."
~Rudolf Nureyev, New York Times, July, 1973~

BIG GEORGE

George and Rudolf greeting young Katherine Healy outside New York State Theatre, NYC, July, 1979. Photo: William J. Reilly

Being famous had its downside, as Rudolf Nureyev quickly discovered. His popularity attracted devoted fans as well as some slightly unstable characters. I recall one in particular that hung around the Stage Door at the Royal Opera House in London. Every night she handed him flowers, which he accepted, but didn't engage her in conversation. She crossed the line, however, whenever Rudolf exited the theatre. She continuously annoyed him by stroking his head and arm. The fans told her to stop. Once, she punched someone in the stomach, screaming, "I'll stroke him if I want to!" On another occasion, she attacked the person helping Rudolf get to his car. The police were there and wanted to arrest her, but Nureyev said, "No, let her go." She immediately shouted, "You see, he defended me!"

Before leaving the Opera House, he would often peer through the glass of the Stage Door to see if she was waiting. He seemed apprehensive as to what she would do, especially when she waited by the car after a performance. In these instances, the rest of the fans surrounded Rudolf protectively, proclaiming, "We're your bodyguards." Eventually this obsessive fan got a job working in the Opera House canteen and apparently became quite good at it. She often walked out of the theatre with Nureyev, which made her feel important. Rudolf cautiously allowed this, not wanting to arouse her often-irrational behavior.

Another obsessive fan used to call Rudolf's unlisted phone number at all hours. Nureyev kept changing the number, but somehow she always discovered his new one. This nuisance even made the London papers.

In the mid '70s when the first of the *Nureyev and Friends* seasons began, they were held in the heart of New York's theatre district instead of the large Metropolitan Opera House at Lincoln Center. The Times Square area at that time was quite derelict, with plenty of drunks, prostitutes and sometimes even dangerous characters hanging around. This did not prevent dedicated theatergoers from attending performances. Big-name Broadway stars usually had chauffeurs and limousines waiting at their Stage Doors. When Elizabeth Taylor was starring on Broadway and Richard Burton left the theatre with her after each show, barricades were set up along the street and police on horseback helped with crowd control. Traffic was often snarled for hours.

Nureyev had no such protection. Ballet on Broadway was fairly new to the theatre district. Since Rudolf was not licensed to drive in New York City, he either took a taxi or joined friends in a waiting car or limousine, often heading to a dinner party or late business meetings with producers.

His 1975 *Nureyev and Friends* season was historic, not only because he brought ballet to Broadway and introduced it to new audiences, but he was also reunited with his longtime partner, Margot Fonteyn. They danced together in *Marguerite and Armand*, the *Corsaire* pas de deux and Ashton's *Foresta Amazonica*. Additionally, Rudolf danced in Bejart's *Songs of a Wayfarer*, and *Moments* by Murray Louis, performing in five ballets every night of the two-week run.

Performing artists and politicians were often gathered in the audience enthusiastically watching this historic program. Those huddled at the Stage Door saw many famous people as they emerged from their backstage visits. One night, both Baryshnikov and Nureyev came out together to a waiting limousine. Nureyev seemed amused by Misha's funny hat and kept trying to knock it off his head. Both dancers were laughing and backslapping like school chums who hadn't seen each other in years.

Unfortunately, there were also some mentally disturbed individuals wandering around New York City, who should have been hospitalized. One such woman appeared on the scene in 1975, when she tried slamming a taxi door on Nureyev's foot and then picked a fight with the fan who stopped her. She then proclaimed, "I love violent things!" She later told someone that she lived with Nureyev and "assisted" him with his choreography.

The disturbed woman had apparently been hospitalized previously for attempting to stab a TV sports announcer with an ice pick. After being released, she frequently reappeared at the Stage Door announcing that she and Nureyev had danced together with the Kirov Ballet in St. Petersburg. One night she was waiting for him dressed in a tutu and point shoes. When Nureyev arrived, she grabbed him and insisted, "Dance with me – NOW." He registered the crazed look in her eyes and immediately dashed inside the theatre. She later announced she was going to kill him, if he wasn't going to pay attention to her. Supposedly she sent Nureyev a photo of him smeared in blood. Hearing such threats, the fans became alarmed and demanded that the theatre management provide police protection for their star. The following night, a police car was promptly waiting by the Stage Door when Rudolf left the theatre.

Both Rudolf and his fans dubbed the disturbed woman "Mafiosa" as a kind of code word in case anyone spotted her. She boldly asked the police, "Are you looking for me?"

At this time a giant of a man named "Big George" arrived on the scene. His nickname served him well, since he was over seven feet tall. A former football player, George Robinson worked as a bouncer at the Bottom Line music club in Greenwich Village, before being employed at various Broadway theatres to watch over the leading stars.

That season, Rudolf was understandably nervous when he arrived at the theatre before performances, despite the presence of Big George and the fans who protectively surrounded him. If police hadn't arrived yet, Nureyev would smile at us, and swiftly dash inside. If the police came late, the fans asked them to arrive earlier for future performances. Rudolf normally took about 20-30 minutes by the time he showered and greeted visitors backstage, but that season he exited the theatre just five minutes after his performance finished. One night the car provided by management wasn't ready, nor had the police arrived. We noticed Mafiosa lurking in a doorway across the street, her wild eyes making her look like a crazed maniac. She was carrying a parcel. Our eyes were on her, not Rudolf, to watch out and see if she would run toward him. Looking like a caged animal, Rudolf kept pacing, asking his driver, "Where's the car? Let's get out of here." He walked one way and then another with fans instinctively forming a human barricade around him. Finally, Big George, not expecting Nureyev to be outside so soon, came dashing out and escorted him to a taxi. We all breathed a sigh of relief. The deranged woman hung around awhile, but disappeared as soon as the police car finally arrived.

  The police continued guarding the Stage Door, but could do nothing unless she tried to directly attack Nureyev. We overheard one bored young officer complain, "Why do I always get these assignments? I have to keep my eyes out for some idiot woman with an ice pick!" Fortunately, nothing happened that season and the woman never returned due to the presence of Big George, the police, and diligent fans. Every night, when escorting him outside or greeting him warmly when he arrived, George stood next to Nureyev, a protective arm around his shoulder.

  New York City was an autograph hunter's dream. I recall one of the bag lady types who waited around various Broadway theatres collecting signatures. One night she approached Nureyev while he was signing autographs outside the Stage Door. She told him she hadn't seen him dance, but wanted his autograph anyway. He laughed and joked with her, while giving a quick glance to Big George. The lady was strange but harmless and both George and Rudolf sensed it.

  George got to know many of the familiar faces at the Stage Door and knew which people he could trust and which people to keep a watchful eye on. Most of Nureyev's public just wanted to wish him well and see him up close after his performances. Others, however, made us very thankful for Big George's protective presence.

Big George took his job very seriously. I remember how one night when leaving the theatre, he placed both arms around Rudolf and whisked him away, saying "He's tired." Nureyev looked like he wanted to stay and chat, but while in George's watchful grasp, he merely shrugged his shoulders in a "What can I do?" gesture and said, "Bye-bye, everyone!"

Another night while leaving the theatre in excellent spirits, Rudolf greeted the crowds by cheerily shouting, "Howdy doody, everyone" as George escorted him to his taxi. Once inside, Rudolf paused to wave at the crowd, but the taxi driver sped off with such force that Rudolf virtually fell back into his seat.

At the last performance of that season, the crush of people at the Stage Door was enormous. Fonteyn had no choice but to sign a few autographs en route to her vehicle. When Rudolf appeared, the crowd surged toward him and he gave a hearty laugh. Big George put both arms around him and practically carried him to the waiting taxi to escape the forceful throng of people. I was like a leaf caught in a huge whirlwind, swept along against my will. When Rudolf passed by a fan next to me, she offered some helpful navigation, "This way Rudolf, it's safer." He turned and said calmly, "It's all right," confident in George's expertise. When he finally made it to the taxi, he seemed deliriously happy, waving to one and all as his taxi disappeared into the distance.

Three derelicts were leaning against the theatre drinking, and said, "Is that someone famous?" "That was Rudolf Nureyev," we replied. "Oh, that ballet dancer?" They seemed curious as they watched fans holding roses, another wearing Rudolf's laurel wreath around his neck, and assistants leaving the theatre carrying laundry, teapots, and belongings from Rudolf's dressing room. Many fans then went out for a late meal and drinks and talked for hours. After all that excitement, I walked home alone at three o'clock in the morning, totally elated and unable to sleep.

Rudolf flew off to dance in London. Less than a week later he was back on Broadway, this time during Martha Graham's 50th anniversary season at the beautiful Mark Hellinger Theatre, across the street from the Uris Theatre which still had *Nureyev and Friends* listed on the marquee. As a result, Nureyev's name appeared simultaneously on the marquees of both theatres that winter. It seemed everywhere you looked, his name was illuminated in lights. The Stage

Door crowds at the Hellinger were not as large as for Nureyev's *Friends* season, but were nevertheless considerable.

At that time, Big George was guarding singer Paul Anka who was performing in New York City. One evening, the Graham performance had just finished and several fans gathered at the Hellinger's Stage Door. We spotted George escorting Anka to a waiting car. From across the street we shouted "Bravo!" to him. One of Nureyev's fans braved the traffic to hand George a photo of himself in action protecting Nureyev. He laughed, kissed her, and seemed glad to see the fans again, even if we were at different Stage Doors.

Nureyev and Friends returned to Broadway in 1977, this time with dancers from the Royal Danish Ballet. Big George was once again engaged as Rudolf's bodyguard. One night someone spotted the crazed woman in the theatre, carrying an open vial that she claimed was perfume. We feared it was acid. Word spread quickly, everyone was on high alert and the entire company was on edge. Two company dancers remained on both sides of the stage in case anyone tried to climb onto it during curtain calls. The fans tried arranging for a waiting taxi to secure Rudolf's safety at the Stage Door. Some nights we were more successful than others.

On the night of Nureyev's 39th birthday, all sorts of festivities took place, from a balloon drop on stage to the audience singing "Happy Birthday." Rudolf emerged from the theatre looking a bit tipsy from post-performance champagne, while fans tossed confetti at him. "Look at all the pretty colors," he said, pointing to the balloons, flowers, streamers and hats as we greeted him at the Stage Door.

However, lurking in the background was the crazed Mafiosa and one fan noticed a bottle in her hands. The festive atmosphere at the Stage Door turned into one of anxiety as everyone jockeyed for position when Nureyev left the theatre. Big George firmly guided Rudolf to a long white limousine filled with fellow colleagues. As the two made their way those few steps to the waiting limo, a sudden disturbance was felt in the crowd. In an instant George grabbed at someone. Before we realized what had happened, Mafiosa was on the pavement, receiving a tongue-lashing from Rudolf's bodyguard who said, "And don't you come back again!" The woman scrambled to her feet and fearfully ran off. To our amazement, she listened to George and was not seen again that season.

George had incredible patience with the mobs of people, but was always very aware of his charge, hovering protectively to keep them at a reasonable distance. Whenever escorting Nureyev in or out of the theatre, George placed both hands on Rudolf's shoulders to ensure his safety. Everyone felt more at ease when they saw his large, protective presence, especially Rudolf. When there was no taxi in sight, George walked with Rudolf to the nearest cross street to help him find one. The crowds naturally tagged along, completely enveloping Rudolf, but the towering figure of Big George acted as a beacon gently leading the way. Once a taxi arrived and Rudolf was packed into it and sent off with a wave, the crowds would disburse saying, "See you tomorrow, George." The next day, George would return to his familiar post by the Stage Door, and patiently await the arrival of the star.

It was wonderful to know that this huge man loved the ballet and would frequently slip in to the theatre and watch Rudolf's performances. We were grateful, however, that George sat in an aisle seat; otherwise we would never see over his head! The disparity in their sizes was truly amusing. Towering more than a foot over Rudolf, George often wore a Sherlock Holmes cap. After one matinee, George followed Rudolf down the middle of West 51st Street to Broadway in search of a taxi. Heads turned to see this odd couple. One young man did a double take, saying to his friend, "Look, there's Doctor Watson and Sherlock Holmes."

Sometimes after dancing at a Saturday matinee, Rudolf would arrive quite late for the evening performance. He usually went home to his 72nd Street apartment to rest in between performances. While waiting for Rudolf to reappear, Big George paced up and down like an expectant father, until he saw him arriving via taxi or, on occasion, walking up the street complaining of the traffic.

One of the reasons Nureyev signed autographs outside the Uris Theatre was that it was often difficult to obtain a taxi, due to all the performances in nearby theatres finishing at the same time. One night the taxi situation led to total chaos. Big George managed to stop and secure one, as it came past the Stage Door. Meanwhile, Luigi Pignotti, Rudolf's masseur, had walked to the next corner and also managed to get one. Rudolf was busy signing autographs and spotted a girl in a wheelchair sitting nearby so he began talking with her. She told him how much she enjoyed his performance and he made a humorous face, saying, "Well, it wasn't as bad as some of the others I've done." Everyone laughed. He chatted and joked with the crowd and suddenly the driver in the taxi Big George had secured decided not to wait any longer. At about the same time, Luigi signaled to George that HE had gotten a cab. The fans told Luigi to hold his taxi because George's cab had already departed. Rudolf thought it was all a great game. He then rambled over to Eighth Avenue with a flock of people trailing him, got in the taxi, waved, and off he went.

Occasionally a limousine was provided, particularly if there was a party after a performance. This, too, often presented problems. Big George once escorted Nureyev out of the theatre after a matinee, only to discover that the chauffeur wasn't there and the limo was locked. While someone went to fetch the chauffeur and the limo key, Rudolf turned around and signed a few autographs. When the missing chauffeur eventually arrived, Big George put a protective arm around Rudolf's shoulder and addressed the crowd by asking, "You ARE aware that he has another performance tonight?" and whisked Rudolf into the finally unlocked vehicle.

After another performance in 1977, George confided to the fans waiting for Nureyev, "I can't believe how beautiful Rudolf is in *Pierrot Lunaire*. He's really come a long way, hasn't he? I remember his first attempts in *Lucifer* and kept thinking he shouldn't do modern dance, but now he performs it like it was made for him." Later George spoke about Rudolf's character. "With Nureyev, he can say all those horrible things with that filthy mouth of his, but you know he doesn't mean it. He's like a little boy and is basically a sweet, charming man. He also respects me, which is more than I can say for some of the others I've worked for." He told us he quit working for Yul Brynner because he was "too difficult." "Rudolf is generous," he confided. "He invites me to his performances and to closing night parties."

As George got to know us, he often acted as a go-between in getting things delivered to Rudolf. Once I asked George for his help in getting Rudolf to autograph a photo for a friend's birthday. He took it willingly. After the performance when Rudolf had left, George handed me the photo, dutifully signed by Rudolf. I thanked George for his help, explaining that I didn't like to bother Rudolf on the street. "Why not?" he replied, "Everyone else does." George was very talkative and related, "When I gave him the picture, he seemed a bit confused, wondering what it was all about, so I just told him to sign

Happy Birthday on it and he did." The next day, my friend, who is over six feet tall, thanked George for his help. Big George put his arms around him and gave him a birthday hug, making my friend look TINY next to him!

If Rudolf wanted a particular photo from one of the many photographers who documented his performances, George arranged to obtain them. One of the photographers wanted to personally give Rudolf a photo and asked George if he could detain Rudolf long enough so she could hand it to him. As Nureyev got out of his limousine, George paused long enough for her to hand Rudolf the envelope, which he took with a big grin and a heartfelt thank-you.

When during a Broadway season Rudolf danced on his birthday, everyone bombarded him with gifts. One fan baked cookies, which she gave to George to deliver to Rudolf. Winking at her, he said, "I'll test them first!"

George knew a great deal about ballet from watching so many performances and enjoyed discussing with fans whether he thought Rudolf was better at one performance over another. On some occasions, he brought his charming elderly mother to the theatre. He told us that he went home to practice the balances from *Moments,* the Murray Louis work Nureyev performed during his 1978 Broadway season. George said he just couldn't do it nor could he figure out how Rudolf did. He told us, "I've always had a great deal of respect for Nureyev, but now my respect is limitless. Anyone who thinks those balances are easier than the grand jetés he does, should just give it a try! " We tried to imagine this seven foot giant going in front of a mirror and practicing a Nureyev balance!

In the crush at the Stage Door, sometimes Luigi got left behind. George quipped, "Luigi is a big boy and can take care of himself." We shot back in unison, "Not as big as George!" Luigi was strong, but was about Rudolf's height. We once spotted Luigi standing on a bench backstage having a discussion with George, and he was later explaining, "He's so tall, it's the only way I can talk to him!" On the way to the car, a fan overheard Rudolf's amusing remark, "I'd like to see Luigi and George dance together!"

The Stage Door entrance to the New York State Theatre at Lincoln Center is down a flight of stairs. In the summer of 1979, on opening night of the Joffrey Ballet's "encore" Diaghilev program, a fan waiting for Rudolf's arrival carried an enormous basket of roses. When it was presented to him,

Nureyev staggered back a few steps, and in a subtle reaction exclaimed, "My GOD!" The basket was so enormous that Rudolf took one side of the handle and Big George took the other side and they pretended it was a terrifically heavy burden while struggling down the stairs to the Stage Door entrance. Luigi, bringing up the rear and carrying the bags, began to laugh. Just as they got into the doorway, Rudolf turned to Big George and quipped, "Now we're wedded!"

In addition to the Diaghilev program being filmed for television, Nureyev gave a very insightful interview on Nijinsky. The fans told Big George all about it. One of them invited George to her nearby office at lunchtime, where he could watch a video recording of the interview. In appreciation, he took her to lunch.

Nureyev's London-based manager, Sandor Gorlinsky, came to New York for the Joffrey season. One night, Gorlinsky waited in a limousine for Rudolf to join him. Running up the Stage Door stairs two at a time, Rudolf ran to the waiting limo, apologizing to those waiting, that he had an important appointment. Big George was several paces behind, but got to the limo in time to prevent an overly eager fan from following Nureyev into the vehicle.

Luigi was also in New York for that season and several times left with his wife and four year-old daughter. She would often exit the theatre carrying Rudolf's bouquets, but was intimidated by the size of Big George, and hid behind her father.

When Rudolf left town, Big George was on duty for numerous other celebrities. After Alexander Godunov defected from the Bolshoi Ballet in 1979, George was called to guard the dancer from Stage Door reporters and crowds. He was also on duty to guard Natalia Makarova and even drove her to performances at the American Ballet Theatre.

Rudolf was back on Broadway in 1980, this time with the Boston Ballet in *La Sylphide*. Sometimes Big George performed double duty. After tucking Rudolf into a waiting limo following the performance, George would walk ballerina Ghislaine Thesmar to the corner, where it often took more than fifteen minutes to get a taxi.

That season was extremely successful. Once again, everyone in the dance world seemed to be in the audience. After one performance, Big George escorted Rudolf and Boston Ballet Director Violet Verdy to a nearby dinner party via a "shortcut" through an adjacent bank. The fans joked that they were making a night deposit from the sold-out houses.

In 1981, George had his work cut out for him when the LaScala Ballet performed *Romeo and Juliet* at the Met with Carla Fracci as Juliet and Margot Fonteyn as Lady Capulet. Jacqueline Kennedy was in a limo waiting for Rudolf at the Stage Door, utterly mesmerized as she watched Nureyev work the crowd, attentively signing autographs and amiably chatting. She kept craning her neck to see him, a brilliant smile over her face. As Big George guided Nureyev to the limousine, he said something about fetching Margot, while Jackie and Rudi chatted animatedly. Shortly after, Big George escorted Fonteyn out of the theatre stage door. The crowd began to applaud vigorously, many asking for her autograph. Rudolf had shifted to the jump seat in the limo, making room for Margot. Now he craned his neck, laughing in utter delight to see Margot magically working the crowd. Finally, they all drove off together, with the "royal couple" waving at the sea of admirers left behind.

After the final performance of *Romeo and Juliet*, Dame Margot supervised the people carrying her paralyzed husband to the limousine and instructed them where to put his wheelchair, all the while placing her arm tenderly around him. Big George appeared and escorted Rudolf through the crowd to a waiting taxi. Some of the fans had stretched colored streamers across the driveway and Rudolf instructed the driver to plow through them. He seemed in good spirits but in a great hurry to leave.

The LaScala troupe also performed *Giselle* that season. Elizabeth Taylor, who was appearing on Broadway in *Little Foxes*, watched the performance with Ian MacKellen from a parterre box. When she went backstage, an army of paparazzi surrounded her and they swarmed en masse into Rudolf's dressing room. After about five minutes of nonstop clicks from countless cameras, Rudolf waved at them, saying, "How many more are you going to take?" The press was relentless and wanted to photograph Nureyev fondling her diamond necklace, but Liz sternly snapped, "Don't be vulgar." When the press followed them down the stairs to exit the theatre, Liz warned, "You're going to fall backwards down those stairs, the price you'll have to pay for being paparazzi."

Outside, the security personnel were going crazy, shoving fans here and there to clear a path. Big George quickly escorted Taylor to further protect her from the press and she entered the limousine with such speed, we barely saw her. Another limo pulled up behind hers, while additional police tried to keep the press at bay. George reemerged from the theatre this time escorting Rudolf, who seemed almost apologetic for being the subject of this kind of security circus. Before getting in to the limo, he took a quick pause and blew everyone a long kiss.

A similar scene ensued when Rudolf's neighbor, Yoko Ono, emerged from the Stage Door with her own bodyguard. It was one of her first public appearances since the death of her husband, John Lennon. Another neighbor from Rudolf's Dakota apartment was Leonard Bernstein, who likewise emerged from the theatre after a winter Broadway *Friends* season. Various producers left with Rudolf while Big George rode in the limo's front seat. We later learned that Nureyev enthusiastically went to a disco after tirelessly dancing eight shows that week!

One evening Rudolf emerged from the Stage Door, sheltered by Big George, when an enthusiastic, rather hysterical woman nearly trampled us in her efforts to get close to Nureyev. She was carrying on in Italian and Nureyev began to laugh at her uncontrollable antics. Big George quickly whisked Rudolf away before things got out of hand.

In January of 1983, the Boston Ballet teamed up with Rudolf for another Broadway season, this time performing Nureyev's production of *Don Quixote*. During one bitterly cold night, Boston Ballet Director Violet Verdy, joined the eager fans waiting at the Stage Door for Rudolf's arrival. To everyone's surprise, Rudolf arrived on foot, walking in the snow with Luigi. Verdy greeted him by reporting, "Rudolf, all your fans are waiting for you." "Yes, I know," he replied with a smile, and pulled her into the theatre with him. Following the performance there was a backstage party. When Rudolf emerged, he jovially announced to everyone, "I'm demolished!" as George steered him to his limo.

On another bone-chilling evening as Rudolf emerged from the car, a gust of wind blew off his hat. Big George was right there, quickly picked it up and put it back on Rudolf's head with a gentle pat.

One night before George was on duty, the crazed Mafiosa made an unexpected re-appearance. She somehow cornered Nureyev and eagerly whispered in his ear. He replied in a tone indicating, "Okay, now leave me alone!" The next night she returned, but George had been alerted and swiftly pushed her away from Nureyev. Rudolf had been in a good mood, which instantly changed when he spotted the Mafiosa. Big George hurriedly escorted him to his car.

Big George didn't just work outside the theatre. On certain occasions he was needed inside the auditorium as well. During the 1984 *Friends* season, a few rowdy businessmen disrupted the performance with incessant whistling at the ballerinas and applauding every single thing, including the tragic moments in *Songs of a Wayfarer*. They even left through the street exit door in mid-performance and then returned, causing a great distraction. Everyone complained to the management. After the second interval, we saw Big George escort them out of the theatre.

In the summer of 1984, during this last *Nureyev and Friends* season, Nureyev was directing the Paris Opera Ballet, while continuing his own career. Rudolf gave the performance of a lifetime on closing night and naturally, we wanted to go backstage. George told the fans that "half the Paris Opera is back there with him and you'll have to stay outside." We asked George to sign a thank-you card we prepared for Rudolf's closing performance and George gladly wrote: "Continue to do what you do best!" At the Stage Door, Big George appeared to be chatting with fans, but he always kept his eye on everyone. He also told us he was supposed to work at the Palace Theatre where the Broadway show *La Cage Aux Folles* was playing, but left to work for Rudolf, whom he adored.

The crowds surged forward to get autographs from Jean Guizerix and Eva Evdokimova who had joined Rudolf's *Friends* season that year. Rudolf was right behind them but, as the crowd rushed forward, he was pushed against a wall. Big George swung into action, saying firmly, "Alright, nobody push. I want a clear passageway from here to the car." Rudolf looked up and said in a mock-sheepish voice, "Thank you, George." He patiently signed autographs, but someone exiting the theatre bumped his arm, causing one signature to be messed up. Rudolf looked at it and said, "What kind of Arabic is THAT?"

Big George is no longer with us, but one of my most vivid memories of him is of a *Nureyev and Friends* closing night performance in December of 1975. We saw the real and touching bond of affection between Nureyev and his bodyguard. As usual, there was an enormous, crushing tidal wave of people pressing at the Stage Door when Rudolf emerged. The New York weather was terribly cold. Like a doting father, George made sure Rudolf had his scarf carefully wrapped around his neck. He wanted to sign a few autographs, but George insisted he leave. Big George literally wrapped both arms around Rudolf and nearly carried him to a taxi. Through the crowd of people, I managed to witness their interaction. Before Rudolf got in, I saw two arms reach up around Big George's neck. He bent down smiling, as Rudolf kissed him affectionately on both cheeks. "Thank you for taking care of me," he said, patting George's arm. Once Rudolf was "tucked in" the cab, he turned around and cheerfully waved to one and all and, especially, to Big George.

*"I think it's good for the public there is a need always to worship,
to appreciate, and to cherish."*
~Rudolf Nureyev, Chicago Tribune, October 2, 1977~

AUTOGRAPHS

*Nureyev signing autographs for children,
Hartford, CT, 1989. Photo: Gina Wexler*

Rudolf Nureyev signed thousands of autographs during his long career. He once joked that because he signed so many, his signature would be worthless. Yet those post-performance autograph sessions were his way of meeting his public. Eyes darting everywhere at once, he observed each face in the crowd, sometimes chatting and sometimes silent. People asked him to sign all sorts of things: ticket stubs, books, programs, posters, ballet shoes, T-shirts, newspapers, envelopes, business cards, store receipts, dollar bills, address books, grocery lists, and leg casts. He always seemed slightly perplexed by the endless demand for his signature. Someone once asked him to sign a blank check, claiming it was the only piece of paper available. One woman handed him a doll in his likeness. He was highly amused and autographed the doll's leg. An excited teenager dared him to autograph her T-shirt while she was wearing it. Accepting the challenge, Rudolf scrawled his name right across her chest.

One night following a performance with Margot Fonteyn, Rudolf rushed to a waiting car, obviously heading to a post-performance reception. "Sign my program," pleaded one woman, to which Nureyev replied, "No time." "Then just put an X on it!" she insisted. And that's what she got.

After one New York performance with a crush of people waiting in ninety-degree heat, Nureyev emerged from the Stage Door in corduroy pants, boots, a ski hat and sweater. He seemed in a relaxed mood and signed autographs for over twenty minutes when someone handed him an envelope. He signed it, turned it over and discovered it was some kind of form so he asked, "What is it, income tax?"

Exhausted from a long series of performances, the dancer finished one autograph session by simply drawing three dollar signs $$$, followed by "Randolf Neveroff," his nickname because he seldom cancelled a performance.

Once an autograph seeker, who just received a signature from Rudolf returned it to him, asking him to date it. Nureyev was somewhat annoyed, because every time his name appeared in print, it was followed by his age along with the inevitable interview question, "When will you stop dancing?" Handing the autograph back to the person, he quipped, "No date. Ageless!"

Pink ribbons play a large part in *La Fille Mal Gardee*, a delightful ballet by Frederick Ashton. After one Royal Ballet performances in London, a friend and I each unfurled a long pink ribbon from either side of the upper reaches of "the gods" as part of the curtain calls. This was so effective that it was even mentioned in one critic's review. After the performance, when Nureyev and his partner, Merle Park, sat behind the Stage Door desk signing autographs, I gave Park one of the ribbons to sign. Without hesitating, she signed it and passed it to Nureyev. He looked at it quizzically, and then looked at me, and then again at Merle. "Sign it!" she urged, nudging him with her elbow. He dutifully obliged.

Rudolf was in a delightfully playful mood after a performance when one of his fans handed him a souvenir book, opened to the front page. Instead of signing there, Rudolf leafed through the book, found a photo of himself in *Swan Lake*, and signed that. Another fan quickly opened her program to the same page, but the teasing dancer leafed through it and this time signed on a

Giselle photo. When I handed him the same book opened to the blank front page, he autographed it there. He was most amused by how we compared signatures.

Nureyev's unique signature, all loops and using the French spelling "Noureev," had many evolutions. In his early years, he signed his name in Russian and those signatures are quite rare. From the mid-60s to mid-70s, he signed "R. Noureev." Somewhere after that, he began writing out his first name. I remember getting my first full "Rudolf Noureev" signature at the London Coliseum. Examining it, I joked to a friend, "He's learned to spell Rudolf." I also remarked that his signature had changed and seemed more expansive than it had been. The friend repeated my remark to Nureyev when asking for an autograph. "Well why not?" he quipped. "Change is good, no?"

These autograph interactions often provided the only opportunity to ask Rudolf about his performance schedule. Without pausing from signing, he would rattle off dates for the next year and beyond, provided they were confirmed. He always told us if something was "in the works" and felt obliged not to discuss it, until it was finalized.

Planning ahead was imperative for the fans, especially if travel was involved. Once while getting my program signed, I casually asked him if the dates for his next *Nureyev Festival* in London were finalized. "Yes," he replied, his eyes twinkling. He saw that I was expecting something more specific, so he laughed and rattled off the dates. A couple of other fans inquired about an upcoming season of *Nutcracker* performances and asked, "Are you dancing all of them in New York?" "No," he replied matter-of-factly without looking up. Then, seeing who had asked, replied "All but one, unfortunately." When someone in the crowd asked him for his schedule the following year, he said firmly, "Let's finish THIS year first!"

One of his fans went backstage one evening, pen and paper in hand, and said to him, "Okay, we need all your dates for the next fifteen months." So Rudolf recited his performance schedule from memory. After his schedule was all written down, it made things much easier for the rest of us to plan well ahead.

I often felt that Rudolf Nureyev had the patience of a saint. But his mercurial mood could change in an instant. During a 1978 summer season at the Met, a very strange crowd waited for him at the Stage Door. With a security guard trying to keep the crowd away from the door so the dancers could exit, Rudolf found himself surrounded by a crush of people jockeying for position to have their programs signed. "Step back and give me room," Rudolf instructed. After a half hour of this ordeal, Rudolf abruptly stopped signing and said, "Whose pen?" Nobody claimed it so he said, "Bye" and darted off toward the waiting taxi.

Some people asked for autographs after every performance, but I didn't want to impose on him. If Nureyev was making a debut in a new role, I liked getting that program signed. When he performed a new role with the Murray Louis Company, I had my program ready to be signed, just as Rudolf stopped to sign the cast of someone who had broken her foot. Someone else cut in front of me and handed Rudolf a huge stack of programs. He made a face, but nevertheless obligingly signed them. As he was signing the sixth or seventh program for the woman, she innocently remarked, "You must get tired signing your name over and over again." Nureyev pursed his lips and said sharply, "First you ask me to sign and then you insult me!" The woman replied, "Oh, I didn't mean to insult you and I'm sorry if I did." Rudolf mellowed a bit, but held up the pen someone gave him, asking "Whose pen?" indicating that he was finished signing. I still didn't get my program signed so I just handed it to him. He gave me a lovely smile and scribbled a quick final autograph before saying "Bye!"

Once while signing, Nureyev borrowed two of my pens and when finished, asked his usual "Whose pens?" He laughed when he realized they were both mine. Another time someone asked him to return her pen and he jokingly said, "Stingy!"

Nureyev behaved differently in New York than he did in London, where he was much more relaxed signing autographs. The physical set-up in London made it obvious. At both the Royal Opera House and the London Coliseum, he was able to sit behind a desk or table while the crowds formed orderly queues and filed outside the Stage Door after they obtained a signature. In New York, and especially at the Metropolitan Opera House, the Stage Door area is not at all conducive to dealing with crowds. The dark underground passageway, with exhaust fumes from cars leaving the parking garage, was unbearable, particularly on those hot and humid summer nights. When Nureyev emerged from the Met Stage Door, huge curious crowds shoved pens, programs or gifts in his face. Many people, eager to chat with him, planted themselves firmly in front of him and wouldn't move, causing others to struggle for an autograph. Crowds were not always orderly, and many times Rudolf had to tell them to back up or he would lose his footing on the edge of the curb. One night the crowds were so thick that he couldn't get from the Stage Door to his car and promptly stumbled off the curb. In his accented English, he yelled out, "Sheet!"

On another occasion he exited a New York theatre in an extremely good mood and was ready to sign autographs. However, two friends were in a waiting taxi and reminded him of a dinner reservation. "Shit!" Rudolf blurted out and climbed in to the taxi giving the crowd a rather reluctant wave.

After one performance, the crowds surrounded him and became so excited that he exclaimed, "Don't suffocate me." A bit later he quipped, "What's the point of signing if you keep bumping my arm?" His vulnerability in such situations made him uneasy and eager to get to the safety of his waiting car. Indeed, in the later years, he often signed autographs while seated in the limousine.

At Washington's Kennedy Center, with its spacious anteroom – perfectly conducive for waiting as well as signing autographs – Rudolf often leaned against the counter and signed endless programs and posed for photographs. His entrances and exits were amusing, because the theatre had glass sliding doors that opened automatically when you stepped on the mat in front of it. He loved to jump on it and grinned with glee as the doors parted, sometimes remarking "Open sesame" or "Voila!"

During a 1978 Paris season at the Palais des Sports, Rudolf told those waiting for his arrival at the Stage Door that he promised to sign, but only after the performance. In the meantime, a sudden snowstorm left a few inches of snow on the ground and to no great surprise, it was still snowing when he emerged from the Stage Door. To appease the crowds, Rudolf went back inside the sports palace and signed autographs in the only convenient space available – on the hotdog and ice cream stand.

At some theatres, Rudolf made his own arrangements. He "held court" in Klagenfurt, Austria, by sitting on the edge of a table that was in a backstage corridor, adjacent to a stairwell. Having danced three ballets in one evening, he didn't feel like standing for another forty-five minutes while signing autographs.

The crowd was modest and orderly and it was one of the rare and fortunate times I had the chance to speak with him. When I asked if he would perform in any more modern works, he replied, "I have to maintain a balance; I must do the classics or they will say I can't dance any more." A man behind me crudely interrupted: "Who said you can't dance any more?" Ignoring him, Rudolf continued to explain to me the types of programs he was performing. "Public can't think for themselves; you must educate them," he disclosed.

After a *Don Quixote* performance in Vienna, Rudolf was in a hurry and didn't stop to sign. A long line of people followed him from the Opera House to the nearby Imperial Hotel. He recognized an American fan in the crowd and asked, "Did you get in?" He had spotted her earlier in the standing room line when he arrived for that afternoon's rehearsal. She assured him she saw the performance. He stopped to sign something, but as soon as the crowds realized that Nureyev was indeed signing autographs, they gathered around him until they were blocking traffic. Rudolf realized this and said in German, "The shop is closed!" and disappeared into his hotel. He used this expression on several occasions when he was rushed, tired, cold or hungry, but would often nevertheless sign a few autographs to satisfy the "new faces" in the crowd.

Sometimes Rudolf's generosity with his public backfired. A coach full of elderly ladies attending a 1973 matinee in Paris, got a delightful surprise when Rudolf, in good spirits after the performance, decided to board their bus and greet them. Clad in his fur hat and coat, he bounded onto the bus and waved his hat in the air before stopping to shake each hand and extend a personal greeting in French. The crowds waiting in the street heard squeals of "ooh la la" through the bus windows as the elderly ladies eagerly rose from their seats to shake Nureyev's hand, pat his back, chat and laugh with him. The driver, at first bored, was captivated at the phenomenon that was taking place. As Nureyev was about to disembark, he removed his fur cap and waved it in the air to this "new" group of fans.

Once he got off the coach, he was instantly bombarded by requests for autographs from the gathering crowd. There wasn't much light, so someone offered a pocket flashlight while Rudolf signed. Slowly coming back to their senses, the ladies on the coach decided that they, too, merited an autograph. One by one, they began descending the bus and joined the thick mob that surrounded Rudolf. As he continued signing, he looked up and saw the bus emptying out with ladies clutching their programs and joked, "What have I started?"

We observed a similar situation in Washington, D.C. following a matinee of *Romeo and Juliet* at the Kennedy Center. Fans followed a discreet distance behind him during his brief walk to the Watergate Hotel, where he was staying. A tour bus filled with elderly ladies was parked outside, and for the benefit of all, Rudolf paused and cheerily waved to them. Just as Rudolf was about to enter the hotel, he turned and waved to us, knowing full well he still had an "audience."

Following one particularly brilliant performance, Nureyev was in a rather euphoric mood at the Stage Door and bestowed kisses on everyone in sight. Standing to one side with some friends, I joked, "Do you think we should get in the queue?" Rudolf heard me and gave a teasing grin. A father with his child got autographs and Rudolf said to him, "What's the matter, father? Don't be shy. Don't hold back" and gave him a kiss. Yet while signing autographs the following night, when he had enough he yelled "Basta!" and walked off to get his dinner. We never knew what kind of mood he would be in, which always made it very interesting.

Many nights, particularly when he could sit down, he signed autographs up to an hour, until every last person left. Yet somehow, in that computer brain of his, he knew when people returned a second time, and he straightaway reminded them, "You already had one." If you told him you needed an extra autograph for a friend or for "Aunt Betty, who couldn't make it tonight," he would generously oblige. But generally, unless he was in a very good mood, the unspoken rule was "one per customer."

Sometimes Nureyev facilitated the autograph process, so as not to waste a second of his time thumbing through programs to find an appropriate page to sign. "Okay, everyone," he announced one night at the Met Stage Door, "Open your books to this page," holding one up to illustrate. Amazingly, everyone complied. Another evening Rudolf instructed one autograph-seeker to "find the right page" in the program. He continued signing for the crowd and returned to see that she was still leafing through the program, teasing, "Didn't you find it yet?"

During a long run on Broadway, a woman stopped him as he was racing to his waiting taxi. "You wouldn't mind signing, would you?" "Yes, I would," he replied and continued to the cab. On another occasion when asked for his autograph, he replied, "But I'll be here for two more weeks!" In good spirits another night, he mischievously teased the crowd, "Well, I danced for you, why don't you dance for me?"

Ever observant of the crowds, even while signing after one matinee performance, he spotted a fellow dancer just behind me and said to him, "Call me. I may be sleeping, but call me anyway!"

Even the Stage Door attendants liked to get into the act. One night in London after Rudolf signed autographs for more than an hour before finally heading to his car, the attendant yelled after him, "Good night, sweet prince. Now there goes a swell chap!"

Once at the Met, the stagehands were trying to exit the theatre, but the crush around Nureyev prevented them. They bumped into him and joked with him. Soon the conductor had the same problem, teasing Rudolf that the crowds were there for him and not the dancer. Much of the crowd disbursed quickly, however, at the sight of a large New York cockroach crawling near their feet!

After Rudolf performed a full-length ballet and was standing outside the Met signing autographs for nearly another hour, Alexander Grant, at that time the Director of the National Ballet of Canada, emerged from the Stage Door. He was going to dinner with Nureyev and was about to head for the car, when he noticed Rudolf still standing on his tireless feet. He said incredulously to Luigi, "Rudolf wants to WALK?"

On another occasion two ladies with Southern drawls stopped Rudolf as he entered the theatre, asking for autographs. "No," he replied politely, because he seldom signed before a performance. "Oh, gee," one said, "He's not going to sign." Rudolf turned to them, eyes twinkling, and in a nasal Southern drawl said, "Noooo, he's not!" Everyone laughed, including the two Southern belles.

Some of his fans handed him presents or cards when he entered the Stage Door, which he accepted with a polite "Thank you!" and continued on walking. Once he was handed a stuffed Snoopy dog and when the fan inquired about it later on, Rudolf humorously explained, "You know I don't play with my toys before a performance."

While Nureyev appreciated the loyalty of his fans at these Stage Door gatherings, his ritual was not to stop for autographs on the way in to the theatre. He was focused on getting inside, making up, warming up, and performing. Yet no matter how rushed Nureyev was when he arrived at the theatre, he always took time to greet any children. He seemed to have an affinity for small children and the elderly. If they wanted his signature, he politely explained, "I can't now. I have performance. I'll sign after, okay?"

After the performance was a different story. Rudolf was incredibly generous with his time spent signing autographs, always giving special attention to the children. Some youngsters in the crowd hesitated and the fans urged, "Go ahead, he won't bite." Nureyev affectionately bent down to their eye level and asked each child's name, adding it to his autograph for a more personalized touch. He was especially attentive to young dance students, keenly asking them "Are you studying hard?" or "Are you practicing every day?"

One little girl began to cry when Rudolf didn't stop before the performance. I assured her that he WOULD sign autographs afterwards. Later after the performance, I spotted her near the Stage Door, and Rudolf indeed signed for her. She skipped away joyfully clutching her autographed program.

After one long wait following a London opening night party, I asked a woman with two daughters aged six and eight, "How long have you been seeing Nureyev?" "Not long enough!" she replied. She told me she saw him in Manchester and Nureyev was very sweet with her children. Her daughters were getting cold from waiting so long, so she asked the Stage Door attendant, when Nureyev would be emerging. "When he's ready" came the reply. The woman and her children were just about ready to leave when Rudolf finally emerged. The champagne from the party put him in a lovely mood. The eight-year-old girl handed him a rose. He bent down and cooed, "Hello, my angel, how are you?" He asked for her name. "Erlinda," she replied. "Erlinda?" he repeated, rolling his rs. "What kind of name is that?" The mother responded, "A made up one!" "Ah," he said, "And how is it spelled?" She spelled it for him and he wrote a very long message on her program. Needless to say, both mother and daughters were thrilled. Since Rudolf was in such high spirits, he decided to walk to the car. Arm-in-arm with one of his fans, he joked, "We go left here, and left again. Left, left, left….like the Communists."

When Patricia Neary, then Director of the Zurich Ballet, emerged from the Chicago Auditorium's Stage Door to cheers and applause from the fans, she verbalized, "Rudolf must be coming out." There was no sign of Nureyev as she turned around and asked, "Who are you applauding for?" "You!" I told her and she seemed somewhat embarrassed. Soon groups of children, staff, and senior citizens emerged from the Stage Door, giddy as schoolgirls, telling waiting friends, "And Nureyev was just sitting there, being absolutely charming and so patient, signing for everyone!"

A few minutes later, another group exited and explained, "Right in the middle, he threw his arms up and said, "Dismissed!" and we all had to leave." When Rudolf finally emerged, he seemed eager to get into the waiting car. Once free from the crush of people, his mood instantly changed again as he waved to familiar fans.

The fans related their escapades to Rudolf after another cast party. We weren't sure if Rudolf would leave from the Stage Door or front of the theatre, so the fans split into two groups. One group stationed themselves by the side of the theatre and the other at the front. If Nureyev exited from the front, they would signal us. After waiting for some time, a policeman came by and looked at us suspiciously, thinking we were prostitutes. Upon hearing this afterwards, Rudolf nearly collapsed with laughter.

By this time Rudolf's assistant Luigi, had the car waiting at the front of the theatre. It became quite a comedy until one woman said, "Rudi, you stay put and I'll go round and tell Luigi you're here." Rudolf darted into the building's doorway "out of the draft" since the wind picked up and it began to drizzle. One of his fans asked where he was performing next. The champagne obviously reached his tongue when he spontaneously replied, "I don't give a shit where I dance, so long as I dance." At last the car linked up with Rudolf and he kissed all of us goodnight. As he parted, he excitedly declared, "It's so good to be back to a ROUTINE again." He was once again performing in one of his long *Nureyev Festival* seasons instead of dancing sporadically.

Thousands of autographs were doled out over the ten *Nureyev Festivals* held at the London Coliseum. Spending my vacation in London to coincide with the 1976 Festival, I had many requests from friends in the States for copies of the special souvenir book that was issued. Nearly every night, I dutifully joined the queue to have another book autographed for someone "back home." After several nights of "explaining" this to Rudolf, he automatically spotted me and signed yet another book, probably thinking I was hawking them to the highest bidder. It became rather embarrassing when more friends requested books and it seemed as though I was asking for an autographed souvenir book nearly every night. These books were so popular that the supply was sold out in two weeks, resulting in a second printing.

I always waited until the very end of the queue, preferring to let others go first who had never seen Rudolf Nureyev up close. Then, when the crowds started to thin out, I positioned myself at the very end. Rudolf soon took this as his signal, saying, "Ah, the end of the queue! Now I can go home!" This became a standing joke among friends who said that unless he saw me "at the end of the queue," he wouldn't know when to stop signing autographs and go home. Once someone joined the line behind me. Rudolf's face became crestfallen, thinking that whenever he saw me, he was finished signing autographs. In fact one night when Rudolf saw me, he turned and asked Luigi, "How many more?" Luigi poked his head outside to see if I really was at the end of the line. The Stage Door attendant, no doubt eager to close up for the night, asked the crowd, "Does anyone have anything else to be signed? Checks? Bankbooks?"

Large posters from these annual *Nureyev Festivals* were sold at the London Coliseum bookstore and proved cumbersome to get signed, despite Rudolf sitting behind a desk at the Stage Door. One fan unwound her poster and had difficulty getting it to remain flat. Rudolf played with it a few minutes and finally got annoyed, squashed it flat and signed all over his leg in the photo. Those in the queue made sure their posters remained rolled, exposing just the bottom portion to be autographed.

Rather than purchase a poster, one fan tore the huge poster off the wall outside the theatre and asked Rudolf to sign it. Amused at the fan's ingenuity, he asked, "Where did you pinch this from?" We found it curious that many of the photos or posters promoting the *Nureyev Festival* were stolen throughout the season, including an oversized one from the wall of the nearby Underground station.

In June of 1977, thundering fireworks along the Thames for the Queen's Silver Jubilee celebration were heard during the performance of *Romeo and Juliet* at the London Coliseum. When Rudolf emerged from the Stage Door, throngs of people en route from the fireworks passed by and exclaimed in their unique accents, "'ere, it's that Nureyev bloke!" and joined the crush around him. Poor Rudolf continued signing for another half hour.

During a biting cold January season in New York, Rudolf signed autographs outside. In an overly exaggerated way, he lamented, "I'm exhausted!" After a few moments, he gleefully continued, "You obviously don't want me to eat my dinner tonight." Since he was in a playful mood, he obligingly stayed until everyone had an autograph.

A fan who was an avid collector once asked Rudolf to sign a 1962 program from the DeCuevas Ballet, the first company Nureyev joined following his defection in Paris. Rudolf took one look at it and wanted it for himself, then changed his mind and said, "No, you keep it, it's yours," and the retort was, "No, you have it." After Rudolf autographed the program and returned it, the fan presented him with a rare review from Nureyev's days at the Kirov in 1959. Rudolf glanced at it, then replied gratefully, "This is more than enough."

Taking advantage of Rudolf's good mood at the Stage Door, someone requested: "It's my birthday tomorrow. Why don't you wish me Happy Birthday on this card?" and handed him a blank card. Rudolf not only wrote "Happy Birthday," but an entire page of good wishes.

Rudolf's presence at the Ballet Shop near Lincoln Center in New York drew enormous crowds, to the point where the shop closed, in order to allow Nureyev to browse undisturbed. The shop's owners frequently asked him to sign posters, photos or books, to which Rudolf said with a sardonic grin, "So you can charge more money?" He then wittily bargained for a discount on merchandise he purchased, in exchange for his autograph. During one of these visits, another patron was inside the shop while Rudolf was signing posters and she asked him for an autograph. "I'm busy!" he teased, so she left abruptly.

One summer day I was on my way to Lincoln Center when I spotted Rudolf, wearing shorts and a new cap, heading for his daily class. Later that day I learned that he stopped to browse at the Ballet Shop and was criticizing the way some of his photos were framed. "You should leave more space around the photo so I can sign them," he suggested.

On Monday, July 26, 1974, Nureyev made a special appearance at the now-defunct Korvette's Department Store in New York, spending his free afternoon signing record albums to promote classical ballet music. Enormous crowds began lining up at noon, but were told to return at 5:30 p.m. By that time, lines stretched throughout the fourth floor, which happened to be in the lingerie and maternity wear department. A small area was roped off where a table and chair was set up for the guest of honor. Two security guards stood nearby to keep some sense of order.

To accommodate him, the store's air conditioning was turned off, which made the long wait rather uncomfortable for everyone but Nureyev. As the crowds waited behind roped barricades, Rudolf made a spectacular entrance wearing tight blue pants and jacket and one of his trademark caps, which he waved when he saw the crowd. After posing for the press, he arranged himself behind a table where he sipped tea and signed record albums for more than an hour. It was reported that over 800 *Swan Lake* and *Sleeping Beauty* albums were sold that afternoon.

A somewhat unbalanced woman turned up and planted herself directly in front of him. Several of the fans warned the security guards that this woman had been stalking Nureyev so they kept a close eye on her, as did Rudolf. Several of the taller fans stood in front of her, at which time the woman became agitated and told them to move. When they refused, the woman became frustrated and finally left. Shortly afterwards an announcement was made that "Mr. Nureyev has to get to a pressing rehearsal," and as he walked toward the elevator, relentless mobs followed him. We later learned his "pressing rehearsal" was actually to see a performance of Gelsey Kirkland in *La Sylphide* with American Ballet Theatre.

The following evening after Rudolf's performance, a friend who was unable to get to Korvette's, brought a record album for Nureyev to sign. He looked at her and jokingly asked, "Haven't you had enough of that yesterday?" "But I missed you yesterday!" she explained. He obligingly signed.

When the Clive Barnes book on Nureyev was published, Doubleday Bookstore arranged for a book signing on January 31, 1983. It was a Monday and Rudolf had the day off from performing. He was expected at the Fifth Avenue and 57th Street store shortly after two o'clock. The press was on hand when Rudolf finally arrived in a taxi almost forty-five minutes late. Clad in his Blackgama fur over a leather jacket with hat and boots, he greeted his fans like old friends and proceeded to the store's mezzanine level, where a table was waiting. We could see him from the street through the glass storefront as he draped his fur coat over the back of the folding chair. Before settling down to the business of posing for the press and signing books, he turned to those of us in the street and gave a little wave.

Those who hadn't seen the newspaper ad about the book signing, wandered into the building after seeing the lines of people snaking around the store and out onto Fifth Avenue. As he signed and chatted, thanking everyone for endless compliments, he then took a momentary pause at four o'clock, to nibble on a sandwich, which he seemed to pluck from out of nowhere. Then leaning forward, he instructed, "Okay, next wave!"

An elderly friend in line ahead of me had written on the flyleaf of the book, "When you dance, my spirits soar." He saw it and said to her, "That's wonderful" and had a long chat with her while signing "To dear Pearl, with my best wishes" in her book. Just as it was my turn, a security guard handed him a note that a film director who directed the film titled *Exposed* was there to see him. Rudolf stopped and looked downstairs, out onto the street. "The director is here? Where? Tell him to come up." So he took a swig of tea and then returned his attention to me. While he scrawled his signature on my book, I took the opportunity to ask about bringing his new production of *The Tempest* to New York. "No," he snapped, "They are pigs!" Then turning to the person behind me, he barked, "Next!" It upset him that producers wouldn't bring his productions to New York, but he always said what was on his mind, whenever I asked him something.

The film director finally made his way through the crowd and greeted Nureyev, who kept turning to wave to his fans on the street. About ten minutes later, he gave an interview to a reporter, posed for more press, talked to various store employees, and then ambled downstairs. We headed off to City Center for a memorial gala for critic Walter Terry while Nureyev and the film director went shopping on Fifth Avenue to a store boasting a "Half Price Sale" sign.

When Nureyev embarked on his *King and I* tour in 1989, we attended a performance in Hartford, Connecticut. The children performing in the show were all Asian, and waited for him outside the Stage Door following the matinee. When Rudolf emerged, he stood in the middle of the group, striking his King of Siam pose, while the parents and many of the fans took photos. He seemed so proud of these young performers and willingly obliged their doting parents with a photo opportunity as well as numerous autographs.

One of Nureyev's long-time fans, Bob Gable, amassed one of the largest collections on Rudolf Nureyev's career. When not attending performances, he spent hours and a considerable amount of money on his collection. During one of Nureyev's seasons at the Met, an elderly friend in a wheelchair asked Bob to get tickets to one of the performances. Bob obliged, even though it wasn't easy arranging for an aisle seat. He attentively helped the friend in and out of the taxi, and made sure the wheelchair would fit into the elevator. The friend was thrilled and asked Bob after the performance, "Do you think I can meet Nureyev?" Bob, who knew of the enormous Stage Door crowds, said, "Yes, we'll try, but I won't promise you anything."

He pushed the wheelchair as near to the Stage Door as possible. The crowds, as usual, surrounded Nureyev while pleading for autographs. After waiting a few minutes, Bob edged forward and asked, "Rudolf, would you meet a friend of mine?" and motioned toward the wheelchair. "Of course," Rudolf answered. He broke away from what he was doing, stepped over to the wheelchair, shook the man's hand, kindly greeted him, and signed a photograph for him. Bob's friend was thrilled and said, "I never dreamed I'd even meet him, but he shook hands and gave me a photograph." Many years later, this friend repaid the kindness. In his will, funds were provided for Bob to continue working on his Rudolf Nureyev Collection, which has since been donated to the Library for the Performing Arts at Lincoln Center.

On another occasion, Bob asked Rudolf to sign a copy of the Clive Barnes book on the very last page that showed a triumphant Nureyev emerging from the Stage Door, surrounded by a crowd with Bob Gable prominently in view next to Rudolf. "This is my favorite page, Rudolf," he joked. Rudolf responded, "I wonder why, Bob?" Bob had a uniquely throaty voice and Rudolf often said to him, "I heard you bravoing, Bob!"

During a New York *Friends* season, one of his faithful fans missed quite a few performances when she was hospitalized for surgery. When told of this, Rudolf signed a personalized message: "With my best wishes. Get well soon." The last part was written in darker, more emphatic letters and under it was "I second that" and signed "Big George," Rudolf's New York bodyguard. This message of inspiration was subsequently framed on her living room wall.

At another *Nureyev Festival* in the 1980s, a Venezuelan fan that wrote for her Caracas Ballet newsletter, asked Rudolf to sign a special message for the

Friends of the Teresa Carreno Theatre. Always willing to promote ballet, he wrote a special dedication to the group, which was later published.

My own personalized autograph came via a friend in London. In the spring of 1979, Nureyev performed *Le Bourgeois Gentilhomme* at the New York State Theatre, the only work created for him by George Balanchine. Several friends came from London and stayed with me. My modest apartment resembled a dormitory, with mattresses strewn side-by-side on the living room floor. Considering the prices of New York hotels, it was the only way my British friends could have managed such a trip. When we all decided to get the freshly published reviews in the Sunday *New York Times*, my friend who offered to carry six copies at one time looked like a weightlifter!

Before returning to London, my friend went backstage and told Rudolf that he and his friends wouldn't be able to come to New York had they not stayed with me. He asked Nureyev to sign a personalized photo for me. Rudolf asked my for name and when told, he replied, "Oh, I know Nancy." Over the years, I have never asked Nureyev for a personalized autograph. Consequently, my photo with inscription "To Nancy, with all my best wishes" always brings back many happy memories of the lively times when my British friends were camping out on my living room floor.

"Get on with it. A wide-angle lens? Ah, what a monster it will make of me!"
~Rudolf Nureyev, Philadelphia Sunday Bulletin, June 1, 1967~

PHOTOGRAPHS

Nureyev holding hat in wind, outside Uris Theatre, NYC, November, 1980. Photo: William J. Reilly

Rudolf Nureyev was the most photographed dancer in history. If he wasn't photographed during a performance, his picture appeared in newspapers or magazines attending other performances, escorting friends Jackie Kennedy Onassis or Lee Radziwill to a gala, an exhibition, or other social event. He was "newsworthy" on or off the stage.

A frequent visitor to the famed New York's *Studio 54* nightclub, Nureyev was photographed disco dancing with anyone from Liza Minnelli to Elizabeth Taylor. If the press spotted him in the Russian Tea Room after a New York performance, his photograph promptly appeared in the morning papers. He joked about the press on various TV talk shows when one host mocked a "breaking news" headline, "Nureyev Eats Hamburger."

He claimed he never cultivated the press, nor did he have a press agent. But Nureyev became a pop icon of his time and having a beautiful male ballet dancer as a celebrity, meant that the press flocked to him. He tolerated the press, especially if the publicity helped sell tickets to his performances or promoted dance in general. The press also served as protection. As he was the first major defector from the Soviet Union, the KGB often followed Nureyev. Continuous visibility in the press was somewhat reassuring to his family in Russia as well as his public around the world.

In the earlier years when impresario Sol Hurok presented visiting companies like the Royal Ballet and National Ballet of Canada, professional photographers held photo shoots of the dancers for the company's souvenir books. The Hurok office also sold the photos for a small price to willing and eager dance fans. There was always a ready market for Nureyev photos.

He was, however, very sensitive about dance photographs. He knew that each time he performed, photographers could capture a single moment on stage for all time. These same photographers then hawked their wares at the Stage Door, where they had a captive crowd waiting for Nureyev. Hordes of people looked through the latest photos from the most recent performance, bought them, and asked the dancer to sign them. This was tricky, however, since Nureyev hadn't seen or approved any of the photographs. If he was interested in a particular photo, he always said so, but if he didn't like it, he certainly let us know.

My first experience with a "rejected" photograph occurred while living in London in the early 70s. The Royal Opera House sold postcard-sized photos of the company's principal dancers including their "guest star," Rudolf Nureyev. In my early days of photo collecting, I thought the Opera House photograph of Nureyev in *Le Corsaire* was perfectly fine. After all, it had been taken by an in-house photographer and must have been sanctioned by Nureyev himself. Handing it to Rudolf one evening after a performance, he looked at it, pursed his lips, and with bold strokes of a thick blue magic marker, scrawled his name all over the body of the photo, practically obliterating it. I was so shocked I remained speechless, since I really didn't see what was wrong with it.

On another occasion, also at Covent Garden, I asked Nureyev to sign a photo of himself in a grand jeté from *Swan Lake*. He took the photo, looked at it carefully, and made a motion that he was going to tear it up. The look on my face stopped him, so instead he scrawled his name over one entire leg in the photograph, remarking sarcastically, "At least they could have waited until I got up there." When I examined the photo more closely, I could see what he meant. He wasn't at the height of his jump so his supporting leg was at a peculiar angle. By scrawling his name across the offensive "bad leg," he was illustrating what was wrong with it.

One night in New York, a friend had purchased various photographs from a Stage Door photographer and waited backstage at the Met for Nureyev to emerge from his dressing room. She had several photos stuffed into a large envelope, and someone waiting with her wanted to know which photos she bought. She was hesitant about taking them out, since she knew that one photo of Rudolf - perched in mid-air with his back to the camera in the middle of a double tour - would not pass inspection. But the friend persisted, so they briefly looked over the photographs. Just as she was about to stuff them back into the envelope, Nureyev emerged from his dressing room. Always curious, he asked to see which photos she had, and before she could hide them, they were in his hands. He nodded approval at the two she had selected for him to sign, but when he saw the one with his back to the camera, he exclaimed, "No, no, that's no good" and tore it into four pieces. Horrified, my friend exclaimed, "But I like that photograph!" Nureyev snapped, "I'll have to teach you how to select a good photograph."

By this time, a small crowd had gathered around him in the corridor. While he was busy signing autographs, my friend looked at the ripped photograph lying on a nearby bench, thinking, "After Rudi leaves, I'm going to grab it and tape it back together again." Despite the fact that she never mentioned this to him, and he was busy signing other autographs, he perceptively caught her glancing at the discarded photo. He walked over to it and ripped it into tinier and tinier pieces. "It was as if he could read my mind," she remarked. Outraged, my friend exclaimed, "I paid good money for that photograph, and the least you can do is put something special on my picture." "You're right," Nureyev agreed half apologetically, and on a photo he'd already signed, added above his name a lovely personal message, finishing "with love and best wishes."

Rudolf Nureyev loved to tease his fans, especially those like myself who seldom spoke to him. On one occasion, I waited in the long queue at the

London Coliseum to get his signature on a copy of the *Nureyev in Paris* book. Beautifully packaged in its own case, this was a book of photographs taken by Jurgen Vollmer during the filming of *Jeune Homme et la Morte* from 1972. Since I didn't want to get the book dirty, I kept it in its case until the very last minute. I turned to the inside title page depicting Nureyev, clad in ballet slippers and jeans, in a pose from the beginning of the ballet. I spread the book out on the ledge where he was writing and he examined the book thoroughly. Rudolf had obviously seen the book before since several people had asked him to sign it. Then, totally disregarding the place where I wanted him to sign, he wrote his name on the book's cover. With teasing eyes, he put down the pen and handed me the book, but refused to let go of it. I tugged on it and he tugged back. I looked at him quizzically. He returned my glance, still tugging on the book. After a few seconds of this, I saw a twinkle in his eyes as he said, "So...why do you like that picture?" He was referring to the photo on the inside cover that I hoped he would sign. Knowing he wouldn't let go of the book without an explanation, I replied, "I don't like the picture THAT much. I just wanted you to sign on the inside page so the book won't get dirty." "Oh," he replied, satisfied, and released his grip on the book, grinning like a Cheshire cat.

When Nigel Gosling (a.k.a. Alexander Bland) worked on his book *Fonteyn and Nureyev – The Story of a Partnership*, he looked through my extensive collection of Nureyev photos, as he did with other private collectors, and chose several he wanted to use for his book. Before I lent them to him, I pleaded, "Make sure Rudolf won't tear them up if he doesn't like them!" I pointed out something in a photo that may have appealed to me simply as a memory of that ballet, but might not meet with Nureyev's approval. As the deadline for publication loomed, neither Gosling nor his photo editor had managed to sit down with Fonteyn and Nureyev to get their approval of the selected photographs. As a final resource, a ballet friend visiting from London for one of Nureyev's New York seasons went backstage one evening with a stack of photos selected by Gosling and was given the task to get Rudolf's okay for the book. "There I was in his dressing room," he recalled, "sitting at Rudolf's feet, flinging photos back and forth. He liked one of Margot, but not of himself. Another he liked for the mood, but not for the actual dance pose. There seemed to be more in the 'no' pile than in the 'yes' pile. But I noticed that even if he didn't like the way HE looked, if it was a good picture of Margot, it went into the 'yes' pile." And that's how the photos were approved for the book. He was exceptionally gracious and considerate of Margot.

If Rudolf liked a photo he saw, he generally asked for a copy. Many of the photographers hawking pictures at the Stage Door handed him several photos during any given season. One friendly photographer snapped Rudolf leaving the Met with a parade of fans following him across the street to a nearby restaurant, where they bid him goodnight. One night, several of the fans in the picture asked Rudolf to sign this photo and when he saw it, he inquired within everyone's earshot, "How come I don't have one of these?" The obliging photographer quickly handed him a copy. Rudolf once remarked, "There are so many photographs I want, I'll have to get the photographer's addresses!"

At the curtain calls of his 39th birthday performance on Broadway, the fans surprised the dancer with a balloon drop while the orchestra struck up the "Happy Birthday" song. Rudolf was truly surprised and gave a charming salute to the audience. The next evening while signing autographs at the Stage Door, Rudolf spotted one of the photographers in the crowd. He asked, "Did you get a picture when I saluted?" Indeed, that very photo appeared in the next issue of *Dance and Dancers* Magazine.

Nureyev himself, as well as Luigi Pignotti, his masseur and assistant, developed a rapport with the photographers who regularly turned up at the Stage Door. Luigi once asked a photographer, "Got any new pictures tonight?" A man selling T-shirts nearby with Nureyev's image on the front asked Luigi, "How about a nice T-shirt of your boss?"

One photographer joked with Rudolf, "If I win the lottery, I'll come to London for your *Romeo and Juliet*." Rudolf looked up from signing autographs and teased, "What? With all the money you make off me with your photos, you should be able to go NOW."

Many of the fans turned to photography and began taking their own pictures during performances. They went to great lengths sneaking in their cameras under coats, bags, and the likes. One even used special material to help muffle the sound of the "click" so as not to draw attention. There were also a few who bribed the ushers in order to film the performance from the standing room area. In those days, the cameras were bulky and the film cartridges had to be changed every eight minutes. Working in team effort, one did the filming while the other had a new cartridge ready. The film was edited and when complete, shown at "viewing parties" during an off-season. Some of these silent films have since been secured in the Nureyev Collection of New York's Performing Arts Library.

One night, a fan-turned-photographer asked Nureyev to sign a photo she had taken during a performance of *Spectre de la Rose*. She captured Rudolf in a split second "in between" pose in which his body seemed to be going in several different directions at once, making it look very three-dimensional. The photograph was from a brief moment near the end of the ballet, when Nureyev appeared to blow a kiss to his partner. The photographer pulled this photo out of a manila envelope and gave it to Nureyev for signature. Rudolf took one look at it and eagerly inquired, "My God, where did you get this photo?" "I took it," she replied hesitatingly. "You're going to give this to me, aren't you?" His eyes were excited and determined. There was no use protesting, because Rudolf had it in his hands and right away showed it to those in his immediate entourage. The photographer reminded him that she wanted his signature, so he took the envelope from her, wrote a very long, personal message, and returned it to her, while commenting, "You're very generous." To this day, she's the only one I know with a personalized autographed manila envelope. The photo later appeared in the Nureyev biography by John Percival.

Several years later, this same photographer went backstage to give Nureyev a few photographs she had taken. When Nureyev saw her, he graciously invited her to join his friends Luigi Pignotti and Erik Bruhn for a glass of champagne.

Another photographer showed Nureyev a photo from the seduction scene in *Miss Julie*, a ballet he had performed with Cynthia Gregory at American Ballet Theatre. In the photo, Gregory, in the title role, stood on a table in a seductive pose, one leg extended toward Nureyev who played the butler. In the photo, Nureyev appeared to be licking Gregory's knee. When he took the photo, he exclaimed in mock horror, "My GOD, what am I doing to her here? You know you shouldn't show me things like this!"

Nureyev was always cultivating and educating his fans. When one of them went backstage, Nureyev praised her work but also suggested creative ways she could improve her photographs. "When shooting a jump, get more of the floor in the picture," he explained, which showed the height of the jump in relation to the floor. When he looked at a photo taken from his *Raymonda* production for American Ballet Theatre in which Cynthia Gregory as the lead character was being fought over by Rudolf on one side and Erik Bruhn as the Saracen on the other, he criticized the look of stress on Gregory's face. The photographer wittily shot back, "You'd be stressed, too, if you were between two beautiful men!"

"This is a curious photo," Nureyev remarked one summer when presented with a photo of himself dressed in a denim jacket, jeans and white shoes, not his usual style of earth colors and boots. When another fan gave him the same photo, he remarked, "I don't like this photo; give me something else to sign," and said still later, "Not that photo again." He certainly made it very clear when he didn't like a particular photo.

Once he was handed a photo from Kenneth MacMillan's production of *Romeo and Juliet* when Rudolf had just performed his own version of the same ballet. He took one look at the picture and declared, "Wrong production!"

One thing Nureyev did object to, was having someone shove a flash camera in his face while he signed autographs. At such close range, it often blinded him from what he was doing. One fan who always asked if she could take his photo, only to get Rudolf's negative reply, was so surprised one night when he actually replied, "Yes, but no flash," that she didn't have her camera ready and had to frantically retrieve it from her bag.

A photographer covering the dress rehearsal of his *Sleeping Beauty* production with the National Ballet of Canada managed to capture Nureyev having fun performing Aurora's third-act variation. Dancers learned best when he demonstrated, and it didn't matter if the role was for the man or woman, because Nureyev simply knew every step of every part. Later on, a fan obtained the photos from the photographer and showed them to Rudolf. He looked at them with a perplexed expression as though not recognizing the ballet and finally said, "What's wrong with me?" She had to explain and remind him that he was dancing Aurora's variation at the rehearsal, wearing his Prince's costume and legwarmers.

During "photo calls" when the press was invited to so-called "dress rehearsals," nearly all the cast dressed in full costume and make-up except Rudolf. Usually sporting a wooly cap on his head and wearing his tattered legwarmers, photographers were continually frustrated about not being able to capture a decent photo of him. Press photographers, needing to meet urgent deadlines, generally printed the rehearsal photographs and then Rudolf wondered why there wasn't a better photograph chosen. For his 50th Birthday Gala at the Met, he showed up at the dress rehearsal wearing clogs and a polka-dot dressing gown over shorts and that's exactly the image that was used in the press.

TV news crews often used snippets from dress rehearsals or performance footage to promote Box Office sales. "Now playing at the Met" ads ran frequently in New York, but whether Rudolf ever "approved" of them is another matter. Sometimes we wondered if the press purposely chose the most unflattering photos of him or his dancing partner.

At his dress rehearsal of *Manfred* at the London Coliseum, the press was in full force, along with a handful of fans. Both Rudolf and the fans could tell by the clicking cameras that the press photographers were taking photos at all the wrong moments. During one particularly unflattering moment, Rudolf was on his knees and swooped his ballerina around his shoulders. The lift didn't go well and he caught her upside-down, exposing her panties while all the photographers eagerly snapped pictures. "You pigs!" he shouted with fury. "You take picture of girl upside down?" Needless to say, Nureyev had far and few friends among the press.

Margot Fonteyn was just as irritated as Nureyev by photographers clicking away during a performance. There were several times when both of them became distracted and sharply glared into the audience, trying to find the offending camera. They usually got word to the stage manager to send someone "out front" and confiscate the camera. One wonders what they would think these days about the cell phones rudely ringing during a performance, if the slightest sound of a camera click bothered them so much. Even the glare from electronic screens is disturbing.

In 1982, during one performance in Italy, Rudolf stopped in the middle of the *Don Quixote* pas de deux, sat down on a chair, and told the TV cameraman he wouldn't continue to dance until the camera was put away. He then stepped off the stage and walked out into the audience, where others were taking photos. He physically turned their cameras around to face them, calmly returned to the stage and finally went on with the performance.

A photographer taking pictures during a performance of Nureyev's production of *Romeo and Juliet* in Washington, D.C. nearly brought the show to an end. In the ballroom scene, there is a moment when Nureyev as Romeo faces the audience while Tybalt, recognizing Romeo as a Montague, performs an enraged dance behind him. Instead of daydreaming about having just met Juliet, Rudolf's gaze turned to the audience as he snarled through his clenched teeth, "Who has the camera? Where is it?" He continued the performance, but when donning his blindfold for the "Wheel of Fortune" dance, he audibly remarked, "There it is again!" Even during the balcony scene, he strained his head toward the public on the persistent lookout for the distracting clicking of the camera, wherever it was.

This particular performance caused a lapse of attention in the production's "despair dance" when Benvolio brings news to Romeo of Juliet's supposed death. The flash from a camera resulted in a nasty fall by Kenneth McCombie as Benvolio, and Nureyev, in turn, fell on top of him. They covered the mishap well, but an audience just doesn't realize how distracting noisy or flashing cameras can affect the performance and endanger the dancers.

In the 1980s, when he began his annual *Nureyev Festivals* in London, I made friends with some of the British photographers and acquired a significant number of photos of Rudolf performing in new roles. When I returned to New York, the stateside fans asked if the photographers could make extra copies. Thus began a kind of trans-Atlantic photo shuttle service, with myself in the middle. On the back of each photograph, I marked how many copies the New Yorkers wanted and then sent them to the UK via several flight attendants that would rendezvous with the photographer once they arrived in London. Multiple copies of photographs were printed and returned "via air express" by the same method. This resulted in many meetings at various hotels in order to collect packages from airline personnel and then finally distribute them to New York fans. I also kept track of collected payments to be returned to the UK. This went on for several years and as a result, the photo collections of many fans immediately doubled.

Nureyev was not above using his image for other purposes. He once posed after a dress rehearsal while holding a sign for the *New York Post*, advertising their lottery. On another occasion following a lengthy newspaper strike, he was photographed with a sign that read "Welcome back *New York Post*." A photo shoot with Martha Graham and Margot Fonteyn, all clad in Blackgama furs, provided citywide publicity for a Graham Gala. As a sign of appreciation, they all got to keep their coats. A few years later, a gigantic image of Nureyev was plastered all over New York City's bus shelters and in numerous magazines advertising Suntori Vodka. He said he did it in order to help finance his revised 1981 production of *Manfred,* when expected funding didn't come through. And after taping a TV interview in New York, he did a brief public service announcement for public television.

One Christmas time, a London newspaper persuaded Rudolf to pose with a Santa's beard and cap. The photo was captioned, "Guess who?" His image was also used on the cover of a magazine next to Santa's sleigh and a red-nosed reindeer, simply captioned, "Rudolph and Rudolf."

Another amusing photo showed a grinning Nureyev in a stretchy pair of legwarmers, wrapped up to his armpits like a cocoon. Some of the fans held a contest to see who could come up with the best caption.

His fascination with all things dance, led Rudolf to the Ballet Shop whenever he was in New York City. On one visit he spent nearly $1,000 on books, prints, artwork, photographs, and other dance memorabilia. He often teased the owners that he deserved a discount, because of the money he made for the shop and once jokingly admonished them for replacing his image in the window with one of Baryshnikov.

Photographer Bill Reilly used his creative talents long before digital imaging became available. He once superimposed Nureyev's face on an oversize $100 bill. Another time he created a double image of both Nijinsky and Nureyev in the opening pose from *Spectre de la Rose*. It became so popular that he printed additional copies to sell at the Ballet Shop. Nureyev stopped in one day to browse and bought both items. When he saw his photo on the $100 bill, he laughed, "Only $100?" Rudolf was also amused by another Reilly creation depicting Tamara Karsavina, Nijinsky's partner in *Spectre*, dancing with Nureyev.

Bill's Christmas cards were so clever that we eagerly looked forward to them every year. They often pictured Nureyev surrounded by enormous crowds with balloon captions on them. There was even one of me, looking quite astonished, while Rudolf raced past me to a waiting car. The caption said, "Who was THAT?" It always made me laugh out loud. Another showed a crowd waiting at the Stage Door titled, "All we want for Christmas." Still another, taken in the summer, pictured a horde of fans following Nureyev down the street after a matinee. This one was called "Christmas in July." Rudolf

Nureyev driving Santa's sleigh high above the New York City skyline was a particular favorite. While Bill Reilly only drew two reindeer, he labeled it "On, Dancer!"

Some of the more talented fans utilized Nureyev's image in works of art. One New Yorker was an excellent painter and did several oil paintings of Rudolf from various photos that appeared in the press. Another turned her sketches into greeting cards, which were sold at the Ballet Shop. Still others had buttons made of Rudolf's image. Another made poster-size collages with multiple images arranged to create designs, which Rudolf would later autograph.

One fan, a former teacher, made card-size signs often attached to bouquets that were handed to Nureyev before or after a performance. The signs always related to current events, locations or performances. Nureyev always looked forward to these signs, frequently asking, "What's tonight?" whenever he saw the fan waiting. One sign got such a reaction from him that he roared with laughter. He had just performed *Romeo and Juliet* and was about to dance *Spectre de la Rose*. The sign depicted Nureyev in his *Spectre* costume posed at the window, but the message read, "Hark, what light through yonder window breaks?" A small flashlight was attached behind the sign. Rudolf loved that sign so much, he turned the flashlight on and off exclaiming, "That tops them all!"

In the summer of 1982 Nureyev performed *Manfred,* his original production based on the Byron poem to Tchaikovsky's music, in the Herod Atticus in Athens. One of the signs given to him depicted the Olympic rings and inside each circle was a photo of Nureyev, Byron, and Tchaikovsky, with the caption, "Manfred: An Olympic Achievement." Another utilized a photo of Rudolf dancing around the Acropolis announcing: "The glory is in Greece." Still another of Rudolf as *Apollo* flying over the New York City skyline informing him that "Your chariot awaits!" Nureyev's friend Douce Francoise found that creative fan one evening and said, "I just have to tell you how much Rudolf enjoys your signs. He's saved all of them. Thank you." Indeed, on the last night of a Broadway *Friends* season, Luigi Pignotti was packing up the trunk of the car while Rudolf signed autographs and we noticed every one of the season's specially created signs was carefully placed on top of the luggage.

Long before selfies, Rudolf posed for photographs with his public, although not that frequently. After a performance, he was usually busy signing autographs or racing to a waiting car or taxi. I recall one time in London that he posed between two Jewish boys while their proud relative took the picture. With an arm draped around each boy's shoulder, Rudolf quipped, "How kosher!"

Rudolf Nureyev was photographed by some of the great photographers of his era: Richard Avedon, Henri Cartier Bresson, Cecil Beaton, Serge Lido, Karsh of Ottawa, and Lord Snowdon, among others. He was also featured in countless fashion shoots in *Harper's, Vogue* and numerous magazine publications. In one *Vogue* photo shoot, Rudolf posed nude in some particularly artistic photos captured by Richard Avedon. Curiously, these photos were ripped out of the library's copies of *Vogue* Magazine whenever we asked for them. Those who managed to secure an original copy have a true collector's item.

But some of my favorite photographs of Rudolf were those taken by his loyal and adoring fans, either at curtain calls when he was proudly cradling a bouquet of flowers, or smiling among the throngs of well wishers at varied Stage Doors around the world.

After Rudolf died, we discovered some of these photos in a large box or "lot" at the Christie's auction. Many photos were the ones he had requested from photographers at the Stage Door; others were countless snapshots taken by fans. Nureyev may have been fanatical and thorough about the use of his photographic image, but the fact that he appreciated and saved photos from his public was indeed heartwarming.

*"The audience can make you feel that self-satisfaction.
That is their contribution. It is part of the performance."*
~Rudolf Nureyev, London Sun Times, April 30, 1972~

BANNERS AND FLOWERS

*Moor's Pavane curtain call, Uris Theatre, NYC, August 26, 1984
Photo: Beatriz Sanz*

BANNERS

Following a 1973 Fonteyn and Nureyev performance at Covent Garden, one of the ballet enthusiasts unfurled a large banner over the balcony railing which read "Rudolf + Margot 4 Ever." Thus started the custom of banners, generally displayed for closing nights. After a long absence from the Royal Ballet, Rudolf returned to dance his production of *La Bayadere, Act Three* with Antoinette Sibley. During the curtain calls, a fan prepared to drape an extremely long banner over the railing, when an usher approached to determine if it was some sort of protest sign. This particular one merely said "Welcome

Home Nureyev." It immediately caught Rudolf's eye but, blinded by the spotlight, he turned to Sibley to ask what it said. She smiled and whispered to Rudolf, who flushed slightly and then grinned with his fabulous smile. Despite his troublesome relationship with the Royal Ballet, he did consider the company his first true "home" in the West.

Most of the banners from fans were made from bed-sheets and black tape. Many were small and simple, expressing a "Bravo" or a "Thank You" or even a questioning message, such as "Same Time Next Year?" Others were more elaborate. A few were based on various quotations Rudolf had given in the press and were sometimes obscure to the rest of the audience. In one 1976 interview in London's *Daily Mail*, Rudolf stated: "I have been an electric rabbit – the ones the greyhounds chase." This was in response to a critic saying that greyhounds have been "chasing that electric rabbit and had the problem of derailing it." For the closing night of that year's *Nureyev Festival*, I prepared a small banner that read, "Long Live the Electric Rabbit." Most of the audience was perplexed, but Rudolf's wide smile and chuckle when he saw it was priceless.

In early 1976, Nureyev had pneumonia, and his health made front-page news, especially because he so seldom cancelled a performance. When he literally danced his way back to health, culminating in a brilliant season at the Metropolitan Opera House that summer, *New York Times* critic Clive Barnes wrote that Rudolf was like a Promethean Fire Giver, galvanizing whatever company he performed with. On closing night, my banner read, "Promethean Fire Giver Does it Again!" Since Nureyev was departing to film *Valentino* on location in Spain the very next day, I made a smaller banner with the words "Hurry Back, Sheik." Everyone was amused, especially Nureyev.

Various banners after his *Romeo and Juliet* production read, "Shakespeare is in Good Hands," and "Parting is Such Sweet Sorrow." At the conclusion of the 1977 *Nureyev Festival*, I made a banner that read, "This was OUR Jubilee" since it was the year that marked Queen Elizabeth's 25th year on the throne. Another fan's read "A Loyal Salute to the Marathon King."

For the 1978 *Nureyev Festival* closing, I made a small banner "You are THE dance." The crush of people who ran "down front" towards the stage prevented me from getting through. So I passed the banner to friends in the front row and they held it up when Rudolf took his final curtain calls. He beamed all over, while everyone in the wings stepped out to see what it said, including critic John Percival who was backstage that evening.

After one particularly memorable Broadway season, I decided to make public what so many of us felt. I chose a strategic spot in the theatre where Rudolf and most of the audience "downstairs" could see my banner. I draped it over the balcony railing with the message "Thank you for being born in our lifetime." Many of the fans as well as total strangers approached me afterward and said it was exactly how they felt. We realized we were witnessing a phenomenon and wanted to relish every minute of it.

Since flower throws became customary for most closing night performances, 1979 was particularly tough on the fans' budgets. Nureyev appeared with several companies in New York City and many of us were completely broke from the sheer number of tickets we purchased. In March, Rudolf joined the Joffrey Ballet in a month-long *Diaghilev Program* on Broadway. He danced *Spectre de la Rose*, *l'apres-midi d'un Faune* and *Petrushka*, roles made famous by Vaslav Nijinsky. The company had been in financial difficulty and by partnering with Nureyev, they were assured of sold-out houses. A week later he made his debut in Balanchine's *Le Bourgeois Gentilhomme* with the New York City Opera. He gave additional performances in both New York City and Washington interspersed with guest appearances with American Ballet Theatre. His closing performance with the Joffrey Ballet happened to be a Sunday matinee on the first day of April. "What are we going to do for closing?" we asked each other at the Stage Door. "None of us has any money left for flowers."

I decided to make a small banner with an explanatory note on it that I would hold up while Nureyev took his bow. As the Joffrey company gathered for their curtain calls following *Petrushka*, Rudolf, joined by cast members Denise Jackson and Christian Holder, spotted some familiar faces "down front" by the edge of the orchestra pit. Nureyev gave the impression that he was waiting for his customary flower throw. When nothing happened, he had a slightly bemused expression on his face. He acknowledged our applause and then spotted the 3 x 3 foot banner I unfurled over the edge of the orchestra pit. The size of the banner prohibited much text, but it did the trick. In white-face as the puppet Petrushka, Rudolf burst into a huge laugh as he poked Jackson in the ribs and said, "Take a look at that banner." Its message: "April Fool. No Fleurs. A Bientot."

The following week Nigel and Maude Gosling came to New York City to see Rudolf in *Le Bourgeois Gentilhomme*. One of the fans asked Maude what Rudolf does with all of the banners. "Oh," she explained, "We have them all folded in a huge cupboard. A pity some of them aren't dated, but he keeps every one." After that, all banners were duly dated.

Prior to the 1982 *Nureyev Festival*, London was filled with special events, such as a visit from the Pope as well as the birth of the Royal Baby, William. Rudolf dedicated the season to his mentor, Nigel Gosling, who had died just prior to the start of the Festival. Nureyev performed in his revised production of *Manfred* with the Zurich Ballet at the Coliseum. Since so many of us converged from all parts of the globe, we wanted to commemorate the universality of dance and Nureyev's part in it.

Before leaving for London, I got the idea to make a huge banner and decorate it with flags from all the countries where Rudolf had danced. After much research, I tracked down a company in New York that sold small flags from several different countries. On the evening of June 17, 1982, Nureyev arrived at the Coliseum in casual attire, wearing brown trousers, a striped sweater and his trademark cap. After he went inside to warm up and apply stage makeup, we made our own preparations. We spread the banner across the entire front row of the orchestra stalls and asked each person in the audience that was sitting there, to help unfurl it at the appropriate moment during the final curtain calls. They were excited and eager to help with the surprise. In addition to our flag-laden banner, every one of the international fans brought small flags representing their native countries.

In Scene 4 of *Manfred*, Nureyev changed into his Greek costume, got in the huge cart and quickly discovered that the Greek flag he waved to lead the revolt was missing. He gritted his teeth in anger, probably trying to suppress a shout to the wings that this key prop was misplaced, then took off his turban and waved it in the air before heaving it into the wings with all the force he possessed. Despite the glitches, the performance was well received. After the formality of two company and two solo calls, the entire front row stood up and unfurled the 25-foot-wide banner reading "21 Years of Uniting the World Through Dance," which was decorated with flags representing the thirty-two countries where Nureyev had danced up to that time. My concern that the banner would be upside down diminished, since it unfurled like clockwork. Rudolf squinted from the glaring spotlights trying to read it and then, putting his tongue in his cheek, tried to suppress a huge grin. He inched forward to get a closer look and saw all of his fans waving flags from their respective countries. He smiled widely and beamed with profound happiness.

FLOWERS

From his earliest days at the Kirov School in St. Petersburg, Rudolf Nureyev worked tirelessly on perfecting the art of taking a bow. Spending hours in front of the studio mirror, he practiced every gesture until it became a performance in itself.

Nureyev's curtain calls embraced the entire audience. Standing alone, he raised one or both arms, acknowledged the upper reaches of the theatre, and made a point of looking at every part of the auditorium. People often remarked, "It looks like he's bowing just to me." Nureyev was the best judge of his own performances, and when he felt he didn't dance the way he wanted, his curtain calls were polite but brief. When he knew he had danced exceptionally well, he proudly acknowledged the audience. One woman seated behind me following a particularly brilliant performance in London remarked, "He's so proud of himself, he makes me feel proud for him, too." His uplifting energy was simply contagious.

These curtain calls were also in character of whatever role he performed. For his roles as a Prince, they were formal and elegant; for the forlorn puppet in *Petrushka*, he waddled out pigeon-toed with his hands to his sides and bowed deeply from the waist. As a deranged ballet teacher in *The Lesson*, he acknowledged the applause stiffly, mimicking the character's quirks in the ballet.

As Nureyev perfected this "last act" of each performance, his intuitive sense of timing served him well. While the American and Austrian audiences seemed to make a contest out of calling him out repeatedly, and European audiences broke into spontaneous rhythmic clapping, the British public applauded and cheered enthusiastically and then, like a faucet turning off, the applause came to an abrupt halt. Nureyev seemed to know just when to finish his bows according to the venue.

After gratefully acknowledging the audience, if the applause went on too long, he would signal for the curtain to come down. On some occasions, the stagehands ignored him or played tricks on him, to his discomfort. He had a certain protocol he followed, especially for his own productions, and didn't want it to appear he was milking the audience for more applause. At first he would smile and nod toward the wings, and then simply glared. Occasionally he just walked off the stage, if he couldn't get the attention of the person working the curtain. When he knew he had danced well, he remained on stage a bit longer; when he felt he didn't deserve much applause, his curtain calls were brief or on some occasions nonexistent. He would "direct" the audience's applause. When he felt it was enough, he would step back behind the curtain with one arm extended, as though waving goodbye. This was his signal that "it's time to leave."

When he performed with Margot Fonteyn, their curtain calls became legendary. Flowers were an integral part of the ritual. Someone from the theatre would present Fonteyn with an armload of flowers, which she received with her usual radiant smile. Plucking one from her bouquet, she kissed it and offered it to Nureyev with a deep curtsy. Nureyev, in turn, accepted it by taking her hand in his, holding it for a brief moment and then giving it a gentle, loving kiss. At some performances, additional bouquets were left at their feet or devotedly tossed from the audience. I once overheard an excited young child tell her mother, "I want to be a dancer when I grow up so I can get flowers."

Following one particularly moving performance of *Marguerite and Armand,* Fonteyn gave a single rose to each of her supporting dancers in the ballroom scene, after her usual curtain call ritual with Nureyev. Someone behind me remarked, "They really know how to take curtain calls, don't they?"

One of the first times I experienced this flower phenomenon occurred after a Fonteyn and Nureyev performance at New York's Metropolitan Opera

House. Not only did the applause last for forty-five minutes, dozens of flowers were feverishly tossed from all parts of the house. One newcomer to the ballet world remarked that she thought everyone in attendance must have brought flowers. Only later did I learn that these elaborate "flower throws," usually done on closing night, were highly organized by serious balletomanes, as a way of thanking the performers for a wonderful season.

As the years went by and I became more immersed in the ballet scene, I likewise became involved in these flower throws. The ballet fans would take up a collection and the organizer was responsible for purchasing the flowers. These were arranged in small bouquets tied with bright ribbons. Both flowers and ribbons were properly color-coordinated to match the costume Nureyev wore in the closing-night ballet.

Since most closing-night performances were on Saturday evenings following a matinee, the flower team prepared the flowers early in the morning or in a great rush in between the matinee and evening performances. Flowers were carefully trimmed, neatly banded together into bouquets tied with correct ribbons, and placed into shopping bags prior to the performance. Usually hidden under the seats until the last intermission, they were then distributed to other fans. Once Nureyev came forward for a solo call, he would be pelted with an abundance of flowers from the orchestra stalls or side boxes.

It was quite a magnificent sight seeing all those colorful flowers with their bright ribbons flying through the lights en route to Rudolf's feet on stage. Sometimes an overly exuberant fan threw too high and Rudolf would reach out and swiftly catch a bouquet or two in mid-flight to avoid being clobbered. Often he simply reached out without even looking; he seemed to magically sense where the bouquets were in the air. Once he amusingly remarked, "It's like baseball game for public, no?"

Despite the "game," there was an actual protocol for the curtain calls that is still followed in most ballet companies today. At the conclusion of a performance, the full company bows to acknowledge the applause. Next is the corps de ballet, the body of any classical ballet, followed by soloists, leading characters, followed in order from less to more prominent roles, and finally the two leading dancers. The starring ballerina is usually presented with a bouquet of flowers. If the performance merits additional curtain calls, the main soloists or leading character dancers bow in front of the curtain, followed by the leading couple.

The fans respected the ritual of the curtain call. However, there were a few occasions when this protocol wasn't followed. During the 70s, Nureyev guest starred with the American Ballet Theatre at the Metropolitan Opera House in New York. Cynthia Gregory was at the height of her popularity and was much loved by her fans, especially the Cubans. When Nureyev and Gregory performed in *Swan Lake*, her fans exuberantly shouted "Cynthia, Cynthia!" while stomping their feet in unison. Following the Black Swan pas de deux, Nureyev actually backed up a few steps, because the enthusiastic screaming was so deafening. At the curtain calls, Cynthia's fans shredded programs and tossed them from the upper reaches of the Family Circle. After one performance, someone brought out a three-foot high floral arrangement in the shape of "C" and "R." When Rudolf saw it, he cracked up. This was certainly not the curtain call protocol he had perfected.

At a performance of *La Sylphide* on Broadway with the Boston Ballet in the early 80s, an enormous display of red, white and yellow mums in the shape of a huge "R" was placed at Rudolf's feet during curtain calls. Rudolf stood center stage with a puzzled but amused grin on his face, and then just stared at it. Finally, he bent down, patted it, and tried his best not to laugh out loud.

In 1977, London Festival Ballet, premiered Nureyev's original production of *Romeo and Juliet* at the London Coliseum. After twenty-five consecutive performances, the company was exhausted from "breaking it in," before embarking on a tour of Australia. On closing night after all the usual curtain call protocols and flower throws, a gigantic Koala bear was brought on stage with "Perth," the first stop on the Australian tour, written on top of the bear's hat. At first Rudolf stared at it with a comical "What next?" expression, but then he couldn't help laughing. Protocol was broken even further, when all the dancers tossed dazzling flowers at him from both sides of the wings.

Despite Nureyev's carefully rehearsed curtain calls, not all of them worked the way he planned, even with his beloved Margot Fonteyn. After a performance of *Marguerite and Armand* in London, she was given three enormous bouquets, which she promptly and unintentionally dropped, due to their overbearing weight. Nureyev, his tongue firmly planted in his cheek, tried not to laugh since his long-time partner mucked up a curtain call. At one point the curtain came up too soon and revealed Fonteyn hastily dashing off to the wings, while Rudolf stood center stage looking somewhat bewildered. He invitingly held out his arm to beckon her back. She skipped out like a young girl, thrust her entire bouquet in his arms and burst into a fit of giggles. He was so surprised that he, too, laughed out loud and bowed his head to kiss her wrist but simply couldn't, because they were both laughing, as was the entire jubilant audience. Someone yelled out "Bravo Fonteyn and Nureyev, the Queen and King of ballet!" Rudolf caught some flowers on the fly and the audience euphorically cheered. The British audience lost their usual reserve and applauded wildly, with curtain calls lasting over thirty minutes.

Once at another performance, one of the brightly uniformed footmen who usually presented Fonteyn and Nureyev with bouquets, came out much too soon. "Not now!" Rudolf growled at him, and the man made a hasty backward retreat until the "proper" protocol was instigated.

With the "ballet boom" in full swing, Rudolf began his many *Nureyev and Friends* programs, both on Broadway and around the world. For his November 1975 season, he invited Fonteyn to perform with him in New York City. Their popularity was so high that the program was billed simply as *Fonteyn and Nureyev*, without further explanation necessary. His masterfully rehearsed curtain calls went awry after a performance of *Amazon Forest*, a ballet specially choreographed for them by Sir Frederick Ashton. At the curtain calls Rudolf was presented with an enormous bouquet of luxurious roses, which he immediately gave to Margot. She was just in the process of pulling out a single rose from her own bouquet, when he plopped his elaborate bouquet on top of hers, causing the stem to break on the rose she was about to hand him. When he somehow managed to take the broken rose from Margot's hand and began kissing her wrist, he was practically pulled to the floor, because at the same instant Margot knelt down to curtsy to him. It was one of their more amusing and unpredictable curtain calls.

That Broadway season opened with Ashton's *Marguerite and Armand*, and was followed by *Le Corsaire*, again danced by Fonteyn and Nureyev. After a quick costume change, Nureyev then joined Bejart dancer Daniel Lommel in Bejart's *Songs of a Wayfarer*, and changed again to perform with Fonteyn in *Amazon Forest*. The program closed with Murray Louis' *Moments*. This meant that Nureyev danced in five different works each evening for the two week run.

We wanted to reward Nureyev and the company for getting through this dance marathon and so six hundred bright yellow roses were dethorned for closing night. Normally Fonteyn would not be performing in the final piece of the evening, so the fans asked Rudolf if the program order could be switched so that *Amazon Forest* came last. Fonteyn could therefore be included in the flower throw. He replied, "No problem, but ask Margot first. I stay away from expressions of emotion."

Amazon Forest was indeed the last piece on closing night. Rudolf seemed amused, knowing full well that the presentation bouquets were just the beginning compared to what the multitude of fans were going to do. We decided to wait for two or three curtain calls before tossing the roses and by this time Nureyev's expression changed from amusement to slight apprehension, as if wondering whether or not there would actually be a flower throw. When the first three hundred fragrant roses were tossed at him from all directions, he just beamed and flushed with delight. Fonteyn received the rest and the entire company was showered with a delightful assortment of flowers. After the last curtain call, I glanced behind the opened curtain to see Rudolf looking tired but profoundly overjoyed. So much for staying away from "expressions of emotion."

In 1978, Nureyev was scheduled to dance a performance of *Don Quixote* with Gelsey Kirkland at the American Ballet Theatre in New York. She became indisposed with bronchitis and a young dancer, Yoko Ichino, stepped in at the last minute. Since they had never danced together, Rudolf was very nervous, but the performance went so well that he was thrilled. However, the curtain calls were apparently not rehearsed. Ichino was so excited she eagerly scooped up all the flowers that were tossed to them and presented them to Rudolf with a deep curtsy. Backstage, he praised her performance, but commented about presenting him with flowers, by clarifying, "That's MY act!" He later signed a photo to her, "To dear Yoko, with my love and gratitude."

Dancers Alexandra Radius and Maria Arati from the Dutch National Ballet joined Nureyev's 1978 Broadway *Friends* season. The program featured a mix of classical and modern works. Rudolf performed the *Corsaire* pas de deux nightly, alternating with Radius and Arati. The latter was terribly nervous for her debut, but at the curtain calls, Rudolf generously demonstrated how proud he was of her and brought her forward to acknowledge the applause. At the conclusion of their next performance, Arati knelt to him and presented him with her bouquet, breaching the protocol. Nureyev swiftly pulled her to her feet, gently kissed her cheek and insisted she receive the flowers and ovations.

Another break in protocol occurred at a gala performance at the Royal Opera House, in early 1975. At the zero hour, Baryshnikov cancelled his much-anticipated London appearance and the Royal Ballet's ballerina, Antoinette Sibley, bowed out on doctor's orders, because she was pregnant with her first child. Management frantically tried arranging last-minute replacements to pacify all those ballet lovers who had literally fought for gala tickets. Unfortunately Bolshoi dancers Ekaterina Maximova and Vladimir Vasiliev couldn't get exit visas in time and Marcia Haydee and Richard Cragun had previous commitments in Stuttgart. As a result, Anthony Dowell and Nureyev danced Bejart's *Songs of a Wayfarer*, the only time they performed it together. Nureyev also staged the pas de trois from *Le Corsaire* for the occasion. The first half of the performance finished with Fonteyn and Nureyev in John Neumeier's *Don Juan* pas de deux. Since Jerome Robbins' *The Concert* took up the second half of the gala, the fans asked for and were granted permission to have a flower throw prior to the intermission. While the audience was eagerly waiting for their bow, the large crimson curtain remained closed for some time and Fonteyn and Nureyev didn't appear. When the curtain finally parted, we realized why. About fifty magnificent bouquets, overflowing baskets of flowers and potted plants were placed in the middle of the stage. Then the fans tossed over one thousand bright yellow daffodils on the stage. What a sight to behold! The curtain calls lasted as long as the pas de deux that preceded it, and the second half of the gala was delayed until the stage could be properly cleaned of the flower deluge. According to critic John Percival, the Gala relied heavily on the talents of "that *other* famous defector" for making it a success.

Nureyev was the best judge of his own dancing. While he loved the applause, if he was not happy with his performance, he showed it. After one performance of *Sleeping Beauty* with the National Ballet of Canada in New York when everything seemed to go wrong, Rudolf was presented with a bouquet at curtain calls. He immediately handed it to young Kevin Pugh, making his *Bluebird* debut that night, who provided the evening's best dancing. Rudolf was very proud of Kevin who looked astonished as he accepted the flowers and gratefully bowed. The audience loved this gesture and started bravoing, which brought a hint of a smile to Rudolf's face. Later, someone jokingly told Kevin to frame the flowers.

Another time Nureyev was in a foul mood because the performance wasn't going the way he had hoped and he simply never took a curtain call. A woman nearby explained to her child how famous Nureyev was. The child asked innocently, "Then why didn't he let us clap for him?"

Over the years, the fans prepared thousands of flowers. Probably the most impressive was a closing night in 1974, with the Canadians at the Met. A cascade of red roses was painfully dethorned and prepared ahead of time. Rudolf, clad in his red *Moor's Pavane* costume, stood center stage, bowing with outstretched arms while hundreds of roses pungently filled the stage, and turned the floor bright crimson.

Fortunately, flowers were scooped up after performances and re-used. Sometimes other members of the company exited the theatre carrying armloads of blossoms. Rudolf frequently brought them to his host or hostess wherever he stayed, and large bouquets filled the back seat of his taxi when he left the theatre. At other times the bouquets were carefully placed atop the car Rudolf had waiting for him after his performance. Any flowers left over were kept for souvenirs or shared with friends. So the magical spirit of the performance – and the flowers – lingered for days.

When I moved to London in 1972, I was surprised to learn that flower throws were not done, at least not on a massive scale. Presentation bouquets were the norm at Covent Garden, although a few daring enthusiasts managed to toss smaller posies from the upper regions of the house. After one exceptional performance of *The Nutcracker* with Merle Park, fans in the Upper Slips tossed shredded paper in lieu of flowers. Rudolf looked amused. At the second performance from our perch in the Upper Slips, we noticed a twinkle-eyed Nureyev as Drosselmeyer bouncing Clara on his knee during the party scene and pointing up in our direction, telling her, "They threw paper at me!" At curtain calls we tried repeating this paper shower when Sir John Tooley, then the head of the Royal Opera House, came upstairs and politely told us we must not toss paper "as you can appreciate how long it takes to clean it up." That was the end of that idea.

When Rudolf's partnership with Fonteyn at the Royal Ballet began winding down, he began his annual *Nureyev Festivals* at the London Coliseum.

These six to seven week summer seasons featured Nureyev performing nightly in a variety of works with visiting companies. The annual *Nureyev Festival* became, as one fan quipped, "A one-person employment office" since many of the companies would not have had a sold-out season without Rudolf Nureyev's name as their main Box Office draw. Since London is a mecca for tourists, the combination of Nureyev and tourist season meant guaranteed full houses and golden profit numbers.

Dance enthusiasts benefited, too, because many of the visiting companies had never been seen in London. These annual seasons also coincided with Wimbledon, so visitors could watch their prized tennis stars in the afternoon and their favorite dance stars in the evening. London in the summer became a second home for many American fans who arranged their vacations accordingly. Thus, the tradition of closing night flower throws actively continued on the other side of the Atlantic.

The first massive flower throw occurred in 1975 when Rudolf performed *Sleeping Beauty* with the London Festival Ballet. I had seen the New York flower throws, and with some willing accomplices, decided to emulate them. At the crack of dawn, a small crew of us assembled at the market to purchase flowers with the contributions diligently collected during the season. Deliberating on the choice of color and type of flower took some time. The "weight" of the flowers was decisively important, because the bouquets had to carry well when tossed over the orchestra pit. The owner of the flower stall, delighted at such a massive sale, dropped his jaw in amazement when we explained, "We're going to throw them."

The flowers were then painstakingly bundled into a car and delivered to the home of whoever had the largest living room. Newspapers and plastic sheets were spread over the carpeting while everyone set to work, usually with some ballet music in the background, while separating and trimming the flowers. The finishing touches came with colorful and carefully chosen ribbons. These flower prepping sessions generally lasted all morning. Then we'd have to clean up the discarded stems and petals, have lunch, get changed, and dash to the theatre for the matinee. But what could we do with the flowers until the evening performance?

The hundreds and hundreds of bouquets ended up in bathtubs in homes and hotel rooms around the world. The flowers stood in several inches of water all afternoon. After the matinee, we made a mad dash to retrieve them, correctly bag them, have dinner, and store the flowers either in someone's car or in the cloakroom of the theatre. On that first flower throw in 1975, the Coliseum house manager kindly stored the boxes of flowers in his office, although he kept muttering, "Seems a terrible waste of money, if you ask me." It was undoubtedly worth it to see Nureyev, ankle-deep in flowers, clutching small bouquets with tears filling his eyes in gratitude. One woman, who was seeing Nureyev for the first time, was more touched by his emotional curtain calls than the riveting performance.

On numerous occasions, flowers became difficult to find. I remember one season where an entire supply of flowers was wiped out from a nearby flower shop. A friend went in to buy a small bouquet and the owner simply said, "No flowers. Nureyev's dancing."

Once during a series of performances at the Kennedy Center in Washington, we simply could not find any flowers since it was very close to Mother's Day. In a supermarket in the Watergate Hotel complex near the Center, a friend and I found some potted plants. Prior to the evening performance, we took the flowers out of their pots, rinsed them off, and made them into bouquets.

During the height of the "ballet boom," in the 70s, one fan quipped, "You can tell we're in the middle of an economic crunch when we have to toss daisies instead of roses." Still, we had over one thousand bouquets of daisies, many of which Rudolf caught in mid-flight, grinning like a Cheshire cat all the while.

Ever since seeing Paul Taylor's *Auerole* in the mid-60s, Rudolf begged the choreographer to let him perform it. Taylor finally relented and Nureyev first danced the piece in Mexico City in 1972, and again at a New York City fund-raising gala for the Taylor Company in October of 1974. Rudolf had been performing with the Paris Opera in his own Act 3 of *La Bayadere* as well as in Balanchine's *Prodigal Son* and *Apollo*. However, he took time to fly to New York City "in between" his Paris engagements for a matinee and evening performance of *Auerole*. He was very jet-lagged and nervous at the matinee, but much improved in the evening. That night, the order of the program was switched to accommodate Rudolf's tight schedule so he could catch the evening flight back to Paris. At the curtain calls, Nureyev generously insisted on giving all his bouquets to the Taylor dancers.

Some New York City critics, already panning Rudolf's performances for years and urging him to stop dancing, wrote scathing articles saying his appearance with the Taylor dancers added nothing and in fact hurt the company's finances. However, critic Clive Barnes pointed out that Rudolf took no salary for his appearance and that it was a pity his good-deed for the company was so under-appreciated.

In 1973, Nureyev joined the Taylor Company again in London at the Sadlers Wells Theatre. In addition to performing *Auerole*, he did a small role as the Squonk in *Book of Beasts*. Seeing the great Rudolf Nureyev dressed in a gorilla-type costume cavorting around the stage was certainly unusual, but it was obvious he had fun doing it.

While waiting for the train at the nearby Underground station and talking animatedly with my London friends, I was approached by someone who asked, "Are you Nancy Sifton, the one who writes all those letters?" While living in London, I wrote lengthy letters to friends back in New York about performances I had seen and I guess my reputation preceded me. Later this fellow fan became a friend and we traveled frequently to see Nureyev perform. She and other New Yorkers provided international fans with full reports of Rudolf's first Broadway *Nureyev and Friends* season from December 26, 1974 to January 25, 1975.

I had to rely on letters from friends for reports, although I did see the "tryout" for that Broadway season in Paris earlier that year. The detailed letters I received stated how well Nureyev danced and how the public, not accustomed to seeing "Ballet on Broadway," strongly and enthusiastically responded.

The New Year's Eve performance must have been "interesting" in the break with protocol, for it seemed obvious to the fans that the dancers had started celebrating early. One fan wrote that occasionally Rudolf was "looking at the floor as if surprised it was still there." At the curtain calls, the company sang *Auld Lang Syne*, cheerfully joined by the audience. Nureyev clearly didn't know the words so he just mouthed them. The cast tossed the flowers back to the audience and even tossed paper streamers. Rudolf couldn't figure out how to throw his and it kept going backwards.

The closing night ovations were thunderous, rewarding the dancers for thirty-four memorable performances. While more than three thousand vibrant flowers were being tossed, a man shouted to one of the fans, "You should be watching the Beatles." "I'm ten years too late for that," the fan replied. Another inquired, "You seem to know each other. Are you part of a family?" The answer came back, "Yes, we're just one big happy family." Following the flower throw, each cast member from the Paul Taylor company lined up one by one and presented Nureyev with a yellow rose and a kiss. There was a genuine feeling of mutual respect and admiration from the dancers. An usher ran down to the front for a closer look and informed the fans that *Nureyev and Friends* was the biggest Box Office success at the Uris Theatre to date.

Meanwhile, across the pond, I began to give serious thought about returning to the States. Nureyev's partnership with Fonteyn was winding down and matters weren't helped by a "No guest artist" policy instituted by the Royal Ballet's management. While I had thoroughly enjoyed my time in London, I knew I could get a better paycheck in New York. I followed Rudolf's advice because he was not one to "sit around on my ass waiting for work," so he inventively created work for himself. He offered his production of *Sleeping Beauty* to the Royal but when they refused, London Festival Ballet gladly accepted it.

Nureyev was headed towards the historic moment of bridging the gap between classical ballet and modern dance that, up until that time, had remained totally separated. Nureyev had performed modern works by Glen Tetley, Rudi van Danzig and others with the Royal Ballet, but the real "test" came on June 19, 1975, when the goddess of modern dance, Martha Graham, created *Lucifer* for him at a star-studded fund-raising gala in New York.

By late spring of 1975, I managed to tie up loose ends in London and returned to New York City to witness a wealth of dance. I registered with an agency that provided temporary office assistance. This enabled me to keep my own hours as well as earn a higher weekly wage than in London. The change meant I could take time off to travel since I could choose when I didn't want to work. The common American policy of a two-week annual vacation never appealed to me.

I saw Martha Graham's "encore" season later that year featuring Nureyev repeating his performance in *Lucifer*. His skimpy gold costume had been "downsized" to one simple jewel rather than the two that decorated it at the gala premiere. I was far more impressed with Nureyev's debut as the Preacher in *Appalachian Spring* and saw every single performance that December as well as numerous works in the Graham rep.

I was back in London for the 1977 *Nureyev Festival*. It was the Queen's Silver Jubilee and all of London was festooned with Union Jacks, floral displays and a myriad of celebratory festivities. Nureyev did an unprecedented seven-week season, which included the premiere of his *Romeo and Juliet* production as well as a week of *Giselle* with London Festival Ballet, followed by a *Friends* program with Margot Fonteyn, Natalia Makarova, and Lynn Seymour. The season finished with Makarova's debut in *The Lesson* joined by members of the Royal Danish Ballet.

After collecting money throughout that season, the fans purchased six large boxes of flowers in preparation for closing night. At the curtain calls, Nureyev, made up as an old man for Fleming Flint's *The Lesson,* broke his character and grinned all the while catching bouquets on the fly. When cast members Vivi Flindt and Anne-Marie Vessel came for front calls, we peeked around the parted curtain and saw Rudolf sitting cross-legged on a chair looking extremely happy and slightly overwhelmed. He leaned sideways on his chair, laughed and waved back at one of the fans waving to him. Enormous crowds handed him countless flowers at the Stage Door. Some tossed bouquets at him from a close distance until people protested, "Stop, you'll hurt him." Once in his car, he looked dazed with so many people all handing him flowers, banners, gifts, or wanting to shake his hand, while trying to balance the enormous armload of flowers on his lap.

When the Dutch National Ballet joined the 1978 *Nureyev Festival* in London, we repeated our ritual of going to the market to select and prepare celebratory flowers. On closing night, the house manager let us store the bags of flowers in the elevator until the interval. When we ran to retrieve them, he quipped, "I thought you said a FEW flowers?" as bag after bag emerged. He said he had to present a bouquet to Rudolf on stage that night, adding, "So please don't throw your flowers until I get offstage." He also asked us to throw them early as the staff "wants to leave within an hour."

In July of 1979 Nureyev joined the Joffrey Ballet in an encore presentation of the Diaghilev Program, this time at the New York State

Theatre. On closing night, we did an enormous flower throw of red and yellow blossoms with blue ribbons to match Nureyev's *Petrushka* costume. Some of the avid fans that were pitching flowers were a bit too enthusiastic and Rudolf was unintentionally hit in the face or on the neck as he bowed. He looked up carefully and squinted, as if saying, "Is it safe to stand up now?" The fans bagged all the flowers left on the stage and audience members – even those in the top parts of the house – pleaded to have one as a souvenir. Fans eagerly tossed flowers as Nureyev exited the theatre and more were placed on the car, causing one of Rudolf's friends to remark, "Oh look, they've put flowers on the car," finding it both amazing and amusing.

That same year Rudolf joined the Canadians in New York, dancing with Mary Jago, who had never performed the leading role of *Giselle* with him. The performance went extremely well and he was so proud of her that at the final curtain call, he gave her his own flowers with a heartfelt kiss. Everyone waited outside to shower him with even more flowers. He was cheered all the way to his waiting limo, which had blossoms piled inches thick on the rooftop. As the car slowly disappeared down the street, Rudolf waved a long-stemmed rose out the window as a trail of flowers filled the street. It was a sight to behold.

Just to do things differently, we decided to do a flower throw on the opening night of the 1979 *Nureyev Festival*. I joined a group of fans who were dethorning roses behind the London Coliseum near the Stage Door when Luigi Pignotti, Nureyev's assistant, arrived. "What's going on?" he inquired. I handed him a rose. "For tonight?" he asked, knowing that we usually did flower throws on the closing night. "Why not?" I replied. Then he kindly greeted us all, one by one, trying to sort us out. "Why aren't you in New York?" he asked me, or "I thought you were moving abroad?" to another fan. Since so many of us were traveling back and forth, it's no wonder he was confused.

By the 1982 *Nureyev Festival*, it was becoming increasingly difficult to arrange my time off to attend every performance. I was the Office Manager for a prominent New York City psychiatrist, making appointments for him and three other therapists, typing up numerous book manuscripts, taking care of billing and insurance issues, and making sure the office ran smoothly. Luckily my boss fully appreciated me and understood my passion for ballet. Not a dance lover himself, he agreed to attend a performance and was incredibly impressed with Rudolf Nureyev's stage presence, irresistible charisma, and especially his unwavering mental focus and stamina, seldom cancelling a performance even when injured. A while later, my boss injured his foot. When I teasingly asked why he was limping, he replied, "I'm no Rudolf Nureyev!"

It was never easy, however, to attend Rudolf's performances across the Atlantic, since I had to find and properly train a temporary assistant to fill in during the weeks I was away and arrange to pay my rent in advance. This often meant working long hours so that by the time I departed, I was just about exhausted.

As part of that 1982 *Festival*, the Ballet du Nancy from France danced the Diaghilev program with Rudolf. I decided to return to New York City a day before the Saturday closing night performance in order to be rested for work on Monday. On my last night in London, I bought a small bouquet of roses and planned to toss them after *Petrushka,* the last ballet on the program. A few others also decided to toss flowers that night so altogether we had about a dozen bouquets. Mine landed directly at Rudolf's feet, but somehow he didn't pick it up. In front of the curtain, when most fans tossed their flowers, he gathered up all the bouquets except mine, which was now behind his feet and caught in the bottom of the curtain's fringe. After acknowledging the fans, he started backing off between the open curtains when he finally spotted my roses. He carefully scooped them up and came forward once again, giving me a lovely acknowledgement.

At the Stage Door, I had saved a single rose from the bouquet and placed it on the desk when I went in to get my program signed. I gave my little speech about not being able to stay for closing night and thanked him for a wonderful season. As I left, he stared up at me in a rather peculiar way. Only later did I find out, that a friend of mine had gone in ahead of me and explained to Rudolf, that I couldn't stay for closing night and asked him to sign a photo for me. When I was handed the newly signed photo, I finally understood why Nureyev gave me a peculiar look, because he had already heard the "explanation" just minutes before I told him.

His final *Nureyev and Friends* season at Broadway's Uris Theatre was in sweltering heat of August 1984. He was joined by French dancers Jean Guizerix, Evelyne DeSutter, and Marie-Christine Mouis, along with Eva Evdokimova and New York City Ballet's Stephanie Saland in a program of *Apollo, Flower Festival, Pas de Quatre,* and *Moor's Pavane.* On closing night, two thousand red blossoms flooded the stage in wave after wave, like a cascading waterfall. Guizerix stood throughout the curtain calls with his mouth wide open; but the others had experienced our flower throws before. The entire house was on its feet in spellbinding excitement; some shouting "Encore, encore." A spotlight came on and Rudolf took a final solo call in front of the curtain. Tears of indescribable joy filled his eyes as he held up both hands and waved but then signaled, "That's enough; I really can't do any more." As always, we respected his wishes and the applause came to a halt.

Outside the theatre, a party atmosphere prevailed, with red flowers smothering Rudolf's limousine, including a yellow floral "smiley face" on the vehicle's front grill and a single majestic rose atop the antenna. The street was packed with people, including those hanging out of their apartment windows across the street. One determined neighbor brought out a stepladder and perched on it to get a better view. Stagehands emerged from the theatre carrying flowers and stopped to watch Rudolf's exit. Flowers began to fly, cheers went up through the throng, and Rudolf was handed a heart-shaped helium balloon. Since I was too short to see over the enormous crowd, that was the only way I spotted him. He paused at the limousine door before getting in and gave a huge wave to everyone, a look of absolute euphoria on his face. The car departed with trails of red flowers blowing off the hood and hoards of fans rushing to the corner, all shouting "Bravo!" Rudolf was headed to the airport for yet another performance across the Atlantic. That was a departure worthy of a king.

We tried including fellow audience members in our flower throws whenever possible. A child shouted excitedly to her mother, "Mommy, my flower got on stage!" One thoughtful fan made several bouquets from her garden. At curtain calls, Rudolf focused on these delicate blooms rather than the floral presentation arrangements still wrapped in plastic.

London experienced a heat wave one summer with temperatures in the 90s. After one performance, a fan clutched a wilted, very potent bouquet of garden flowers that was tossed during the curtain calls. The flowers were clearly, as the British say, "Past their sell-by date." When Rudolf stepped in front of the curtain to acknowledge the applause, we kept saying "Don't pick it up, please, Rudolf. It's just for show." But of course he reached down and retrieved it.

When he placed this wilted bouquet in the crook of his arm, he actually drew his head back because the aroma must have overwhelmed him.

A fan attending an outdoor performance in California's Hollywood Bowl once told me that when someone tossed flowers onto the stage, Nureyev tossed them right back because they smelled so terrible from sitting out in the hot sun all day.

In London the summer heat worked in our favor, however, because it caused all the roses to bloom at once so local florists were practically giving them away. We bought three-dozen red roses for one British pound and used them for closing night.

During his *Nureyev Festival* seasons at the Palais des Sports in Paris, bouquets were often thrown from the audience. Nureyev gathered them together and presented them to his leading ballerina with a deep bow. This lovely gesture always charmed the French public. On many occasions I overheard phrases such as "Tres elegant" or "ooh la la" from the Parisians during curtain calls. The flowers became a large part of the curtain call ritual. Rudolf was generous with them, giving bouquets to his ballerinas and other cast members or, on occasion, a singer or even the conductor. At one performance, he was given a large bouquet while his two leading ballerinas received none, so he tore his in half and graciously gave one to each.

At the Palais des Sports with its thrust stage and seats on three sides, Nureyev often had throngs of people standing near the stage edge handing him flowers. One group of overly enthusiastic teenagers tossed flowers at Nureyev's feet and then reached up to touch him. Rudolf was highly amused and bent down to shake their hands. When he emerged for another curtain call, there were pens and autograph books neatly placed on the edge of the stage. He promptly burst out laughing.

After a lovely performance with the Royal Ballet's Lynn Seymour in Paris, a fan tossed a bouquet, but the flowers dislodged mid-flight and all that remained was the plastic shell. Rudolf turned it round and looked at it rather sarcastically, but gave it to Lynn anyway. Just as he bowed to kiss her hand, a tossed bouquet landed on top of the empty plastic case and they both cracked up. Another fan tossed two bouquets of roses. When Nureyev tried to catch them, all the petals fell off and he scratched his hand because the roses were not dethorned.

Those of us who attended these Paris *Nureyev Festivals* became friendly with Madame Blot at the Box Office. Prior to online booking, obtaining tickets there was a daunting task. Each performance ticket was held at the Box Office until we arrived to pay for them. If we didn't arrive by 6 p.m., our tickets were sold. Madame Blot became accustomed to our nightly rush to collect our tickets, and on the last night she said, "See you next year." There was no question we would be back somehow.

For one of these *Nureyev Festivals*, a fan arranged individual bouquets to toss to the four performers after *Moor's Pavane*, the closing piece on the program. As the cast of four lined up for their curtain calls, Rudolf watched attentively while a single bouquet landed precisely at the feet of each dancer. Nureyev extended his arm to give the fan a special bow, obviously impressed with her pitching skills. A French fan tossed his hat on stage at curtain calls and Rudolf playfully tossed it back.

Rudolf always made a point to acknowledge individuals in his audience. When one man shouted "Spasebo," he turned and acknowledged him. This also included his fans, those down front as well as up "in the gods." Since the applause lasted so long, I used to make my way down from the upper regions of the theatre during curtain calls, pausing at each level to bravo, until I ended up "down front" near the stage. Rudolf recognized my bravo, and it seemed to amuse him to hear my bravo "traveling" from the top to the bottom of the auditorium. The mother of one fan broke her nose when she ran into a door while frantically running downstairs for curtain calls. It made a good story when asked how she broke it.

In Vienna, flowers were verboten by the management. But the ingenuity of Nureyev's public never ceased to amaze. Flowers were smuggled into the theatre in coat sleeves, handbags, briefcases, and by other devious means. Knowing that flowers were forbidden made Rudolf appreciate them all the more. If someone tossed him a bouquet that suddenly appeared from under a coat, he reached down – often fishing it out of the footlights – and gathered it into his arms while acknowledging the members of his appreciative public. If the bouquets missed the stage and landed in the wide orchestra pit, members of the Vienna Philharmonic, which played for the ballet, fished them out and tossed them on to the stage for Rudolf or in some cases reached up and simply handed him his bouquet. Once a senior member of the Philharmonic remained in the orchestra pit applauding when a tossed bouquet landed on the floor near him. He kindly handed the bouquet up to Rudolf, who gave the gentleman a deep bow of gratitude.

Sometimes being in the orchestra pit proved hazardous. Following a performance of *Petrushka,* one of the fans made posies for each member of the large cast. They were individually weighted in wet newspapers in order to reach across the orchestra pit to the stage. After endless pitching, one of the orchestra members requested that she toss them higher because the musicians were getting wet. It didn't bother Rudolf, who caught many bouquets mid-flight or scooped them up to present to his fellow cast members. On his last curtain call, he waved both of his mittened *Petrushka* hands to signal it was time to leave. When he emerged from the theatre, the Stage Door attendant piled Rudolf's arms with bouquets. While he was escorted to a waiting car, someone put yet another bouquet on top. Nureyev rolled his eyes as if to say, "Just what I need." He was driven off to a party, sitting alone in the back seat next to a colorful pile of gorgeous flowers, most of which he gave to his party hostess.

Rudolf's innate sense of timing served him well during the curtain calls. Once several enormous bouquets were presented to him, which Rudolf placed on the floor indicating they were for the entire cast. Joining hands with the other dancers, the ensemble came forward to acknowledge the applause. Without taking his eyes off the audience, Rudolf automatically stepped forward to bow and then stepped backward over the bouquets, just "knowing" where they were. When a fan tossed a huge bouquet after one performance, Nureyev caught it behind his back as it whizzed past him. He grabbed it by the ribbons and whipped it around to "present" to the public, who cheered his quick reflexes.

At curtain calls with Carla Fracci, a bouquet tossed from the audience came speeding toward Fracci's stomach. Rudolf's face registered surprise, at first unsure what it was. Without removing his arm from around Fracci's waist, he simply reached out and grabbed it with his free hand before it could hit her. His natural reflexes were impeccable and quite extraordinary. The audience loved it and both dancers laughed.

Despite numerous performances together, Fracci and Nureyev had never danced *Giselle* in New York until 1981. The curtain calls took on the form of a contest between Fracci's fans, who showered her with pink carnations, confetti and shredded programs, and Nureyev's fans, who pelted the stage with white flowers. The Fracci contingent ran out of flowers before the Nureyev one. That season they also starred together in Nureyev's *Romeo and Juliet*. Rudolf coaxed Margot Fonteyn to come out of retirement to perform the role of Lady Capulet. On closing night, the dancers kept bowing extremely low in order to escape getting hit by the ongoing avalanche of flying flowers. When the flowers were depleted, the fans tossed colored streamers.

One incident at a curtain call occurred in 1974 when Nureyev performed the title role in John Neumeier's *Don Juan* with the National Ballet of Canada at the Metropolitan Opera House. This was one of Rudolf's best roles. His stunning all-black costume with a white collar made him look exquisitely elegant. An enthusiastic audience brought Nureyev out for curtain calls again and again. In addition to flowers, plastic wristbands were being tossed on stage. Rudolf obligingly picked one up and put it on his wrist. Before anyone realized it, an overly enthusiastic man climbed onto the stage, and held Rudolf in a gigantic bear hug. As he did this, he swung Rudolf around so that his legs were dangling over the orchestra pit, causing gasps from the astonished audience. Finally, the man put him down and ran offstage. Rudolf jokingly made the Sign of the Cross once he realized he wasn't being dropped into the pit. That was the final curtain call for that performance. The following night, the Hurok Organization, which sponsored the tour, had security guards strategically positioned at both sides of the stage. Nobody was going to climb onto the Met stage for the remainder of that season.

After Nureyev premiered his production of *Manfred* for the Paris Opera in 1979, he desperately wanted it to be seen in New York and London. However, when the production was scheduled for New York, the French dancers decided to strike. The producers couldn't take the financial risk of bringing the company in if the dancers wouldn't perform. Rudolf was disappointed but reworked the production for the Zurich Ballet and it was finally shown in London three years later. It never made it to New York, though not for lack of trying, but was finally presented along with his production of *Don Quixote,* and made its American premiere at Washington's Kennedy Center and then at Chicago's mammoth 3,900-seat Auditorium Theatre.

At least a dozen New Yorkers flew to Chicago to see it. Despite decent reviews, *Manfred* was poorly attended, with audiences preferring to buy tickets for what they knew, such as *Don Quixote*. In between the matinee and evening performance on the last day, we retrieved the flowers purchased that morning that were soaking in the bathtub of our hotel room and arranged them into numerous stunning bouquets with ribbons. The performance went so well that we broke our usual protocol and tossed smaller bouquets already at the first company call. Because the fans were on both sides of the theatre, about a dozen small bouquets were tossed across the entire width of the stage at the company's feet. I still picture it after all these years.

Rudolf acknowledged each of us with outstretched arms and then immediately gathered up as many bouquets as he could, arranged them quickly, and presented them to Elise Flagg and Janet Popelesky, two of his leading ladies in the ballet. Christine Redpath was at the very end of the line-up, so Rudolf walked a few steps to scoop up more flowers and presented them to her, blowing a sweet kiss. The audience refused to leave but, after endless calls, the curtain came down and we heard the company applauding and cheering behind the curtain.

Nureyev was an expert "flower arranger." After a performance with Fonteyn when loose flowers were tossed at her feet, Rudolf gathered them up and arranged them incredibly quickly. When he presented them to her, the white flowers all tastefully surrounded a single pink one to make a perfect bouquet.

Throughout the years, our flower throws extended to other dancers. When the Royal Ballet performed Ashton's *La Fille Mal Gardee* in Washington, we learned it would be the farewell performance of Alexander Grant who created the role of Alain. The fans thoughtfully arranged a large flower throw after his last performance. When he came in front of the curtain to bow, he was pelted with flowers. He immediately burst into tears and ran off the stage. Rudolf insisted on bringing this veteran performer out in front of the curtain, picked up every single bouquet and presented them to Grant with a kiss, stepped back and applauded him. Grant stood there clutching his new red umbrella with flowers on top that we gave as a joke when this key prop broke at a previous performance. Whenever someone tossed a bouquet to Rudolf, he immediately handed it to Grant, who was so overcome with emotions he could only sob. The curtain came up once more and Rudolf motioned for the company to join in the applause.

When Grant performed in Ashton's *A Month in the Country* in Washington, D.C. for the last time before retiring, the fans arranged a commemorative plaque to be presented at curtain calls. It read, "To Alexander Grant, for his vast contribution to the ballet, with love and appreciation from your American friends." At the Stage Door, he told us how very touched he was because, in all the years he had performed, he always watched others get flowers and never had a flower throw himself. It was very touching and heartwarming.

After attending so many performances, especially with the long *Nureyev Festival* seasons, the faithful fans got rather punchy from lack of sleep. Most of us were either in school or working. We needed to feed off Nureyev's energy to get us through. When others asked me how I could see so many repeat performances, sometimes remarking, "But you've seen *Swan Lake*," I would retort, "But you've seen a baseball game." The point was made. Every live performance, whether ballet or a sports event, is different, with varied audiences and alternating "players." Half the excitement is that none of us ever knew, not even Rudolf himself, how a performance would turn out. We also knew that a dancer's career is incredibly short and we cherished each performance because it could be their last. In order to keep things fresh, sometimes we did really crazy things just to keep everyone "alert."

Once at a Vienna performance, we smuggled in Austrian cowbells and rang them at curtain calls before the ushers could confiscate them. Rudolf nearly doubled over with laughter.

His 1979 London *Nureyev Festival,* finished with the Murray Louis Dance Company. The program closed with the light-hearted comedy *Brighton Venus,* titled *Canarsie Venus* to identify a more local beach for its 1978 New York premiere. It was set to the music of Cole Porter. Nureyev played a fussy lad arriving on a cluttered and crowded beach, dabbing suntan lotion on himself, wearing sunglasses and a sailor hat, and donning immaculate white gloves before being seduced by "Venus" performed by Anne McLeod. The fans gave everyone a huge send-off. Murray Louis looked positively stunned by all the flowers when taking the final curtain call with Rudolf. Nureyev glanced at him and then at the flowers as if to say, "See? I told you so." When the house lights came up, they took one look at the fans "down front" and cracked up at our antics. A group of us wore white gloves and sailor hats, just as Rudolf did in performance, and unfurled three small towels, each with the words from the

Cole Porter song, "You're De-lightful, You're De-licous, You're De-lovely." Ovations lasted over twenty-five minutes until Rudolf, taking a solo call at center stage, waved and signaled for them to stop. He had a plane to catch the very next morning. We continued our upbeat mood with a street party behind the Coliseum until the midnight hour when, like Cinderella, we had to catch our trains and go our separate ways.

A fan in London once had a T-shirt made up at the end of an extremely long *Nureyev Festival* season. It read, "Dear Rudi, we are broke but richer." She held it up as he took his bow on closing night and he beamed from ear to ear. When Nureyev left the theatre that evening, the closing night crowds were so enormous that it was difficult for him to get to his car. Sizing up the situation, the fan with the T-shirt went to the end of the road and, as the car passed by, she held it up. The car came to a sudden stop as Rudolf wound the window down and exclaimed, "I want THAT one!" He drove off into the night clutching the shirt and the fan went home - happy, broke, but richer. It was another splendidly memorable "drive off" into the night.

In 1986, as Director of the Paris Opera, Nureyev brought his dancers to the United States, first to the Met and later to Washington's Kennedy Center. The fans organized a massive flower throw for the final New York City performance and we then headed to see them perform in D.C.. For that last performance on a Sunday matinee, we arranged for the entire company to be presented with a single red rose. It required some logistics purchasing the flowers early on a Sunday morning, properly dethorning them, wrapping them in tricolor ribbons, and promptly delivering them to the theatre's stage manager. This all had to be completed by noon when we had to check out of our hotel. It also meant that we were rushed to have lunch before the performance began; the line at the Kennedy Center cafe was enormous.

Pressed for time before the matinee, we ran to the nearby Watergate Hotel coffee shop. I carried one red rose as a souvenir. Just as I came to the hotel entrance, Nureyev came out the door, ready to walk to the theatre. He was in a dreamy mood and I spontaneously handed him the rose and said "Good morning!" He seemed jolted from his reverie, took the flower and gave me a lovely smile. Later some of the others related that Rudolf arrived at the Stage Door carrying his rose and everyone wondered who gave it to him. I merely smiled to myself.

Despite all of our efforts to give the entire Paris Opera corps de ballet a rose, the management refused to present them on stage. However, some of the dancers emerged from the Stage Door clutching a single rose with red, white and blue ribbons, so we knew our efforts were not in vain.

Nureyev's tenure as Director of the Paris Opera wasn't all roses, however. Various claques who disliked him attended his performances to boo him at curtain calls. A picture exists of Rudolf shading his eyes from the spotlight trying to find out where a particular booer was. After several experiences of this, it became a game. At one performance Rudolf boldly gave the booer the finger, which caused the audience to laugh and cheer while the man was drowned out. Another time a claque loudly booed him from the balcony. The boos grew louder with each curtain call until Rudolf finally looked up and made another rude gesture, but this time trying to hide a smile. This was after a performance of *Pierrot Lunaire*, a ballet by Glen Tetley that Rudolf really liked, but its Schonberg music was difficult for the general public. "I suppose I'm wasting my time," he later remarked, "after sweating blood and trying to educate public. There's more to dance than jumping, and boos are my reward."

In the late 80s and early 90s, Rudolf performed his *Nureyev and Friends* program everywhere, often with dancers from the Paris Opera. Fans had heard the rumors that he had AIDS and none of us knew for certain when we would see him again. However, when he continued to dance for several more years, we dismissed the rumors. After one of these performances, someone handed him a bouquet of lilies. He was not amused and returned them, saying, "I'm not dead yet!"

By 1991, we could see that his health and strength had deteriorated, but his interpretation of *Songs of a Wayfarer* only seemed to deepen. This duet finishes with the Wayfarer played by Nureyev, dressed in blue facing the audience and blowing a kiss while the figure in red takes his hand and slowly walks him to the back of the stage. Just before reaching the back wall, Nureyev turns with an outstretched hand to the audience. So much was read in to the ballet ever since it was first performed in 1971, but at that final New York performance on March 21, 1991, we all sensed he was saying goodbye and Fate was taking him on his final journey. It was a powerful and poignant moment.

Since several of us attended that performance, we organized a flower throw. Many in the audience that day had never seen Nureyev perform. In fact one audience member even asked me, "Was Nureyev the guy in blue?" During the interval, we solicited those sitting nearby to help in tossing flowers during the curtain calls. Everyone willingly agreed. Nureyev was pleased and touched at this send-off. When the performance finished, an elderly woman thanked me profusely for asking her to help toss the flowers. "I've never seen him before but this is something I will never, ever forget. He moved me to tears. It was like watching someone's soul dance." That was certainly profound and very perceptive.

Following the performance, some faithful fans went en masse backstage. Rudolf finally emerged, wrapped in layers of sweaters, scarves and his usual cap. He lingered awhile, attentively chatting with us all, and we sensed a slight reluctance on his part to leave. It was the very last time many of us had the pleasure of seeing him, but as he walked out of the theatre, we noticed he was tenderly clutching our flowers.

"It is nice to be remembered."
~Rudolf Nureyev interview with Mavis Staines, BBC Television, 1981~

ANNIVERSARIES AND BIRTHDAYS

50th Birthday Gala, Metropolitan Opera House, with Paris Opera and guests, NYC, June 27, 1988. Photo: William J. Reilly

ANNIVERSARIES

Watching Nureyev perform year after year, we progressively realized how very special he was. No other dancer seemed to inhabit a role the way he did. His charisma galvanized both his public and the companies he danced with. Because a dancer's performing career is unusually short, we were well aware that it could all come to an abrupt end. We tried not to take any of his performances for granted, and were extremely grateful for all the joy and beauty he brought into our lives.

For all that Nureyev gave us, we wanted to give something back to him. We seized every opportunity to celebrate his triumphs, but of particular importance was the anniversary of his first day in the West – on June 17th.

Whenever possible, the occasion was marked by a flower throw. No matter where he was performing, we made sure that he received a card thanking him for all his performances.

For his 19th anniversary in the West in 1980, Rudolf took his curtain calls as if "expecting" something. We obliged by giving him a huge flower throw. When he emerged from the London Coliseum Stage Door, his car was blanketed in flowers, many with cards attached. While waiting for Rudolf, his assistant Luigi began reading the cards and when he came across a name not familiar to him, he called out "Who is this?" Nureyev was always acquiring new fans as his career progressed. When he eventually emerged from the Stage Door, he asked in mock surprise, "What's all this?" Some of the flowers were even tossed into the car at Rudolf's feet until the very last moment, when the car door closed and Luigi drove them away.

Shortly before his 20th anniversary in 1981, some of the fans thought it would be interesting to make a chronology of Nureyev's performances in the West. We mobilized ourselves worldwide and spent considerable time researching dates, pouring through old dance magazines and programs, as well as the public library's resources. With fans sending information from the world's major dance capitals, the chronology ultimately came together. Of course this was accomplished by mail and telephone, prior to the Internet. Then came the laborious task of typing the more than two-hundred and fifty pages of data. I labored each day on my lunch hour while co-workers just assumed I was terribly busy. The detailed chronology included performance dates, city, theatre, title of ballet performed, Nureyev's partners, and the company he performed with. The chronology was finally completed, but I was still compiling some of the statistics while waiting for and during my flight from New York to London. To illustrate how frequently Rudolf Nureyev performed, by 1972 he had logged in more than two hundred performances of *Sleeping Beauty* alone – a number most other dancers would not achieve in their entire performing careers.

In typical fashion, Nureyev commemorated his 20th anniversary by dancing *Giselle* with Eva Evdokimova and the London Festival Ballet during his 1981 *Nureyev Festival*. Several fans came from New York, Paris, Vienna, Zurich, Milan, Lisbon, and other dance capitals to mark the special occasion. The performance was incredibly beautiful, and the fans did a large flower throw.

The company's Stage Manager arranged for a "streamer shower" from the stage boxes, stalls, and upper regions of the house, in addition to a marvelous balloon drop. Company director John Field came out and made a brief speech, thanking Nureyev for his twenty years of performing. When the rest of the audience realized this was a special anniversary, the cheers grew even louder. The stagehands unfurled streamers and soon the stage was awash in a mesmerizing sea of colorful streamers and flowers. When the balloons cascaded down from the flies, Nureyev blew kisses. Field gently pushed Rudolf forward to accept the applause, but when balloons began to pop, Rudolf's face changed from a grateful smile to "eek!"

Nureyev seemed in a happy daze as he accepted gifts and shook everyone's hand at the Stage Door. He signed autographs for an unusually long time while seated in a chair behind an enclosed partition used by the Stage Door attendant. An orderly queue formed while he patiently signed everyone's program.

Purposefully waiting until the crowd had thinned out, I went inside with a couple of friends for moral support to present Rudolf with his 20th Anniversary Chronology Book. I placed the huge three-ring binder onto the ledge. Nureyev clutched his pen, and looked quizzically at us as if to say "What is this and where do I sign?" He opened the book and began thumbing through it while I explained "We'd like to give you this as a record of all your performances in the West." As the words sunk in, he exclaimed, "My GOD," and we all laughed. He stammered, "I....I" to which I added, "It will never be up to date; that's impossible." He just kept staring at the pages and tried controlling himself from tearing it open and reading it properly. He couldn't quite contain his overwhelming enthusiasm. After a few moments he called, "Luigi, look at this!" and Luigi quickly obliged. Another fan joked, "And here's the bag to carry it in!" and everyone chuckled. Luigi groaned but gave us a smile as he put the heavy book into the bag to carry to the car. Rudolf, all smiles, gave us a genuine heartfelt "Thank you!"

He lingered a while, as if not wanting the evening to finish. When he stepped outside to his car, he laughed to see that it was covered with bouquets, collected from the stage after the festivities. He was so laden down with gifts, flowers, and other goodies that it was a wonder he could get into the car. With deep emotion in his eyes he paused to shake hands one last time and waved as the car rounded the corner into the night. The aura of his presence still lingered in the air.

The following year's Festival celebrated Nureyev's 21st anniversary and a huge flag-laden banner was displayed at curtain calls for the occasion. The company, applauding Rudolf from the wings, craned their necks to read it. Rudolf gestured for them to join him on stage. Elise Flagg who danced the Contessa in his production of *Manfred,* stood next to Rudolf holding his hand. Overwhelmed by the reception, the company didn't realize it was Nureyev's anniversary and gathered around to congratulate and kiss him. He pretended to do a mock faint at all the attention. The entire audience was on its feet when Nureyev emerged again, this time pelted with flowers. Dancer Christine Redpath found a single carnation on the floor, picked it up, and worked her way toward Rudolf and handed it to him. He took it and gave her a kiss. Everything was so spontaneous that Rudolf was slightly embarrassed by this breach in curtain call etiquette.

Earlier in the evening, I overheard a man behind me remark that the Zurich Ballet was well drilled and rehearsed but "would the ballet make me stand up and cheer?" Now, as I turned around, there he was standing up and cheering. When the houselights came up and Rudolf saw the entire Coliseum audience on its feet, the smile of his face was positively beaming.

At the Stage Door, we arranged to have champagne and hoped that Rudolf would pause momentarily for a celebratory toast. We ordered drinks from the Lemon Tree pub on the corner, but used the glasses for a champagne toast. One fan began uncorking the first of several champagne bottles and even provided a tea towel and a lovely fluted glass. Someone offered a glass of champagne to Luigi when he went to fetch Rudolf's car and we asked if he could help detain Rudolf momentarily. This wasn't necessary since Nureyev decided to sign autographs, which took quite a while. We had hoped that the bulk of people would leave after getting their autographs, but the party atmosphere in the street was contagious and nearly everyone remained. When Rudolf finally emerged, the enormous crowd parted like the Red Sea. The crowd had already consumed five of the eight bottles of champagne, but we saved the "good stuff" for Rudolf.

When he was about four feet in front of us, the good champagne was uncorked and I held the fluted glass while my friend poured it. Rudolf staggered back two steps, mockingly, and put one hand up to his face and exclaimed, "My God!" The bubbly ran over as I handed the glass to Rudolf. To our relief, he took it willingly and the crowd gathered around, making a little circle of friends and fans, all holding out their champagne-filled paper cups for a toast, as we began singing "Happy Anniversary to You." Rudolf's face registered a myriad of emotions: slightly embarrassed, then amused, then relishing every moment, appreciatively looking at each of us. He held his glass out and said enthusiastically, "Some more" as no doubt the first glass contained more bubbles than actual champagne. Photographs taken that night show him sticking out his tongue in anticipation of the bubbly, and grinning madly at this impromptu celebration in the middle of the street.

He seemed quite thirsty and gulped it down, permeating his dehydrated mouth while joking, "How am I going to talk with Berlin Ballet after all that?" We knew he was in negotiations for an upcoming Berlin Ballet production of "Wagner in Venice" as part of a Wagner Centennial, which never materialized. We merely replied, "You'll manage."

Making a joke of all the banners Rudolf had received in previous seasons, my friend quipped, "You'll never be short of sheets, Rudolf," causing him to laugh. "Go on, Nancy, give him your banner," he urged. I had been holding the folded flag-studded banner, but it was obvious Rudolf didn't have a free hand, holding flowers in one hand and his champagne in the other. So he matter-of-factly raised the elbow of his right arm, indicating, "Put it under my arm." He said softly, "I want THAT one!" I tucked it under and gave it a little pat. One of his fans quipped, "Rudolf, we didn't arrange for the Greek flag not to be there during tonight's performance – honest!" and everyone cracked up. A fan offered her small Greek flag to him in case the flag, a key prop, was missing at the following performance.

When Rudolf's glass was empty, he hesitated and looked at Luigi in the waiting car. The gathered crowd waited in anticipation, as he glanced at everyone once again and said, "Well, bless you." He sauntered over to the car as the applause started up again and cheerily kissed each of the fans gathered around the vehicle. Luigi drove off and got as far as the corner pub when the car stopped. One of the fans, champagne bottle and glass still in hand, was leaning in the window, chatting. I heard him laugh and say to Rudolf, "I'm sorry, I'll try and arrange it next year." Apparently Rudolf had stopped and asked for another glass of champagne and added, "Do you have any ice?" He then spotted one of the company members standing outside the pub and requested, "We need another glass!" She dashed into the pub for a glass at the same time that several fans offered theirs, but Rudolf shared his glass with Luigi. Finally one of the stagehands pulled up behind Rudolf's car, honking, and the driver teased, "C'mon, Luigi, move it. This ain't no place for a party!" Everyone was in a jovial mood and when Rudolf finished his second glass of bubbly, he promptly handed the glass back and was driven off out of sight. The evening was a complete success.

Through the efforts of Nigel Gosling, Rudolf Nureyev was finally invited to perform once again with the Royal Ballet after a long absence. He prepared a new work for the company, *The Tempest*. In addition to other performances, Nureyev revived his third acts of *Raymonda* and *Bayadere*. In a television interview filmed while he rehearsed Bryony Brind for *Bayadere*, he stated that, "I've always come to expect nothing from people but a bucket of shit." The interviewer replied, "I'm sorry to hear that. Was there manure flying every which way when the Royal broke off with you?" Rudolf laughed but retorted, "Now they got what they want – and so have I." Needless to say, Rudolf's fearless and direct way of expressing himself was quite entertaining.

In 1983, his anniversary again occurred during a London *Nureyev Festival*. A large group of us planned on having a picnic at Sussex Downs. We invited Rudolf who said, "We'll see." On the Sunday of our picnic, we went ahead without him and despite his absence, had a most enjoyable day in the country. We later learned that he was in nearby Glynbourne, enjoying the opera on his day off.

For his anniversary in 1986, we prepared a special tribute book. This took a lot of coordination, but basically each of Rudolf's loyal supporters participated. The idea was to write a personal message about the first time they saw him dance, their own reaction, and anything else they wanted to convey for all the years of performances he gave them. Some wrote brief paragraphs, while a more imaginative fan wrote a poem. In all, some fifty fans contributed to the book, including Katherine Healy, who had watched Rudolf dance as a young child and later became a professional ballerina. The tribute book was compiled along with several photographs taken over the years of the enormous

Stage Door crowds surrounding Rudolf. Some of the fans pictured in those crowds were identified, even though Rudolf knew who we were.

The book was mailed to his Quai Voltaire apartment in Paris, and a few days later I received a "proof of delivery" receipt, signed by Rudolf himself. On a subsequent trip to Paris, I stayed with an elderly fan. She told me that she asked Rudolf if he was pleased with the book. He seemed somewhat embarrassed, but replied, "Very pleased," and repeated his "Nice to have support" comment that he said to us on his 46th birthday.

On the actual night of his 25th anniversary, Rudolf danced the role of the butler in *Miss Julie* with Northern Theatre Ballet in Manchester, England. When the performance finished, Nureyev took his bow with the company and they then left, surrendering the stage to him. He took his solo bow and beckoned the dancers to rejoin him, but they remained in the wings. The company director, Robert de Warren, came on stage and told the audience it was Nureyev's 25th anniversary. Halfway through his speech, the audience began to laugh as twenty-five young girls came on stage and formed a semi-circle behind Rudolf. They each held a large white card with a big number in red – from number one on the left side of the line to twenty-five on the right side. Rudolf turned and immediately went back along the line, gently kissing every girl. Two more came out with a large card saying: "Congratulations and Happy 25th Anniversary." A small boy followed carrying an enormous bottle of champagne that was almost as big as he was. Finally a floral tribute, about five feet high, was placed in front of Nureyev after more cheers and roaring applause from the enthusiastic audience.

Afterwards there was a party backstage with a big cake from the local baker. Rudolf was asked to cut it. He plunged the knife in and said, "Everybody make a wish." He then asked, "Do I have to cut it all up?" The director stepped in and did the honors. About an hour later, Rudolf left with friends to have supper because he was, as usual, leaving at six the following morning to catch a plane to dance somewhere else.

The following year, for his 26th anniversary in the West, we organized an even more ambitious project. This time we presented him with a beautiful scroll, congratulating Rudolf on his anniversary, signed by as many fans as possible. The document was envisioned as something like the Declaration of

Independence, with fine calligraphy at the top and filled with signatures at the bottom.

One of the fans consulted with a calligrapher as well as an artist familiar with making leather-bound scrolls. The difficulty was in getting everyone's signature on the same parchment paper. I sent letters to overseas fans explaining the project and asked for their signatures so the calligrapher could trace them onto the parchment. Local signatures were gathered and combined with those from overseas. The project took longer than expected, but it was finally ready by closing night at the Met when Nureyev danced his final *Swan Lake* with the Paris Opera.

Our original intention was to have the scroll presented to him on stage after the performance, but it became impossible. I had written Jane Hermann at the Met and her reply stated that Nureyev "didn't want any fuss." She suggested we give it to her at the Stage Door and she would see that Rudolf got it. That didn't work out either, so after the flower throw and the applause, we all waited at the Stage Door.

To our astonishment, security barricades lined the area. Apparently the Met management finally decided that crowd control was necessary, but it made our "presentation" a bit challenging. Huge crowds jockeyed for position when Rudolf came out, but one of his most loyal fans was able to thrust the precious scroll into Rudolf's hand. The dancer held on to it tightly as he struggled to get out the Stage Door and into a waiting car. Once there, he gave us a broad smile and waved the scroll triumphantly in the air before being whisked away. Our mission was accomplished!

BIRTHDAYS

One of Nureyev's first birthday bashes in New York occurred during his 1977 *Friends* season at the Uris - now Gershwin Theatre. It was his 39th birthday and reaching that milestone can be traumatic for anyone, but particularly for a dancer. Nureyev stated in many interviews the words his father once told him: that he would be washed up at age 40. Yet he was still dancing exceptionally well and during this season had a most interesting and somewhat complicated program consisting of Glen Tetley's *Pierrot Lunaire* to the music of Arnold Schonberg as an opener. Even some of the diehard ballet enthusiasts had difficulties with the music; so the uninitiated public was getting a "baptism by fire" with this piece opening the evening's triple bill.

Following an interval, Rudolf danced Maurice Bejart's *Songs of a Wayfarer*. It was sung in German to Gustav Mahler's songs and was originally created on Rudolf and Paulo Bortoluzzi in 1971. However, this time it was danced with Bejart dancer Daniel Lommel. This ballet, one of the most performed of Nureyev's repertoire, fit him like a glove. Rudolf seemed to perform from "inside out" by expressing a myriad of emotions representing each of the "Songs."

The final work of this program was *The Lesson*, by Fleming Flindt with music by contemporary French composer Georges Delerue, who was most noted for his film scores. Nureyev played the mad ballet master in a version based on the Ionesco play. Every night he had to murder his dance pupil, performed by Danish dancer Anne-Marie Vessel. There were some nights of such feverish intensity that we feared for her safety.

For a Broadway audience in 1977, the program proved challenging, but audiences seemed to love it. Several people warned Rudolf not to do this program on Broadway because an evening of three "heavy" works to music of Schonberg, Mahler, and a relatively unknown composer would not sell. But Rudolf loved taking risks and after trying the program out in Paris to great success, he felt he could equally engage a New York public. He was right, of course. According to Variety, the three-week run broke even after just four days and played to 90% capacity.

Alexander Grant, then director of the National Ballet of Canada, flew to New York for discussions about an upcoming season and Rudolf told him,

"Good, you can be here for my birthday." On March 17, 1977, we thought it seemed like a good idea to relieve the "heaviness" of the program with some lighthearted birthday festivities. We spoke to the theatre manager and received permission to do something special, as long as we provided all the supplies and manpower. During the afternoon of the big day, a few fans gathered in the theatre with an air pump and strong lungs and set to work blowing up about three hundred multi-colored balloons. These were then placed in a net suspended high above the stage lights. On a given signal from conductor Stanley Sussman, the stagehands would release the balloons when Nureyev took his curtain calls.

When Rudolf arrived at the theatre that evening, he was as surprised as we were to see three strolling troubadours in Renaissance garb with long capes playing classical instruments while serenading his arrival. Everyone ran to greet him with presents. One fan gave him a coffee mug for his tea with a silhouette of Fred Astaire on it. Under the image were the words: "When you've got it, they remember your name!"

Throughout the entire performance, and particularly during the opening sections of *Pierrot* when Nureyev was perched high atop his structure looking upwards catching "moonbeams," we had visions of Rudolf spotting the balloons or – even worse – having them pop from the hot lights and ruining the performance. Fortunately, no such thing happened, and the balloons remained a well-kept secret.

The Lesson finished with all its ferocity and the crazed ballet master came center stage to take his solo curtain call. As was his custom, his curtain calls were always done in character, so he walked briskly to center stage and with fixed mouth, bowed stiffly. Stanley Sussman tapped his baton for the orchestra to begin playing "Happy Birthday" and the applause died down when the audience heard the familiar tune. Rudolf's face registered a genuine surprise. This was not part of his carefully choreographed curtain calls. He seemed to fumble with his arms, more like *Petrushka* than a maniacal instructor who'd just murdered his pupil. He then raised his right hand to his ear, as if straining to hear the tune, and slightly embarrassed, "saluted" the audience until we finished singing to him.

After the "Happy Birthday" salute, he bowed deeply from the waist. As he did so, hundreds of balloons gently cascaded down from their concealed netting. Rudolf was not aware of them until they fell into his line of vision, but he knew from the audience reaction that something special was happening. Once he spotted the balloons, his mouth dropped wide open. He put one hand to his mouth and the other to his chest in a shocked expression and seemed to take two small steps backward. Then he looked up and grinned like a child as he watched the colorful balloons cascade all around him. Once they had landed and he appeared knee-deep in a sea of balloons, he blew a big kiss to the audience. He called out his supporting players, Vivi Flindt and Ann-Marie Vessel, and they gingerly stepped over the balloons to get to his side. Laughing all the while, Vessel jumped up and down excitedly and Flint playfully waved her finger at him as if to say, "Didn't we surprise you?" Buoyant streamers and gorgeous flowers were tossed from the audience until the stage was simply ablaze with color. The photos from that night are strange indeed: a man wearing a salt-and-pepper wig and old age makeup, celebrating his 39th birthday, while his manner and delight in the evening's festivities were that of a schoolboy having the best time at his own birthday party.

Rudolf scooped up the countless flowers and waved to everyone, blinking back tears. At the Stage Door, a waiting taxi was loaded with decorations until everyone realized Nureyev and his entourage would be departing in a limo, so the taxi was immediately stripped of its décor and the balloons and streamers were shifted to the limousine. When the birthday boy finally emerged, the entire crowd that overflowed into the street sang "Happy Birthday." Big George gently steered him to his waiting car while Rudolf joyfully exclaimed, "I'm demolished!"

The fans had even taken up a collection to pay the stagehands overtime to clean up the balloons and streamers. The Uris theatre manager adored Nureyev and agreed to it. The papers the next day commented, "Meanwhile at the Uris, Nureyev celebrated his 39th birthday in style," commenting on the many balloons, streamers, and so on. "The birthday boy mustered a sheepish grin, making him look sixteen."

The photographers must have worked straight through the night, because their photos of the birthday event were ready the next evening. Before Nureyev had spotted the balloons, he saluted the audience, so he asked the photographers, "Did anyone get a photo of when I saluted?" Indeed they did and after presenting the photograph to Nureyev, it ended up in the next issue of *Dance and Dancers* Magazine.

The Uris Theatre's stage manager spent that evening looking over photos taken from the birthday performance, and asked for copies, commenting, "It was a night to remember, wasn't it?" And yes, indeed it was.

Two years later, Nureyev was back on Broadway, this time in the Diaghilev program with the Joffrey Ballet, dancing in Nijinsky's *L'Apres Midi d'un Faune* and in Fokine's *La Spectre de la Rose* and *Petrushka*. Once again he was dancing on his birthday and a gigantic flower throw was planned. At the ballet's conclusion, when Petrushka's spirit left him and he collapsed over the puppet theatre, little ant-like movements took place in the audience as dozens of us scurried to our places for the planned flower throw. Protocol required the company to take calls in a certain order so the supporting players came out, each in turn, for their bows: all the character dancers, the nursemaids, the Magician, and finally the Moor, the Doll, and Petrushka. Naturally, Nureyev spotted all those extra bodies along the front row retrieving bouquets from the many shopping bags stored there since the final intermission. But the protocol for flowers, and especially since it was his birthday, had to wait until he was on stage all alone.

After a few more company calls, he finally took a solo call and the flowers flew madly. Nureyev remained in the character, bowing from the waist, his toes slightly turned in, his gloved hands outstretched, and a thin black pencil line of a mouth nearly obscuring his own. Yet somehow while remaining in character, he managed to reach out and catch several bouquets in mid-flight and, as always, arranged them in the crook of his arm to "present" them to the public. As the flowers continued to fly, hundreds landed at his feet and his sad Petrushka mouth gradually gave way to an ever-widening jubilant smile. When he was in the middle of a deep bow – and a total surprise to the audience -- the stagehands dumped about a season's worth of paper snowflakes directly behind Rudolf. The snow literally thudded to the stage floor, making a spray of thin paper in its wake. In mid-bow, Rudolf turned his body sideways to see what was happening and once he stood up, had a bemused smirk on his face.

Earlier that night, we arranged a very special birthday surprise – his name in lights in Times Square. In 1979, anyone who paid the $25 fee could "rent" the Times Square sign for whatever message they chose. I made some inquiries and discussed it with the other fans. We took up a collection and I met with the sign representatives for a proper birthday message. We agreed on a giant birthday cake with flickering candles in front of an animated curtain that pulled back to reveal the message: "Another year of greatness for Rudolf Nureyev. Happy 41st Birthday from the Big Apple." At exactly 6:30 p.m. on March 17, 1979, the sign remained high above the Times Square traffic for sixty seconds.

I wrote a note inside Rudolf's birthday card and handed it to Big George when Rudolf arrived for the matinee, laden down with gifts. I thought that when he arrived for his evening performance, he might be able to pass the Broadway area at the time the sign was illuminated. Dozens of spectators set up cameras on Broadway, patiently waiting for the sign to appear and soon a curious crowd gathered around to see what was going on. A few St. Patrick's Day revelers also assembled to see what they were missing. The scheduled start time was delayed slightly, but after a few minutes, the message appeared and a resounding cheer went up along Broadway. Several tourists stopped to look up and see what the fuss was all about: Rudolf Nureyev's name high above Manhattan, higher than any marquee. The renowned location is currently used for the New Year's Eve "ball drop" festivities that are witnessed by the entire world.

Louis Peres, who photographed both the curtain calls as well as the Times Square sign, made a composite photo that he sold at the Stage Door the following evening. Everyone gathered and crowded around when Nureyev emerged, babbling at once about his name "in lights" over Times Square. "Yes, yes," he replied, "I know all about the sign. I just want to SEE it." Several copies of the photo were offered to Rudolf for his signature and as soon as he saw them, he exclaimed, "I hope someone is going to give ME one of those!" Naturally, the photographer obliged. Once in the car, Rudolf eagerly showed the photos to his friends who were joining him for dinner. The handsome smile never left his face.

I learned much later that Rudolf did in fact see his name in lights. A fellow dancer was in the car with Nureyev en route to the theatre and told me that they both saw the Times Square sign wishing Rudolf a Happy Birthday. I guess Rudolf always had impeccable and fortuitous timing!

The following year, Nureyev celebrated his 42nd birthday in Vienna and for months I scrimped and saved in order to be there. He and guest artist Cynthia Gregory danced in Nureyev's *Swan Lake* production. It was created for the Viennese company in the 60s and subsequently filmed with Margot Fonteyn. Nureyev also danced in two works never performed in America: *Ulysses* and *Four Last Songs*.

When New York friends knew I would be in Vienna for his birthday, they handed me assorted cards and gifts to present to him. There was a rehearsal on Nureyev's birthday, so my Viennese friend and I nervously waited at the Stage Door to present him with various goodies. We seldom spoke to Nureyev at these brief encounters but when he arrived, we wished him Happy Birthday. He paused, and gently took my hand that held the bag full of cards as well as the Viennese "delicacies" that my friend had made. "My God!" he exclaimed, kindly thanked us and went inside. We were unsure if he was pleased with his gifts or just in shock that two of his most reticent fans spoke to him.

That evening, charming troubadours serenaded Rudolf at the Stage Door when he entered the theatre and fans presented him with champagne and flowers. Even though he seemed tired at that performance of *Swan Lake* compared to others we had seen that week, a woman sitting next to me said in beautiful English, "This was the essence of dance. I never saw human arms used that way." I could not have said it better myself.

For his 44th birthday, Rudolf was in Boston performing in his production of *Don Quixote* with the Boston Ballet. There were so many fans from New York making the bus trip that we signed a joint birthday card with "Greetings from bus 5280 from New York." It seemed that everyone on the bus was going to the performance. Despite the fact that his birthday was in the middle of the week and many of us had to return to work the following morning, we organized a beautiful flower throw. Since I could only afford to sit in the balcony, I decided to bring along some green and white streamers and helped organize a streamer throw from the balcony to coincide with the flower throw downstairs.

At the intermission, I spoke to a few Bostonians in the first row of the balcony and enlisted their help in throwing streamers at the appropriate time during the curtain calls. They were delighted to participate in his birthday celebration and I had to caution them not to throw the streamers until they saw the flowers being tossed onto the stage. Someone asked me how old Rudolf was and I replied, "Forty-four." The man looked at me incredulously and replied, "No, you're kidding. Somebody forty-four couldn't dance like that!" Needless to say, the flowers and streamers went over very well, but unfortunately Rudolf couldn't hear the choruses of "Happy Birthday" over the thundering applause of the sold-out 4200-seat Metropolitan Center.

When he turned 45, Nureyev danced *Swan Lake* in Tokyo with Yoko Morishita and the Matsuyama Ballet. The performance revealed to the Japanese audiences the perfect blend of East meeting West with the partnership he had built with Yoko. A friend was able to attend that performance so all of our birthday cards were given to her for delivery to Rudolf. During the curtain calls, the appreciative company had arranged for an enormous backdrop banner resplendent with a large red heart, saying, "Happy Birthday, Rudolf, We love you." Prince Siegfried aside, the alluring smile on Nureyev's face nearly wrapped around his head. Later the friend gave the envelope of birthday cards to Rudolf and he tore them open eagerly like a child.

By far the most extravagant birthday celebration was the one given for his 50th birthday during the Paris Opera's season at the Met in New York City. On his actual birthday, March 17th, 1988, Nureyev danced the role of Albrecht with Marianna Tcherkassky in the American Ballet Theatre production in Los Angeles. He had stepped in on short notice for an injured Mikhail Baryshnikov, and thus spent his half-century doing what he enjoyed most – dancing. Since he wasn't in New York, on his real birthday, it was duly commemorated on June 27 with a gala.

At that time Nureyev was directing the Paris Opera and so the entire company performed at the Met that evening. They opened with *Suite en Blanc* by Serge Lifar, followed by a rousing pas de trois from *Paquita*, and the William Forsythe contemporary work, *In the Middle Somewhat Elevated*. Nureyev himself danced with Charles Jude to the Mahler *Songs of a Wayfarer*, beautifully sung on stage by soprano and Rudolf's good friend, Jessye Norman. Following *Wayfarer*, Mayor Ed Koch presented Rudolf with a Tiffany Crystal Apple in appreciation for his artistic contributions to "the Big Apple," New York City. They both stood in front of an enormous red sign, taking up the entire width and height of the Metropolitan Opera curtain space, with NUREYEV spelled out in gigantic gold letters. It must have cost a fortune and was used only briefly.

The evening concluded with the *Grand Defile*, a ceremonial procession only performed at the Paris Opera, but with Nureyev in charge to break a few rules, it was presented on the Met stage that evening. A glorious excuse for pomp and circumstance, it utilized the music from *Les Troyans* by Berlioz to full effect. The Met stage was opened nearly to the street for the ceremony's full pageantry. The traditional order of the processional is followed rigidly, with the younger students or "petit rats" solemnly walking from the furthest point at the back of the stage towards the footlights to take a bow and promenading to their assigned spots on the side. Followed in order of rank are the corps de ballet, soloists, demi-soloists, and coryphées, and so on through the hierarchy assigned by the Opera until the *Etoiles* or "star" dancers enter. The *Grand Defilé* is then "frozen" in a beautiful arrangement of dancers filling the huge stage.

Extending the *Grand Defilé*, invited guests marched out in elegant evening attire, each one of them announced over the public address system so the audience would know who they were. The grand line-up was a "who's who" of the dance world: Dame Margot Fonteyn, Carla Fracci, Mikhail Baryshnikov, Lincoln Kirstein, Peter Martins, Alwin Nikolais, Murray Louis, Eva Evdokimova, Karen Kain, Paul Taylor, Jerome Robbins, Violet Verdy, Sir Kenneth MacMillan – and even Miss Piggy – all of whom were associated with Nureyev's career. Star-shaped spotlights, confetti, silver glitter, balloons and streamers cascaded down on Rudolf as he took center stage and then proceeded to bow to his guests and kiss them one by one. It was a once in a lifetime affair, truly quite an occasion – thanks to Met producer Jane Hermann for making that happen.

Since Nureyev loved performing so much, many of his birthdays were spent dancing in theatres around the world. His fans were fortunate to have seen many of them, from "out front" in the audience. Perhaps the most memorable celebration occurred on the occasion of his 46th birthday, for we were invited to share in his birthday celebration at his exquisite Paris apartment … and that is the story of our next chapter.

"It's nice to have support."
~Rudolf Nureyev to his fans, March 1984~

23 QUAI VOLTAIRE

Fans with Nureyev at his apartment, Paris, March 17, 1984
Photo: Douce Francoise

P aris became a frequent destination when Nureyev took over the Directorship of the Paris Opera Ballet in 1983. Touring the City of Lights by day and seeing a performance at night seemed the perfect vacation. In 1984, Nureyev had mounted numerous new ballets for the Paris Opera and it afforded a wonderful opportunity to see the company as well as Rudolf in works never seen before.

In addition to his directorial duties at the Paris Opera, Nureyev was equally busy with his own performing career. In January 1984, he invited the Martha Graham Dance Company to perform at the ornate Palais Garnier. Nureyev gave two performances of *Phaedra's Dream* with Christine Dakin and George White during the Graham Company's Paris season.

At a gala commemorating Graham's 90th birthday in March of 1984, the Graham Company performed at the New York State Theatre. It marked the

New York debut of *Phaedra's Dream*. Rudolf flew via the Concorde from Paris to New York City in very bad weather conditions for an afternoon rehearsal before the evening performance.

Nureyev showed a newfound confidence in the Graham technique, assuredly handling the contractions, back falls and numerous props, including an enormous symbolic wheel. The piece received an enthusiastic reception and at the conclusion of the evening, Rudolf came out in an elegant tuxedo and tie, taking a curtain call center stage with Martha Graham. By this time, Graham had discontinued her custom of walking out to center stage for a bow. As she became increasingly frail, one of her company members brought her from the wings and only when she was properly positioned center stage did the curtain rise so she could acknowledge the applause. Graham and Nureyev bowed to each other and to the audience and seemed to be giggling in childish delight over some private joke. Rudolf's face was flushed from champagne and as he clasped Graham's arm, one of the fans asked jokingly, "Who's holding who up?"

A champagne reception to benefit the Graham School immediately followed the performance. Graham and Nureyev arrived on the Promenade of the State Theatre while security guards became adamant about clearing everyone out of the theatre. Several of the fans attended the reception, having paid for their higher-priced gala tickets. Since I was leaving for Paris the next evening, I returned home to pack, flushed with excitement as well as the flu. Those who stayed, however, remarked that no matter who attended the reception, whether society people or fans, heads turned when Rudolf Nureyev made his entrance. Everyone continued to gawk at him all evening, remarking how good he looked and what great shape he was in. Some of the fans crowded around him when he remarked, "The public was fantastic tonight!" After the various claques booing his performances at the Paris Opera, the New York public was a pleasant and welcome change.

The next morning, Rudolf urgently returned to Paris on the Concorde. I was scheduled to leave for Paris later that day on an overnight flight. All week I was fighting a nasty bout of flu and admittedly pushed myself too much, so the bug returned with a vengeance right on time for my departure. I spent the day in bed and by late afternoon had to make a decision as to whether to cancel the trip or not. Finally I thought I'd rather be sick in Paris than at home missing everything, so I headed to the airport with a large supply of ginger ale.

The trip was endless since the flight was delayed five hours due to weather conditions. The plane was full and cramped and all I wanted to do was sleep, but felt so uncomfortable I couldn't. I arrived in Brussels the next morning and somehow missed my connection to Paris, so I had to take the train. The delay meant arriving in Paris during the maddening rush hour rather than mid-afternoon, but I began to feel better when I emerged from the Metro steps and saw the majestic view of the Paris Opera. Arriving at the Box Office, I discovered that the Paris Opera dancers were threatening yet another strike. I later learned that one of the reasons Rudolf so swiftly flew back to Paris the morning after the Graham Gala, was to try to avert the strike.

As I checked into my hotel where my two American friends were awaiting my arrival, I breathed a sigh of relief because one of them had collected my tickets for me. After grabbing a banana for my dinner, I headed back to the opera house and discovered that Rudolf was scheduled to dance both *The Tempest* and *La Bayadere*. I simply don't know how he did it; I was having trouble just watching him, I was so exhausted.

Sporting an impressive turban with a brand new feather, Nureyev danced the role of Solor with Monique Loudieres as his Nikiya in the Shades scene of his production. He looked incredibly tired, but was the consummate partner. His solo seemed lackluster and forced, struggling as he was from obvious fatigue. But during the coda, he miraculously found his second wind and executed multiple pirouettes with such a speed, that a young girl seated near us let out an audible gasp bordering on a scream, causing titters from the audience. Fans didn't call Nureyev "the Coda King" for nothing.

The Tempest was next on the program. Originally created for Anthony Dowell and the Royal Ballet in 1981, the production was reworked since its London run and looked completely transformed on the enormous stage at the Palais Garnier. Among those in the cast were Elisabeth Maurin as Miranda and Eric VuAn as Caliban, both pulled from the corps and promoted to major roles. The many teenagers in the audience snickered and giggled at some of the stage effects, such as the boat being tossed in the storm with the stagehands' legs clearly visible, or the banqueting table that suddenly came "walking" out on stage, again with human figures crouched underneath. Yet for all their carrying on, these young people stayed on until the very last curtain call, cheering everyone including Rudolf.

The evening finished with Serge Lifar's *Les Mirages*, but we decided not to stay because of sheer exhaustion. We headed for the Stage Door to say hello to Rudolf, but he remained in the theatre to watch his dancers in the last ballet, so we had a long wait. Once he came out, we headed back to the hotel where I could finally catch some sleep after being up for nearly 48 hours.

Seeing "Dr. Nureyev" and sleeping most of the next day finally revived me. However, we discovered that Rudolf was dancing in *Harlequinade* at the Opera Comique that evening in a "make-up" performance from the one cancelled on March 8th. He told two of the fans at the Graham Gala reception that they should come to Paris "early" because he was dancing in "this little gem," but they didn't understand what he meant. We just assumed we would miss this ballet, so getting to see it was an unexpected bonus and we bought tickets for that evening's performance.

I still didn't have much appetite, having tea and toast for my dinner before the performance, and climbed the endless stairs of the Opera Comique to my amphitheatre seat. I opened my program and discovered that Patrick Dupond was dancing in all three ballets that evening. A French woman sitting next to me asked to look at my program and exclaimed in English, "I thought Nureyev was dancing tonight," so everyone was perplexed. No announcement was made and I had the sinking feeling I was at the wrong theatre and Rudolf was performing in *La Bayadere* and *The Tempest* at the Opera House that night. Nevertheless, it turned out that the wrong cast sheets were inserted in the programs. Dupond danced two out of the three pieces on the program, but Rudolf did dance *Harlequinade*. Then he dashed over to the Garnier to perform in *The Tempest* that same night. His stamina was simply astounding.

This Commedia d'ell Arte piece was indeed "a little gem." Reconstructed by Ivo Cramer, *Harlequinade* utilized the old-fashioned sets that transformed instantly from a wooded glen to a drawing room to a street scene, because the sets moved in and out on tracks. The opening scene was very dark. Three figures, masked and wearing three-cornered hats and cloaks, were obviously hiding from someone. Okay, I thought. I'll have to wait until one of them moves, to find out if it was Nureyev or Dupond. Suddenly one figure turned and looked up. I saw those unmistakable twinkling eyes catching the light. Rudolf Nureyev was indeed performing and he projected his energy to the top row of the theatre while wearing a mask and standing still.

Rudolf was dressed in the diamond-patterned Harlequin costume with buckled shoes and wore the mask throughout the entire ballet. The role offered him the chance to appear in many different disguises in order to court his sweetheart, here played by Maurin, his "daughter" from the previous evening's performance of *The Tempest*. He played a masked courtesan, complete with a fan, flirting with the Old Count; a chef - and a prim and fussy fat lady. At one point he even perched on a cloud and rose up into the flies. He was very mischievous and obviously relished every moment of it. When we gathered at the interval, everyone remarked that our face muscles hurt from laughing so much.

The rest of the program was Fokine's *Carnaval* followed by *Le Bourgeois Gentilhomme* by Balanchine, both danced by Patrick Dupond, who had a terrific following in Paris. Rudolf's mad dash after *Harlequinade* to perform in *The Tempest* at the Garnier illustrated the flurry of activity Nureyev generated as Director of the Paris Opera, with a company of outstanding dancers large enough to perform in two theatres in different programs on the same night.

Rudolf Nureyev turned 46 years old on Saturday, March 17, 1984. True to form, he celebrated by dancing both matinee and evening performances. Both were sold out and we had to queue for returns. My flu bug was still with me and having to queue, felt like torture. All of us finally got in, although my place in the third-row of a box meant I had to stand for the entire performance, because I simply couldn't see over the two rows in front of me. *La Bayadere* was first on the program featuring an eager young cast of Shades, the first one by the name of Sylvie Guillem. Because the matinee was filled with young people and was being televised, Nureyev set out to prove that at the age of 46 he could still "deliver the goods." When he performed his series of double assembles, he executed not six, but seven! My friend turned to me and said, "Did he just do what I think he did?" The audience went wild.

I began to feel better and risked eating my first meal in well over a week. I needed my strength to battle the hordes of people in front of the Opera House that were attempting to get tickets for the evening performance. Despite waiting forty-five minutes, the pushing and shoving caused us to lose our place in line and I feared being trampled once the doors opened and everyone raced to the Box Office. The control kept shouting at the crowd to form one line, but to no avail; it became a free for all. Miraculously all of us got tickets, though I was forced to stand again at the back of a loge.

Jean Guizerix danced *La Bayadere* with Elisabeth Platel. After the interval, Nureyev danced *The Tempest* with a different cast, this time featuring another newcomer, Laurent Hilaire. Rudolf gave a remarkable 46th birthday performance, living up to his usual form of dancing better on a Saturday night after dancing at the matinee. He received a warm, enthusiastic reception from the French audience.

The fans gathered at the Stage Door and we waited for almost an hour before Rudolf finally emerged with some of his friends. We merrily serenaded him with a chorus of "Happy Birthday." Since we had formed a circle around him, he kissed each of us in turn and thanked us for coming, and said, "It's nice to have support." Then he asked, "So, did you all get in?" "Yes," we chanted, adding, "Rudolf, we followed your advice – we found a door and just pushed." "Well, that's how it started for me, just pushing open a door. And many doors have opened since. But many are still closed." He reminded us of a situation with the Met and how the invitations to dance and perform in New York were dwindling. "Nobody wants me," he said, matter-of-factly, adding, "Would be so easy, no, to bring company for Diaghilev program on Broadway," practically suggesting that we do it for him.

He asked, "So how did you like *Harlequin*?" When one American fan admitted she missed it due to seeing performances at the Palais Garnier, Rudolf's face registered a myriad of expressions, from surprise to amusement until he teased her by saying, "I was good!" He looked at the rest of us who did see it and we heartily agreed that indeed he was. He then told us that he was flying to Berlin the very next morning to perform in the Peter Schaufuss production of *La Sylphide,* doing a little dance while adding, "If I keep at it, maybe I'll hit it." Noticing how cold it was on this March evening, and that one of the fans had no hat, he reached into his leather coat pocket and pulled out a red knit cap. He placed it on her head, gently pulled it over her ears and patted it saying, "There, now you won't get cold."

Someone handed him a copy of the *New York Times* review of *Phaedra's Dream* with the comment, "Look, they liked you." Rolling his eyes, Nureyev replied, "I'm impressed. Maybe when I get to be as old as Alicia Alonso, I'll get it right." Alonso, then in her mid-60s, was currently in Paris performing *Giselle*. Rudolf had obviously seen her because he asked us, "Did you ever see her do her curtain calls? It's like this…" And he began to give his interpretation of an Alonso call. He tucked my present under his chin, as Alonso did with her bouquets, and extending his arms, executed a deep curtsey.

Despite the fact that several of Rudolf's friends were sitting in a nearby car waiting for him, he seemed in no hurry to rush off. He continued chatting with us until the subject was changed to having champagne and helping him celebrate his birthday. He persisted in his playful mood by pointing an accusing finger to one of the fans that worked for the airlines, saying "But not American champagne! They serve American champagne on the plane!" She quipped, "So, we have the champagne. Can we help you celebrate your birthday or should we all go back to our hotels and do something boring?" He roared with laughter, glanced at the car where his friends patiently sat in expectation, and explained, "I have people waiting." Then his eyes lit up as if he just had a brilliant idea. "Call me in two hours," and proceeded to rattle off his phone number. Cries of "Wait, wait, I'll never remember" to "I know it" ensued and Rudolf said, "Good, so call me in two hours." With that, he joined his friends in the car and disappeared.

We stood there in a state of shock, wondering if he was serious. We decided to buy some good quality champagne and spent the next two hours in The Drugstore, a café adjacent to the Opera House. Everyone ordered a drink except me – I was sticking to ginger ale – as we excitedly pondered Rudolf's invitation to share in his birthday celebration. Someone placed Rudolf's red knit cap in the center of the table and we arranged our glasses around it for a photo entitled "Still life with hat." Then we began composing a joint poem for Rudolf's birthday, but we never finished it because we were having too much fun.

At 2 a.m., one of the fans dutifully phoned Rudolf and came back exclaiming, "He said yes. Come on!" She related how Rudolf answered the phone and asked, "How many of you are there?" "Eleven," she replied. She heard him shout, "There's eleven of them coming. We need more plates!"

We hurriedly grabbed three different taxis and agreed to meet just outside 23 Quai Voltaire along the Seine. That was indeed where Rudolf resided. We needed to punch the computer-coded doorbell, which opened the big double green doors leading to an inviting cobblestone courtyard with some parked cars. The block of flats formed a square and to the left was the entrance hall for Rudolf's building. I looked up and saw warm lights coming from an apartment about three floors up and thought, "I bet that's his," and sure enough, it was. There was a small lift to the third floor which some took; the rest of us walked up the circular concrete stairs.

At the top of the stairs, Rudolf's friend, Douce Francois, opened the great double doors leading to an inner foyer where she asked us to deposit our coats on a large sofa to the right of the door. We gave her our bottle of good quality champagne and after an enormous pile of coats amassed on the couch, she opened the other set of double doors that led directly into the spacious dining area. Rudolf immediately got up from the dinner table where he was lingering with six or seven other guests. He was in a multi-colored sweater and brown slacks and wore red slippers and a bright red knit cap. Because Rudolf always felt cold, the apartment was so warm that my glasses fogged up. He tried to make all of us comfortable by saying it was nice we could come and asked if we wanted to see the apartment. He then led us into the living area where quite a few guests looked on in amazement as eleven people arrived en masse.

Rudolf pointed out a few things to us, but as he spoke so softly, I barely heard him. He pointed out some Japanese obies that he was particularly fond of, but his pride and joy was an adjacent room he fondly called "The map room." It was a small room with a single bed against the wall, covered in a rich red and gold fabric. A small antique table was to the left. Covering the walls from floor to ceiling were antique maps in dark wood frames that he explained he'd been collecting for about twelve years. He beamed with enthusiasm as he pointed to various maps as well as old theatre prints, such as the Opera Comique where he had performed the night before. One of the Paris fans asked him a question about his theatre collection and he instantly replied in French. As he led us out of the room, he carefully patted the small antique table and said, "That's from my house in England." This table turned out to be a miniature harpsichord.

There was a full size harpsichord in the living room in front of the enormous stately windows that overlooked the Seine and the historic Louvre beyond it. He drew our attention to a few other antiques, such as the double-sided luxurious sofas that once belonged to Maria Callas. He discovered a wad of birthday wrapping paper on the floor, so he paused, picked it up, and cautioned, "Just a minute, don't trip on this."

One of the fans decided to read him our "unfinished" poem composed while waiting at the Drugstore, and he grinned, saying, "Ah, Shakespeare!" He then proceeded to warmly kiss everyone, before one of his friends brought out a camera and took a group photo. We were such a large group that there was much rearranging and Rudolf remarked, "This group is asymmetrical!"

Then he inquired, 'Do you want a drink?" and signaled toward the kitchen, where two gentlemen in white dinner jackets promptly appeared with champagne in flute glasses on a fine silver tray. Rudolf politely excused himself, saying he had to return to his dinner guests, and the waiters appeared again, offering each of us a mouth-watering apple tart. We mingled with Rudolf's guests in the living room, which included his dear friend from London, Maude Gosling; British critic John Percival; Charles Jude and other Paris Opera dancers; as well as Rudolf's niece, Gouzel, who had recently moved to Paris and was studying at the Sorbonne.

Once we were seated we had time to take in our exquisite surroundings, including the magnificent view of the Louvre from the floor-to-ceiling windows. We learned that the stunning draperies were made from leather scraps in Rudolf's favorite earth colors of brown, green, mustard, and accented with burgundy and teal blue. They looked enormously heavy as they were pulled back and secured with large black cords. A marvelous throne chair was in one corner near the harpsichord where most of the dancers congregated. As I sat on one of the Maria Callas sofas facing the window, there was a fireplace to my left and a large antique globe on a stand in the corner. Acting as a kind of room divider to conceal videotapes and other clutter was an enormous Renaissance portrait on an easel. A smaller portrait of a beautiful boy in a plumed hat was perched atop the mantle and bore a striking resemblance to Nureyev.

An enormous table laden with birthday gifts, some opened and some still wrapped, was behind the sofa. The ever-gracious Maude Gosling included us in her conversation and related that she had been in Paris for nearly two weeks and "Rudolf runs me ragged. I can't keep up with him. He's always wanting me to go here and there." She informed us that she stayed in "the map room." "Rudolf sleeps in the back, away from the street, as he wakes up at the slightest noise, despite the double glazed windows," she explained. She also related that Rudolf "was the perfect house guest" whenever he stayed with her in London. "He eats anything that's put in front of him. Eating out with him can be a trial. If the meat is not cooked exactly, it goes back." Nureyev loved his steaks extremely rare and often stuck his finger in it to see if it was overcooked. When someone else joined the group, she introduced us as "Some of Rudolf's most devoted fans. They've come from London, New York, California, Paris – all over."

We decided we had better leave after an hour or so, since some of the other guests were departing as well. As we said our good-byes to those seated at the dining room table, I observed Rudolf's enormous bookcase that lined one wall. Videotapes, all neatly labeled, were on the top shelf almost near the very high ceiling. The shelves were filled with art books, many on the Renaissance, as well as books on history and theatre in French, Russian and English. On the corner of the lowest shelf were snapshots just back from being developed and still spilling out of the envelope.

After waiting in the outer foyer in my winter gear, Marie-Susanne, Rudolf's assistant at the Paris Opera who was also at the party, came out and said, "Rudolf is just there. Why don't you say goodnight to him?" He had emerged, sans his red hat, looking very sleepy but happy, as he was shaking hands and bidding everyone goodnight. "I have to get up early tomorrow to fly to Berlin, so I'm going to bed. You can stay if you want." We decided we'd better not wear out our welcome.

And so about 3 a.m., we all filed downstairs into the street. The private visit to Rudolf's stunning abode had been an incredible privilege and gift, perfectly wrapped into the softness of a dreamy Parisian night. We felt so elated that we decided to walk back to our respective hotels. Once there, we had some of the champagne that we did NOT give to Rudolf and suddenly my flu bug was a thing of the past. I joked that I had to go all the way to Paris to consult my "doctor."

With a short break in Nureyev's Paris schedule, we took advantage of the other dance companies in Paris and went to the Palais des Congress to see Bejart's company. At the triple bill consisting of *Rite of Spring*, we noticed Rudolf's niece and remarked that Uncle Rudolf probably told her that he had danced in that ballet and she should go see it. Just four days later, Rudolf was back at the Opera. During that time he flew to Berlin to rehearse *La Sylphide*, returned to Paris the next day for a rehearsal, flew back to Berlin for the performance, before returning once again for the Paris premiere of *Marco Spada*. His schedule was a continuous marathon.

Pierre LaCotte originally reconstructed this work for the Rome Opera Ballet in 1981. Rudolf played the title role of the bandit while LaCotte's wife, Ghislaine Thesmar, played Marco Spada's daughter. For some reason, this ballet did not translate well on the Paris Opera dancers. I think they felt it too "old-fashioned" and didn't take a lot of the mime as seriously as the Italian dancers did. The ballet received a lukewarm reception on its first night and Rudolf looked disappointed. "You must return tomorrow," remarked one of the dancers departing the Stage Door. "Tonight was only the first night," indicating that all did not go well. Some of the dancers also admitted they didn't like the ballet.

At Rudolf's next performance, a Saturday matinee, Alicia Alonso was spotted in the audience. Rudolf was tired and in a bizarre mood, possibly due to strange circumstances. Conductor Ashley Lawrence didn't arrive until the second act, so there was a different conductor for the first act. Several little things went wrong and Rudolf seemed a bit preoccupied. But he always managed to do a brilliantly moving death scene in the third act. The claques were in full force again, and Nureyev was booed at the curtain calls.

Following the matinee, Rudolf remained in the theatre until 10 p.m. rehearsing a work he was about to premiere entitled *Bach Suite*. Meanwhile, that evening we saw an alternate cast of *Marco Spada* with Patrick Dupond, whose claques chanted "Du-pond, Du-pond" at curtain calls. A well traveled fan that just recently arrived from America remarked, "I'm certainly glad I've seen three performances already, so I know what the choreography is supposed to look like" since Dupond tended to put in extra technical tricks whenever possible.

The following day – our last in Paris after nearly two weeks of performances – we returned for another Bejart performance at the Palais de Congress. At the interval while buying an ice cream, we spotted Rudolf chatting with London dance critic John Percival. Rudolf was there to see *Divine*, a creation for his friend, Marcia Haydee, dancing with Jorge Donn. He applauded enthusiastically and dashed backstage to say hello. Even on his day off, Nureyev was devouring dance.

"Practice till exhausted. Die. Come to life."
~Rudolf Nureyev, The Observer, May 16, 1976~

REHEARSALS

Nureyev arrives for Birthday Gala rehearsal, Metropolitan Opera House, NYC, July 27, 1988. Photo: Susanne Richelle Whitehead

One of the best things about watching Rudolf Nureyev throughout the years was observing him in rehearsals. They were a great opportunity to learn, and see Nureyev the teacher, working with dancers, coaching them, cajoling them, and helping them discover untapped abilities. We watched Nureyev the producer and director, insisting on and getting high production standards. We witnessed Nureyev the conductor, sometimes playing the piano to set the tempi for the orchestra or on rare occasions conducting from the orchestra pit. We were awed by his encyclopedic knowledge. His outrageous sense of humor came through at every opportunity. We sensed how completely at home he was in the theatre.

Nureyev seldom invited us to his rehearsals, but didn't kick us out if we found ingenious ways of obtaining entry. In fact, he was somewhat amused, knowing how hard we had to work at it, and frequently remarked, "Oh, I see you got in!"

Before theatres became so security conscious, it was relatively easy to enter through a rear or side door and find a seat at the back of a box where we would not be noticed. Occasionally fans got into a theatre only to discover that the rehearsal time had changed, so they were forced to spend time waiting in the restrooms, hoping not to be discovered. In one theatre where Nureyev frequently performed, we eventually learned our way into the auditorium via a door that always remained open for ventilation. It was nerve-wracking because, if we took a wrong turn in the maze of backstage corridors, we would end up near one of the dressing rooms. Once a group of us posed as ballet students who had been invited to attend the rehearsal. No credentials were checked, nor did they ask Nureyev to authorize our entry. We were simply escorted into the theatre.

Some theatres were easier to enter than others. New York's Metropolitan Opera House was impossible to access due to its tight security. The New York State Theatre was slightly better. In 1975, I remember sitting in the back row of the orchestra watching Nureyev rehearse two acts of his *Raymonda* production for American Ballet Theatre, before I was asked to leave. The Palais des Sports, a circular sports arena in Paris, was relatively easy to enter due to its numerous entry doors.

When I lived in London in the early 70s, attending dress rehearsals became one of the highlights of the dance season. Often friends had a spare rehearsal ticket. In some cases, we just snuck in with the entering crowds.

One of my earliest rehearsal experiences was in 1973 while watching Nureyev practice Balanchine's *Prodigal Son* with the Royal Ballet. Statuesque Deanne Bergsma portrayed the Siren. She often seemed to be cast in duets where she and Rudolf were complexly entwined, as in 1971's *Field Figures* choreographed by Glen Tetley. When the Siren wrapped one leg around the Prodigal Son and pulled his head to her chest, Nureyev turned mischievously to the rehearsal audience and quipped, "Now it's getting sexy!"

At another Royal Ballet rehearsal, Rudolf worked on Balanchine's *Apollo* with Georgina Parkinson. They were having difficulty with the "swimming on the back" lift in the pas de deux. Apollo is on one knee and Terpsichore is lifted onto his upper back and neck, where she has to balance precariously while both perform swimming movements with their arms. Getting down from this pose is equally tricky, because Apollo must stand up and immediately brace his stretched leg so she can balance against it, while they both bend backwards for the concluding pose. Parkinson was rather well endowed for a ballerina. At one point Rudolf suggested to her, "Just hang your boobs over my shoulders and you won't fall."

In 1973, Natalia Makarova joined Nureyev and the Paris Opera Ballet for a series of *Swan Lake* performances in the Louvre courtyard. A fan charmed a lighting technician into letting her watch rehearsals that week. Each day she arrived at the courtyard's gate with a large bag and entered with the dancers. Instead of heading for the dressing room tent, she joined her new friends, the technicians, in the lighting booth. When Nureyev left for a tea break and headed into a nearby café, she followed along. Nureyev thought she was with the others, and the others thought she was with him. He finally realized what she was up to, but said nothing, only giving her amused glances at her "game."

Nureyev performed every night, alternating with Makarova, and Paris Opera dancers Noella Pontois and Ghislaine Thesmar. They rehearsed long hours from noon until midnight for an entire week. On the first day, Nureyev arrived late, complaining that a taxi driver, taking advantage of Nureyev's accented French, took him all over Paris instead of the direct route from the Opera House to the Louvre. "He turned right and then left, and right again. I kept saying that's not the way. And I had to pay ten francs!" Everyone was amused when Nureyev said repeatedly, "Dix francs, dix francs!" when explaining his late arrival.

During the rehearsal week, there were numerous problems with the lights. "I can't see the edge of the stage," The technicians didn't want to take the time to reset them, but Nureyev insisted, "If I can't see the stage, I can't dance. If the lights are not right for dress rehearsal, who will guarantee that tomorrow the lights will be right?" After much grumbling, the lights were fixed.

Another day, Nureyev tried out the sightlines from various bleacher seats. "This is a bad seat. They can't see stage left" or "From here, it's not elevated enough." The seating arrangements were adjusted. The stage space was enormous and the production of Swan Lake utilized fifty-two swans. Rudolf wanted to optimize the sightlines for the entire paying public.

Nureyev made his debut as Colas in Frederick Ashton's delightful ballet *La Fille Mal Gardee* in 1974, when the Royal Ballet performed at the Metropolitan Opera House. Prior to the tour, fans had attended the open rehearsal in London. Merle Park, in the role of Lise, told us that Rudolf had great difficulty tying the ribbon onto the staff and making a bow, so she instructed him, "It's just like tying your shoes." "Our shoes had buttons," he explained matter-of-factly, referring to his life in war-torn Russia. "Then you must practice, practice," she scolded him.

Sir Fred himself watched his ballet from the company box. As the dancers practiced their curtain calls, they all turned to bow to the choreographer. Rudolf had a puzzled expression on his face, because the entire rehearsal audience faced the Royal Box until he realized the reason why.

In 1974, Rudolf set "The Kingdom of the Shades" scene from *La Bayadere* on the Paris Opera stage. The technicians needed to time the lighting cues, but at the rehearsal the corps de ballet was not available. "That's okay," Rudolf told the technicians. "I'll dance the whole thing for you." He did every arabesque from the corps' initial entrance down the ramp, followed by the pas deux with an imaginary partner, and all the variations for an "audience" of two technicians, plus a fan who snuck in to watch the rehearsal.

While rehearsing his 1975 production of *Raymonda* for American Ballet Theatre, some of the fans tried to watch Rudolf in the studio. One group posed as ballet students and stood in the studio doorway hoping to get a peek. Rudolf spotted them immediately and, to quote one fan, came toward the group, "like Gary Cooper in *High Noon*" to shut the door. A few stood their ground when they saw Rudolf's eyes twinkling and they tried not to laugh. Nevertheless, the door was shut, but the determined fans managed to find a second-floor window that overlooked the studio. Of course, Rudolf spotted them right away and laughed at their persistence. Since they were quiet, they were allowed to watch. Many dancers wrapped themselves in plastic garbage bags to keep their muscles warm. At another rehearsal, Rudolf arrived wrapped in a plastic sweat suit, instead of his usual multiple layers of legwarmers and sweaters. "Like garbage can liner," he joked and strutted around, as if he were wearing an elegant Prince's costume.

While working with ABT ballerina Cynthia Gregory, he stopped and explained that she needed to have a stronger reaction at seeing Rudolf's character, Jean De Brienne, when she awoke from her dream. In his own unique way, he explained, "Cynthia, think of it as ooh-la-la – kissy-kissy time!" Rudolf also coached the young Fernando Bujones in the lead role who complained about the many steps in Nureyev's choreography. "Then why don't you dance at the Bolshoi?" Rudolf retorted because he obviously did not favor that company's lack of choreographic invention.

A few days after the *Raymonda* performances, Rudolf joined Margot Fonteyn in his *Friends* program in Washington, D.C. My friends who attended the rehearsal said that, in the middle of *Marguerite and Armand*, the injured Nureyev complained that Margot was too heavy and should do her own dancing instead of leaning on him. With an elegant smile, Margot retorted, "Just for that I'm going to gain twenty pounds." She always managed to humor him out of his moods.

Later that year, Nureyev was in Madrid rehearsing *La Sylphide*, a ballet he clearly loved. However, in one section the tempo was so fast that Rudolf asked the conductor to slow it down slightly "because my golden days are over!"

Once at a *Swan Lake* rehearsal with the Royal Ballet, Merle Park accidentally kicked his knee. Later, she kicked his thigh. Rudolf stopped, gave her a long stare and asked, "What next, Merle?"

When the Royal Ballet instituted a "no guest artists policy" in 1975, Nureyev contacted London Festival Ballet's director, former ballerina Beryl Grey, and subsequently mounted his sumptuous production of *Sleeping Beauty* on the company. Prior to its April premiere at the London Coliseum, we were able to see multiple rehearsals. One of the boys in plastic sweatpants caught Nureyev's attention. "Hey, plastic bags," he instructed, "get some air under your legs when you jump."

There were many *Sleeping Beauty* rehearsals over the years, especially when new cast members were performing roles for the first time. In 1979, two friends and I had the rare experience of watching Nureyev supervise the dancers in the studios near the Royal Albert Hall. We slipped past the receptionist, acting as if we knew where we were going. We heard music from *Sleeping Beauty* coming from a second floor studio, and discovered Rudolf rehearsing the corps in the Act One Waltz. We parked ourselves in the open doorway. With the aid of the studio's full-length wall mirrors, we were able to see the entire rehearsal process. Nobody questioned us. Even though Nureyev spotted us, he said nothing.

Wearing his usual red legwarmers and clogs, he sat on a folding chair in front of the ensemble sipping endless cups of tea from a giant thermos. He got up to demonstrate what he wanted during a difficult section, offering partnering tips to the boys. Nureyev insisted on "more effacé." Patting his upper chest, he instructed the dancers to "Present yourselves to public." Then he clapped his hands for attention instructing, "Let's do the Soda" rather than the Coda, or called for the "triplets" rather than the pas de trois. He used amusing code names to cue the pianist, such as "let's take it from poopsy-woopsy" or "oopsy-daisy." Surprisingly, the pianist usually knew what he wanted. If not, Rudolf would sing it for him.

We saw Rudolf nearly collide with us in the doorway when he performed his rapid diagonal of pas de chat/brise combinations in the Vision Scene. The other dancers took a break at two o'clock while Rudolf and Eva Evdokimoa, one of the Auroras, rehearsed the Grand Pas with the pianist. After performing the entire pas de deux, repeating certain troublesome spots such as the final "no-hands" fishdive pose, he ran through the entire thing again with Patricia Ruanne, another Aurora. Toward the end, she had some questions. Nureyev tried explaining to her and she said, "Show me, Rudolf," which he did. She instantly understood what he meant.

Nureyev took a very brief break at three o'clock, walking past us; when he returned, he avoided eye contact, but showed no sign of being annoyed by our presence. We took that as permission to remain for the rest of the rehearsal. Luigi, Rudolf's assistant, initiated a conversation with the three of us. Admitting that he preferred opera or sports to ballet, he added, "I don't often get to see the performance. What you see out front and what you see from backstage is so different. I prefer out front."

We stood in the doorway that day for eight hours. Rudolf emerged twice for a break and more tea. He slipped past us with a curious expression but never spoke to us, obviously too busy perfecting his production. When the rehearsal finished, he thanked the dancers and we left for some much-needed food. We hadn't eaten all day. Then again, neither had Nureyev or the dancers. When he was working, nothing else mattered.

The next day during the stage rehearsal, he told the boys rehearsing the Prologue, "Don't force the legs. They bend anyway and nature will take care of things." Two of the Prologue soloists practiced their variation. One dancer had difficulty executing her rond de jambes, the step where the leg extends out to the side and bends at the knee, making circles in the air. It was a favorite step of Nureyev's. When she asked him about it, he executed the step for her, explaining, "You must stir the leg, like teaspoon in a cup. See?" and he repeated the stirring motion. She tried it and it worked like a charm, to which Rudolf smiled and said, "Voila!" His instructions were simply exceptional.

Evelyn deSutter, who had just joined London Festival Ballet from the Paris Opera, rehearsed the Bluebird pas de deux with Kenneth McCombie, who remained on the sidelines watching her variation. Rudolf told him, "You can't just stand there. You must call to her," and proceeded to demonstrate beckoning gestures with his wing-like arms. He began walking McCombie through the variation. Even though Nureyev didn't do the jumps, the essence of the Bluebird was in the carriage of his body and the use of his arms. I had never seen him dance that role but, after this rehearsal, I felt I had.

Once the sets were in place, Rudolf rehearsed the three girls with the knitting needles for the scene that precedes The Waltz. One was quite small and had difficulty when she "peeked" around the backs of the other two. Rudolf told her, "You're short for this group and also overeager. But I can't SEE you peeking around. Let's try it together." He grabbed the girls' hands and joined them. When it was time for the shorter girl to peek behind Rudolf, he said, "Peek-a-boo NOW – behind my fat ass!" That helped her relax and she got it right.

During The Waltz Rudolf insisted the dancers "keep those diagonals," or "let me SEE those arabesques." The conductor asked if the tempo was okay and Rudolf replied, "It can be faster – they know it by now."

Always aware of how things would look to the public, he scolded his Aurora at one point by shouting, "Eyes!" He explained, "You gaze that way and it will be right into a light; you must look THIS way" and demonstrated for her. When Evdokimova rehearsed the Rose Adagio with her four Suitors, they seemed to squeeze her hand too tightly, annoying her. Losing patience, Rudolf said, "They should have done this two weeks ago and not wait till night before the performance!" After Aurora pricked her finger and fell asleep, the four Suitors held her aloft, swaying her back and forth, but not in time with the music. Nureyev interrupted them by saying, 'You're putting her into the grave too soon!" He arranged the groupings around Evdokimova and made sure they turned away in sadness on the right musical sequence, almost like a "wave" of grief. When Carabosse returned, Rudolf shouted to the corps, "Horror, horror, not heil, Hitler!" A burst of laughter broke the tension. At another time, he advised, "Don't force it – you should have FUN with your dancing."

  He wanted to rehearse the Sarabande, but some of the corps dancers were missing because the rehearsal schedule had been altered. "How can we do this if they're not all here?" Rudolf asked. Afraid of a scene, the Ballet Mistress suggested the available dancers show Rudolf another section while someone else went to fetch the missing ones. The dancer portraying the King had difficulty with the opening of the Sarabande. Rudolf explained the arm positions as, "The sun rises this way and THEN sets." He meticulously rehearsed the mime scenes so that the performers understood them.

  Jay Jolley, a new company member, got a lot of personal coaching for the pas de cinq. Rudolf danced the entire solo and then demonstrated certain accents. He explained that the "first double assemble has to look like a surprise, since audience doesn't expect it." Demonstrating for the "triplets," he then did all the point work, in his clogs.

  After a set and costume change, Andria Hall danced the Bluebird pas de deux. As she enters, Princess Florine "hears" the Bluebird before he makes his entrance, but as Rudolf jokingly explained, "she can't see you yet, because you're just hoovering around." He meant, "hovering" but he loved to play with English words. The boy fell over at the end of his big solo, to which Rudolf commented, "You're not going to do that tomorrow, I hope!" He told the dancer that the Bluebird's feet must "skim the floor, like you're flying," and then got up to demonstrate with such speed, that everyone looked on in amazement. In the final pose with Andria balanced on the boy's shoulder, he told her, "You're flying away, not coming down." At seven p.m. after seven solid hours and a short break, Rudolf gathered his shoes and tea flasks and left.

  Dissatisfied during much of the next morning's dress rehearsal, Rudolf sprung into action, repositioning the King's throne and Aurora's cradle, while demanding, "We'll need more light here!" At one point in the Prologue, the various fairies cradled the infant Aurora and paraded her around the stage for all to see, before returning her to the nanny. Ever watchful of the spacing, Rudolf cautioned them when they appeared to be bunched up, "No baby bashing!" For the Fairy variations, Andria Hall was first and proceeded to walk to center stage to begin her solo. Rudolf shouted, "Why don't you fall off the stage?" Andria looked over to see if Rudolf was speaking to her, while he repeated, "Where are you? In corner? Why don't you fall off stage? What are you DOING?" Not understanding what he meant, she replied, "I'm reaching the center." "But you DANCE to the center; if you start there, you fall off stage." Her variation consisted of many on-point dance steps forward; if she had started in the center, she would indeed be in the orchestra pit halfway through.

He was considerably more relaxed by Act Two, although he noticed his own shadow on the stage floor during his dance with the Countess and asserted the overhead spot should be somewhat softened. Instead of doing a lovely mime with the Countess, he jokingly mimed he'd rather be home sleeping, while she, in turn, tried to keep a straight face.

After Rudolf marked the lyrical solo in which the Lilac Fairy showed him the vision of the Sleeping Beauty, the corps de ballet ran down the grand staircase to get into position. He clapped his hands for everything to stop and insisted they redo their entire entrance, because the staircase on which they were posed was pushed in too late and gave the girls insufficient time to get into position. Throughout the scene, Rudolf would reposition the girls, especially correcting their arms, calling them "amoebas." When the Lilac Fairy appeared on the boat, he humorously mimed he wanted to hitch a ride with her.

During this rehearsal, the transformation scene was a mess. The boat crashed into the trees, the lighting cues were all mixed up, and the lowered front drop narrowly missed everyone's heads. Rudolf lost patience and screamed, "What's happening here? I want to be sure THEY know this bit." The boat was backed up and everything was repeated, though not looking any better.

After the Awakening, Rudolf rehearsed a few problem areas of the Vision Scene with Eva, while the stagehands changed the set for Act Three. He sat on a chair drinking tea, watching the dancers like a hawk. He and Evdokimova then danced the entire wedding pas de deux, during which it was fascinating to hear Nureyev's corrections. He suggested Eva come off point quickly after the third fishdive to help de-emphasize her height. When it came to Nureyev's own solo, the conductor took it at such accelerated speed that, in the section following his double tours just before his ménage – his "breathing room" section – Rudolf had to run. He stood at the front of the stage and said in a clear voice, "Can I have a small vacation before rushing into this madness?" Everyone laughed. Rudolf hummed the tempo he wanted, and then landed in a mock collapse on the floor beating his heaving chest. After catching his breath, he repeated the entire variation again, full out, finishing in a perfect fifth position, holding one hand out to signal to the conductor, "Okay, much better." The corps burst into applause. It all seemed effortless to him.

When the corps began rehearsing the Sarabande, the designer, Nicholas Georgiadis, called out to Rudolf that some of the girls had hooked the trains of their dresses up, when they should have been down. Nureyev made the necessary adjustments himself. When Jay Jolley had difficulty with the solo from the pas de cinq, Rudolf kicked off his clogs and danced it alongside him, so Jolley would understand the proper accenting of the steps. When they finished, Rudolf pointed to Jay's tunic, indicating it wasn't long enough, because of Jay's long legs and made him look "scrunched up." Rudolf advised him to talk to wardrobe before the evening's performance.

Considering the dancers had four rehearsals in two days, the actual premiere went very well. Nureyev was proud of them, bowing to the entire company. One of the fans remarked at the Stage Door, "What you've done with Festival Ballet is incredible." Rudolf merely said, "It was expected, no?" "Yes," the fan responded, "but I didn't expect miracles." Our friendly usher, who became our "lifeline" through that long season when tickets were difficult to obtain, was incredibly impressed with Nureyev's sense of stagecraft. We discussed the production endlessly. At one point he asked us how old Nureyev was. He was astonished to learn that Rudolf Nureyev was 37. You're joking," he replied. "I thought he was in his 20s." He remained silent a while and confided, "He's changing my life." That was the effect Rudolf had on many who witnessed his genius.

Legendary modern dance choreographer Martha Graham created *Scarlet Letter* for Nureyev in 1975. His partner was Graham dancer Janet Eilber. At one point when they were rehearsing, Rudolf was on the floor and asked Janet,

"What do I do now? How do I get up? Eilber advised, "If I were you, considering the position you're in, I'd put one hand on the floor and push myself up." Rudolf broke up laughing, having thought there was a special "recovery" method of getting up.

Margot Fonteyn, Natalia Makarova and Lynn Seymour joined Rudolf for his 1977 Coliseum season. The opening ballet, *Les Sylphides*, showcased all the dancers. At the rehearsal near the end of the opening pas de trois with Fonteyn on one side of him and Makarova on the other, the two ballerinas didn't finish together so they stopped and asked, "Who's right?" Rudolf wanted to live to see another day, so he diplomatically stated, "I think it would be nice if you both ended on the music at the same time!" While the other dancers did their part, Rudolf posed on high demi-point, arms beautifully curved over his head. Suddenly he did a mock step as though wilting from exhaustion and crawled into the wings on all fours.

Makarova performed the pas de deux with Rudolf. He momentarily had a mental block during one lift. He turned to Margot and asked, "What did we used to do here?" She couldn't quite remember so she and Rudolf effortlessly danced it together, their "muscle memory" returning to illustrate the passage for Makarova. Later, during a lull in the rehearsal, Makarova lit up a cigarette. Rudolf went around to the rest of the company pretending to carry a large box, saying, "Cigars? Cigarettes?" and everyone broke up.

Just before his solo, Rudolf came to the front of the stage and teased the conductor by saying, "Now you're going to see this solo done at the fastest speed known to mankind." At another point he snuck up behind Makarova and goosed her. His playful mood was infectious. Even Margot fooled around at times, once looking down at the floor as if she'd lost a contact lens.

We managed to attend a few other rehearsals of Nureyev's original production of *Romeo and Juliet*. At one rehearsal his dissatisfaction with the lights caused him to vent his frustration, "Shit! Nobody cares about anything anymore. I have to do it all myself." Still later, when watching from the audience, he again repeated, "If I have to do it all myself, I will," and bounded onto the stage barking out more lighting cues to the technicians.

Ballet Mistress Elizabeth Anderton shouted directions to the corps over the microphone from her table in the orchestra stalls. At one point she instructed, "You're ladies of the court. Fix your dresses, as they look like dirty laundry!" Rudolf interrupted her and said sternly, "Can I speak now? I want those lighting cues up. I know it and you know it." Pointing to the lighting crew, he continued, "But I want to make sure THEY know it,"

Despite these production details, Nureyev often danced better at rehearsals because the glares of live-audience's "thousand's of eyes" weren't pressuring him. During the balcony scene, he did a long, slow, seemingly endless pirouette that caused a stagehand to whistle in amazement. Everything he danced appeared so effortless that even the company members gasped in ohhs and ahhs. Of course, as soon as they did, he fell out of one of his turns. Just milliseconds before a big catch-lift with Ruanne, he paused to roll down the straps of his leotard and tuck them in at the waist, still catching her with split-second timing.

Once again the lights were incorrect. He pointed to the floor and barked, "It's not supposed to be midday. I need more blue light. It's supposed to be night. Come on, guys. We're not in provinces now!" Even while dancing, he continued to supervise the lights, and signaled that the follow spot wasn't turned on. When it did come on, it followed Rudolf to the wings and remained on him while he sipped a cup of tea.

There were further problems with lights during the wedding scene between Romeo and Juliet. He stopped the orchestra, shouting, "We do from beginning. Light should ONLY be in front. We don't get married outside!" In the marketplace scene, which is supposed to be well lit, he shouted, "More orange lights. It should be later in the day by now." The message was repeated through the microphone, "Did you get that? He says it should be brighter, because it's later in the day by now." Rudolf declared, "Ah, they are finally understanding!"

At another morning rehearsal, Rudolf and Patricia Ruanne, his Juliet, performed their first meeting scene in the ballroom. At one point, she clasped both arms around his neck, apparently holding on too tight. He made an exaggerated fall forward, causing her to fall on her backside, while still clinging to him with her feet in the air. He deliberately came down on top of her and they both collapsed into fits of laughter. Later, Rudolf removed several legwarmers and sweaters and danced in an all-white leotard, as did Ruanne. Although the costumes were integral to the performance, it was fascinating to see the movement stripped to its essence.

While the stagehands continued with the sets, Rudolf practiced his pirouette turns. He repeatedly changed his ballet shoes, still not finding the right ones. Resigned, he scooped up the shoe pile and headed for his dressing room. The stage manager followed behind, retrieving Rudolf's dropped shoes, legwarmers, and cap.

When Rudolf left, Evelyne DeSutter rehearsed the third act without her Romeo, who left for a brief nap at home. After swallowing the potion, she sat on the bed watching the minstrels' entrance. "Be very sad, boys," the Ballet Mistress instructed. They began audibly sniffling and crying out, "boo hoo." As they lifted the "dead" Juliet, one of the boys held out DeSutter's arm and waved it to those of us in the audience and shouted, "Bye folks!"

At another rehearsal, Nureyev complained about the lights. "That light is wrong; it should be more to center." A spotlight was aimed at the wall and not on the dancers. To illustrate the absurdity of the situation, Rudolf told them, "Okay, boys, climb the wall; they want you to be in the light." The dancers pretended to climb the wall into the spotlight. Rudolf shaded his eyes and instructed the lighting technician, "I don't want you to CHANGE it, just put it where it was before."

Some of the girls had trouble manipulating their long heavy dresses in the ballroom scene. He stood next to a new dancer to see the placement of her feet. Wearing his clogs, he demonstrated for her while they executed the step together. Still in clogs and holding a teacup in one hand, he later danced beside DeSutter, demonstrating the accents for her agonized dance over Tybalt's dead body.

When London Festival Ballet premiered *Romeo and Juliet* in Paris, I was invited to attend the photo call dress rehearsal with one of the photographers. Nureyev had a busy afternoon because, in addition to a press conference and photo shoot, he was restaging the production for the Palais des Sports. At one point he came into the auditorium to check something and stood directly in front of me, wearing his green Romeo tunic and legwarmers over his white tights. He was just inches away. I was fascinated by how small his waistline was. If one would place both hands around his waist, they would surely meet. The contrast of how small and vulnerable Rudolf appeared offstage and up close, compared to his overwhelming stage presence was truly remarkable.

In 1981, *Romeo and Juliet* was staged for LaScala Ballet in Milan. Friends who attended the rehearsal there said Rudolf complained, "Why can't these Italians act more like Italians?" The marketplace scenes lacked the dynamic realism that the English dancers brought to the production, whereas the true Italians seemed tame and timid. During this particular rehearsal, the dancer portraying Mercutio became fed up with Nureyev's demands and left the stage in a rage, saying he wasn't going to perform that evening. Insults were exchanged and they had to finish the scene without him. In the third act, Carla Fracci, who was portraying Juliet, accidentally hit Nureyev in the face. The exasperated dancer took off his ballet shoes, put on his clogs, and stated, "No more dancing for me," and he, too, left the stage. Fracci improvised with another dancer as Romeo.

Rudolf, who may have left the stage but not the theatre, sat in the wings. Margot Fonteyn, portraying Lady Capulet, tried to calm him down. Rudolf only grew more upset, almost like a hurt child about to cry. Fonteyn sat next to him while he talked animatedly until he became less agitated. She eventually humored him and the rehearsal continued. Dancers returned for the evening performance and everything seemed to click. In this instance it truly was an example of "bad rehearsal, good performance."

During the 1979 *Nureyev Festival*, the Murray Louis Dance Company joined Rudolf. One rehearsal began with *Moments* first. Murray Louis explained that, while they were waiting for the lighting crew and musicians, the company would rehearse *Schubert*. He told Nureyev, "You stay warm while we do this and then we'll rehearse *Venus*." Rudolf questioned, "How can I stay warm like this?" He was merely wearing three layers of legwarmers, so he immediately donned a cap, a floor-length blanket robe, socks and his clogs and sat in the wings sipping hot tea while watching the company piece.

While Louis worked with one of the dancers, a new company member was practicing a step and kept falling out of her turns. Rudolf had been watching and said one word to her: "Torso." He got up and demonstrated how to turn and stop quickly without losing balance. She tried it and said excitedly, "Hey, it works!" and he merely gestured, "See?" and sat down matter-of-factly. She conveyed to him, "You should be our company instructor!" Other company members flocked around him, chatting away with great camaraderie.

The duet in *Venus* to the Cole Porter tunes went well. When Nureyev performed his macho walk offstage, he suddenly bent over like a feeble old man while everyone laughed. While the company repeated certain sections, he put his clogs on again and fooled around by going up on point like the clog dance in *La Fille Mal Gardee*.

The rehearsal was taking rather long so Rudolf announced, "At 3 o'clock I want to be in my bedski!" The company said they would fine-tune things later, giving Rudolf time to rehearse *Vivace*, another piece specially created for him by Louis. While waiting for the pianist, Rudolf got out the Bach *Toccata and Fugue* sheet music and began to play the piano. Louis was surprised, "I didn't know you could play." The pianist emerged along with Luigi and a few dancers. Soon they gathered around the piano while Rudolf played uninterruptedly for at least ten minutes, because he was so involved with the music, he simply could not stop. When he finished, the onlookers all marveled with a heartfelt, "Ahhh."

After the pianist arrived, Rudolf took his spot in center stage to rehearse *Vivace*. He danced the entire solo flat out, only marking the very last section. Louis asked if he wanted to repeat anything and Rudolf continued to work on a few steps. Addressing those in the audience, Louis explained, "This is the transition Rudolf makes between rehearsal and performance, when he decides he's going to DO it!"

"Let's take it from hoodgy koodgy" Rudolf instructed the pianist. Then he danced with electrifying energy. At one point he clapped both hands to signal the pianist to stop and said in a mock drunken accent, "Oopsh, schmall mishtake." When finished, he gave everyone a mock bow and then yelled out "Lunch!"

Murray remarked, "Weird lighting, isn't it?" "They're playing with the lights," the lighting director said over the loudspeaker. In a mocking voice, Nureyev said, "PLAYING with the LIGHTS? Tell him to FIX the lights and play with himself." He explained, "This will be horrendous for my balances because I can't see anything on this side. Use number three light – minimum here." When all the technical details were sorted out, he again did a hilarious theatrical bow and repeated, "Lunch – are you coming?" He looked straight at us in the audience, which was our cue to leave.

During the many *Nureyev Festivals*, we attended numerous rehearsals of Nureyev's *Don Quixote* production with various companies. A light-hearted work in which Rudolf showed his comic side, his rehearsal antics often carried over into the performance. Just after his entrance in Act One, he enjoyed tossing his guitar high into the air and hoping someone would catch it. At one rehearsal, a Japanese boy in the corps tried to anticipate the throw. Rudolf shouted, "Okay, Japan, get ready," and tossed the guitar with great abandon, setting the poor boy on a "catch as catch can" mission. When the guitar wasn't needed for a scene, Nureyev tried playing it, which sounded quite out of tune as he plucked and strummed it amusedly.

Toward the end of the first act, when the orchestrated chaos ensued and the characters of Kitri and Basilio ran off together, Rudolf stopped the ensemble to demonstrate to Kitri's father how to hit Sancho Panza over the head with a huge rubber fish. Grabbing the fish, Rudolf instructed, "You must really show public you're hitting him, like this," and he wound his arm like a baseball pitcher, shouting audibly, "Whack, whack, whack!" Poor Sancho went down on the floor, a little harder than he was supposed to.

Rudolf rehearsed the Act Two mantilla pas de deux with Eva Evdokimova, his Kitri. At one point, she accidentally stepped on his toe and Rudolf remarked, "That WAS my toe," but nevertheless remained in good spirits and laughed. After Eva completed a stunning series of pirouettes, Rudolf, watching intently, said in a sweet-natured voice, "Eva Diva, do you think when you do this movement, you can do this with your arm?" He demonstrated what he wanted, which beautifully articulated the step. Each time they needed to repeat something, the rehearsal pianist had difficulty finding the exact spot unless Rudolf hummed the music or asked in his unique code language, "Can we do the cha cha boopsy daisy bit now?"

It was not unusual for Rudolf to rehearse one act with one dancer and another act with an alternate cast. In Act Two, Yoko Morishita danced the role of Kitri, having never before danced it with him. In the windmill scene, Kitri and Basilio danced a moonlit pas de deux. The so-called lighting was nonexistent. Rudolf turned to the front and said for everyone's benefit, "I want to make sure you're aware that there's supposed to be more light for this scene!" The lighting technicians did nothing, so the entire pas de deux was rehearsed in the dark. Morishita had difficulty assuming a quick sitting position and Rudolf's instructions were, "Knee straight – that's it – now cross this leg over. No, not like that or I won't have time to put you down before my solo. When you get a few blisters on your bum, you'll know it!"

He instructed the rehearsal pianist to "play slowly so we can talk and I can work with her." His instructions were about angles, lifts, and counts. They walked through it together, despite the dimly lit stage. At the end of this dance, a cloak was spread out on the floor and they both laid down on it in an embrace. In the ballet storyline, the gypsies at the camp discover them and pull them apart. However, at this particular rehearsal, their timing was off and Rudolf quipped, "You must separate us straight away; otherwise we have a baby right in the middle of the stage!"

Nureyev went out front to watch the gypsy dancers, but was not satisfied so he jumped up on the stage and demonstratively stomped out the counts for them with his boots on. "It's a mess; too hysterical. Don't rush it. Listen to the music." To the girls who were rehearsing in leotards, he tutored, "Don't be afraid to shake your tits. Your costume jewelry will be right here," pointing to his chest. Even the dancers on the sidelines got instructed to "move into the light." When on stage, he glanced at the lights and informed the technicians, "Whatever you just changed, I don't like it." He then instructed the conductor, "Don't start playing until you see the puppet theatre is built," which gave the gypsy dancers time to take a bow. A cart was transformed into a small puppet theatre, with young children showing the story of Basilio and Kitri's love. Rudolf explained, "Move the cart back so it's in the light," and demonstrated their little pantomime along with them.

After Don Quixote attacked the windmill, the Vision Scene followed. Nureyev gave corrections to the corps dancers, particularly in maintaining the diagonals, saying "present yourselves to the public – open the chest." When Morishita began her solo, Rudolf asked her to hop in a diagonal in the opposite direction, "Otherwise it's all on the same track." He also reminded her to follow her extended arm line with her eyes. One of the most beautiful moments occurred, when Rudolf demonstrated to the corps de ballet the sequence of steps just prior to their exit. He displayed a soft pas de chat while letting his arms float upwards. When the rehearsal finished and the houselights came up, Nureyev spotted us in the audience and first waved, then humorously shook his finger at us in a "naughty, naughty" fashion, but smiled at our ingenuity for once again sneaking in for the rehearsal.

Switching partners again for Act Three with Evdokimova, Rudolf was intent on working out any difficulties in the pas de deux. Once he stopped her too soon in a pirouette and apologized, "Sorry, my fault." Eva did her solo, but suddenly stopped to ask, "I don't know what I'm supposed to do with this fan – is it open or shut here?" Rudolf borrowed it and did the whole variation side by side with her, explaining, "You must do the first three passés clearly and honestly when you have the energy. The others you can play with a bit." However, she couldn't get the fan coordinated correctly, so Rudolf demonstrated again. "Here, it's open and down in front, like this," holding it across his chest in a regal fashion. She still had difficulties. Realizing the rehearsal time was nearly over, Nureyev handed her the fan and said, "Well, it's on your conscience!" As she slammed the fan shut into her hand, she laughed out loud, "Ouch!"

After a dinner break there was a full dress rehearsal in costumes and make-up. The Prologue began with Don Quixote in his room. Nureyev, sitting out front, was very unhappy with the lighting. "The whole thing looks like porridge" he complained. "You can't see a thing. Where's special light for Don Quixote? Where's light for fireplace? It's all too flat." The stagehands came onstage to prepare the set for Act One, but Rudolf quickly interfered, "Hold it! Don't touch anything!" He bounded onto the stage and proceeded to move table, chairs, and books and reset everything himself. He then repositioned the dancers and the Prologue was promptly repeated to his satisfaction.

Nureyev continued moving furniture and dancers to block the spacing for Act One. Then he danced the first act pas de deux with Evdokimova as Kitri. More relaxed while dancing, he put Eva into the one-arm lift but it went awry, so he immediately brought her down, while laughing. At the end of the pas de deux, Rudolf placed Evdokimova in a fishdive. She overbalanced, put both hands on the floor and started giggling. There wasn't a graceful way of getting up without doing a handstand. They both laughed while Rudolf helped her up, joking, "Are you pregnant?" He thought her center of gravity seemed somehow "off."

The rehearsal was to have ended at 9:30 p.m. but Act Three was just beginning at 10 pm. During the Tavern Scene, one of the soloists unintentionally pirouetted into a table at the side of the stage. Rudolf immediately halted the rehearsal, moved the furniture and repositioned everyone so as not to impinge on the dancer's space.

During the wedding pas de deux, Eva accidentally kicked Rudolf. This occurred during the Coda, fondly called by Rudolf "the Soda." The conductor, fed up with having to stop and start, played at such speed, that Evdokimova whipped off double and triple fouettes. Rudolf then spun off so many tours that Eva, still catching her breath, inquired, "Was I fast enough for you?" During the dancing finale, Eva seemed to have confused some of the steps with the *Sleeping Beauty* finale, so it was repeated. By this point, Rudolf had put on his clogs and stomped out the counts for her, looking quite hilarious.

The next morning there was yet another rehearsal. This was an important engagement for the Zurich Ballet in London and everyone wanted to be well prepared. For many dancers in the company, this was their first experience with a perfectionist like Nureyev and they certainly learned of his work ethic.

When we arrived at the rehearsal, Rudolf was already on stage rehearsing the first act crowd scenes. Rudolf's instruction to the supers was emphatic, "Don't just stand there, you must DO something. Play cards or wave fans, but look alive." He hated it when the corps or supers in the background just stood around like they were "waiting for a bus." Even at a rehearsal, he wanted them totally involved.

Yoko Morishita, who danced Kitri was in full costume, while Rudolf rehearsed Act One without even removing his boots. In the one-arm lifts at the end of the first act, Rudolf instructed her: "Don't push my hand, because that really kills me. I can lift you without you helping me." Yoko was petite, so he easily lifted her very high.

When the three lead Dryad girls – Rudolf called them the "Three Shepherds" – began the Vision Scene, Rudolf directed, "Contraire, contraire, you're doing just the opposite." There was some confusion between their right and Rudolf's right. After that was straightened out, he finally left for his afternoon nap.

The following week, we watched the Zurich Ballet rehearse their second program, a Balanchine triple bill of *Who Cares?*, *Rubies*, and *Le Bourgeois Gentilhomme*. When we arrived, the company was rehearsing *Who Cares?* Rudolf, clad in several layers of legwarmers, a jacket and his ever-present cap, was off to the side warming up. He spotted us immediately, but said nothing. We thought we might have to leave, since Nureyev was making his debut in the *Rubies* section from Balanchine's *Jewels*, and normally didn't like visitors when still learning a new role.

The rehearsal pianist played the pas de deux and Rudolf and Elyse Flagg went through the entire dance without stopping. Occasionally he marked steps, but they repeated some tricky pirouettes where she turned positioned at his side, because it was unusual partnering for him. She was very secure, having performed with New York City Ballet before moving to Zurich.

There were spacing problems in the running section. One of the American corps boys said to Rudolf, "You must chase us." Rudolf clapped to stop the pianist so they could repeat it. Looking slightly embarrassed, scratching the side of his nose in a sign of nervousness, Rudolf shouted, "Coleen, how many runs do I do here?" Former New York City Ballet dancer Colleen Neary came on stage and did it for him, counting aloud, and instructed, "Eight, then you jump here." Rudolf clapped his hands together, exclaiming "Ah," and understood immediately. They repeated this section as the 42-year-old Nureyev playfully trotted after the corps dancers counting aloud, "Eight and jump!"

Opening night was the following day, but the dress rehearsal took place that afternoon. We entered through our usual door. The staff, so used to seeing us, merely asked, "Can you please close the door after you?" Director Pat Neary was commanding orders to her company, "I want British arms for this London tour – keep those arms in position!" Rudolf and Elyse Flagg ran through the *Rubies* pas de deux, this time to a cassette recording of the Stravinsky music. Both remarked that it was too fast, but Pat chuckled and said it was from a Balanchine performance, so they made do with it. Both Elyse and Rudolf entered from opposite wings to begin. When Neary instructed, "Move back to the last wing," Rudolf asked, "Move back? Are you trying to hide us?" After the pas de deux, the wardrobe mistress came out to fit Rudolf's costume, and once dressed up, he spread his palm onto his chest saying in a mocking falsetto voice, "Oooh, it's tight!"

In the finale, Rudolf got confused, asking them to stop the tape. "Sorry, kiddiepoos," he said to the corps and laughed. "It's first time I hear full orchestra," since he had only rehearsed with a piano. "That's why we wanted to use the tape today," Pat explained. Coleen Neary counted the finale with him, which Nureyev did loudly, and then danced it again. While the company repeated a section of the finale, he went to the side, and fiddled with the pieces of dangling fabric on the *Rubies* tunic. Clad in this red costume with his red legwarmers and a cap, he looked like a performer in *Prince Igor*.

Rudolf worked out the fine details of the duet with Elyse. After it went to everyone's satisfaction, he came to the front of the stage, spotting several of his fans in the audience, and asked director Patricia Neary if it had been okay. She replied from halfway back in the auditorium, "It looked very Balanchinian." More for our benefit than his own, he cocked his hand to his ear and teased, "What was that? I didn't hear you!" so she repeated it loudly for all to hear. "Yes?" he questioned, beaming. "Yes!" She yelled again, teasingly adding, "Nobody will know the difference but us."

George Balanchine created *Le Bourgeois Gentilhomme* for Nureyev in 1979. A photographer friend was at the dress rehearsal in New York and observed a "fabulous rapport" between "Mr. B" and Nureyev. Every time Balanchine discussed something with him, Rudolf's face "just lit up." The two spoke in Russian. Occasionally Rudolf laughed heartily over a remark made by Balanchine.

After Balanchine's death, the rights to this ballet went to Nureyev, who performed it with the Paris Opera and then with the Zurich Ballet as part of the 1981 *Nureyev Festival*. Rudolf wanted to make sure it looked the way Balanchine had intended, so he supervised most of the London rehearsals. The stage crew demanded a great deal of his time, asking him a long list of questions until Rudolf finally told them, "I have to dance now."

The ballet has a series of on-stage costume changes in which Rudolf, as Cleonte, disguises himself as assorted characters in order to enter the bourgeois' house to woo his daughter Lucille. One of the Zurich corps dancers was chosen to act as his onstage dresser. Rudolf instructed the boy on the split-second timing needed for various props used. In between set changes, Rudolf and his masseur, Luigi, sat center stage on two chairs. Nureyev sat cross-legged, fixing his shoes. One of the fans watching, whispered rather prophetically, "Look, it's the King and I!"

A key scene comes when the bourgeois, disguised as a pasha, rides atop an "elephant," comprised of four boys under an enormous blanket. Grabbing the hand of the dancer at the front of the elephant representing the creature's trunk, Rudolf playfully led him around the stage. Then the elephant "collapsed" and the pasha was wrapped in the blanket. Rudolf explained, "This is important effect and must be done right. Let's do it again." In all, there were three rehearsals for this program. At each rehearsal, the elephant sequence was repeated. Rudolf grabbed a corner of the large "curtain" as they called it, and demonstrated how to fling it upward before the boys ducked under it. Finally the elephant formations worked by opening night.

At the dress rehearsal, Rudolf supervised the hanging of the front curtain for *Bourgeois*, as well as the lighting cues. Growing frustrated, he called out, "Lighting man….somebody….can you fix it? Come here." Neary urged Rudolf to come out front to see how it looked, but he replied, "I can see from here – that pool of light needs adjusting." Finally, a technician made the necessary changes and the rehearsal continued. Still displeased, he noticed that the front dropcloth wasn't lowered enough over the proscenium, exposing the overhead lights. "We'll fix it tonight," assured the technician. Nureyev insisted, "No, I want it now to be sure it's correct." The technicians conferred with the stagehands while Rudolf, by this time quite exhausted, repeated, "I want to see it now, not tomorrow." So the rehearsal was stopped and Rudolf stood in the front row and ordered, "Lower it another three inches." When it was to his satisfaction, he instructed, "Now mark it for tonight." Nothing escaped his eagle eye when it came to stagecraft. Finally satisfied, he left for his afternoon nap.

A bonus to that season was watching the company class on stage, prior to the rehearsal. Nureyev arrived late, wrapped in layers of sweaters, legwarmers, and scarves, and then fiddled with his ballet shoes. Pat Neary gave a complex combination of steps. Rudolf, still switching ballet shoes, requested, "Sorry, wasn't listening. Can you repeat the combination?" After it was demonstrated again, Rudolf wiped his neck with a towel and heartily remarked, "We're going to be very busy today!" Once he started, he became completely focused. Toward the end of the class, Neary demonstrated an intricate jump-combination and instructed everyone, "We'll do this in two groups." However, everyone did it in one group and Rudolf did the combination on his own. He covered so much stage space that he nearly ended up on top of the rehearsal pianist at the side of the stage. He moved like the lighting, enveloping everything around him.

When the Boston Ballet brought their production of *Swan Lake* to London, Nureyev partnered ballerinas Laura Young and Marie-Christine Mouis, on alternating nights. Mouis, formerly with the Paris Opera, was one of the tallest dancers Nureyev worked with, while Young was rather petite. It must have proved challenging for him to adjust to the different sizes each night. While rehearsing the White Act pas de deux, Young audibly gasped when Nureyev lifted her high overhead. As he put her down, he cordially asked if everything was all right. "Yes, I just didn't expect to be lifted that high."

The role of Albrecht in the ballet *Giselle* was one of Nureyev's favorite roles. He performed it throughout his career with numerous ballerinas from Margot Fonteyn to Sylvie Guillem and danced it as late as 1989 – a total of more than 350 times. Mary Skeaping was a former dancer with Anna Pavlova's companies and ballet mistress for the Sadlers Wells' Ballet in its formative years. In 1971 she created a production of *Giselle* for London Festival Ballet. In this production, while rehearsing with Evdokimova, Rudolf was in a specially playful mood. He pretended to eat Giselle's daisies before she plucked the petals for her "loves me, loves me not" section in Act One. Toward the end of the act when his fiancé Bathilde questions him about his "disguise," Albrecht justifies his peasant garb by miming he was out hunting or, in Nureyev's case, he just wasn't thinking. At this rehearsal, instead of doing the mime, he pointed to the holes in his tattered legwarmers and said aloud, "Why doesn't somebody fix these?" Company director Beryl Grey and Skeaping, both watching from out front with serious expressions on their faces, firmly told him to stop fooling around.

At a 1977 *Giselle* rehearsal in Paris with the Scottish Ballet, Nureyev seemed to give those of us in the audience a private performance. His Royal Ballet colleague Lynn Seymour danced the title role. Neither she nor Nureyev had ever done this particular version before. Nureyev made his rehearsal entrance wearing five layers of dirty legwarmers and a rather worn gray leotard top. He literally stamped his way onto the stage. We could tell he was in a very devilish mood. When knocking on Giselle's cottage door, he pretended to bang furiously with his hand and then turned and used his backside. Seymour entered with both feet bandaged from injuries while Nureyev sat on the bench fiddling with his ballet shoes, changing them several times. At one point he came into the audience to chat with friends but, with his innate sense of timing, returned to the stage right on time for his entrance.

When Hilarion tried to interrupt Albrecht and Giselle, Rudolf sat defiantly on a table pretending to munch the harvest grapes. During an orchestral break, he rehearsed with the dancer playing Albrecht's squire. After adjusting the dancer's hat, he demonstrated some royal mime gestures, contrasting them with the sloppy hand gestures and nods in all directions, that the young man had done. During the crowd scenes, Rudolf continued warming up by executing leg kicks while holding on to Giselle's cottage. In Giselle's "mad" scene, he broke into a tango. At another point, he seemed bored and broke into a little soft shoe dance.

He remained in the audience while the stagehands set Act Two. Back on stage for his grief-stricken entrance, he reached Giselle's grave and began doing Graham-style contractions. It was well past Rudolf's lunchtime and he began carrying on. He removed the floral crown from the cross on the grave and jokingly put it on his head, examined it, and pretended to eat it.

Scottish ballerina Elaine MacDonald danced Myrtha, and entered chewing gum and carrying her handbag. She wore fluffy bedroom slippers over her point shoes, removing the former, but not her thick legwarmers, causing Rudolf to quip, "She has fat legs!" Then, to the technical crew, he remarked, "This lighting looks idiotic to me."

In the Second Act, the Willis in this version wore long-sleeved Victorian dresses. They also wore blond wigs with side curls that made them look somewhat like Kewpie dolls. Additionally, they waved white scarves at anyone who entered their "territory." All of this highly amused Rudolf. At one point he borrowed one of those scarves and shook it at them as if trying to scare them away. Instead of doing his poetic run around the stage in search of Giselle, he did a flat-footed stomp, "called" to her, and then put his hands around his throat as if strangling himself. He watched Seymour's entrance from a kneeling position and became more serious for the rest of the rehearsal, stopping the orchestra occasionally for adjustments. At one point when the tempo wasn't quite right, he burst into a frenzied tap dance to get the conductor's attention.

During Seymour's solo, Nureyev tap-danced to keep warm. Then he performed his own variation full out and effortlessly. Shading his eyes from the spotlight, he came forward and said it caused a blind spot and he couldn't see the edge of the stage. He then repeated his solo once again, to his satisfaction. His professionalism always took over whenever he had to partner or dance, but he admittedly didn't like rehearsals – especially when they were not of his own productions – so he frequently added humorous antics to break things up and entertain himself.

At this Paris *Nureyev Festival*, each performance of *Giselle* was followed by two additional pieces. Lynn Seymour performed the Isadora Duncan solos that Sir Frederick Ashton had created for her, and Nureyev danced *Moments* by Murray Louis with four boys from the Scottish Ballet. It made for a very long program, since the actual performance started at 8:30 p.m. and finished at 1 a.m. The Paris Metro stopped running at 1 a.m. Due to the late finish we often hitched a ride back to our hotels with Luigi, while Nureyev went out for a late dinner.

Manfred was finally introduced to London audiences during the 1981 *Nureyev Festival*. Several fans turned up for the morning rehearsal. Luigi went inside to ask Rudolf if it was okay to observe and received an affirmative, so we were in "officially." That felt really kind of special. The Zurich company was in the middle of rehearsing Balanchine's *Western Symphony*, while Rudolf did his own class holding on to a piece of scenery on the side. He instructed the dancers to move forward, because they were all crowded in the back third of the stage. Later, while the tech crew fiddled with the lights, Rudolf remained in one beam of light doing his adagio, almost like a stunning otherworldly vision.

Nureyev alternated between his own dancing and supervising *Manfred*. During the final scene, the stage is engulfed in waves of parachute silk and Rudolf walked to the orchestra bridge to supervise. The dancers underneath the silk were not spreading the waves over the full width of the stage, since they were accustomed to a smaller stage in Zurich, where this version originally premiered. Their arm movements in helping spread the silk were too choppy and violent, so Rudolf had them repeat it. All hands on deck, including Rudolf, returned to carefully refold the "waves" and they did it once again.

During the rehearsal when the production was later staged at the amphitheatre in Athens, Rudolf wasn't satisfied with how the waves worked. He simply took a pair of scissors and cut holes in them to make them billow in the wind.

Often our attempts to see rehearsals required ingenuity. France's Ballet du Nancy joined Rudolf for his 1982 *Nureyev Festival*. At that time London Transport was on strike. A few of us managed to find a bus – they usually kept some lines running, but on extremely erratic schedules – but were still late arriving at the Coliseum. We snuck in but were promptly stopped in a backstage corridor. One quick-thinking fan in our group immediately began speaking French and the Stage Door attendant advised, "I think you'd better speak to Sally." Sally, a member of the staff, soon arrived and played along with us, because she had seen us numerous times and knew what we were up to. She led us into the auditorium and discreetly disappeared.

Rudolf was already on stage rehearsing *Spectre de la Rose* wearing blue legwarmers and an adorned orange turban. For the benefit of all those in the auditorium, he made all sorts of remarks about the horrible lighting. Three huge pink spots on the stage floor were reminiscent of a gigantic traffic signal and did little to enhance the mood of the piece. When the rose follow-spot came on to Rudolf, he immediately knew it was wrong and directed, "Too bright; half." Since he wasn't supervising one of his own productions, he was in a very playful, relaxed mood and let everyone else deal with the tedious production details, but the lighting certainly had to be corrected. Dominique Khalfouni danced the role of the Young Girl. She kept asking conductor Andre Presser to stop during a difficult passage but he, nose pressed to the score, simply ignored her. Rudolf knew better and made a mental note to speak with him later, since they wanted to run through it all in one go.

A photographer out front was taking flash pictures. Rudolf looked surprised, but didn't say anything. After the third or fourth disruptive flash, Presser stopped the orchestra, turned around from the pit and screamed at full volume, "Stop the flash! Stop it at once!" Rudolf gave a wicked grin as if to say, "My, my, such temper – and I didn't have to say a word!"

Everything he did at that rehearsal was almost like a "show" for his loyal fans and admirers out front. When he executed his double assembles, he purposely nearly crashed into the set to make it obvious that the chair was positioned incorrectly and he wouldn't be able to clear it. At the moment when the Young Girl returns to her chair and the Spectre momentarily reclines at her feet, the tempo was so fast, that Rudolf just made up his own dance. He pretended to partner an imaginary ballerina, spinning her around, lifting her up, and carried on with a hilarious mime section. Finally, the conductor looked up, stopped, and Rudolf, all business by now, instructed him, "You have to wait for me here – I can't get up that fast." He had to go from a floor pose directly into entrechats and needed a slight pause.

When the ballet finished, Rudolf, in very good spirits, carried on another conversation with Presser, humming parts that needed tempo adjustments. "Also I thought there was a kind of drum or something in this bit, as kind of crescendo," Rudolf relayed carefully. Andre uttered an emphatic "No," and Rudolf just said, "Hmm, strange." Yet later, during the performance, a drum made a slight crescendo and Rudolf's eyes lit up. At the rehearsal, after discussing all of his memorized notes with Presser, he instructed, "Again, from my entrance, okay?" and did his entire section flat out. At one point he yelled out, "Come, Dominique, now!" because she missed her cue and wasn't where she should be. After this second run-through, she still wasn't satisfied and asked Andre if she could have the first part repeated. Rudolf decided however, that they would rehearse it with the piano later, since the rehearsal needed to continue while they still had the orchestra.

When he rehearsed *Faune*, this production was slightly different from the one he premiered with the Joffey Ballet in 1979. The somewhat modified set meant that the Faune had a new rock on which he perched. The steps leading up to the rock were well hidden and had a textured surface. Not having adjusted to it, Rudolf navigated the steps tentatively. The first step was far too big, while the others were too narrow. He memorized the steps with his feet and adjusted his steps accordingly. He wasn't in costume and wore tatty old ballet slippers instead of the sandals so we could really see his feet when he walked. He stretched out his arms to indicate to the conductor that he wanted the music stretched out a bit more. Presser's nose was buried into the score once again so Rudolf shrugged and carefully climbed back up the stairs to his rock. When the curtain went back up, Rudolf was talking with one of the stagehands about adjusting the uneven spacing of the steps and securing the front piece to the rock.

After a long interval, the stage was set for *Petrushka*. Serge Golovine, whose production they performed, raced around trying to round up the children and supers for the opening crowd scene. Rudolf came along and told all of them to move forward and better utilize the stage space. However, he basically let Golovine handle things.

Between the crowd scene and the one for Petrushka's cell, a snare drum is played for as long as it takes to properly change the scenery. At this rehearsal, that period was interminable. Just before the second cell scene with the Doll and the Moor, Rudolf impishly came to the front of the stage, directly over the tireless drummer. He began drumming himself, pretended to look at his watch, continued drumming and mimed, "Long time, eh?"

Maurice Bejart created *Songs of a Wayfarer* for Nureyev and Paulo Bortoluzzi in 1971. Rudolf performed it with various dancers throughout the many years. During the 1983 *Nureyev Festival* in London, an incident occurred that made the front pages of the London newspapers.

A young dancer named Patrick Armand was performing *Wayfarer* with Nureyev for the first time. The various "songs" have different moods and are reflected by changes in the lighting. Shortly into the rehearsal, Nureyev shouted, "Here lights should come up." The lighting person kept insisting that the lighting cue was correct. Nureyev became more and more agitated, insisting that Bejart's original lighting cues were not being respected.

He shaded his eyes and said to the lighting technician, "Johnny, do I have to scream or what? I said I wanted these lights fixed!" He came onstage while Rudolf explained, "Here, no backlighting, and here should be special. And look at that" he said, pointing upward, very dissatisfied. None of the lights were changed, but the technician made notes.

Rudolf returned to dancing, but stopped soon after and interrogated, "Johnny, what are we going to do? Do you want to dance and I'll do the lights?" Johnny snapped, "I'm not doing anything. Those lights were set according to the plan." Rudolf retorted, "Look, I have to dance, too, so let's go, eh?" Johnny's finger thumped repeatedly on Rudolf's chest to emphasize once more, "I'm doing nothing," and then he stormed off. Rudolf stood there and said, "I've been ready and you do nothing. Ok, that's it – cancel performance," and he walked off to the wings. The curtain was lowered and there was an explosion of voices in the wings. Rudolf had left the theatre, leaving everyone to rehearse without him. "After such a scene, there's no coming back," one of the fans remarked.

The conductor went on with *Wayfarer* for the sake of the baritone who wanted to rehearse, while Patrick Armand danced the Shadow all by himself – his first performance ever with Nureyev and the star had gone home. The lighting technicians must have stormed off as well, because they merely used the overhead neon work lights without even trying the lighting cues needed for each "song."

The evening papers were filled with news of Rudolf's outburst and speculated, "Will Nureyev dance tonight?" The house was sold out. Everyone wanted to find out if he would indeed dance. Of course, Rudolf returned to the theatre, looking refreshed from his outburst and his usual afternoon nap, and danced spectacularly very well with Armand. Also, the lighting cues had been corrected.

Nureyev was a tireless worker, always striving to make things better. I recall one closing night when Nureyev had performed Jose Limon's *Moor's Pavane*. As soon as the curtain came down, he had the dancers remain on stage because he wasn't happy with how it had gone. Limon had personally taught the role to Rudolf and the ballet dancers hadn't given their characters the right "weight" that the choreography required. Rudolf worked with them on stage while a huge crowd gathered at the Stage Door. We noticed the loading dock door was open and observed Rudolf working with the dancers until *Moor's Pavane* was to his satisfaction. Dancers continually try to give their very best performance. Nureyev always insisted on it.

"Of course I get tired. Of course jet lag bothers me, but I make my head rule my body. I just go on dancing no matter how I feel. That's what being a professional is all about."
~Rudolf Nureyev, London Evening News, June 1, 1977~

RANDOLF NEVEROFF

Last act of Giselle, Metropolitan Opera House, NYC, 1974
Photo: William J. Reilly

If ever there were someone who was proof positive of "mind over matter," that someone was Rudolf Nureyev. Dance was his oxygen - he couldn't live without it. "From the age of six, I can truthfully say I was possessed," he wrote in his autobiography. When a reporter once asked him if his love for dance was an obsession, he replied without hesitation, "True. Guilty, so indict me!" He added, "My obsession saved me, because I knew early on what I wanted to do."

This thirst for dance meant that in more than thirty years of dancing, he seldom missed a performance. If the public paid money to see Rudolf Nureyev dance, he danced, often with both legs wrapped in bandages. A fan once asked him when he had danced on an injured foot, "Are you really better tonight?" He sighed and replied, "My foot won't listen to me." He continued, "You wrap up your foot - and the important thing is - you think of something else and go out and dance."

I was often unaware that Nureyev danced while injured. He refused to cancel a performance nor would he let the public ever see him limp on stage. Often we only found out, when his partner or fellow dancers mentioned it at the Stage Door.

Rudolf preferred dancing as much as he possibly could because he was convinced, "The more I dance, the better I become." It also helped him conquer stage fright, knowing that each performance could be better than the last. In 1985, he stated to the London *Sunday Times* : "The mind is ready, but the body isn't – it doesn't follow the pattern you want it to. That is why it is so important to dance as often as possible."

Nureyev's workload increased dramatically in the 70s. In February 1974 he embarked on a three month American tour with the National Ballet of Canada, performing his production of *Sleeping Beauty*. After that tour culminated at New York's Metropolitan Opera House, Nureyev then remained in New york City, where the Royal Ballet joined him for a nearly month-long season at the Met and then consecutively at Washington's Kennedy Center.

Two of my friends and I decided to travel from London to New York for the Royal Ballet's tour that was appearing there. We saw Nureyev in *Swan Lake, Romeo and Juliet, Apollo, La Bayadere,* and his debuts in Ashton's *La Fille Mal Gardee* and MacMillan's *Manon*. It was a feast of dancing and Nureyev danced all his scheduled performances.

Five days later, he embarked on a new venture in Paris, called *Nureyev and Friends*. Joined by his Royal Ballet colleague Merle Park, in addition to dancers from the Paris Opera, the program consisted of Balanchine's *Apollo*; Bournonville's *Flower Festival* pas de deux; Paul Taylor's *Aureole*, performed in bare feet; and concluded with Jose Limon's *Moor's Pavane*. I visited Paris for a weekend and could see clearly that Nureyev danced the entire season while injured. This was in fact a tryout for his first *Nureyev and Friends* program later that year on Broadway. In Paris, while performing barefoot in *Aureole*, his bare feet were so heavily bandaged, they were barely recognizable. He never made it easy on himself, either, for he refused to modify the choreography and performed all four ballets on the program during that two-week season.

In one performance of *Moor's Pavane*, Rudolf must have had a muscle spasm; at the ballet's conclusion, he moved with such intensity, that it appeared he had really killed his Desdemona. All was well, however, since the dancers rose for curtain calls while the 5,000 spectators in the Palais des Sports applauded with palpable enthusiasm.

A few nights later, Nureyev danced in his *Swan Lake* production in Vienna, then went off to fulfill engagements in Milan and swiftly returned back to London for more performances. This backbreaking schedule was followed by another three-week season with the Canadians in New York City.

When a reporter asked about his obsession with dance, Nureyev declared that he was a masochist and at times the audience were the sadists who came to see how he would dance. Margot Fonteyn once referred to a performance as a bullfight, where the spectators were out for blood.

Meanwhile, on the other side of the Atlantic, Mikhail Baryshnikov defected from the Kirov while on tour in Canada in June of 1974. Later that year, he spent time with Nureyev in London. Rudolf became a kind of mentor to him at that time and the two former Kirov Ballet stars were often seen together in the audience at the Royal Ballet. When Nureyev wasn't dancing, he was watching dance performances.

We visited the Paris Opera again in mid-November of 1974 to see an injury-free Nureyev perform in *Tristan*, a new work by modern choreographer Glen Tetley, which he performed with Carolyn Carlson. Two days later, we were back across the Channel to see Nureyev's London debut in *Manon*. Critic Richard Buckle wrote an interesting review, writing that Nureyev "did something so special nobody else in that role had done." I wrote to the critic, asking him to reveal what Rudolf had done, because I had seen his New York debut earlier that year. We had a running exchange of letters for a while, until he wrote to disclose that "the something special" was Nureyev's boyish reaction at cheating in the card game, in the second act, "like a kid caught with his hand in the candy jar."

When I returned from Paris, I was detained at British customs for over thirty minutes. My work permit was coming to an end. While it hadn't expired and a new one was being processed, I shouldn't have been traveling. They admitted me after a warning and marked my passport "good for six months" pending receipt of the permit.

When my permit eventually arrived, I began to give serious thought as to how long I could remain in London. The cost of living in Britain had nearly doubled during the three years I was there and the government had imposed a "Value Added Tax" on purchases, including theatre tickets. Union stagehands at the Royal Ballet demanded an additional 60% increase in their contract, to which management balked. Because tickets had been sold in advance, the Royal was forced to find another venue, which turned out to be "in the tent" at Battersea Park, definitely not an ideal situation. There were always some patrons who fainted from the stifling summer heat while the noise from overhead planes or helicopters disrupted many performances. But at least the "tent season" allowed the dancers to continue performing.

The difficult economic situation led the Royal Ballet to refrain from renewing Nureyev's contract. Rudolf loved the Royal, but stated he had to keep working.

As for myself, I was also facing an important decision. Since my work permit was tied to a specific job, it meant I wasn't permitted to work elsewhere. When my boss in London announced that he was leaving, I began to set my sights on New York City, which seemed to be the center of the dance world. And I'd have a higher paycheck.

I couldn't attend Nureyev's five-week *Friends* program on Broadway just after Christmas in 1974, but friends eagerly testified how well he was dancing. They also reported that by the end of that season, both Rudolf and Paul Taylor dancer Lisa Bradley, who danced in *Auerole*, wore matching band-aids on their fingers. "Isn't it strange," one friend wrote me, "That after five grueling weeks of performances, Nureyev ends up with a measly band-aid, but his fans are ready to drop dead from exhaustion!" When Merle Park returned from New York to London at the end of January, she told us, "After five weeks of dancing, I'm still suffering jet lag. I don't know how Rudolf does it."

In addition to dancing his previously scheduled performances at Covent Garden and the Paris Opera, Rudolf was preparing his own season at the London Coliseum with the National Ballet of Canada, performing in *Coppelia*, *Giselle*, *Flower Festival* and *Don Juan*. All of this, while rehearsing with the London Festival Ballet for his *Sleeping Beauty* production. After his two-week Canadian season at the London Coliseum, Nureyev embarked on a multi-city tour of Australia. He was also staging his production of *Raymonda* for American Ballet Theatre. This meant that within two months, he was mounting two full-length productions on two different continents, while taking lessons from Martha Graham for a fund-raising gala for her company in July. It was no surprise then, that Nureyev was injured by the time he premiered *Raymonda*.

We found out that he had hurt his foot while stepping off the plane in New York! Both legs were taped from ankle to knee, but he refused to cancel. Since he wasn't scheduled to dance every performance, his so-called "time off" afforded him the opportunity to rehearse young Fernando Bujones in the title role of Jean deBrienne as well as prepare for his upcoming two-week *Friends* season with Margot Fonteyn in Washington.

I tied up loose ends in London and arrived in New York City just prior to the *Raymonda* premiere. I quickly arranged a trip to Washington to see Fonteyn and Nureyev. Margot agreed with Rudolf's philosophy "the more I dance, the better I become." She began somewhat tentatively on that first night, but by the second or third performance in *Marguerite and Armand*, she was magnificent. Photos from that season show that both of Nureyev's legs were heavily bandaged, but despite injuries, he never cancelled.

Barely three days after his Washington season, Nureyev was back again at the Met for another three weeks with the Canadians, still injured and heavily bandaged. A reporter asked why he danced while injured. Nureyev mischievously remarked that he had to "exorcise the devil" by dancing daily.

The summer season of 1975 was simply insane for ballet lovers. It was the absolute height of the "ballet boom." ABT performed opposite Nureyev and the Canadians at Lincoln Center. Many of the fans wanted to see Baryshnikov and Kirkland dance *La Bayadere* at the State Theatre. Dedicated Nureyev fans skipped a *Sleeping Beauty* at the Met to attend ABT, and then ran to the Met in time for curtain calls.

Both companies were performing *La Sylphide*. Erik Bruhn portrayed Madge the Witch in BOTH productions, forcing him to run across the plaza from ABT's matinee to join the Canadians for the evening. Baryshnikov danced *La Sylphide* at one ABT matinee and was later spotted in standing room in time for Nureyev's evening *Beauty* performance.

As if things weren't already busy enough, on his night off from the Canadians, Rudolf joined several ABT dancers in a gala performance. He danced the pas de trois from Bournonville's *La Ventana* with Erik Bruhn and Cynthia Gregory and also partnered Gelsey Kirkland in the *Corsaire* pas de deux. The lifts with Kirkland were unbelievable; at one point, she went up so effortlessly that it seemed she would just keep going. Rudolf merely supported her pirouettes with one finger. The look of amazement on his face, captured by an in-house photographer, was priceless. His expression seemed to say, "I've found a dancer!" At the curtain calls, he immediately presented her with his own flowers and gave her a fatherly kiss on the cheek. The applause went on for some time. Critic Clive Barnes wrote, "Nureyev seemed so enchanted with his ballerina, that he looked like he could carry her off forever."

For that gala, Alicia Alonso returned from Cuba to perform the adagio from *Swan Lake* at age 53. The fans queued for three days just to get a ticket. Police prevented us from lining up outside the Met, so we were forced to wait in the park opposite Lincoln Center. We got very little sleep, but somehow we all managed to get tickets, despite all standing room being three rows deep.

The following night, Rudolf made his debut in Erik Bruhn's production of *Coppelia*. He had been rehearsing all day with Martha Graham for an upcoming season before his evening performance. In Act Two, Nureyev's character, Franz, sneaks into the toymaker's workshop and is stopped by Dr. Coppelius, played by Bruhn. In his attempt to escape, Franz jumps over a chaise lounge. While doing so, Rudolf clipped his foot on the furniture's wooden edge. Luckily Franz lies down in a stupor, until being revived near the end of the act. I could imagine Rudolf's thoughts while propping up his throbbing foot, wondering if he could finish the performance. We heard he had lost a toenail.

In the third act, the Burgonmeister performed the marriage ceremony of Franz and Swanilda, She was kneeling in place without her groom, when suddenly this blur in white dashed onstage and plopped down on the cushion, next to his partner. An embarrassed Rudolf had a sheepish grin on his face, because he was nearly late for the wedding. He asked the preacher to help fasten his sleeve and stared so adoringly at his bride that he missed gesturing "I do" for the ceremony. Luigi told us later that Rudolf had a massage and was re-bandaged during the interval, but his dancing showed no signs of injury.

At the Stage Door, however, Nureyev could barely walk. When asked for autographs by the enormous crowd, he said, "I'll sign, but I must get off my feet," and he hobbled to a waiting car and patiently signed. When a relative newcomer to the Stage Door asked the fans why he danced with an injury while other dancers under similar circumstances immediately cancelled, we offered the only explanation: "He just does more performances and often dances better when injured!" At the next performance, Rudolf not only danced all the difficult steps in the Coda, but in the middle of his entrechats, when someone in the audience yelled "Higher!" Rudolf vigorously obliged.

Just before one of his final *Sleeping Beauty* performances that season, he sustained yet another injury, while warming up in the wings. Panic ensued backstage as Nureyev paged the faithful Luigi from his dinner and told Frank Augustyn to cover for him. The interval was delayed twenty-five minutes while Rudolf had a massage and his ankle was taped. Those sitting in the first row heard conductor George Crum telling the musicians to cut certain sections of the score that contained a lot of jumps, and omit the Coda in the third act. Nureyev practically dragged himself through his entrance and opening solo. However, as the performance wore on, his confidence and sheer willpower returned and he valiantly danced through the pain. His variation in Act Three was amazing and we were told he later said, "Why did I cut the Coda? I could have done it – I know I could!" He simply believed he was invincible.

After such a hectic season, Nureyev went off for a brief rest, before performing with the Royal Ballet touring company at the Edinburgh Festival in early September. At first we welcomed the break, to recoup our finances and catch up on mundane things like laundry. But part of me wanted to be in Edinburgh with friends who wrote that Nureyev danced amazingly well, particularly in *Prodigal Son*. He also made his debut in Ashton's *The Dream*, originally created for Anthony Dowell. Those who saw him said he was terribly nervous and with just two performances, didn't quite seem comfortable with the role.

Fairly rested, and injury-free after a two week break, Nureyev teamed up in Madrid with the Scottish Ballet for debuts in new roles: Bejart's *Sonate a Trois*, Flemming Flindt's *The Lesson*, and *Moments* by Murray Louis before a long European tour with the Dutch National Ballet in *Corsaire* and another new work, *Blown in a Gentle Wind*. I knew I could never keep up with his performing schedule. Once I had a few paychecks, I shared an apartment with a friend. We both began saving for Rudolf's appearances in November for ABT's "encore" season of *Raymonda*, immediately followed by his Broadway *Friends* program with Fonteyn. Conveniently, Nureyev didn't even have to change theatres because both programs played in Broadway's Uris Theatre.

Fonteyn and Nureyev performed the *Corsaire* pas de deux, Ashton's *Marguerite* and *Armand* and *Foresta Amazonica*, while Nureyev also performed *Songs of a Wayfarer* and *Moments* during the two week run. Despite dancing in each ballet every night, Nureyev never missed a single performance. During that New York season, Dutch ballerina Alexandra Radius was "standing in" for Fonteyn in case the senior ballerina was unable to perform. Indeed, at age 56, Fonteyn's first *Corsaire* was a bit "shaky," but she was as determined as Nureyev to fulfill her performances. As the season progressed, Fonteyn became stronger and stronger, amazing everyone with her artistry. Radius remained in the wings, although she did get an opportunity to dance *Corsaire* with Rudolf at a later *Friends* season in London with the Dutch company.

A few days later Nureyev was back in London fulfilling commitments there, before returning to New York to appear with the Martha Graham Dance Company. Nureyev's legs were bandaged, primarily for support, in repeat performances of *Lucifer*. He also debuted in *Night Journey, Appalachian Spring*, and a new work Graham created for him, *Scarlet Letter*.

In a good mood at the Stage Door, Rudolf asked his fans if we slept well. Someone asked if he would dance in Philadelphia and he replied, "No, I'm doing my OWN season," which is how we discovered that his first *Nureyev Festival* would take place at the Palais des Sports in Paris.

I had saved up enough money to see a few performances of *Sleeping Beauty* in Paris, this time with the London Festival Ballet. Quite a few of the Londoners and some European fans also attended. This first *Nureyev Festival* in 1976 ran for three weeks, with Nureyev dancing at every single performance. The long season gave us the opportunity to study the production from every possible angle, because we changed our seats every night. The fishdives – where the ballerina pirouettes and plunges headfirst to the floor to be caught by her partner – never looked so precarious as they did the night we viewed them from behind, in seats at the side of the thrust stage.

Our nightly seat-hopping also afforded us the opportunity to study Nureyev up close, as a partner. Eva Evdokimova alternated in the role of Aurora. Being longer-limbed than Patricia Ruanne, she did not perform fishdives. Instead, she did a series of pirouettes and Nureyev choreographed her into a side bend. Nureyev had to be very focused, so as not to mix up his leading ladies on their alternating nights and perform the wrong step with either of them.

The French public loved Nureyev's production of *Sleeping Beauty* and the way it evoked the court of Louis XIV. They passionately applauded his entrance as he removed his plumed hat and bowed to his entourage, and again when he tossed the dart at the target, scoring a bull's-eye. While his dancing merited applause from the French, the public admired even more his courtly manners, as when he saluted the King and Queen upon exiting after his big solo in the last act. Awed cries of "Ooh la la" could be heard during his Princely curtain calls, while he elegantly promenaded his ballerina around the stage, giving a formal bow to the entire company before bringing everyone forward to acknowledge the boisterous applause.

We did notice, however, that Nureyev seemed to be perspiring far more than usual during this marathon engagement. He kept a handkerchief tucked inside one of his sleeves and, whenever possible, wiped the perspiration from his face and neck. Because he worked up such a sweat whenever he danced, we didn't think too much of it, until we began to hear coughing in the wings. These coughs were deep and hoarse, the bronchial kind, that signaled something more than a mere cold.

Toward the end of the three-week season, Nureyev began coughing on stage. It did not affect his dancing; he still danced flat out and the public's wildly enthusiastic receptions kept him going. When he left the theatre, however, he was bundled up from head to toe. We didn't think much of that, either. Rudolf off stage always dressed warmly, even in summer, because he hated the cold. This was, after all, February, and he was flying directly from Paris to California, where he would join American Ballet Theatre for repeat performances of *Raymonda*.

Despite his persistent cough, Nureyev refused to cancel a single performance. During the final week of his three-week run, he received so much applause for his third-act variation, that Evdokimova peeked from the wings to see when she could begin her own solo. Rudolf reappeared on stage once again to acknowledge the applause and exited after saluting the King and Queen. By the fourth time he was forced to come out to irrepressible applause, he flashed his dazzling smile and began to laugh and then pointed to Eva to begin her variation. When she finally came out, the unstoppable applause reignited. The enthusiastic public was on fire. Even while sick, Rudolf managed to wow his audiences.

After finishing the season on February 14, 1976, he flew to Los Angeles, where he opened on the 16th with Gelsey Kirkland in *Raymonda*. He struggled to get through the demanding role of Jean deBrienne and then finally admitted, "I can't go on like this."

That night, at a friend's home, Rudolf complained of having difficulty breathing, and suddenly collapsed. He was rushed to the hospital and placed on oxygen. As he was being wheeled off to have his chest X-rayed, he insisted on returning to his room to retrieve one of his woolen hats in order to "avoid a draft." He must have been a difficult patient, because he stubbornly demanded to be released, so he could dance *Raymonda* with Martine van Hamel, a dancer he hadn't partnered in that role before. He was even caught walking the corridor looking for the exit. When confronted by a nurse, he said he was just going to take class and promised to return. He was escorted back to his room, much against his will.

A staff member entering his room, exclaimed, "Hey, I know you! You're Randolf...Randolf..." and without missing a beat, Nureyev answered, "Neveroff." Early on, the British press coined the nickname "Randolf Neveroff" for him and it stuck. He was even presented with a jacket with those very words emblazoned on it.

Nureyev's pneumonia and subsequent cancellation of his ABT performances was in all the newspapers. The *New York Daily News* ran a photo of a bikini-clad Rudolf Nureyev in Martha Graham's *Night Journey* captioned "Up From His Sickbed." One fan that had never seen his skimpy costume from that ballet remarked, "No WONDER he got pneumonia!"

A good friend of Rudolf's bought him a stack of books to read while he recovered. He sat on the floor sorting those he would read right away, those to read on the plane, and the ones to keep for later. Midway through sorting, he told his friend, "This is hard work. The doctors said I'm supposed to rest!"

Nureyev outfoxed the press by saying he was going to Monte Carlo to recuperate, but flew to Morocco instead. Monte Carlo in February was too damp while Morocco offered him the warmth needed for a speedier recovery. Before his flight to Morocco, he stopped in New York, and met briefly with a Hurok representative to go over his upcoming Met season. He explained, "I need to do more performances of *Giselle* or I'll lose my permit to do so." He also rang one of the fans, asking that a message be passed along to the others. We were told to "stop worrying" because he was feeling better and resting. He admitted he would enjoy his first long vacation in seven years. Rudolf also cautioned that some future performance dates might change and we shouldn't rush to buy tickets just yet.

This was disturbing news because, up until then, we never hesitated about booking performance tickets, airline or hotel reservations to see Nureyev perform. We were so accustomed to Nureyev's dancing through pain and injuries that it seemed inconceivable he would cancel a performance. That thought never crossed anyone's mind. Now he was under doctor's orders to rest for at least two months.

He did rest for a bit, but resumed dancing one month later in the very demanding roles of Ashton's *La Fille Mal Gardeé* and *The Dream*. He fulfilled these previously contracted performances, out of concern that the Royal Ballet wouldn't invite him back, had he cancelled. He was determined to get through them, but his stamina wasn't quite there yet. *The Dream* has a very fast and long scherzo section, challenging enough for a dancer in top form, but at rehearsals Rudolf couldn't manage it all in one go because of breathing problems. He repeated it again and again until he felt he could get through it. After the performance, we heard one of his Royal Ballet colleagues say to him, "Rudolf, I thought you'd kill yourself today with all those rehearsals." They had apparently gone on for twelve hours.

Then he rejoined American Ballet Theatre in Washington, where he finally got to dance with Martine van Hamel in *Raymonda*. He caught a cold, probably from the theatre's air-conditioning, and developed a fever. "It's nothing," he insisted, while ignoring everyone who urged him to get another chest X-ray. It was early April and mild weather, but when he emerged from the theatre, he was bundled in his fur coat and hat and still shivering. We asked him point blank how he was. Rudolf replied, "I'm melting!" He had a temperature of 101. We suggested, while hopeful, "You'll probably get a chance to rest a week before the Royal Ballet performances start at the Met, won't you?" He laughed and replied, "No, I'm catching the first plane to Amsterdam in the morning. I must rehearse the new piece with Rudi Van Dantzig."

Rudolf was already preparing for his marathon season that summer in London, but his schedule with the Royal Ballet tour in New York and Washington fortunately allowed him some down time between performances, to rebuild his stamina.

While in Amsterdam, he injured his ankle during a rehearsal. He rested briefly in Monte Carlo, but because it was unusually cold, he flew back to New York, which was experiencing an early heat wave.

Nureyev knew that the Met Box Office and the Royal depended on him. Only with fierce determination was he able to fulfill all his scheduled performances. He was absolutely driven and all too aware of the passage of time. When questioned by a reporter why he worked so hard, Rudolf replied, "Because I love to dance." When the reporter replied "other dancers say they love to dance and yet they don't drive themselves the way you do," Nureyev responded, "Their love is not sufficient."

The Royal Ballet opened their Met season on April 20, 1976, with a gala performance of *Romeo and Juliet*. Nureyev, both legs bandaged for support, danced with Merle Park as his Juliet. At galas most people are there to be seen, with the performance being secondary, but once this performance began you could hear a pin drop. After endless curtain calls, a nearby audience member proclaimed, "Nureyev is unbelievable. The energy he put into that performance is miraculous – this man is a superman to just get out of his sickbed and perform like that!" Anna Kisselgoff wrote in the *New York Times* that Nureyev seemed to "suddenly and almost violently regain his old fire; the magic had returned again." We learned that when the performance finished, some of the Royal Ballet dancers tossed Rudolf in the air and cheered, because he inspired the entire company.

Two nights later, Park and Nureyev starred in *Swan Lake*. Rudolf arrived at the theatre, pleased to see his fans, and generously shook everyone's hand. He danced an "electric" performance, despite having his left leg bandaged from ankle to calf. He seemed to have rethought his interpretation of Prince

Siegfried, as if his illness and subsequent recovery had made him so glad to be dancing again, that his roles took on a deeper meaning.

At a second performance of *Romeo and Juliet*, in the scene after killing Juliet's cousin Tybalt and begging Lady Capulet to forgive him, Nureyev's intensity was gut-wrenching. What Nureyev lacked in technique due to injury, was often outweighed with his ability to emit extraordinary dramatic power. At the intermission, we spotted a young man in the lobby on his knees, imitating the scene he'd just witnessed. Clutching his girlfriend's skirt, he blurted out, "And then Romeo buried his head in her skirt like this and . . . oh, it was just too beautiful!"

Three nights later, Nureyev, still bandaged, performed *La Bayadere*, Act Three. The audience gasped as he executed superb slow-motion pirouettes and weightlessly sunk into a soft fourth position. In his big variation, he was determined to do all six double assembles around the circumference of the Met stage. As he came around from number five, we heard him audibly counting and after the sixth, he shouted "SIX!" and the audience burst into thundering applause. Nureyev was euphoric that he'd accomplished the impossible and got so wildly elated that he nearly skidded off the stage; how he managed to effortlessly land on one knee, only he and God will ever know. It was both frightening and exciting, but that variation alone merited three curtain calls.

When he wasn't rehearsing for his upcoming *Nureyev Festival* in London on his days off, Rudolf was also spotted in the audience watching Ashton's *Month in the Country*. The ballet received a fifteen-minute ovation for Sir Fred, who basked in the applause. Rudolf applauded wildly and said to a friend, "Well, the bastard's gone and done it again." That was Nureyev's charming and unique way of expressing Ashton's genius.

Three days later he danced the Washington portion of his Royal Ballet tour, performing in *Swan Lake, La Bayadere, La Fille Mal Gardee*, and the death figure in MacMillan's *Song of the Earth*. A group of us took the bus to D.C. Between getting up early for standing room, rushing around sightseeing during the day, and staying up quite late after each performance, I existed on a total of three hours sleep in three days. When Rudolf arrived for the matinee performance, he clutched his fur coat to his chest and looked somewhat "distant and faraway." We learned he had a relapse of his pneumonia and was on antibiotics. Yet, he refused to cancel.

Three days later he was in London beginning his marathon *Nureyev Festival*, which advertised, "Nureyev will dance all performances." An unexpected heat wave in London made it very uncomfortable, because in those days, theatres were not air-conditioned. However, the heat was a tonic for the dancers, and helped keep their muscles loose and warm. It was especially helpful to Nureyev, who quickly regained his strength. He danced in his *Sleeping Beauty* production for three weeks, followed by two weeks of a *Friends* program. He danced *Apollo, Le Corsaire, Songs of a Wayfarer* and *Moor's Pavane*, alternating with *Flower Festival* and Paul Taylor's *Auerole*. Then the Scottish Ballet joined him for two weeks of *La Sylphide* coupled with performances of Flemming Flindt's *The Lesson* and *Moments* by Murray Louis.

Just days before his final 1976 *Nureyev Festival* performance, Rudolf sustained a "very painful" ankle injury. Three different doctors looked at it and advised him not to dance. But Nureyev – being Mr. "Neveroff" – determinedly flew to New York to open in *Sleeping Beauty* with the Canadians. Because of the precise footwork required for *La Sylphide*, he was forced to cancel the first couple of scheduled performances. Of course, the audience was not happy, but Nureyev did perform in *Four Schumann Pieces*.

Interspersed with performances of *Swan Lake* and *Giselle*, Rudolf announced that he was going to dance both *Four Schumann Pieces* and *La Sylphide* in the same evening, as originally scheduled. Both of his legs were visibly taped underneath his Scottish socks. At the Stage Door, one of Nureyev's colleagues remarked, "He must think he's a man of steel and I'm beginning to think he is!" Indeed, Clive Barnes referred to him in one review as the "Champion Weightlifter."

On his first day off after dancing for seventeen weeks, Nureyev looked at properties in northern New York, returned to the city to see a film, attended the nightclub act of friend Monique von Vooren and took in another film at 4 a.m.

After dancing his way back to health, Nureyev's "Neveroff" commitment resulted in an August 8, 1976 closing night performance of *Sleeping Beauty*. It was "one for the history books." His Act Three solo merited applause well before he finished. The entire Met audience euphorically jumped to its feet and cheered.

Nureyev remained in fifth position, arms outstretched, as he calmly took in this standing ovation. "What must he be thinking?" we asked ourselves. Here he had recently recovered from injuries and pneumonia to make such a triumphant return, knowing full well, that the next day he was leaving for Spain. He was set to begin work on Ken Russell's *Valentino* film, bidding farewell to the stage for the duration of the three months, while the filming took place. As Rudolf later remarked, "Had I known I would go from pneumonia to dancing this well, I never would have agreed to do the *Valentino* film." He had committed to the film solely because he thought it would give him the "enforced rest" that he needed to fully recover.

The audience laughed incredulously while watching the *Sleeping Beauty* finale and gave Nureyev a forty-minute ovation. Rudolf became quite emotional as he bowed to the company, who applauded him enthusiastically. He insisted that company director Alexander Grant share in the triumphant evening. A friend of mine who had watched from the company box, said Grant was gasping in amazement at Nureyev's virtuosity that evening.

Luigi later told us that Rudolf was furious after reading an unfavorable review that stated, "Nureyev can no longer manage the choreography and had to make changes in his own production of *Sleeping Beauty*." Nureyev had modified the steps to favor his uninjured foot, so he wouldn't have to cancel. Just before the matinee, he decidedly informed Luigi, "I'm putting back all the original choreography, even if I kill myself."

The inevitable comparisons between Nureyev and Baryshnikov made for good press. That season Baryshnikov had cancelled so many performances that the Box Office staff began to call him unreliable. I overheard several ticket buyers comment, "At least with Nureyev you know you'll see him; he never cancels." The conversation continued: "When Nureyev gives a bad performance, critics say, 'He's finished.' When other dancers give a bad performance, they merely report, 'He's off form.'" With these kinds of remarks, the critics only fed Nureyev's determination to prove that, at age 38, he could still "deliver the goods."

Of course, Nureyev's enforced "rest" during the *Valentino* filming didn't mean he just sat around between takes. He spent the time reading and researching for his original production of *Romeo and Juliet* scheduled to premiere with London Festival Ballet. In addition, he rehearsed with a group of the dancers, late each evening after a long day of filming. He did his own daily class to keep in shape and also worked with choreographer Glen Tetley to learn *Pierrot Lunaire*, a work he greatly admired and wanted to perform.

When filming in London ran overtime, he was still able to fulfill some of his Royal Ballet engagements by dashing from the set, straight to the Opera House, still sporting his slicked-back Valentino haircut. Unaccustomed to seeing Nureyev with such short hair, one of my British friends wrote, "How can you look romantic with a haircut that looks as if the U.S. Marines got hold of you?" These same friends attended the dress rehearsal of Ashton's *The Dream*, in which Nureyev danced Oberon. His wreath-like headpiece "was a noticeable improvement over that haircut," they wrote.

Once the *Valentino* film was wrapped, Nureyev plunged into an even more hectic schedule, crisscrossing Europe. This resulted in further injuries, because he simply refused to stop and rest.

In January of 1977, during a performance of *The Nutcracker* at Covent Garden, something seemed to go wrong toward the end of the grand pas de deux. In the final pose, choreographed by Nureyev, he balanced in arabesque with his left leg extended while supporting the ballerina on his hip. To our eyes, his supporting leg seemed to be cramping. Small choreographic changes ensued in his variation and in the coda. When he came forward to acknowledge the applause, his eyes were tearing and he gritted his teeth upon leaving the stage. He was obviously in severe pain.

At the Stage Door, everyone tried to determine just how seriously injured Nureyev was. Park exited the theatre and vaguely disclosed to the waiting crowd, "He's got a bad calf muscle." When Rudolf finally emerged, he was limping badly as he got into his car. He turned to the anxious faces that surrounded him and declared, "Well, kiddie-poos, looks like a long vacation." He then drove off to hopefully recuperate. The "long vacation" was not just for his benefit, but also for ours. Many had gone to great expense flying to London, and an injured Rudolf Nureyev was not in the cards. He never cancelled. This was unheard of!

Two scheduled performances of *The Nutcracker* went on without him. Nureyev being Nureyev, returned only a few days later, dancing the demanding role of Colas in Ashton's *La Fille Mal Gardeé*. One of his fans asked Nureyev how he felt. His cryptic response, "We'll know tomorrow" regarding how his calf muscle "reacts to so much dancing." Both legs were taped up, but he was dancing nevertheless.

Three days later, many of us headed to Paris to see his three-week *Nureyev Festival*, where he danced *La Sylphide*, this time with fellow Kirov ballerina Natalia Makarova. The season also included performances of van Manen's *Four Schumann Pieces*, *Giselle* with Royal Ballet's Lynn Seymour, and a mixed program featuring Tetley's *Pierrot Lunaire*, which Rudolf had diligently rehearsed with the choreographer while filming *Valentino*.

During a performance of *Giselle*, Rudolf either had a muscle spasm or sustained an injury. When he landed from a jump, he stomped his foot, winced, and uttered an audible "Shit!" He couldn't put any weight on his right foot. We could read on his face the fear that, "This kills the second act and perhaps the rest of the season." He looked apprehensive about continuing, then switched to mere annoyance, as he struggled through the remainder of the scene. He eventually resumed putting weight on the bothersome foot and was bandaged for the second act, but never omitted a step.

Rudolf danced in Toronto with the Canadians for the remainder of February and on March 1st began his three-week Broadway *Friends* season, performing every night with members of the Royal Danish Ballet.

Switching gears, he remained in New York with Martha Graham's company. He performed in *Appalachian Spring* and *El Penitente*, the latter a work where Rudolf bit into an apple in the Adam and Eve section. On the last night at the Stage Door, I handed him a lunch bag containing two real apples, remarking, "This is the REAL thing. See you in London." He found it amusing.

We both headed for London on separate flights for the Queen's Silver Jubilee Gala on May 30, 1977. Nureyev premiered a new Ashton work, *Hamlet Prelude*, with Margot Fonteyn. Three days later, he was in good form for the premiere of his *Romeo and Juliet* production, dancing twenty-five consecutive performances. The remainder of that *Nureyev Festival* lasted until mid-July, an unprecedented seven weeks of performances.

I had the great pleasure to be there for all of them. That *Nureyev Festival* reunited Nureyev with Margot Fonteyn in *Marguerite and Armand* and with Natalia Makarova along with Lynn Seymour in *Les Sylphides*. Makarova also danced with Nureyev in *Le Corsaire*, *The Lesson* and *The Toreador*, a work rarely seen outside of Denmark. The Danish company joined Nureyev for the final week of his season.

The day after the Festival season, I returned to New York. I was exhausted simply from traveling and attending all the performances, but "Mr. Neveroff" took his *Romeo and Juliet* production all the way to Australia for a multi-city tour. Up next, Rudolf flew to Manila to dance a gala with Fonteyn, before joining the Canadians on a month-long tour across America and Canada.

All too aware of the passage of time, Nureyev began increasing the number of his performances. In the 1970s, he averaged more than two-hundred performances a year compared to less than one-hundred in the 1960s. He was about to turn 40 in 1978 and remembered that his father warned him he would be "finished" by that age.

I, too, was aware of this pending reality and vowed to see him dance as much as I could. I still worked temporary jobs that gave me flexibility, but whenever I was in London for long Festivals, I registered with a temp agency, working all day before seeing a performance each evening. The pay was lower than in New York, but I could afford my nightly standing room or balcony ticket as well as continue to pay rent for my New York apartment during my absence.

In late 1977, I decided to give myself a break and stayed in Europe as long as possible. I contemplated whether I wanted to make a permanent home in New York or in Europe. I traveled to Vienna where I saw Nureyev's brilliant performance in *Don Quixote*. His scheduled appearances there were sporadic and so, in his usual style, he took a group of dancers for a brief *Friends* tour. One of my fondest memories is traveling via train to Klagenfurt with my Viennese friend to see Rudolf perform. Later, we had a rare opportunity to speak with him semi-privately at the Stage Door, since the waiting crowds weren't as numerous as in other cities.

Back in Vienna during a performance of *Don Quixote*, Nureyev accidentally stepped on a metal trap door in the stage floor, hurting his back and twisting his knee. After finishing the performance, X-rays confirmed that nothing was broken, so he danced the remaining performances wrapped in bandages "just in case." In Vienna, I also got the chance to finally watch Rudolf's original production of *Swan Lake*, my first view of it "live" rather than the film version.

En route back to my London base, I stopped in Paris for his production of *Romeo and Juliet* and then in Amsterdam, where many of the fans had a "reunion" while seeing Nureyev perform new works with the Dutch National Ballet.

In what was becoming a yearly tradition, Nureyev once again appeared on Broadway for his fourth *Friends* season. Yul Brynner was playing in a successful run of *The King an I* at the Uris Theatre, so Nureyev had to use the smaller 1600-seat Minskoff Theatre, much to the disappointment of the organizers while the Box Office staff turned away customers.

During that 1978 Minskoff season, Rudolf was joined by the Murray Louis Dance Company and the Dutch company, in several new pieces. Critics complained that the 40-year-old dancer should stop dancing but the constant lines at the Box Office caused one puzzled ticket-buyer to exclaim, "If Nureyev isn't any good at 40, why are all these people waiting for tickets?" Nureyev was doing so much dancing with so many companies that when the Metropolitan Opera House booked the Peking Ballet, the entertainment weekly, *Variety*, speculated, "with Nureyev as guest?"

Following more performances in Europe, he began his 1978 *Nureyev Festival* in London. He repeated the same program as his earlier *Friends* season with the Dutch National Ballet, as well as his production of *Romeo and Juliet,* and in new roles, *Scheherazade* and *Conservatoire* with London Festival Ballet. That company then joined him at the Met and Washington's Kennedy Center. Immediately following that engagement, he embarked on a cross-country American tour with the Dutch company, finishing in Los Angeles with a *Friends* program with dancers from the Dutch, Danish and French companies.

In the autumn, he paused in New York long enough to dance four performances with ABT including Baryshnikov's production of *Don Quixote*. The remainder of the year was spent touring throughout Europe in assorted *Friends* programs.

By this time I was feeling quite frustrated with my temporary office work situation, because I wasn't being challenged. Other than answering phones and doing the occasional project, I spent hours typing letters to friends in order to "look busy." I had read just about every dance book and magazine available and branched out into opera. That provided an incentive to learn more, so I enrolled in a Music Appreciation class at the Juilliard School with an emphasis on the great composers. The arts fed my soul, but it had expensive taste! As a friend facetiously remarked to me one day when we were pondering our future, "We are marked for life by our obsession."

I knew Nureyev was a phenomenon that I wouldn't see again in my lifetime, despite all the other wonderful dancers I was witnessing. At the end of the year, he was performing at the Paris Opera with Natalia Makarova as well as in new roles in Vienna in January of 1979. I desperately wanted to see those performances, but my budget simply wouldn't permit it.

Taking inspiration from Nureyev who had stated, "Nothing happens unless you make it happen," I placed an ad in one of the local papers as an experienced and organized secretary, available for evening work. The very next day a prominent New York psychiatrist interviewed me. I was immediately engaged and put to work typing up various books he had written. One of them happened to be about athletes and performers who work through injuries, based on visualization and "mind over matter" techniques. I was hooked. Thus began an even busier part of my life, consisting of working at my "day job" as a temp and working three nights a week, from 6 p.m. until midnight. This meant I had to be more selective in the choices I made as to what performances I would have to miss. Despite the long hours, my life became somewhat more balanced. My bank account was replenished enough, to enable me to attend selected performances in Paris and Vienna.

One of Nureyev's *Swan Lake* performances at the Paris Opera was unexpectedly cancelled due to another injury. At the Stage Door, one of the fans asked Luigi, "Did you put ice on Rudolf's foot?" He sighed and replied, "We put everything on that foot!" Nonetheless, two nights later Rudolf was back on stage in Vienna in a new work by Rudi van Dantzig called *Ulysses*. He later dubbed it as "Useless Ulysses," because it was not that successful. In between European performances, he flew to California to partner Natalia Makarova in *Swan Lake* when her scheduled partner, Anthony Dowell, cancelled.

During March of 1979, Nureyev danced with the Joffrey Ballet in a "Homage to Diaghilev" in which he performed works made famous by the legendary dancer Vaslav Nijinsky. These included Michel Fokine's *Le Spectre de la Rose,* and *Petrushka,* as well as Nijinsky's *L'Apres midi d'une Faune.* The program was completed with Leonid Massine's *Parade.*

This historic season took place at Broadway's Mark Hellinger Theatre, and the publicity machines worked overtime. Essays were written about the importance of Diaghilev, Nijinsky, and the works Nureyev would perform. In an interview, Rudolf said he always wanted to do these roles in Russia, but they were forbidden. "And you know how we're attracted to forbidden fruits!" he chuckled.

The season was also a way for the Joffrey Ballet to survive. The company was about to go into hiatus, because of financial problems. Producer James Nederlander hired the company outright, guaranteeing pay to the company's male dancers who didn't dance, because Rudolf performed every night. The season was not only historic, but literally saved the Joffrey Ballet from financial collapse.

The star-studded opening night gala on March 7, 1979 began with *Petrushka*, normally performed last on the program. The stagehands claimed they needed extra time to put up the elaborate sets. This was followed by *Parade*, danced by the Joffrey dancers, and the evening concluded with *Spectre de la Rose* and *Faune*. A brief pause in between the two pieces allowed Nureyev to change costumes and the stagehands to change the sets. On the opening night, *Faune* didn't begin until 10:45 and many in the gala audience left immediately, claiming there was "no dancing" in the program!

During the first four evenings, *Petrushka*, a full company piece, opened the program. The role of *Petrushka* is one that is performed with dancer's feet "turned in," a trademark of the puppet's dejected character. For a classically trained dancer like Nureyev, whose muscles were tediously trained to remain "turned out" in order to perform the roles of the classical repertory this was not only challenging, but also physically demanding.

Immediately following the intermission, Nureyev had to transform himself into "the spirit of the rose," a technically taxing role filled with an array of jumps and based exclusively on the classically turned-out vocabulary. Nijinsky's *Faune,* with its turned-in and frieze-like movements, followed the classical *Spectre*. The combination of turning in, out, and inward again, is very stressful and can cause muscles to cramp up. Nureyev was aware of this possibility and informed the producers. He also felt that the program would work better if *Petrushka* were presented last on the program, instead of the quieter *Faune*.

On the fourth night of the four-week run, Nureyev haphazardly pulled a tendon in his right toe. He momentarily slipped in the snow scene during *Petrushka* and was unable to point his foot. Consequentially, the performance of *Spectre* that followed the interval caused him trouble, because he couldn't maintain his balance while on demi-point. By the time he performed *Faune*, his foot was so badly swollen, that he wore different sandals, although the emotional intensity of his character remained very strong.

The next morning, he awoke in "extreme pain" according to the press, and never left his hotel room. The sold-out house at the March 10th matinee eagerly anticipated this history-making program. Fans were deeply concerned when Nureyev didn't arrive for the performance. Many had waited at the Stage Door since noon for the two o'clock matinee, since Rudolf generally arrived ninety minutes before curtain time. About five minutes past two, we went inside, thinking that perhaps he had arrived extra early or had gone in via another entrance.

The public was kept waiting for twenty minutes and growing rather agitated when an announcement was finally made. "Ladies and gentlemen, the management regrets that Mr. Rudolf Nureyev has sustained an injury and will not be able to perform this afternoon. We regrettably must cancel the performance. Please see the Box Office for a refund." Pandemonium broke out as the reality of the situation set in. The audience left en masse, trying to obtain refunds and an explanation from the frenzied Box Office staff. His dedicated fans, of course, raced to the Stage Door. Rudolf's masseur, Luigi Pignotti, had not arrived at the theatre either. The most we could ascertain from Nureyev's bodyguard, Big George, was that Rudolf realized he couldn't put weight on his right foot when he tried to walk. "This is serious," we exclaimed. "Nureyev NEVER cancels." Since the Joffrey Ballet season was riding on the Nureyev name at the Box Office, there was no option for the company to perform without him. It was the first time in seventeen years, that Nureyev had cancelled a New York performance.

One man in the lobby couldn't understand why the matinee had to be aborted. "Couldn't someone else replace Nureyev?" he innocently inquired, to which someone in the line replied, "Mister, NOBODY replaces Nureyev!" As I waited for my refund, wondering if the evening performance would also be cancelled, I overheard two women behind me talking. One said, "Today's

Saturday and there's no performance on Monday. Let's get a ticket for Tuesday." Her friend asked, "How do you know he will dance Tuesday?" "It's Rudolf Nureyev. He heals fast."

The company and orchestra were told to report for the evening performance, but by 6:30 a cancellation notice was posted. The press reported the cancellation of the show, but added that Nureyev would return as soon as possible.

The Saturday and Sunday performances were cancelled, but on Tuesday night heroically Nureyev returned with a heavily bandaged right foot, to complete the month-long engagement. There was, however, one major change. *Le Spectre de la Rose*, the classically turned out ballet, was performed before the turned-in works of *Faune* and *Petrushka*. The stagehands merely set *Petrushka's* scenery behind the smaller-sized productions. The program not only finished earlier, but also closed with the full-company piece.

One of the reasons those three performances were cancelled, was because Nureyev was about to realize his lifelong dream of working with George Balanchine, who was creating *Le Bourgeois Gentilhomme* for him. Nureyev wanted to be sure he was injury-free for that premiere, which took place a week later at the New York State Theatre. Balanchine worked with Rudolf, but then became quite ill; so Jerome Robbins stepped in and put the final touches on the piece. Nureyev was ecstatically happy and performed it with Patricia McBride. Balanchine gave him the rights to perform the ballet, which Rudolf did later when he mounted it on the Paris Opera. The performances of *Bourgeois* were spread out rather than scheduled every night, so in between, Rudolf joined ABT and performed in *Miss Julie*, *Swan Lake*, and *Pierrot Lunaire*.

For his London *Nureyev Festival* in June of 1979, he danced numerous performances of *Romeo and Juliet* and *Sleeping Beauty*, followed by mixed programs of *Conservatoire*, *Scheherazade*, *Spectre* and *Faune*. He even coaxed Margot Fonteyn to return to the stage and perform in unannounced performances of *Spectre* and *Faune*. Three days later, he was back in New York for the month of July, first with the Canadians and then followed by an "encore" Diaghilev Program with the Joffrey.

Earlier that year, we learned the exciting news that Nureyev would create a new ballet based on the life of Lord Byron. Cellist and conductor Mstislav Rostropovich had apparently given Nureyev the idea to use

Tchaikovsky's *Manfred* symphony. But Rudolf felt that the music was too symphonic and wasn't sure he could work with it. After further research, however, he said that "he found a way" to incorporate the life of Lord Byron with incidents from the *Manfred* poem. Without using a pre-existing scenario, Nureyev could freely develop his movement vocabulary to Tchaikovsky's score.

Rostropovich and the National Symphony of Washington performed the *Manfred* symphony at Carnegie Hall some months prior to the ballet's premiere. I found it very powerful. I read several Byron biographies and eagerly anticipated the Paris premiere on November 20, 1979.

In early November, Nureyev danced with Merle Park in his production of *The Nutcracker*, which had been dropped from the Royal Ballet and was next staged for the Berlin Ballet. In the grand pas de deux, disaster struck. According to Nureyev, "Merle tends to be chatty. So there she was, talking away and I wasn't paying attention and my toe caught in one of the cracks on the floor. I finished the performance, but that was it." He had broken his toe.

He returned to Paris in a wheelchair. Sensational photos appeared in papers worldwide of Rudolf Nureyev wearing a cumbersome foot cast and hobbling around with a cane, while putting the final touches on *Manfred*. Ever disciplined, he still took a daily class, but without using his injured foot. He taught the title role to Paris Opera Etoile Jean Guizerix. As was his usual working style, he then learned the role from Guizerix. Nureyev was unable to dance in the premiere of his own work, so Guizerix danced for him.

I wrestled with the decision of traveling to Paris for the premiere, knowing full well that Nureyev would not be dancing. The odds seemed stacked against me, since all the chartered and bargain flights were on strike. I booked a nonrefundable flight on Air France, which also threatened to strike at the last minute. On the night of November 20, 1979, I took my seat at the Palais des Sports to see not Rudolf Nureyev, but Jean Guizerix performing the title role of Lord Byron.

I had an aisle seat about halfway back from the stage. Just seconds before the performance began, who should come hobbling out from the backstage area, but Rudolf Nureyev! His slight frame was swathed in black and his foot was engulfed in a bright red ski boot. He used a cane for support. The audience spotted him right away and reverently applauded as he slowly made his way along the aisle and took a seat directly in front of me.

Watching Nureyev view his own ballet was most intriguing. While he remained very still, his head darted back and forth to follow the movement, almost willing the dancers through it. At the same time, one could sense he was judging the reaction of the audience. I became so involved in the ballet that I soon forgot the choreographer was sitting in front of me, until the conclusion when the audience began to applaud.

My initial reaction to *Manfred* was so gripping that I began to bravo. When Rudolf slowly made his way up the aisle and then up to the stage for a curtain call, I stood and cheered. It was an evening to remember. Even now, when I think of *Manfred*, my thoughts wander to that premiere with Nureyev sitting right in front of me.

During the first week of *Manfred* performances, I found myself face to face with modern dancer and choreographer Murray Louis in the foyer of the Palais des Sports. Being the only Americans in the vicinity, we struck up a conversation during which I learned that Louis was having difficulty seeing over a large head of an audience member in front of him. I told him a seat next to me was empty that offered a clear view of the stage. And so I sat next to Murray Louis while he watched his first performance of *Manfred*. About two-thirds of the way into the ballet, when Guizerix, as Lord Byron, was leading the Greeks in battle, Louis turned to me and said, "This is a killer role; Rudolf's going to kill himself getting through this."

Approximately three weeks after the premiere, at age 41, Rudolf Nureyev danced this "killer role" himself. I couldn't stay to see him, but news from Paris was that Rudolf heard it wasn't good to keep the cast on his foot too long, so one evening he dramatically kicked his foot against a piece of scenery and discarded the cast. Most people would resume activities gradually after breaking a toe, but Nureyev was, by his own admission, no ordinary man. "If I was ordinary, then I wouldn't be Rudolf Nureyev," he once said. Instead of easing his way back into dancing, Rudolf plunged into it by tackling the demanding role of *Manfred*. It was his therapy.

Nureyev was eager to mount *Manfred* elsewhere and offered it to London Festival Ballet, the Joffrey, LaScala and even proposed it to George Balanchine for an upcoming *Tchaikovsky Festival* for New York City Ballet. All offers fell through, until it was taken into the Zurich Ballet's repertoire in 1981 under the leadership of former Balanchine dancer Patricia Neary.

By this time I had secured a permanent position working with the psychiatrist and no longer needed to seek out temporary employment. After streamlining office procedures and revamping his appointment schedule to more suitable hours, I also bargained for my own work hours, starting at 11 a.m. until 7 p.m. This enabled me to get my standing room tickets en route to the office, and at the end of the day, grab some dinner before attending the 8 p.m. evening performances. The doctor fully understood my "obsession" with seeing Randolf Neveroff and actually attended one of his performances. While he didn't understand the technical aspects, he was certainly impressed with Rudolf's charisma, passion for his art, and his ability to "inhabit" the character he portrayed.

I traveled to London in late March of 1980 to see Nureyev in *Sleeping Beauty*, followed by a brief trip "across the Channel" to see him in *Swan Lake* with the Paris Opera. I was only able to do this by explaining to my boss that the trip was booked prior to my starting full-time work. He eventually got used to my frequent departures, which caused careful planning on my part. The singular performance of *Sleeping Beauty* was well worth the trip. Rudolf danced magnificently and a friend, nearly in tears, remarked, "He never ceases to amaze me. Here he is 42 years old and dancing better than ever." The entire audience refused to leave the theatre. Despite a looming transit strike, making the homeward journey questionable, they preferred to reward the dancer who bestowed upon them such a rare offering.

The next month, Nureyev danced with Martha Graham's company, this time at the Metropolitan Opera House, in *Clytemnestra*, *Equitorial* and *Appalachian Spring*, before joining up with the Joffrey in another series of Diaghilev performances in Chicago.

His 1980 *Nureyev Festival* in London began with performances of *Romeo and Juliet*, which Rudolf danced with a bad cold. Two days later, the two o'clock curtain was held for thirty-five minutes and there was much conspicuous scurrying of feet back and forth behind the curtain. The audience became irate at the late start. The house manager finally appeared and announced that "Mr. Nureyev has injured his foot and this performance is cancelled." Fans ignored the many rude comments from the disgruntled public and dashed to the Stage Door to see Rudolf who apologetically disclosed, "I can't jump." Luigi seemed more upset than Rudolf, who was in full makeup and was ready to perform.

Management hastily had called Nicholas Johnson, who usually danced Mercutio but also performed Romeo - however, he wasn't able to cover for Nureyev in time. Everyone's ticket money had to be refunded. One frazzled Coliseum Box Office attendant who had no appreciation for Nureyev, fabricated a whopper and told the very unhappy customers, "He doesn't like doing matinees, you know. He probably just didn't feel like dancing. He does this sort of thing all the time." We knew very well that Rudolf wanted to perform and wouldn't cancel even if both feet were taped up, but the company had to wait for impresario Victor Hochhauser to make the final decision to cancel.

The fans waited around in a state of shock and saw Nicholas Johnson arriving at the theatre to "cover" for the evening performance. Suddenly Rudolf arrived at 6:00 for the 7:30 curtain. We asked Luigi what had happened, and he said, "It was all my fault. I was pulling his legwarmers off and some material caught his foot and twisted it, resulting in a pinched nerve. It doesn't bother him except to jump, so we'll see how he can manage."

At exactly 7:35, an announcement was made, "Mr. Nureyev sustained an injury to his foot this afternoon, causing the cancellation of the matinee. We had hoped that with sufficient rest he'd be able to dance this evening, but unfortunately this is not the case. At tonight's performance, the role of Romeo will be danced by Nicholas Johnson." It was to have been the debut of Evelyn DeSutter as Juliet, but Patricia Ruanne took over the role, because she and Johnson had rehearsed it together. Nureyev stayed in the theatre to watch and emerged later. Luigi continued to apologize to the fans for the two cancelled performances, but despite all the upheaval, Rudolf seemed in good spirits. At the Stage Door, he raised his pant leg to reveal his right foot, explaining, "It only hurts there, but if I can point my foot, I'll dance tomorrow."

The next evening, Nureyev arrived shortly after six o'clock with Luigi smiling and explaining, "90% sure he's dancing." With his leg heavily bandaged, Rudolf began his performance a bit tentatively. He substituted pas de chats for the bigger jumps, permitting him to land on his good foot. As he gained confidence, he dropped all hesitations and danced with real energy, even including the fiendish six double assembles in the balcony scene. He didn't change a single step of the choreography despite a badly swollen ankle.

The following day, June 14th, Evelyne DeSutter made her much-anticipated debut as Juliet to a sold-out house at the Coliseum. By this time the

London critics, with few exceptions, had given Nureyev poor reviews. One even went so far as to say that, if the dancer were egotistical enough to dance every performance, it was no wonder he got injured, completely overlooking the sold-out houses.

While Nureyev continued his nonstop schedule dancing in Europe, it gave American fans the opportunity to save up for his upcoming three-week *Friends* season on Broadway, where he did some of his best dancing in the Pierre LaCotte version of *La Sylphide* with the Boston Ballet. Just about every dancer around came to watch him. I vividly recall sitting in the same row as London Festival Ballet dancer Liliana Belfiore, who kept screaming in amazement at how well Nureyev danced. When someone near her nudged her to be quiet, she questioned, "Don't you SEE what he's doing?"

Directly after that engagement, Nureyev flew to Italy where he mounted his production of *Romeo and Juliet* for LaScala. He also began to form a real partnership with Yoko Morishita, who had danced *Don Quixote* with him during his 1980 *Nureyev Festival*. Rudolf privately told us one evening that "She could be my new Margot."

During some of those *Don Quixote* performances, Rudolf changed the first act one-arm lifts with his ballerina for an equally impressive fishdive. The reason? He had a temperature of 105 degrees and we could hear him coughing in the wings. Yet the nonsensical critics accused him of changing the choreography in his own production!

Following performances in Europe, Nureyev premiered Pierre La Cotte's restaging of a rare ballet called *Marco Spada*. Several of us eagerly flocked to Rome to see it and the work did not disappoint. The choreographer's wife, Ghislaine Thesmar, played the daughter of the bandit, Marco Spada, without realizing that her father was leading a double life. The ballet was filled with lively street dancing, pantomime, humor, tenderness, and pathos in the final scene when soldiers captured and killed the bandit. Being in Rome in March was indeed a tonic for those of us escaping the chilly New York winter. We did lots of sightseeing by day and enjoyed this new ballet by night.

Rudolf performed in Paris and Honolulu in between his Rome performances and then flew to New York for a Paul Taylor fund-raising gala. He performed "for the first time on stage together" with Mikhail Baryshnikov in a spoof of American history, *From Sea to Shining Sea*. The gala audience didn't appreciate this irreverent piece, but dance fans delighted in seeing the two famous dancers cavorting on the stage together.

Then he was back in Europe for more performances before beginning his 1981 *Nureyev Festival* in London. The week prior to my departure for London was a busy one. New York City Ballet held a *Tchaikovsky Festival* where Nureyev had wanted to present his *Manfred* production. I decided to go as often as I could and recorded the music with my pocket cassette recorder. I saved a program from each evening, purchased a souvenir *Tchaikovsky Festival* tote bag, and carried it loaded with the tapes and programs to London, presenting it to Nureyev at the Coliseum Stage Door. Rudolf was celebrating his 20th anniversary of dancing in the West and I wanted to give him something unique. He appreciated my rare gift.

Nureyev then opened at the Met in New York with LaScala Ballet in *Romeo and Juliet*, opposite Carla Fracci as Juliet and Margot Fonteyn as Lady Capulet. Before returning to Europe to finish out the year, Nureyev conquered a new territory of Puerto Rico and Caracas, by performing in *Giselle*.

In November, his revised production of *Manfred* was presented at the Zurich Opera House. Afraid it would never be seen in America, I did something unthinkable: I flew to Zurich for the weekend to see two performances. I informed my boss I might be a bit late for work on Monday as I was "going away for the weekend." He sighed and replied, "Just so long as you're not off to Europe again!" I brought my trusty cassette recorder and taped the performance to compare it with the tape from the original Paris premiere. Returning to New York, I was stopped at customs, not because of having a recorder in my overnight bag, but because I didn't have any other luggage. They scrutinized my passport and asked how someone whose occupation was listed as a secretary, could go to Switzerland for the weekend without luggage. I surmised they would have been less suspicious if I had carried ski equipment.

It had been years since Nureyev had danced with the Royal Ballet. In 1982, Nigel Gosling brokered a "ceasefire" with management that permitted Nureyev to make appearances at Covent Garden once again. Rudolf partnered Lesley Collier in *Giselle*, and coached a young Bryony Brind in his production of *La Bayadere*. Simultaneously, he tirelessly performed various "in between" engagements throughout Europe.

One of the few times Nureyev actually cancelled performances without being injured was in mid-tour when his "adopted father," Nigel Gosling, was dying of cancer. Rudolf flew back to London to spend a few days with him, before his dear friend and mentor died. On the opening night of his 1982 *Nureyev Festival* in London, he dedicated the entire season to Gosling. His passing happened so suddenly that some in the audience knew nothing about his death.

Manfred with the Zurich Ballet was showcased in Athens' Herod Atticus outdoor theatre, billed with Balanchine's *Agon,* which Nureyev had danced nearly a decade earlier. Friends said it was an unforgettable experience seeing this work in the outdoor amphitheatre under a full moon. Byron was much loved in Greece and the huge audience of thousands of people really appreciated the piece.

Meanwhile my parents had left Michigan and moved out West. I began bicoastal trips to visit them in between my full-time job while trying to keep up with Nureyev's performances. Nobody told me that the life of a ballet enthusiast would be easy!

During the Christmas break, I was able to visit London for several Royal Ballet performances, including the premiere of Nureyev's new production, *The Tempest*. Then a friend and I took the ferry to Paris and followed part of another *Friends* tour, stopping in Lille, Grenoble, Avignon, and celebrating the New Year's Eve in Cannes.

Another Broadway *Friends* season began on bitter cold days in January of 1983, when the Boston Ballet joined Nureyev in his production of *Don Quixote*. Nureyev alternated with three different ballerinas, but caught a cold during the run. By the end of the second week, he was audibly coughing, though usually only upstage. After the third act solo, dancers surrounded Nureyev while he walked upstage in a coughing fit, affectionately patting his back to "cover" it. When he recovered, he smoothly sailed into the dancing finale.

The same hacking cough persisted at a Saturday doubleheader. By the evening performance, a rather unappreciative audience seemed to finally wake up at the moment Nureyev did two beautifully secure one-arm lifts with Laura Young. The man next to me gasped and yelped "Jeee-sus!" One audience member became so enthusiastic, that he stood up each time Rudolf finished a solo. After a brief rally, Rudolf's cold unfortunately got worse. We were told he had a temperature of 101, but nevertheless got out of bed to dance with Marie-Christine Mouis. He coughed his way through the entire performance.

In May 1983, Rudolf brought his revised production of *Manfred* with the Zurich Ballet to Washington and Chicago. He arrived limping. During the evening performance it became obvious that he could not sustain any of his turns. His shoes squeaked as if they had too much rosin on them and at one point he just stopped and yelled, "Bastards!" as if cursing his own feet. Yet somehow, after nearly forty-five minutes of nonstop dancing, he got his second wind by the final movement and valiantly finished the ballet. By the next afternoon, he looked like he had spent a week at the beach and gave a stellar performance that merited applause from his first entrance. He turned his pirouettes so well, that at one point he effortlessly executed eight multiple turns, slowing them down ever so gradually, causing the audience to audibly gasp. When Rudolf was "hurting," the company performed less well. When he was really "on," the entire company was inspired, and this transferred to the audience, often resulting in a standing ovation.

The Boston Ballet joined Nureyev for a 1983 European tour. That same year, the Ballet Theatre Francais de Nancy joined *The Nureyev Festival* with the Diaghilev program. One evening, Nureyev arrived extra early to perform in three of the four pieces on the program. Just before the 7:30 p.m. curtain, someone appeared on the Coliseum stage and read a prepared statement: "Ladies and gentlemen, Rudolf Nureyev has sustained an injury to his knee during the course of the evening and will be unable to dance in *Spectre*. However, he will dance in *Faune* and *Petrushka*." While waiting after the performance at the Stage Door, we learned that a doctor had been summoned. Apparently by trying to favor his "good leg," Rudolf injured it just before curtain time. One fan asked about the injury and Rudolf shot back, "This leg is finished forever!" Despite that remark, he danced *Spectre* the very next evening, omitting none of the choreography. His ankle was heavily bandaged into a literal "sandwich" because his bone spur was acting up. He related to Maude Gosling, that he had "A bone sticking out in my ankle." She told him to see a doctor and he replied, "He'd only tell me to stay off my feet for two weeks and I can't, can I?" These long seasons relied on his name to sell tickets during the high tourist season and he wanted to attract new audiences.

Nureyev exited the theatre limping and graciously signed autographs while seated in his car. He had already injured a knee earlier in the week. At the following performance, he wisely omitted all big overhead partnering lifts, so his heavily bandaged knee wouldn't buckle. He actually left the theatre wearing tennis shoes instead of his usual boots or clogs. At the final performance, he was again limping at the Stage Door, when he noticed one of his fans using a cane. Another fan had one foot wrapped up following a foot operation. "Everyone's wobbling!" Rudolf joked.

New Yorkers eagerly awaited his return to the Met immediately following his month-long London season, because Nureyev would be seen in a new role with Natalia Makarova in Roland Petit's *Hunchback of Notre Dame*. The role was not a demanding one, but because he was injured, he wasn't seen to his best advantage.

Then came another run of *Don Quixote* performances in Boston's enormous Wang Center. The ads announced that Rudolf Nureyev would dance all performances. On opening night, August 10, 1983, the curtain rose on the first act when shortly thereafter Nureyev winced and went offstage, where icepacks were applied. A fast-acting young dancer completed Rudolf's solo. Even though Nureyev was obviously injured, he returned to the stage and finished the performance. Concerned fans at the Stage Door asked how he was. "My leg feels funny," was all he said. He had torn a calf muscle and doctors ordered him to rest. The next day headlines from Boston to New York blared, "The $80,000 Calf Muscle." With Nureyev unable to dance as advertised, the Boston Ballet was forced to cancel the entire engagement. Shortly afterwards, I received a letter from the company asking if I wanted a refund, would donate my tickets, or keep them as a souvenir since "Nureyev never cancels." It was basically an appeal for contributions to help offset the deficit caused by the cancelled season.

Rudolf flew back to New York and was seen shortly afterwards on a small exercise bike, riding a few blocks from his Dakota apartment to the Ballet Shop on Broadway, near Lincoln Center. At that time, the shop had employed a new security officer, a large imposing man who prevented Rudolf from entering the shop with his bicycle. One of the co-owners of the shop came running out when he saw the guard trying to stop Rudolf's entry, explaining that it was okay to allow Rudolf Nureyev inside. This was a reminder of his appearance on *The Muppets Show*, when they were anticipating Rudolf's arrival. When he entered the scene dressed in jacket, hat and boots, Eagle tried to toss him out, saying, "Who do these punk kids think they are?" to which Kermit replied, "That one thinks he's Rudolf Nureyev!" Once inside the Ballet Shop, Rudolf raised his leg to show his injury and said, "I could dance in two or three days. Why did they cancel the whole season?"

In the fall of 1983, Nureyev was named Director of the Paris Opera Ballet. His contract stipulated that he be allowed to continue dancing and choreographing. The Cultural Minister, Jack Lang, felt that after the rather "revolving door" of Artistic Directors that followed the reign of Serge Lifar, Nureyev would once again restore the company to world status. Without further New York engagements – by this time the Met was no longer sponsoring dance – Rudolf felt he could be based in Paris while continuing to tour.

Nureyev wasted no time. After fulfilling commitments in London and Vienna, he mounted his own production of the full-length *Raymonda* at the Paris Opera, partnering Noella Pontois in the title role. Despite the ballet's problematic scenario in previous versions for the Zurich Ballet and ABT, this version, according to the press, "galvanized" the Paris Opera.

Nureyev then danced in his production of *Don Quixote* with the Parisians before heading off to dance with the Ballet de Nancy. In January of 1984, he arranged for Martha Graham's company to perform on the huge stage of the Paris Opera's Palais Garnier. Graham had recently lost government funding and Rudolf thought it only fair to present her company in Paris. He danced in *Phaedra's Dream*, ensuring Box Office success for Graham. Next, he flew to New York to dance the same role at another fund-raising gala on March 13th, and then returned to Paris the very next day to perform.

Because Nureyev wanted his top dancers to be seen outside of France, he arranged for "exchange artists." At that time, Anthony Dowell was directing the Royal Ballet so Rudolf sent two of his ballerinas, Elisabeth Platel and Monique Loudieres, to perform at Covent Garden. He felt they would gain valuable experience performing to new audiences and on different stages. The London stage is "flat" whereas the huge stage in Paris is slanted or "raked." This makes it easier for the audience to see the full stage, including the performers upstage. Dancers often have difficult adjusting to the raked stage, especially if they must jump "going uphill."

When Nureyev performed at the Graham gala in New York, he informed us not to miss "a little gem" of a new ballet he would be performing in Paris. *Harlequinade* happened to coincide with Nureyev's birthday and we certainly wanted to be there. He also staged his production of *The Tempest* for the Paris dancers and brought LaCotte's *Marco Spada* into the repertory. In addition, he learned another new work, this time a solo, entitled *Bach Suite*, choreographed by Francine Lancelot. Nureyev was eager to learn all forms of dance; this particular piece showed the development of court dancing all the way through to modern dance, educating audiences in the process.

Nureyev continued to do double duty as both the Director and dancer while in Paris. When one of his star dancers, Charles Jude, was unable to guest-perform in London, Rudolf filled in for him.

During one of his *Bach Suite* performances in Europe, Rudolf unexpectedly injured his metatarsal. This occurred just a week before the San Antonio engagement, and Texas media immediately speculated whether Rudolf Nureyev would perform at the Festival. We scoffed at the press and flew to Texas anyway. A woman sitting next to me on opening night asked anxiously, "Will he dance?" I replied, "We saw him, he's here, he will dance." Nothing in *La Sylphide* was omitted and Mr. Neveroff performed every step, giving no indication of an injury. Afterward the woman in her Texas drawl commented, "Honey, if he dances like that when he's hurtin,' I'd like to see him when he's whole!" Later, Rudolf grumbled to us at the Stage Door, "I can't dance in buckled shoes!" since those he wore in *Bach Suite* had caused his injury.

August 1984 found Rudolf without work, so he gave up his vacation when the opportunity arose to dance once again on Broadway in a *Friends* program. The New York temperatures were brutal and kept audiences away from sold-out performances. Yet the heat brought forth some of Rudolf's best dancing. Some of the matinees were sparsely attended as people headed to the beaches. This allowed the fans to have front-row seats at the former Uris theatre, renamed the Gershwin. Rudolf appeared to be dancing just for the sheer joy of it. Some performances of *Flower Festival*, *Wayfarer* or *Moor's Pavane* left his fans absolutely dazed by their beauty and intensity.

I planned to attend the Edinburgh Festival the very next day, so life was hectic. I had to train a replacement before I left, since my boss was beginning to tire of my absences. The trip to Scotland was well worthwhile, because Nureyev danced *Bach Suite, Le Bourgeois Gentilhomme,* and *Harlequinade* with the Paris Opera.

He staged his production of *Sleeping Beauty* for Vienna and then toured with it throughout Japan. By the end of October, his production of *Romeo and Juliet* was staged for the Paris Opera, although, at age 46, Nureyev danced the role of Mercutio rather than Romeo.

I returned to Paris for the Christmas holidays to reunite with friends and see Nureyev's new production of *Swan Lake*, where he alternated in the roles of the Prince and the antagonist Rothbart. After one performance, he came on stage to proudly announce the promotion of young Sylvie Guillem to the rank of Etoile – Star dancer.

Nureyev continued to direct and choreograph at the Paris Opera and wanted to showcase his company in America, but the dancers threatened to strike if he danced with the company on tour, preferring to rely on their own merits than on Nureyev's name.

In June 1985, he created a new ballet, *Washington Square,* based on the Henry James novel. The dates coincided with a trip I'd planned to see my young friend Katherine Healy. She was set to dance the lead in Frederick Ashton's production of *Romeo and Juliet* with London Festival Ballet, recently renamed English National Ballet. She was fortunate enough to work with Ashton on the role despite being only 16 years old. Ashton beamed in approval as the audience cheered on opening night.

From London I took a day trip to Paris to see one performance of *Washington Square*. I thought it was extremely inventive. The French public, however, did not appreciate the Charles Ives score with its cacophony of different musical styles. Rudolf had wanted to create a work for the entire company. If the ballet had been pared down to its dramatic essence with fewer dancers, it would have been more successful.

Then it was back to London for his *Nureyev Festival,* dancing *Swan Lake* and *Giselle* with Yoko Morishita. Rudolf was recovering from another bout of pneumonia and switched the program order around to begin with *Swan Lake* because, as he confided to the fans, "It's easier." After eleven consecutive performances, he then performed two weeks of *Giselle*, which required more stamina and emotional involvement.

In November of 1985, Nureyev debuted in *La Dansomanie* by Swedish choreographer Ivor Cramer in Paris. Unfortunately I was unable to see it, but those who did, said it was delightful. I did manage to get to Paris over the Christmas holidays to view his production of *Nutcracker*. Rudolf was gradually putting most of his productions into the Paris Opera repertory.

By 1986, I was busy flying from New York to Nevada to spend time with my father, who was diagnosed with cancer. While Rudolf continued to dance around the world, I was busy talking to doctors about my father's condition.

Nureyev partnered Marianna Tcherkassky in *Giselle* at American Ballet Theatre in New York. On July 8th, his wish to showcase Paris Opera was finally realized when, at a joint gala with ABT, he presented a suite of dances from *Raymonda*. The audience was especially impressed with Manuel Legris and Sylvie Guillem in one of the pas de deux. Clive Barnes wrote his review as if keeping score, giving the Paris Opera higher points than ABT.

Returning from my father's funeral on July 9th, I headed straight to the Met, which provided just the tonic I needed. Nureyev introduced the Met audiences to *Quelques Pas Graves de Baptiste*, a Baroque ballet by Francoise Lancelot, on the program with *Raymonda Act Three*. On July 11th, Rudolf set a most unusual precedent. Rather than announcing it in Paris, he came on stage to promote Manuel Legris to the rank of Etoile – Star dancer. His *Washington Square* ballet also debuted at the Met, in which he danced only a single performance. Nureyev then took his company to the Kennedy Center in Washington for performances of *Swan Lake,* where he alternated in the roles of the Prince and the adversary Rothbart, as he had done in Paris.

Before embarking on a summer *Friends* tour with a group of his French dancers, he appeared in *Coppelia* with London Festival Ballet. He relished returning to this company. With their love of nicknames, they fondly called him "Randolfski."

In the autumn of 1986, the tireless dancer premiered his Hollywood version of *Cinderella* in Paris, which garnered favorable reviews. The French love novelty and cheered the production. Rudolf merely remarked, "I gave them what they wanted."

In 1987, Nureyev introduced some of his French protégées to wider audiences, dancing *Swan Lake* with Fabienne Cerruti in England, *Don Quixote* with Sylvie Guillem at LaScala in Milan, and taking his *Friends* group on tour throughout Europe, America, and Israel before showcasing his *Cinderella* at the Met that summer.

Numerous other *Friends* tours with his Paris dancers had him flying from Philadelphia to Panama, Hanover and Tel Aviv. When Mikhail Baryshnikov had a knee surgery and had to cancel his own *Friends* season, Nureyev immediately came to the rescue, performing with ABT dancers Susan Jaffe, Kevin McKenzie, and Amanda McKerrow.

In January of 1988, I made yet another trip to London to see Royal Ballet performances where Nureyev danced with his protégé, Sylvie Guillem, in *Giselle*. She amusingly remarked to the press, "It was like dancing with my teacher."

In June that year, he achieved one of his dreams by dancing with the New York City Ballet. Although Balanchine had died in 1983, director Peter Martins invited Nureyev to dance *Orpheus* with Merrill Ashley. The role didn't require much dancing, but Nureyev brought his usual dramatic strength to the performance.

Nureyev's frequent *Friends* tours became the "norm" throughout the rest of 1988 and '89 as eventually offers to perform dwindled. The dance world was changing rapidly and the "crossover" between classical and modern dance began to breed newer works and choreographers. Fans traveled whenever possible if the *Friends* performances were nearby, taking weekend jaunts rather than trans-Atlantic trips. It became obvious that Nureyev was slowing down and fighting to keep performing.

His 1989 *Friends* program with his Paris Opera dancers in Hartford, Connecticut was advertised as "See This Living Legend," and the 2,000-seat Bushnell Auditorium was effectively sold out. I overheard someone in the audience say, "I didn't know what to expect." Her friend responded, "I don't care, I wanted to see a STAR and we know how rare they are these days." Another remarked, "The man is 50 now, but Nureyev's a more evocative dancer. What he's doing is far more interesting than these younger boys." An elderly man agreed: "I've never seen a ballet, but to my untrained eye, Nureyev's a genius."-

In early 1989, Sylvie Guillem "defected" from the Paris Opera to the Royal Ballet in London, where she felt she had more freedom to control her performance schedule and make guest appearances. That was the first of many crushing blows for Nureyev. Due to frequent dancers' strikes, new management, and continuous contract negotiations, Nureyev finally resigned as Director of the Paris Opera in November. He stated to the press, "I think I have done good work in Paris ... Maybe it's time to leave. One cannot just sit in that office and wrestle with one-hundred and fifty egos."

When choreographer Flemming Flindt told Rudolf he should dance roles more "appropriate" for his age, he promptly replied, "Then why don't you create something for me?" The result was *The Overcoat,* based on Gogol's novel and staged for the Cleveland Ballet. Eager to see him in a new role, several fans flew to Ohio after the work premiered in Florence and an engagement at the Edinburgh Festival. In one scene, Nureyev, as Akakievich, danced a waltz with the white overcoat he dreamed of. It was a haunting image, as if he were dancing with a ghost. In another scene, Rudolf had to leap over a bed and again accidentally clipped his foot on the edge. He could barely walk down the few steps of the Stage Door to a car, but never cancelled any future performances.

Unwilling to stop working, he signed on to perform the lead in *The King and I* which premiered in Syracuse, New York on August 18, 1989. The show continued to tour throughout the States and Canada until mid-February of 1990. I managed to see two performances in Wilmington, Delaware and in Hartford, Connecticut. Even though his singing voice and vocal delivery left much to be desired, his mesmerizing stage persona won over audiences.

One of Nureyev's most unfortunate injuries occurred during his historic return to dance with the Kirov Ballet in November of 1989. Director Oleg Vinogradov invited his former colleague to dance two performances of *La Sylphide* for the occasion. Nureyev, then 51 years of age, was eager to return to Russia and perform once more on the stage of the Mariinsky Theatre. A television crew accompanied Nureyev and his entourage to St. Petersburg. Many of Nureyev's Russian fans eagerly greeted him at the airport. It had been twenty-eight years since they last saw him. It was a deeply emotional reunion for everyone.

During his time in Russia, Rudolf visited the old classroom where he took class as a student. He signed the guest book, "To my beloved school. I wish it many more years." In the school's museum, he had his photo taken in front of a portrait of his former teacher, Alexander Pushkin. In addition, he was reunited with one of his first partners at the Kirov, Natalia Dudinskaya. When he saw that the museum contained a section on Natalia Makarova, Mikhail Baryshnikov, and himself, he was profoundly overcome with emotion, saying later that it felt "very intense." For years, photos of the three dancers who had defected had been banned from the Kirov and erased from the history books, as if they had never existed.

Nureyev arrived in Russia with a bad foot, caused by a previous injury. To make matters worse, midway through the dress rehearsal on November 16, he injured the calf muscle of his other leg. He wasn't going to let that stop him, especially since the anticipation over his return was so extraordinary. When the curtain rose the following evening showing Nureyev "asleep" in a chair, the welcoming applause lasted so long, that the conductor put down his baton. The "sleeping" Nureyev, eyes still closed, smiled broadly. He was clearly overjoyed. The Sylphide, danced by Zhanna Ayupova – a Tartar like me — Rudolf remarked, waited patiently until the ballet could begin.

With both legs heavily bandaged, the 51-year-old Nureyev had considerable difficulty with the intricate choreography. Those expecting to see the dancer they remembered at age 23 were disappointed. Yet there was such depth of character and electricity to his presence that the applause at his curtain calls lasted well over half an hour. Seven ladies presented bouquets as well as floral baskets. Rudolf tossed a bouquet to his 101-year-old former teacher from Ufa, Anna Udeltsova, who sat in the front row and watched him perform for the first time. The reviews were generally mixed, all agreeing that Rudolf was struggling through the intricate choreography, but gave a most vivid interpretation.

On his day off, Nureyev attended a performance of *La Bayadere* by the Kirov. He also asked to make copies of the costume and set designs used at the time of Anna Pavlova, as research for his own future production at the Paris Opera Ballet. Despite his injuries, he also toured the Hermitage Museum, constantly accompanied by the television crew. He instinctively knew, he had to make the most of every minute.

This determination continued through his final illness. In 1985, rumors that Nureyev had AIDS began to circulate. We were devastated, of course, but the fact that he continued to dance for so many more years helped us doubt the facts. A fan once confronted him, by remarking how thin he was. "So I'm thin!" he shot back defensively.

The extraordinary fact was, how Rudolf Nureyev just kept going. While it's true that some of his later performances didn't live up to his own highly demanding standard, he still brought something of tremendous value to the stage.

In what was billed as his "Farewell Tour" in 1991 – his promoter's idea and certainly not Rudolf's – he played smaller cities in less than satisfactory venues, accompanied by pre-recorded music. During the British portion of the tour, some people bluntly demanded their money back, because he no longer performed his famous jumps or leaps. Had they known he was dying, would they have been so carelessly critical? He needed to dance. It kept him going.

As early as the mid-60s, reporters and critics crassly asked Nureyev, "When will you stop dancing?" It seems that whenever artists are successful for so long, oblivious people want to tear them down. Over the years Rudolf gave many responses to these questions. In 1979 when asked how much longer he would continue, he confidently replied, "As long as my legs hold me." "And then?" the interviewer persisted. "Then I do wheelchair ballets."

People once told Margot Fonteyn to stop dancing, because she was spoiling their memories of her earlier dancing days. She merely replied, "It's too late to stop. I've already spoiled their memories." Rudolf felt likewise. As one of his more astute fans pointed out, "Nureyev expresses love through his performances. He feels fulfilled in receiving love, both from fellow dancers and his audience. When he doesn't get it, he becomes frustrated. Sometimes the only way a person that possessed can cope is to overcome the passion. But how? It's a heavy price to pay."

Toward the end of his life, when his physique began to change and he fought to maintain his technique, we became concerned. But Nureyev needed to be on stage. When he could no longer perform as a dancer, he took up the conductor's baton. Music seemed to flow from him to the musicians and back again.

Only when we saw photos of his frail curtain call appearance at the October 8, 1992 premiere in Paris of his *La Bayadere* production did we realize that Rudolf was, in fact, leaving us. How could this be? This was Randolf Neveroff. Even when he was gravely ill, he needed to be on stage.

When the Parisian audience saw the fragile Nureyev, supported between two dancers in order to acknowledge their applause, they immediately rose in a final farewell send-off. Following the *Bayadere* performance, Nureyev was presented with the Legion of Honor in a ceremony on stage, surrounded by his dancers. Too ill to stand, he sat in the Sultan's throne chair used during the performance. Haunting photos, which appeared in the world press, showed a grateful Nureyev and his concerned dancers applauding him, trying not to show their true emotions. Less than three months later, Rudolf Nureyev died at the age of 54.

Even when hospitalized, he was working on a new ballet. Dance was his life, and Nureyev saw his illness as just another obstacle to deal with, like an injury. It was truly a case of "mind over matter." He just "thought about something else" and kept on going. "Just keep pedaling," he often said, "Otherwise you fall off the bicycle."

"Dancing is my medicine."
~Rudolf Nureyev, Vienna Kurier, January, 1979~

DOCTOR NUREYEV

*Bach Suite, Pennsylvania Ballet Gala, Philadelphia, PA,
June 6, 1984. Photo: Susanne Richelle Whitehead*

In a 1981 television interview, Nureyev compared himself to a transmitter while the audience was the receiver. It was truly amazing how he "energized" his public. Even though his "marathon" seasons proved challenging, somehow the fans managed. Some completed their homework while waiting in long standing-room lines for tickets. Those who were working, either dashed to buy tickets on lunch hours or had a "doctor's appointment" scheduled for 10 a.m. when the Box Office opened. We grabbed meals in between matinee and evening performances or else gathered for late-night dinners after an evening performance. Laundry and food shopping was relegated to nonperformance days.

One organized fan stated that she switched into "military mode" to prepare for long seasons. She prepared meals a week in advance as well as did all her laundry. No matter how difficult, we dutifully reported for work or school each morning. Just knowing we had another performance to look forward to reinvigorated us, because stamina was important. We fed off Nureyev's limitless energy.

A letter from a friend in London in the mid-seventies summed up how we all felt: "The old adrenalin has finally returned. The first week of the season was murder; everyone felt like zombies. But 'Dr. Nureyev' cured all that with his performances, and we're going back for more tonic tonight."

Occasionally, a cold or flu would inconvenience us. My philosophy was that if Nureyev performed under these or worse circumstances, I could certainly tolerate an illness or discomfort in order to watch him. The concentrated focus of the performance helped us to forget our maladies.

I vividly remember one New York performance during the 1979 season with the Joffrey Ballet in which Rudolf performed three different ballets. I had dashed from my office job directly to the theatre and breathlessly settled into my balcony seat. Suddenly in the middle of *Spectre de la Rose*, I began to feel quite nauseous; I suspected food poisoning from a hurried late lunch. It took every bit of willpower to remain focused on Nureyev's performance and not my gurgling stomach.

As soon as the curtain calls finished, I ran to the Ladies' Room. Naturally, there was an enormous line and I knew I would be in big trouble if I waited much longer. I made my way through the crowded lobby into the night air to recover. Once back inside, I had a few sips of water, returned to my seat, and enjoyed the rest of the performance as if nothing at all had happened. "Doctor Nureyev" worked his magic.

On another occasion, I arrived at the theatre with a beastly headache after a stressful day at the office. "I don't know how I can enjoy the performance," I complained to a sympathetic friend. Yet following *Marguerite and Armand* with Fonteyn and Nureyev, my friend asked, "How's your headache?" "What headache?" I replied, having forgotten all about it.

During one of Nureyev's Broadway seasons, a friend required surgery and consequently missed a number of performances. One of the fans told Nureyev why she was absent and suggested he write her a Get Well card. Since Rudolf seldom wrote anything other than his autograph, that seemed highly unlikely. Imagine her surprise when she received a personal note encouraging her to heal faster, so she could watch more performances.

Another friend made one of the most remarkable recoveries. Inspired by Nureyev, she began studying ballet as a mature adult. During one class, when landing from a jump, she ripped her Achilles tendon. Doctors told her that she might not dance again. A short time after her injury, Nureyev was performing *Don Quixote* in Boston, where he would be celebrating his 44th birthday. She was determined to be there.

While she was recuperating after surgery, she placed her injured foot on a pillow in front of her TV set, while watching Nureyev videos. She was certain that the energy he transmitted from his performances, even on videotape, helped speed her rehabilitation process. In fact, her doctors said they never saw such a fast recovery.

A large group of New Yorkers traveled by bus to Boston on March 17th for Nureyev's birthday. There, waiting at the Stage Door, was my injured ballet dancer friend, using crutches but nevertheless on her feet, determined to see Rudolf. I'm sure the warm greeting she got from "Doctor Nureyev" also helped her healing.

During long breaks in his schedule when Nureyev was performing in Europe before returning to New York, we consoled ourselves by watching him on the big screen. His *Don Quixote* film was released at a gala opening in a London cinema, attended by Princess Margaret and many of his fans. The film played for several weeks and we saw repeated viewings of it. It was amazing how elated we all felt just by watching him on film.

When videotapes were released and most of my friends bought the latest releases, I made a conscious decision not to buy them. I wanted to remember each "live" performance as long as possible. My philosophy was that money spent on videos meant less money for tickets and travel. Those who had video tape players would frequently have viewing parties. We commented that, even on tape, Nureyev energized us.

In Rudolf's later years, I succumbed and made up for lost time by purchasing as many dance videos as possible. I realized that recorded dance could never capture the feeling and atmosphere of a live performance, but it was better than nothing. Even now when I watch them, it's like discovering Nureyev all over again and the old "magic" returns. We used to joke and wished we could bottle that feeling and share it with the world.

Nureyev's effect on the public was truly amazing. I recall one matinee performance when a mother brought her baby in a carriage to the Stage Door. The baby was fussing, but the minute Nureyev emerged, it stopped crying and smiled. Rudolf could calm or invigorate any crowd just by his mere presence.

When Nureyev had pneumonia in 1976 and was forced to cancel several performances, he returned with a marathon season in London, literally dancing his way back to health. At the Stage Door one evening, I overheard someone say, "He's truly a phenomenon. You name any other dancer who would bounce back from pneumonia and dance a seven-week nightly season."

Former New York City Ballet dancer Patricia Neary, who later directed the Zurich Ballet, remarked to us one evening that, "the man is a miracle" the way he galvanized the Zurich company. Rudolf spent time coaching, rehearsing, and performing with the dancers, all the while continuing his marathon *Nureyev Festival*.

In 1984, several of us planned to be in Paris to see Nureyev in many new roles, with the added bonus of a performance on his birthday. Just prior to leaving for Paris, I came down with a nasty bout of flu. For several days I couldn't keep any food in my stomach and I didn't like the thought of making a transatlantic flight in that condition. But since I had a nonrefundable ticket and didn't want to miss out, I boarded the plane, drinking ginger ale all the way across the Atlantic.

Following the performance on the night of Rudolf's birthday, he paused at the Stage Door to greet each of us and even invited us to his Paris apartment to help him celebrate. I describe this very special and memorable occasion in greater detail in the chapter *23 Quai Voltaire*. At that time, I was a bit hesitant about accepting champagne and an apple tart, but strangely enough, my flu symptoms completely disappeared. It wasn't every day that we could visit "Doctor Nureyev" at his home.

One of Nureyev's many awards was an Honorary Doctorate from the Philadelphia College of Fine Arts. He had performed in New York at the Metropolitan Opera House and traveled to Philadelphia on his night off, to attend the award ceremony on April 27, 1980. Afterward, there was a huge sit-down dinner and a brief recital by dancers from the Pennsylvania Ballet. When Nureyev was officially given his cap and gown, photographers duly commemorated the scene as he fiddled with the tassel on his cap, unsure of which side to place it. Rudolf made a very brief and remarkable speech in which he stated, "I like to doctor dancers." After kindly thanking everyone, he invited the crowd to the party with closing remarks, "May you be drenched in dance."

A fan-turned-photographer was able to capture some of that night's festivities and subtly took photos while Nureyev was dining and conversing with his hosts. At an appropriate break, she approached and thanked him, "I'm so glad you finally came to Philadelphia." Rudolf laughed and acknowledged her. He had recognized her from her regular presence at Stage Doors where she would usually ask, "When are you coming to Philadelphia?"

The next day Nureyev performed in New York. We decided to make a small banner that read, "Bravo, Doctor Nureyev." That night he left the Met with Jacqueline Kennedy Onassis and others, and didn't stop at the Stage Door to sign autographs. I quickly unfurled the banner and as he passed to get into the limousine, he noticed it and smiled. Before getting in to the limo, he recognized his Philadelphia fan. She eagerly asked, "Did we take good care of you in Philadelphia?" Rudolf replied, "Yes, I'd say so!"

Shortly after that, he returned to London for his annual *Nureyev Festival*. One of the fans there decided to play along with the "Doctor" theme, so her opening night sign read, "What's Up, Doc?"

Much of our free time was spent planning for future seasons. It wasn't easy figuring out travel plans or finances to pay for escalating ticket prices. Traveling was tiring, particularly via overnight bus or train to save money on hotels. Sleeping on crowded or bumpy plane rides was also a challenge. The end result, however, was always worth it.

Whenever I traveled to see Rudolf, I usually had so much work to complete before departing, that I was exhausted. Work stress combined with lack of sleep sometimes resulted in a cold or flu. There were several occasions when I began my trip feeling lousy, but once I had seen Nureyev perform, the cold or flu disappeared. On one trip abroad, my symptoms disappeared already while halfway across the Atlantic, in sheer anticipation of seeing "Doctor Nureyev."

One of my most frustrating trips occurred when I had flown to London for a couple of performances, before taking the ferry to Calais and then a train to Paris. The English Channel was very rough and the boat was delayed. I arrived at the theatre with luggage in tow, for a performance of *Sleeping Beauty* that was already half over. The Box Office was closed and I had no way of collecting the ticket that I had booked. Pleading with an usher, I was finally allowed in. Since the Prince doesn't appear until after the intermission, I arrived just in time for Nureyev's entrance. "Doctor Nureyev" revived me, as usual.

Another nightmarish trip made that one seem easy. After having seen Nureyev perform in Paris one weekend in February, I took the Hovercraft across the Channel back to England. Halfway through the extremely rough journey, all the engines failed. We bobbed up and down in the choppy water for hours, until the Coast Guard finally rescued us. Everyone around me was seasick. I steeled myself by reading a book and tried following Rudolf's frequent advice to "think of something else."

Naturally, due to this three-hour delay, I missed my connecting train back to London. Once on British soil, a bus was provided for the now seriously queasy passengers. Unbelievably, the bus broke down about thirty minutes from Dover. Instead of letting the passengers wait in the coach until another could be provided, they made us wait by the roadside. By this time it was dark and had begun to snow. Along with everyone else, I was cold, tired, and still trying to recover my equilibrium from the boat trip. Another bus eventually came, but it was unheated and bitterly cold.

By the time I returned to my friend's house in London, she had gone to bed and left me a note, "Sorry, but there's no heat or hot water. The boiler broke." Thankfully, the gas stove worked, so I fixed myself a cup of tea and prepared a hot water bottle to warm the bed. I eagerly crawled under the covers, only to discover that the hot water bottle had leaked and soaked all the bedding. By this point, all I could do was laugh.

Unable to sleep, I ended up packing my suitcase for my return flight back to New York the next morning, wondering what more could go wrong. Luckily, the plane departed on time and was well heated, so I slept all the way across the Atlantic.

Some time after that, I was back in London for Christmas. I was staying in a friend's flat while she spent the holidays with family. I rang Nigel Gosling, who lived nearby, to inquire about some of my photos he had borrowed for his book on Fonteyn and Nureyev. He kindly invited me to his home for a Christmas drink. He and his wife, Maude, were most gracious hosts and we talked for hours about dance. Nigel related that he sat Rudolf down to look at the photos the dancer himself had previously selected and kept him up until two in the morning until he got his final approval. They finally finished when Rudolf asked, "Can I go to bed now?"

When I related the tale of my disastrous Hovercraft trip culminating with the broken boiler once back in London, Gosling laughed and observed, "You certainly pay for your pleasures!"

Looking back, as fans and ballet enthusiasts, we frequently asked ourselves, "How did we do it?" If we made sacrifices to see Nureyev perform, it was nothing compared to what he gave us in return, with his brilliant presence and utter commitment to his art. Nureyev inspired us with his motto that he frequently shared, "Nothing happens unless you make it happen." He energized us all and helped us overcome whatever ailed us. Besides, if he could dance through sickness and injury, the least we could do was watch.

*"Traveling and working is more interesting than spending time at home.
You think I should sit at home darning socks?"*
~Rudolf Nureyev, London Evening Standard, April 19, 1991~

ON THE ROAD

*Nureyev outside The Ballet Shop, NYC,
August, 1983. Photo: William J. Reilly*

Nureyev's performance schedule grew more hectic with each passing year. He commented that he wanted to dance as much as he could "while the going is good." That often meant finishing one performance and jumping on a plane to dance somewhere else that same night. Once he danced a matinee and evening performance in two different Italian cities. When directing the Paris Opera, he even appeared in one ballet at the beginning of the evening at the Opera House, then raced to perform in another ballet at a different theatre that same evening. He did this also in London, dancing in the evening at Covent Garden and racing across town to perform in a midnight charity gala.

We used to joke that the Concorde was invented and kept in business by Rudolf Nureyev. He crossed the Atlantic whenever possible on this supersonic jet, thus reducing the agonizing hours of flying, which he detested. He affectionately referred to the plane as "Concordski." "She goes up like a bird," he once told us, gesturing with his hand in a steep, upward motion.

I often wished I could have taken the Concorde, but it was too expensive. Thankfully, in those days the flights were very affordable. I was practically a frequent flyer with Laker or People Express, since both airlines offered cheap flights without advance bookings. I showed up at the airport and if the flight wasn't sold out, I got on the plane that very day. If not, I queued the following day. When living in London in the early 70s, I regularly took advantage of cheap airfares to Europe, most frequently to catch Rudolf performing with the Paris Opera.

The trips were tiring, because it meant returning either overnight Sunday by boat or taking the first flight out on Monday morning in order to report to work on time. I vividly recall one such trip where I was chatting with another fan on the plane, while waiting for the rest of the passengers to board our very early Monday flight back to London. Just as I was in midsentence, sleep overtook me and only when we reached cruising altitude did I wake up to my friend's remark, "You were really tired, weren't you?" Luckily I never had sleep problems and could take quick catnaps, but NEVER during a performance!

After a series of performances at Washington's Kennedy Center, Nureyev was on such a tight schedule to catch his 9 p.m. flight to London, that he was supposed to be picked up by helicopter to get to the airport. He had performed *La Bayadere* and was told that for various reasons the helicopter could not be used, but instead he was provided with a police escort in order to catch the last flight back. Consequently, the program order was reversed, omitting the overture and a small section of the three Shades.

He took the briefest of curtain calls and still in full costume and make-up, bolted for the waiting car. Luigi was sent on ahead to process Rudolf through customs. With so little time to get there, Rudolf pulled his boots over his tights and removed his feathered turban in the back of the speeding limo. The plane was held for him when he arrived just moments before departure.

Once on board, the flight attendant was busy relocating people, because in all the rush they neglected to reserve a seat for Nureyev.

Nureyev was scheduled to appear in Jerome Robbins' *Dances at a Gathering* at Covent Garden, but the filming of *Valentino* ran over the expected shooting time. He had been on the *Valentino* set since 5 a.m. and consequently arrived at the Opera House in full film make-up and slicked-back hair because there was "no time to change" until he arrived at the theatre. When one fan asked why he couldn't continue dancing at night and filming the next day, Rudolf replied, "I can't very well do both at once, can I?" But on this rare occasion, he did just that.

Another admirer asked where he was going to perform next. "To America," was his reply. "Are you flying?" the person asked innocently. "Well, I'm not rowing across!" he retorted.

Following a closing matinee in New York, Rudolf dashed out of the Stage Door after a couple of curtain calls and raced to catch a 7 p.m. flight to Milan – the performance had only finished at 6 p.m.! We had no chance to toss flowers so we gave them to the dancers as they left the theatre.

Whenever Nureyev was, as he put it, "between gigs," he rounded up a group of dancers, and took the show on the road. Sometimes his fans followed him, because it was a wonderful opportunity to travel and see the sights during the day and enjoy watching Nureyev perform with great dancers in the evenings.

On a December trip to Vienna in 1977, I was able to see Rudolf in several roles. Like most European theatres, the ballet alternated with the opera, leaving one or two days "in between" his performances. God forbid that Rudolf Nureyev should take a night off. No, he gathered a group of dancers from the Vienna State Opera, including Gisela Cech who danced Kitri with him in *Don Quixote*, and took them on the road. They performed a *Friends* program consisting of *Apollo*, the *Don Quixote* pas de deux and Bejart's *Songs of a Wayfarer*. My Viennese friend and I decided to explore a bit more of Austria by taking the train to Klagenfurt where Nureyev performed.

Our train left Vienna at 11 in the morning through the snow-covered mountains and arrived in Klagenfurt by late afternoon. Rudolf did a double take when he saw us at the Stage Door. We arrived without tickets or hotel, but someone in the company offered us free tickets in the orchestra stalls. The audience was all dressed up and there we sat, in our travel clothes.

Following the performance, we went to the Stage Door and because of the cold temperatures, waited inside a long corridor. The doorman hurried past the crush of people and placed a small table and chair near the stairwell for the dancer to sign autographs. Nureyev improvised by sitting on the edge of the table, signing programs on his knee, and chatted with everyone in a mixture of languages. I sensed his relaxed mood and remarked, "I can't believe I had to come all the way to Klagenfurt to see a *Friends* program." He smiled, especially since everyone else was speaking to him in German. Klagenfurt was a place I never expected to visit, but it was enjoyable because it was a spontaneous adventure.

Of course we paid the price for our little side-trip from Vienna. The return train was delayed for several hours and we were punch drunk from the cold and lack of sleep, while waiting in the freezing train station. We amused each other with stories or observations of the town – anything to stay awake until the train finally arrived. I recalled when Rudolf had said to one of his New York fans, "everyone needs a passion in life." On another occasion, he expressed it rather poetically with "Everyone needs a sylph." Our comfortably heated train finally arrived around five in the morning and we slept all the way back to Vienna.

For New Year's in 1978, I was once again in Paris to see Rudolf Nureyev dance *Swan Lake* with Natalia Makarova at the beautiful Paris Opera. Upon arrival, I learned that the first two performances were cancelled, due to a strike by the stagehands. This was not uncommon for the Paris Opera house, but was particularly disappointing because as a result, I saw only one of the four scheduled performances. For the New Year's Eve performance the unions "allowed" the show to go on, but without scenery. Rudolf was so frustrated he offered to put the sets up himself or dance without them, which is exactly what ended up happening. The dancers simply danced *Swan Lake* on an empty stage, forcing the audience to use their imagination for the lakeside or ballroom scenes.

My return journey from Paris to London turned into a real "saga." I left after the performance and caught my train to Calais, which broke down at one o'clock in the morning. We waited on the freezing platform for over an hour.

By this time the English Channel was too rough for the hovercraft, so I had to take the larger overnight ferry. I arrived in London in the middle of a demonstration by striking bus and ambulance drivers. The entire city seemed to be paralyzed by four inches of snow. Due to a rail strike, it took me nearly half a day to get to the airport for my connecting flight to New York. Subways ran once an hour and police were called in to manage the crowds, making everyone wait outside the stations. They feared the passengers may easily fall from the crowded platforms on to the tracks. I tried to find an airport bus, but drivers refused to drive, due to the airports being closed. Somehow I managed to get to Gatwick to see if my Laker flight had departed. Because London wasn't prepared for snow, we waited for approximately ten hours, before snowplows could be brought all the way from Scotland to clear the runways. Laker was the only flight to get out, but left over one hour late, not due to "snow on the runway," but a sound malfunction for the in-flight movies!

I attended the 1979 *Nureyev Festival* in London, but the trip back to New York was challenging, to say the least. While I presumed Rudolf had taken the Concorde, I spent four days in the stand-by queue waiting to get on an Air India flight, listening to horror stories of passengers waiting a week or more for the more popular airlines. When I finally made it, our flight was delayed two hours due to "catering problems" no less. Once on the plane, I was surrounded by screaming babies on all sides.

It was after 4 p.m. when I arrived back in New York, and discovered there was a bus strike, so I had to take a taxi to my apartment in the midst of our Independence Day holiday traffic. I could barely face the thought of attending that night's performance of *Sleeping Beauty*, but hated to miss it, so I dashed to Lincoln Center with just twenty minutes before curtain time. A crowd waiting for Rudolf at the Stage Door cheered my homecoming and said, "Now Rudolf can arrive." Sure enough, about five minutes later, Nureyev pulled up in a limousine while my friend commented, "Nancy, you've had close calls before with your trans-Atlantic trips, but twenty minutes before curtain time is a bit ridiculous!"

Earlier that year I flew to Vienna to see Nureyev perform in his production of *Swan Lake*, which I had only seen on film. With a stopover in London on the way back, I discovered Rudolf was on the same flight. He always boarded at the very last minute and was in first class. The flight experienced a lot of turbulence flying over the Alps due to very strong headwinds. As soon as the seat belt sign went off, Luigi rushed up front to see how "the boss" was doing. Rudolf was as white as a sheet and once the plane landed, he was the first one off the plane. When we boarded the shuttle bus to return to the main terminal, Nureyev sat near the door and I stood nearby. Respectfully, I didn't speak with him, because I saw from his expression that he was still recovering from the flight. He avoided eye contact by fiddling with his luggage and looking out the bus window.

Once we reached the terminal, he bolted out of the bus and I lost sight of him, until I saw him ahead of me in the "Other Passports" line at customs. "Welcome to London," an announcement came over Heathrow's public address system. "Due to staff shortages, there are no luggage trolleys." We met yet again at baggage claim, but at least Luigi was waiting for Rudolf in a car. On the other hand, I had to lug my suitcase onto the Underground. I was staying with a friend and walking along Victoria Road from the subway, when I saw Nureyev emerging from the home of his good friends Maude and Nigel Gosling, no doubt dashing to a rehearsal. The following morning when I went to the bank, I bumped into him again, and later that night he was watching the same performance that I attended at Covent Garden. It felt like we were traveling on the same timetable.

In 1980, Nureyev began dancing with the Boston Ballet, first on Broadway in *La Sylphide* and then at the 1981 *Nureyev Festival*, in the company's production of *Swan Lake*. In March of the following year, he mounted his production of *Don Quixote* for the Bostonians. A large group of fans traveled from New York to Boston to see Rudolf perform. It was the dancer's 44th birthday, and nearly everyone on the bus was going to the performance, so we circulated a birthday card for all to sign. All 4,200 seats in the Metropolitan Center were sold out with long lines of people waiting for returns. Before the performance, we waited at the Stage Door and gave Nureyev his birthday cards, gifts and other trinkets. Rudolf beamed and in mock innocence asked, "For me?"

There was a "Meet the Dancer" reception for patrons following the closing matinee in Boston. Champagne and refreshments were beautifully laid out on festive tables in the theatre's lobby. Some of us crashed the party, helping ourselves to chocolate covered strawberries and champagne. Suddenly the room began to "buzz" with excitement as Rudolf Nureyev, his long winter coat trailing around his shoulders like a cloak, rushed in "like his last-scene entrance in *Marguerite and Armand*." He dashed through the lobby, shook a few hands, whizzed past us with a smile and breezed out the front door to a waiting taxi for the airport. "Meet the fleeing dancer," we quipped while many patrons who had hoped to meet him were deeply disappointed. We didn't mind since our return bus to New York was departing much later, so we stayed and enjoyed the champagne. They were also giving away the *Don Quixote* posters, so we made the return trip satisfied with our ill-gotten "gifts."

There was another gala at Lehman College in New York, advertised as "Come meet the dancers" after the performance. The trouble was, nobody bothered to mention it to Rudolf, who was nowhere to be seen.

The Boston Ballet then did an extensive tour of *Don Quixote*. While in San Antonio, lawyers and others acted as supers, "extras" in the background. They remarked that being on stage with Nureyev was "more fun than their day job" and something they could tell their grandkids.

The tour manager was dismissed for the way the tour was booked without enough advance publicity. Producer James Nederlander stepped in to manage the second part of the tour, after Nureyev took time off to visit his friend and mentor, Nigel Gosling, who was dying of cancer.

On his 45th birthday Nureyev danced *Swan Lake* with Yoko Morishita in Tokyo. One of the fans with flight privileges attended the performance and discovered that Rudolf was on her return flight back. She called her father, who worked for the airlines, to help arrange for Rudolf a VIP treatment upon his arrival. When they landed, Rudolf was royally welcomed. This was one occasion, when the flight landed ahead of schedule. Because of the early morning hour, staff hadn't arrived to clear him through customs.

While waiting, Rudolf settled into a seat next to father and daughter. He was surprised to learn that the fan's father was the one who arranged his "welcome." He had an interesting discussion with both, telling them of his flight to Japan where he couldn't get a sleeper seat. He had to sit up for fifteen hours and then went directly to the rehearsal and performance. While they were conversing at the airport, the customs staff began to arrive, so the fan reluctantly said her good-bye to Nureyev, adding, "Now the withdrawal pains will begin." He laughed as they escorted him to passport control. Before catching a waiting taxi, he thanked both of them for their kindness in welcoming and waiting with him.

On April 30th 1983, the dance world experienced a shattering loss with the death of George Balanchine. On the morning of May 15, 1983, I attended his funeral in New York City. Then I boarded a bus for Washington D.C. for Nureyev's production of *Manfred* with the Zurich Ballet that same night. *Manfred* was not coming to New York, so we had to travel to see it. Rudolf had affectionately dedicated his performances to Balanchine. The New Yorkers decided shortly after seeing *Manfred* that we would go to Chicago, the next stop on the tour. When waiting for Rudolf outside the Kennedy Center, we told him we'd see him in the Windy City. He stared at us incredulously, asking, "You're… coming to Chicago?" He just beamed with joy over our loyal enthusiasm.

At the 1984 San Antonio Festival, several of us flew to Texas to see him in *La Sylphide* with the Berlin Ballet. In the middle of the week when he wasn't scheduled to dance, Nureyev departed for a gala in Philadelphia, celebrating Pennsylvania Ballet's 20th anniversary. There were no direct flights from San Antonio to Philadelphia and because of the time difference, it required catching a very early flight to be on the east coast in time for the performance. A few of us bit the bullet and left Texas on an 8 a.m. flight.

One of his fans was on an even earlier flight with Rudolf. Terrified of flying, he asked, "Sit with me during take-off." A storm was brewing with plenty of thunder and lightning and she observed that Nureyev assumed the "crash position" until the plane reached the cruising altitude. His terror of flying meant that he sometimes lost the nerve, got off the plane before take-off and booked another flight. Considering he couldn't perform his peripatetic schedule without flying, it's a testimony to his incredible willpower, that he continuously overcame his fear and anxiety, in order to travel for another performance. In this instance, he said that it took less time to fly the Concorde from Paris to New York, than from San Antonio to Philadelphia.

He arrived in Philadelphia just in time for his 3 p.m. rehearsal. For that evening's gala performance, the audience arrived for a costume ball dressed in togas, 17th Century wigs, clown outfits, and assorted get-ups. Suzanne Farrell and Nureyev closed the first half of the program with Balanchine's *Apollo* – the first and only time they danced together. On stage, Rudolf presented her like a rare jewel. Farrell was unaccustomed to Nureyev's curtain calls and had a slightly amused expression as Rudolf delicately kissed her hand and insisted she acknowledge the applause.

After the interval, Nureyev premiered a beautiful Baroque solo called *Bach Suite* by choreographer Francine Lancelot. His costume by Nicholas Georgiadis evoked the "Sun King" period with a plumed hat, gold, red and black brocaded waistcoat and breeches, red stockings and buckled shoes. Set to Bach's *Cello Suite No. 3*, the piece began slowly, with a subtle movement of the hands and feet and gradually built. About midway, Rudolf removed his buckled shoes and seemed to be doing "riffs" of the dance vocabulary, suddenly doing leaps and Graham-style contractions, offering a mini course in dance history in this twenty-two minute solo.

The gala audience seemed mesmerized and an enormous crush of people waited at the Stage Door for him. Rudolf patiently signed autographs for fifteen minutes until a security guard whisked him off to the afterparty.

The next day Rudolf flew back to San Antonio and resumed his performances of *La Sylphide*. Those who flew to Philadelphia and back to San Antonio had a taste of what Rudolf's life was like, since we had taken eight connecting flights in a seven-day period in order to see him.

That evening a few of us presented him with a red cowboy hat with a large plumed feather, explaining that if he ever performed *Bach Suite* in Texas, he would be prepared with this hat. He immediately tried on the hat and posed for photographs with a witty smile. Years later, this same red Stetson turned up at the Christie's Auction in one of the "lots" of his many hats.

Rudolf Nureyev claimed he was not a sentimental person, but we knew otherwise. One fan related how one of the ushers at the Metropolitan Opera House checked on Rudolf following a closing night performance. The usher found him packing up to take yet another flight and noticed some rather expensive gifts sitting on his dressing room table. Some of the items were wristwatches, which Rudolf seldom wore, and other trinkets. Rudolf just left them all behind. The usher exclaimed, "But Mr. Nureyev, don't you want to pack these, too?" "No, give them to somebody. Take them," was his response. As he continued packing, the usher observed that Rudolf placed into his suitcase all the assorted cards and trinkets given to him by fans. That is what he valued the most.

Several of us flew to Toronto to see Rudolf in his production of *Sleeping Beauty*. Since he was also dancing the following night at the Metropolitan Opera's 100th Anniversary Gala, most of us left the next morning. One fan was on the same flight back to New York as Nureyev. She traveled in economy; Rudolf in first class. A talkative flight attendant asked her if she enjoyed her stay in Canada and she replied yes, and that she had gone to see Rudolf Nureyev dance. "Oh, did you know he's on this flight?" "Yes," replied the fan. "I saw him in the lounge." She explained that she had followed Rudolf's career for twenty-two years. The attendant said, "He should know that. I'm going to tell him." "Oh, don't do that. I don't want to bother him," begged the fan, but the flight attendant went into the first-class cabin, pulling the curtain aside a bit. Rudolf politely stood up when she approached and as the flight attendant spoke to him, he kept glancing to the economy section to see which fan was there.

Once the plane took off, Rudolf assumed his usual crash position, hugging his knees. He relaxed a bit when the plane reached cruising altitude, but upon arrival, he thanked the pilot for a good flight and bolted for the door.

Back in New York, the fan noticed Rudolf walking slowly through the airport corridor. She caught up with him, telling him how much she was looking forward to seeing him perform in the gala that evening. "We call these galas *fouette a la seconde* nights," she told him, since most galas contain endless fouettes by dancers performing flashy turning steps. "What?" Rudolf asked quizzically, then laughed and explained that he wouldn't be doing any of those steps with his performance that night. Just before leaving the baggage claim area, he gave her a deep bow and went to a waiting taxi.

On a shuttle flight from Boston to New York, Nureyev was again in first class in the seat behind the pilot's cabin while two of his fans were in "steerage." Jane Hermann, at that time in charge of presenting productions at the Met, sat across the aisle from Rudolf. That night, Lincoln Kirstein was giving a party for Nureyev at his Greenwich Village townhouse. He was a prominent cultural figure who founded the New York City Ballet with George Balanchine. The plane was delayed and Rudolf got off to make a phone call, no doubt telling Kirstein he would be late. He spotted two of his fans sitting in the first row of "steerage" and decided to do a small performance for them. He pretended he was drunk as he got off the plane, staggering from one side of the aisle to the doorway. Rudolf simply loved to clown around and entertain.

A few minutes later, he returned to his seat and the captain announced that they would be taking off. Immediately Rudolf assumed his crash position. The two fans saw the look of concern on the face of Nureyev's travel companion as she glanced back into "steerage" but the fans looked on sympathetically as if to say, "It will be alright."

Once they landed in New York, an announcement was made, "We've had the honor of having Mr. Rudolf Nureyev on our flight," and the passengers burst into applause. Upon deplaning, Rudolf again kindly thanked the pilot for a good flight.

When returning from some London performances, the flight attendant recognized me and said, "I saw you at *The Merry Widow* last night." I had extended my London stay in order to see Margot Fonteyn perform the title role in this ballet, and the flight attendant spotted me during the intermission talking animatedly with friends. On the plane, the attendant told me how much she loved the ballet and we got into a discussion that would have lasted the entire trip, had her duties not intervened. Just about everyone that saw Rudolf perform became a dance enthusiast.

Traveling to see Nureyev took a lot of persistence. After receiving telegrams from the theatre in Florence that all performances were sold out, several determined fans took an overnight train only to be told that no tickets were available. They said they would return later in the day to see if there might be a few returns. Around four o'clock, the fans walked back to the theatre when they spotted Nureyev walking ahead of them. They asked if he could help with tickets and he told them to check with the company's director. When they returned to the Box Office, there were four tickets waiting for them – not from Rudolf, but from the press officer they had met on previous visits. Their persistence paid off.

Nureyev performed in many charity galas and unfortunately we missed one in London that we particularly wanted to see. The prices were beyond our means so we were shut out. During the performance, we all went for a drink and returned to the theatre in time to see the performers leave. Rudolf's first question to us was, "Did you get in?" "No," we complained, but luckily that gala was later broaD.C.ast on television.

On another occasion, fans in Italy discovered that Nureyev performed a gala where tickets cost five million liras – an equivalent of around five thousand dollars. "Not quite in our price range," one fan quipped. Despite not getting in, there was an added and unexpected bonus when at the next stop of the tour, the fans walked through the train station and spotted Nureyev walking down the platform from his arriving train. He saw his fans with their luggage and looked at them with, according to one, "a lovely, inexplicable expression on his face," smiling all the while. He clearly loved and appreciated his fan's loyalty and enthusiasm.

Once in Venice, Rudolf was out sightseeing near San Marco, when he recognized two of his fans nearby smoking cigarettes. As he passed them, he commented, "Tough girls, smoking away," and then went on for a gondola ride.

During a long summer tour through Italy, some of the fans rented a car and drove from city to city. After a performance in Macarata, Rudolf invited a couple of his American fans to join him for dinner. The restaurant was known for its fish and Rudolf took them to the fish display to make their selection. He suggested one and amusingly commented, "That one is smiling a lot…like the Americans."

While following the tour, they discovered that an extra performance had been added at the Baths of Caracalla, so they headed there. A car passed them on the autostrada and "vibes went off" for one of the fans in the car. They sped up to the car that had just passed them, to see Rudolf Nureyev dozing in the back seat. They honked the horn and Rudolf opened one eye, gave a sleepy wave, and nodded off again. Both performer and fans were headed to the same place.

In the early 80s, when Luigi Pignotti began to branch out and try his hand as an impresario, he arranged a *Nureyev and Friends* tour throughout France. I happened to be in London at that time and decided to follow the tour, enabling me to see more of the beautiful country as well as Rudolf's performances.

That 1982 winter tour was a difficult one. Beginning in Lille, the stadium the troupe performed in was freezing cold and the audience kept their coats on throughout the performance. Rudolf, who dreaded being cold, began the program with Balanchine's *Apollo*, in which he is bare-chested. Whenever Nureyev exhaled, you could see his breath. *Apollo* is a difficult opening piece for an audience unfamiliar with ballet, and the taped music was played so softly it was difficult to hear.

Despite the elevated stage, the sightlines were dreadful; it was, after all, a sports palace. The French audience became irate at not being able to see and stood on their folding chairs or in the aisles. Pandemonium soon broke out while others shouted, "Sit down!" or "We can't see!" The taped music was barely audible, but Nureyev valiantly carried on.

Following this performance, one of his faithful fans braved the frigid December temperatures and waited for him. When Nureyev emerged from the stage door, she said through chattering teeth, "I don't know how you could have danced in there tonight. You must have been frozen stiff." He instantly said defensively, "I wasn't stiff!"

Things got worse in a stadium in Grenoble. The performance was delayed by one hour and the irate audience sitting in the bleachers began moving closer to the stage. Many seats were double-booked and fights soon erupted. Just twenty minutes into the program with Rudolf again performing *Apollo*, French patrons crowded around the stage and shouted at Nureyev that they couldn't hear or see. Police were called in to restore order, while Nureyev continued the performance. Immediately after, Luigi whisked Rudolf away, while my friend and I thanked him for his "brave performance."

That performance in Grenoble was postponed for two days, so we found ourselves wandering from café to café simply trying to keep warm. The city was foggy and rainy and unsuitable for sightseeing. We ventured out to the Olympic Village to purchase our tickets and discovered, that the performances would be held in the section of the Sports Palace usually utilized for table tennis matches. Since most of these sports palaces were on the outskirts of the city, it proved very challenging to get back to our hotel late at night. Luigi gave us a ride in one of these instances, all the while complaining, "I will NEVER do another tour in France again." At least in Italy, without language barriers and more familiar theatres, he knew what he was getting into.

This *Friends* tour criss-crossed the country from Grenoble to Avignon, on to Cannes and Montpellier. In Avignon, furious cries of "Rembourser" meaning "Refund" could be heard from the audience, again due to the inappropriate sightlines for a dance performance. As my friend and I wandered through Avignon that afternoon while taking in the sights, we spotted a cartoon showing a Roman arena with the audience shouting "Rembourser!" because the lions weren't attacking the gladiators. We immediately copied it and gave it to Rudolf at the Stage Door that evening.

When we arrived in Cannes, the weather was blessedly sunny and warm and the performances were held in a proper theatre, instead of an unheated stadium. It made such a difference for both the dancers and the audience. Rudolf was in better spirits and the New Year's Eve performance was truly lovely. At the Stage Door, some of his fans walked arm in arm with him all the way back to the hotel, where he cheerfully wished us a "Happy New Year."

In December of 1984, Nureyev took a group of his Paris Opera dancers on a brief *Friends* tour to India – the first time Nureyev performed in that country. I couldn't go, but one of his loyal fans did and gave a detailed report of how his flight from Bombay to Delhi was delayed by four long hours due to crowds and traffic caused by local elections. The heat was unbearable.

Rudolf was driven to his hotel in an Embassy car and gave an immediate press conference. He patiently answered questions from the press, despite the fact that many were entirely unfamiliar with Western ballet. One reporter asked him if he didn't feel strange dancing with Fonteyn, because of the differences in their ages. Fonteyn was in fact nineteen years older than Nureyev. "I was dancing with artistry, not age," he explained. When another reporter, who had seen Rudolf dance in London, asked how he managed to keep each role fresh after dancing it so many times, Rudolf opened up, saying "every performance is as if I'm dancing it for the first time." He practically gave a mini-dance-history course for all that were present. The press conference was followed by a typical Indian buffet and Rudolf inquisitively asked about each of the various dishes. Musicians seated on the floor played the sitar, tabla, and other instruments while he watched with great interest.

Due to the demand for tickets, the December 31st rehearsal was opened to the public. The New Year's Eve performance was completely sold out. One of the pieces performed by the Paris Opera dancers was Maurice Bejart's *Bhakti* to Indian music, which was very well received. Indian audiences did not bravo, but soon they joined in with enthusiastic applause, punctuated by bravos from his loyal fan in attendance. There was a New Year's Eve party at the Ambassador's residence and when guests formed a receiving line to be greeted by Rudolf and the Ambassador, he greeted this fan by saying "Bravo!" because he obviously heard her over the applause. At midnight, everyone exchanged toasts and kisses.

By the second performance in Delhi, the dancers were more rested from the long flight, with Nureyev in particularly good form. He did manage, however, to bark directions to the lighting crew about the poor lighting cues during *Songs of a Wayfarer*.

On January 2nd, the company left by bus for Agra to see the Taj Mahal. Rudolf rode in a separate car with his Paris Opera assistant Marie-Suzanne. There was heavy fog on the road and a truck rammed the dancers' bus from behind, throwing many of them to the floor. Rudolf's car stopped to ensure that his dancers weren't badly injured, and when help arrived, he continued to the next stop. The shaken dancers had to wait another five hours for the relief bus to arrive. After reading about it in the newspapers, Maude Gosling told us, "Nothing would keep Rudolf away from the Taj Mahal."

While in India, Rudolf picked up some sort of stomach virus, but only two days later, the *Friends* troupe performed in Bombay. There they were "garlanded" by local people who placed flowers around the dancer's necks. There was one extra dancer performing who somehow didn't receive a garland. When a second group came out to place more flowers around each of the dancer's necks, Rudolf anticipated the gesture, took the garland in his own hand and draped it around the garland-less dancer's neck. He was always very attentive and considerate.

After the last night of their performances in India, my friend approached the stage where the dancers had gathered and listened to a speech – in French – by their Director, Rudolf Nureyev. He thanked his dancers for giving such superb performances and wished them good luck and bon voyage for their upcoming Singapore jaunt. Everyone applauded him.

Rudolf was endlessly on the move. After a *Swan Lake* performance with Lesley Collier in London, Rudolf dashed out of the theatre to take a private jet at 12:30 a.m. back to his directorial duties in Paris. Not a day of work could be missed.

As his opportunities to perform dwindled, Nureyev continued to rely on his *Friends* programs to showcase his Paris Opera dancers and remain on stage. The venues became rather dicey during this period. One trip in 1987 saw a group of us traveling to see a *Friends* program billed as - See a Living Legend -

in the Circus Maximus Casino in Atlantic City. It was quite an experience trying to watch ballet from a cocktail table, but we had the good sense to blow out the candles on the table once the performance began. It was difficult to concentrate on the dancing with people talking, smoking, getting up and down and - worst of all - the cocktail waitresses coming around taking drink orders. The audience clearly did not know what they were watching and we had the distinct impression that we were the only ones applauding. The "auditorium" was quite large and they had 400 "free" seats at the tables in the front, made available to "invited guests," in this case all from South America. All of them arrived late and got the best seats. Those of us who had to pay $50 for one lousy chair at a tiny table set for eight people – drinks not included – had to queue from 6 p.m. for an 8:30 show. Supposedly it was "first come, first served" seating and we expected a front table. Queuing for ninety minutes and being placed at the back did not make us happy.

Charles Jude and Claude DeVulpian danced the *Sleeping Beauty* pas while latecomers continued to file in. Manuel Legris and Monique Loudieres woke up the talkative audience with the *Don Q* pas de deux. Rudolf danced *Apollo*, but clearly the audience didn't understand what it was all about, despite him being in very good form, totally focused, relaxed and natural. After a long interval, he danced *Wayfarer* with Jude. Both Jude and Nureyev performed the duet *Two Brothers* to complete the program.

While the idea of performing in the great outdoors sounds idyllic, it presents many challenges. Staging a ballet in huge open spaces, such as the many arenas in summer European festivals or in rustic wooded areas closer to home, requires preparing for just about everything. Music needs to be amplified which can cause an echo effect, making it difficult to dance. Prerecorded music may suffer from faulty equipment. Sets need to be incorporated into the existing structure or eliminated completely. With the elements of wind, rain or extreme temperatures, not to mention bugs, planes flying overhead, traffic noises, and talkative audiences, I would have preferred seeing a performance in a proper theatre setting.

Aside from drafty sports palaces, there were numerous open-air performances throughout Nureyev's career. He performed in the moonlight in the Herod Atticus at the foot of the Acropolis; at the Baths of Caracalla in Italy; the Hollywood Bowl in California, and in many summer venues throughout the world, sometimes playing to enormous crowds of 30,000 people or more. Knowing how susceptible he was to the cold, Rudolf was always wrapped in shawls, hats, scarves, heavy coats, bathrobes, legwarmers and whatever else he could find to keep his muscles warm.

One summer a small group of us took a "road trip" to tour some historic sights in Boston, Cape Cod, and the countryside. The highlight was a *Nureyev and Friends* performance in the Great Woods in Mansfield, Massachusetts. Temperatures in northern states can be unpredictable and the August air turned bitterly cold. I thought it ironic that we heard *O Come All Ye Faithful* on the car radio in midsummer en route to the theatre! The performance was held in an open-air theatre with the audience huddled under blankets or heavy coats, sipping hot tea.

When we arrived at our seats, we saw Nureyev on stage. He was wrapped in a terrycloth robe over his costume doing a brief warm-up, all the while talking to the on-stage musicians about how cold it was. At the stage manager's signal, the house lights began to dim for the opening ballet, Balanchine's *Apollo*, and Nureyev headed for the wings for the performance to begin. Suddenly a stagehand noticed that Rudolf had left his thick, multicolored shawl on the floor directly behind the stool that Apollo sits on. He started to pick it up when Nureyev rushed out, instructing, "No, leave it. I need it there." And so, after the initial opening, when this bare-chested Apollo sat on the stool to watch his muses dance, he promptly wrapped himself in his enormous shawl to ward off the frigid night air. We could see into the wings and the muses pulled on legwarmers and heavy sweaters the minute they came off the stage. It was extraordinarily cold, but when not dancing, Nureyev's shawl was his only concession to the climate.

The dancers who performed the *Romeo and Juliet* pas de deux were nearly blown away by the strong winds. We felt sorry for Nureyev and Jude, barefoot and in shorts and T-shirts, performing *Two Brothers*. Once the performance ended, we tried finding the Stage Door and it was in a so-called "security area," but Rudolf was genuinely amused when he saw us all huddling to keep warm. After we returned to our hotel, we headed to the restaurant and ordered hot soup!

At one *Friends* performance at the Greek Theatre in Los Angeles, Nureyev had some competition from Mother Nature. The premiere was nearly rained out in the middle of *Pierrot Lunaire*. The stage was covered, but everything else was out in the open air. As a result, the conductor was getting drenched, so he stopped the performance and asked that the curtain be dropped. This wasn't done immediately, so they left poor Rudolf hanging upside down on his *Pierrot* scaffolding for a few minutes just "improvising" some acrobatic moves in silence. About twenty minutes later, a face with a *Pierrot* hat peered through the curtain to see what was happening. Some of the die-hards wrapped in blankets and huddling under umbrellas shouted, "We're still here!" and Rudolf beamed. His loyal fans weren't dissuaded from staying by a few drops of rain.

The performance eventually continued where they left off – with Nureyev hanging upside down. This time the orchestra was moved to the back of the stage. At the end, when Nureyev was robbed of his *Pierrot* suit and hat and executed a series of slow-motion arabesques across the stage, the audience began to laugh. This was supposed to be a poignant moment in the ballet, but Rudolf soon discovered why the public was laughing. A mother raccoon and two babies had crept onto the stage, obviously attracted by the lights, and remained there watching him. One of the backstage crew shooed them away, but they later reappeared in the middle of his *Aureole* adagio, again breaking Rudolf's concentration due to the audience's laughter. He attentively stopped while the furry family paraded in front of him to the side of the stage and then resumed from the spot, before he was so rudely interrupted.

The New Jersey Symphony played "live" at the back of the stage of the outdoor theatre in Holmdel, New Jersey for another of Nureyev's *Friends* programs. The conductor frequently turned to watch Nureyev or the dancers, to make sure the tempo was correct. While it was great to have the orchestra, it somewhat restricted the stage space. The Paris Opera dancers on this program danced up a storm – literally. About halfway through the program, it began to thunder. Flashes of lightning ripped across the sky. Just as the interval started, the skies opened up and the wind blew the rain sideways. All 5,000 people in the audience huddled together under the covered portion of the roof to keep dry. As quickly as the downpour started, it stopped, just in time for the second half of the program.

The last piece of the evening was the *Two Brothers* duet with Charles Jude and Nureyev. As they danced in bare feet, we only hoped the stage was dry so they wouldn't slip. All went well and it amused us to see Rudolf taking a princely curtain call without shoes and wearing shorts. He wanted to acknowledge the orchestra, but the person in charge of opening the curtain must have gone home, so Rudolf grabbed one side and Jude the other and opened the curtain themselves, bringing the conductor out for a final bow. Rudolf was always wonderfully appreciative of his coworkers.

When performing indoors, Nureyev had to contend with air-conditioning, which he loathed. He hated being cold because his muscles cramped up, making dancing more difficult and prone to injury. During a ninety-minute taping of the *Dick Cavett Show* in 1974, Rudolf began sniffling and Cavett asked if he was catching a cold. "No, it's your air-conditioning," he quickly explained.

At a *Friends* performance in Las Vegas when the outside temperature was a scorching 107 degrees, Nureyev was inside rehearsing and wearing several layers of sweaters. He insisted that the air conditioning be turned off, as he always did in chilly theatres, until the rehearsal was finished. Nureyev was satisfied, but naturally the staff was sweltering. When it came to the actual performance, he carried on valiantly dancing *Apollo, Wayfarer* and other challenging works to the accompaniment of ice clinking in glasses, since drinks were served throughout his performance.

During various summer tours in Italy, Rudolf arrived at one open-air venue in Udine. The performance was postponed when it began to rain at 9 p.m. After the rain subsided about 10:30, Rudolf checked to see if the stage floor was wet and sprinkled rosin on it to prevent slippage. He warmed up on stage with the dancers once again and at 11 p.m. the conductor started up the orchestra. However, the heavens opened up once more. Because of the late hour, the performance was officially cancelled. Rudolf left in good spirits and when the audience recognized him, they applauded. He appreciatively acknowledged them by performing a little improvised dance before departing.

At another open-air venue in Italy, torrential rain again disrupted the performance and Rudolf mingled with the astonished audience while waiting for the rain to stop.

In the Verona Arena filled with 18,000 people, a performance of *Don Quixote* was disrupted by a sudden storm in the middle of the windmill pas in the moonlight. The wind kicked up so suddenly, that the mantilla carried by the ballerina was blowing out of control. The audience began filing out to seek shelter. Savvy vendors sold plastic raincoats to those remaining behind. Rudolf put on his dressing gown and watched, as stagehands covered the stage with a huge tarp. When the rain stopped, Rudolf removed his hat and bowed, as if thanking both the returning audience and the Rain Gods. Shortly after the second interval, however, the skies opened up again and the performance had to be cancelled.

In 1982, Nureyev performed *Don Quixote*, this time in the South of France. It had rained earlier and when the audience arrived, Rudolf was feeling the stage to see if it was dry enough. During the performance it rained again and everyone took shelter, with Rudolf hiding behind some plastic plants. Two performances during that engagement were rained out. One consolation for friends who were there is that Rudolf invited them backstage for champagne.

The infamous 1973 *Swan Lake* performances with the Paris Opera in the Courtyard of the Louvre were exceptionally trying. The July weather for the rehearsal period was seasonable, but temperatures suddenly plummeted just before the opening night's free performance on Bastille Day. When asked how he was, Nureyev replied with one word: "Cold." The audience huddled under blankets in their bleacher seats. I felt sorry for the Swans, posing in the frigid air, and pulling on their sweaters and sweatpants the moment they left the stage. Nureyev as the Prince, wrapped his enormous horse-blanket cape around his legs when sitting on the throne in an attempt to keep his muscles warm.

Then came the famous incident in which Makarova took a nasty fall in the Black Act and went to the press, claiming it was Nureyev's fault and she would "never dance with that man again." A fan watched the performance from the wings and was mystified by what happened. All she knew is that Makarova pirouetted past Nureyev and before he could react, the ballerina was flat on the floor. They finished the pas de deux, but Makarova, quite shaken, omitted her variation. Nureyev performed his solo, even though it allowed little breathing time between the pas de deux and his variation. At the curtain calls, Nureyev insisted that Makarova take a bow, saying, "It's for you," but the tension was so thick, one could cut it with a knife. Makarova left Paris the next day, breaking her contract. Nureyev finished the season performing with Noella Pontois and Ghislaine Thesmar, because "the show had to go on." He later told some of his fans that "nobody defended me," after the blitz of publicity about the incident. Nureyev never publicly commented about it and just kept on dancing.

Some of the most magical ballets were performed in the amphitheatre in Athens. Rudolf's productions of *Swan Lake, Sleeping Beauty, Raymonda* and *Manfred* were presented there. The setting was spectacular, utilizing the natural formations behind the stage area as "scenery" with the full moon illuminating the Acropolis nearby. Fortunately the temperatures in Greece were more conducive for outdoor summer performances.

Because dance was his life, Rudolf didn't really care whether he performed indoors or outdoors, just as long as he could dance. "The stage is my home," he said and where there was a stage, we would find Nureyev. Many of us realized that we would not see another dancer like Rudolf Nureyev in our lifetime. Dancers – even great dancers – come and go, but none captivated us the way Nureyev did.

People frequently remarked how lucky I was to travel as much as I did, claiming they didn't have the funds to see him perform outside of New York. My philosophy was that if you wanted something badly enough, you would find a way to do it. I followed Rudolf's advice that he shared in an early 1970s TV interview. He recalled about wanting to get to the Kirov School in St. Petersburg, but lacking the finances to get there from his hometown of Ufa. "I realized nobody would come and take me by the hand. If I wanted it, I had to do it all myself." That's exactly what I did in my life. I have no regrets.

"It is my mother's greatest wish to see me before she dies."
~Rudolf Nureyev, London Telegraph, June 19, 1977~

THE PETITION

Chalk drawing on New York City sidewalk,
May 14, 1977. Photo: William J. Reilly

Ever since I had been following Nureyev's career, I never knew him to comment about his family. He publicly avoided making political statements that would jeopardize the safety of his mother and sisters back in Russia. Yet on March 28, 1976, London's *Evening Standard* newspaper ran a feature entitled *Nureyev's Plea: Let Me See My Mother*. His agent, Sandor Gorlinsky, was quoted in the article: "We have been trying to get Rudolf six weeks off somewhere, so that his mother could join him. It would mean so much to them. To them both." The world press circulated the story and it felt like a bombshell to me. I photocopied the article and sent it to my fellow fans.

Gorlinsky's statement had particular relevance, since it came during Rudolf's enforced month-long rest following his collapse from pneumonia the previous month. Even while resting, Rudolf's mind was always thinking ahead.

There was no question of the dancer traveling to Russia to see his mother. The Soviets never forgave Nureyev for defecting in 1961. He was tried in court as a traitor to his country, and sentenced to seven years in prison, if he ever returned.

Despite his phone calls being "bugged," Nureyev was allowed to contact his mother by telephone, but longed to see her once more and let her see the kind of success he had acquired in the West. Some of his friends visiting Russia managed to smuggle gifts for his family, including videotapes of his dancing. Even Pushkin, his former teacher at the Kirov School, saw one of these videos and realized his efforts training the young Nureyev paid off.

On one of these occasions, I thought it would be a good illustration of Nureyev's fame and success, by gathering photos showing the massive Stage Door crowds surrounding him. I contacted a photographer friend and he printed up several photos documenting the throngs of admirers. We arranged to have the photos taken to his mother, since she couldn't possibly comprehend the extent of her son's stardom.

Rudolf privately sought the advice of politicians. He made personal appeals to President Gerald Ford and Prime Minister Harold Wilson, about helping his mother obtain a temporary visa. He had hinted in his interviews with the press, that he was going public with his appeal as a "last resort." His mother, Farida, was then in her 70s and her eyesight was failing.

In London there was a very public campaign in support of dancers Valery and Galina Panov, for seeking exit visas. At the time, they were under house arrest in Russia. Demonstrators were everywhere, blocking traffic and even disrupting performances by releasing white mice in the theatre, or opening umbrellas during a performance. The campaign also had the support of many London's leading artists.

During the 1976 *Nureyev Festival* in London, some of the fans discussed ideas about how we could help Rudolf. Not quite sure where to begin, we decided the best strategy was to ask Nureyev himself. Following one of the performances, Rudolf sat at the desk inside the Coliseum Stage Door, signing endless autographs. The crowds were so large that the Stage Door attendant organized a system whereby everyone formed an orderly queue, approached the desk where Nureyev sat, received their autograph, and then filed out through an adjacent hallway to a rear exit. When a couple of the New York fans approached Rudolf, they politely asked him, "Can we discuss this at a more appropriate time?" He responded, "No, no, this is fine." They were in deep discussions about the petition. The Stage Door man grew suspicious that they were talking with him at length, without getting anything signed. Two or three other fans were also present when Rudolf was asked, "Do you want publicity?" "Yes," he responded. They continued talking.

Disturbed that the line wasn't moving so he could go home, the Stage Door attendant said something to the fans and physically tried to escort them out. In a flash, Rudolf's hand shot out, clasped the attendant's arm, as he said matter-of-factly, "I'm talking to them. Leave them alone." Once this brief discussion was completed, the group of fans left the line without an autograph, to the astonishment of the guard. After Rudolf departed, several of us met at a nearby restaurant to discuss what strategies could be used, including the idea of a massive petition campaign. The Londoners were on board and we agreed to begin as soon as possible.

When Rudolf returned to New York to join the Canadians at the Metropolitan Opera House that summer, the newspapers reported that on his rare days off, Nureyev was busy taking trips to New England to look for a farm. On the advice of John Lennon and Yoko Ono, his neighbors at the Dakota apartment, he "invested in cows" and bought a dairy farm in Leesburg, Virginia. Clearly he was making preparations for his future as well as providing a place where his mother could join him.

After Rudolf finished his 1976 Met season, he flew to Spain to begin work on the *Valentino* film. It would be his "enforced rest" after his pneumonia and months of nonstop dancing. Meanwhile, we held our first "official" petition meeting in August 1976. We needed a name for our group in order to coordinate the petition effort. The British fans didn't like what was ultimately chosen, *The Committee to Assist Nureyev*, deeming it "too American." Additionally, the heading on our petition appealed to the U.S. Government to assist Nureyev's mother with her visa. Clearly, if this was an international effort, it didn't matter which country assisted, since the visa ultimately had to come from the Soviet Union. The situation was uniquely problematic, because Nureyev was not a citizen of any country, although he was a resident of Monaco and used French travel documents. Helping a "stateless" person in this cause was definitely challenging, to say the least.

For the rest of that summer and into autumn, *The Committee to Assist Nureyev* met regularly. The fans formed a research committee, seeking professional and legal advice, and learned that Nureyev had previously made several private appeals to heads of state of the British, French, U.S. and Canadian governments. We realized that the petition would not be a formal request to the Soviet Government, but would merely lend support to the already existing efforts.

In addition to a research committee, we established a fund-raising committee charged with finding funds for mass mailings, print costs and other expenses. Another group took responsibility for contacting numerous ballet schools and dance companies. Regional coordinators were established to obtain signatures in various parts of the country. Each of us contacted everyone we knew. Based on my friendships with fans in major dance capitals, I acted as International Secretary for the petition effort. Post Office Boxes were set up in London and New York City, to receive incoming petitions. Each petition was then given a number, tallied, and indexed by country.

An early effort at obtaining signatures took place in September, when we set up a table on the campus of the University of Pennsylvania. Several signatures were obtained and this more or less "tested the waters," before a larger campaign got underway. Our first mailing went out in October of 1976, to ballet and modern dance companies in various geographical locations throughout the States. The effort began to snowball and soon dance companies did their own petitioning, copied additional petition sheets and returned the signed ones to us. Entire dance companies actively sent pages of signed petitions. Other companies planning tours to the Soviet Union hesitated and explained, that while they supported the petition effort, they were reluctant to sign in order not to jeopardize their tours to Russia.

In October, we rented the film *Jeune Homme et la Morte*, starring Nureyev and Zizi Jeanmaire, which naturally attracted many dance enthusiasts. Prior to the screening, we gave attendees a briefing on our petition efforts. Not only did we recruit further volunteers, this mini fundraiser enabled us to temporarily cover the costs of our photocopying and mailing expenses.

When it came to gathering signatures, Nureyev was our best resource. Since it was the height of the "ballet boom," many cinemas showed assorted dance films. The Carnegie Hall Cinema was screening *Romeo and Juliet* with Fonteyn and Nureyev and we successfully gathered numerous signatures from those waiting in line to buy tickets. We also took advantage of the annual bazaar at the Library for the Performing Arts, when the Library sold duplicate copies of material that had been donated. Enthusiasts augmented their collections with rare souvenir programs, Playbills, photographs and other memorabilia. Avid collectors lined up at Lincoln Center for hours before the Library opened its doors. Since most of us were going to the bazaar anyway, we simply arrived early with clipboards and petitions and had another ready-made line of interested people willing to sign.

Volunteers with petitions became a familiar site at the TKTS line on Broadway at 47th Street. Those waiting in line for half-price theatre tickets were generally receptive. We tried not to engage in political discussions with anyone, but sometimes we were asked an oblivious question, "Why doesn't he go back to Russia, if he wants to see his mother?" We had to explain Nureyev's situation and many people were shocked to learn, that he was a stateless person and faced a prison sentence if he returned. In some of our research, we learned that Khrushchev was so furious with Nureyev for starting a mass "exodus" of Soviet artists, that he had a contract out against Nureyev's life.

Other people asked us, "Why should I help one individual, when so many others want to get out of the Soviet Union?" We reminded them that they had the support of many organizations both here and abroad. "But what about the Panovs?" they asked, since the Panovs were finally allowed to leave, largely due to the massive public campaign in London. My friend replied, "Valery Panov is Jewish." "Oh, you got me there," admitted the reluctant gentleman and signed the petition. If others chose not to sign, we politely thanked them and passed the clipboard to the next person. In one weekend, we effectively gathered thousands of signatures.

By Christmas we had contacted the American Dance Guild, which agreed to run a small ad in their newsletter about the petition effort and urged those interested to contact the Committee. We also petitioned outside of various Broadway theatres.

By December, the filming on *Valentino* was nearly completed. Because Rudolf did his daily class, he remained in excellent shape and promptly returned for performances with the Royal Ballet. But members of the British Committee met with some resistance while petitioning. One person abruptly told them, "You don't have a hope in hell of succeeding, so why bother?" Another suggested they try petitioning in Russia.

A man in a Russian hat and coat with flawless English was asked to sign the petition. "Why pardon him? There are many other people who want to leave Russia." They later discovered this man was from the Soviet Embassy. One evening this same man waited at the Stage Door and asked Nureyev for his autograph. He took a long time finding the appropriate page in the program while speaking in Russian, and then walked away. Rudolf seemed slightly agitated, but never said a word to those of us who were petitioning, perhaps not wanting this Russian gentleman to see the connection.

The British effort was well underway, with signed petitions from the entire Actor's Equity as well as members of the Royal Ballet. My friends in Toronto, Zurich, Vienna, and Brussels organized and petitioned in their countries and it seemed I was busier than ever sending material back and forth. We tried to establish a committee in Paris, but couldn't get anyone involved at that time.

On December 27, 1976, *Newsweek* ran an article entitled *A Son and His Mother*, which mentioned Nureyev's efforts to see his mother. It also stated: "Nureyev wants to organize a petition campaign similar to those used to win Kremlin permission to emigrate for a number of prominent Soviet Jews, including dancer Valery Panov and his non-Jewish wife, Galina." Clearly, Nureyev was preparing to "stir the pot" himself, by going public.

By January of 1977, we had collected 13,000 signatures and had the participation of 72 dance companies. Our contact from Switzerland was in New York for a brief vacation and met with the committee members. Since many of the fans planned to attend the *Nureyev Festival* in Paris the following month, we discussed strategies for taking the petition effort to France, where our efforts intensified. Both American and European fans made great progress in the theatre itself. Because the Palais des Sports is literally a sports stadium, it has numerous entrances and exits. Unlike our experience at petitioning outside most theatre entrances, this was not possible in Paris, due to the lack of volunteers to cover each entry. Once inside the theatre, however, the French audiences tended to remain in their seats during intermission, while vendors wandered up and down the aisles selling programs, popcorn, ice cream, and other goodies. Those rows and rows of people gave us the perfect opportunity for collecting signatures.

Working in teams of two, each of us handed the petition to the person in the aisle seat who would sign it and pass it along. The volunteer on the opposite end of the row likewise started passing a petition to the row behind. Just by standing in the aisles, we easily collected hundreds of signatures each evening. With every passing day, many of the audience members had heard via word of mouth that we were organizing a petition to help Nureyev's mother obtain an exit visa and despite the occasional language problem, they readily signed. Nureyev danced *The Lesson* that season, based on the Eugene Ionesco play. The playwright attended a performance and when asked to sign the petition, Ionesco heartily replied, "I do so with pleasure."

By this time, many of us had memorized the phrase, "Would you like to sign a petition for the mother of Nureyev?" in French. On occasion, because we were rushed to get petitions signed during the fifteen-minute interval, our words didn't exactly come out correctly. One startled Frenchman gave a double take and asked me to repeat the question. Apparently I ran the words together and instead of saying "the mother of Nureyev" it came out "merde de Nureyev." For those of you fluent in French, you get the humor. If anyone had told me twelve months earlier that I would be petitioning – in a foreign language no less – just to help Rudolf, I would have laughed.

The French were unbelievably receptive to signing, as soon as they heard the word "mother." When we approached an American tourist, we got a barrage of questions: "Where will you send it? How many signatures have you got? How many do you need? Do you think it will do any good?" This was a lesson in diplomacy and patience, and rather than get involved in time-consuming conversations, we simply thanked them and passed the petition along. Besides, the details were still to be determined.

The French press interviewed Rudolf while we were there, but he seemed reluctant to mention the petition. A day later, a French journalist happened to see me and other fans petitioning at the Box Office queue and asked us a few questions. I gave him a copy of the petition and some press cuttings. We later saw him going backstage to speak to Rudolf about it in person. An article in the next day's edition of *L'Aurore* stated "Parisians are invited to sign a petition at the Palais de Sports." We were bombarded by requests to sign and ran out of petitions. I knew a fan from London was arriving the following day, so asked him to bring more copies. Meanwhile, we frantically ran around Paris trying to get another 150 copies made before the evening performance, when numerous people approached us and asked, "Is that the petition? Can I sign it?"

Back at the hotel room each evening, we counted the petitions and noted any famous people that had signed. The list of "celebrity" signatures continued to grow, since many frequented Nureyev's performances. Our efforts were aborted near the end of Nureyev's three-week Paris Festival, when gendarmes outside the Palais des Sports told us we were not to petition inside the theatre. By that time, even the ushers had signed it and the signature count reached a whopping 42,000.

When that *Nureyev Festival* ended, Rudolf changed his flight to New York, so he was on a later flight than mine. However, one of his former fans that frequently assisted him flew with me and asked if I would keep some luggage in my New York apartment until Rudolf arrived. It was rather amusing when she arrived two hours later to fetch Nureyev's tights from the suitcase, and rushed them to where he had a costume fitting for *Pierrot Lunaire*. His Paris costume didn't fit properly and he wanted a new one made for his New York engagement. As soon as the costume fitting ended, Rudolf met with choreographer Glen Tetley and began rehearsals at once. After an incredibly busy day, he went to the cinema.

Meanwhile I was suffering from an unbelievable jet lag and had to stay up late to finish petition business, before going to work the following morning. As Committee Secretary, I spent most of my so-called "free time" corresponding with overseas contacts, keeping everyone informed, and spending enormous amounts of money on postage and international phone calls. Whenever someone was flying abroad, they became my "messenger" by carrying petitions, press cuttings, and any related material.

Nureyev and Friends opened for a three-week season at New York's Uris Theatre, and Rudolf politely asked us not to petition on the opening night of his Broadway run, because "I want them to review the performance and not the petition." After that, however, we petitioned nightly, either in the lobby at intermission or outside the theatre, when people were waiting in line at the parking garage. It was mid-March and the signature count increased by another 25,000.

At the end of that season, a reporter had contacted a committee member, wanting to interview Nureyev for the New York press. By then Rudolf was in transit so his good friend, Nigel Gosling was called and assured us he would be speaking to Rudolf that day. He added, "It must be very frustrating for you to be doing this without any direct contact with Rudolf. I will tell him how important it is to have this interview." The reporter explained that he wanted to write the article from the viewpoint that "no matter how rich or famous Nureyev is, despite his so-called influential friends, he is still frustrated in his attempts to get the visa." The reporter was contacted and told to call Nigel Gosling about the exact time Rudolf could be interviewed. He was shocked "Me? Speak to Rudolf Nureyev?" He was expecting to go through a representative.

During Nureyev's Broadway season, we met with Patricia Barnes, wife of critic Clive Barnes, who was very involved with the Panov campaign, and we discussed strategies. Patricia met with Nureyev and helped compose an "Open Letter to the Editor" of the *New York Times* on March 31, after Nureyev concluded his New York engagement. In the letter, Rudolf reminded the readers that thirty-five countries, including the Soviet Union, met in Helsinki in August of 1975. The meeting resulted in the signing of the Helsinki Accords, that called for greater freedom of travel, particularly for those wishing to rejoin or visit their relatives abroad. These human rights issues would be discussed at the upcoming Belgrade Conference and Rudolf's letter pleaded his case for getting a visitor's visa for his family. In the letter's final paragraph Rudolf stated, "I feel that I have created only good will for the country of my birth and I urge the Soviet authorities to demonstrate their sincerity at Helsinki, by allowing my family to visit me and granting my mother, sister and niece the required visas without further delay." He signed the letter and asked Barnes to submit it to the editor "after I leave," since he didn't want to be bombarded by the press.

The news that Rudolf wanted his sister and niece to be included as part of the visa request caused us confusion, since the petition stated that it was for his mother. We changed the heading accordingly, but wondered if the signatures already obtained were now worthless. Nigel Gosling was indeed correct. Without having direct contact with Rudolf, who was always on the go, the whole effort proved extremely frustrating.

Patricia Barnes proved invaluable, because she was an active member of the Human Rights Committee. She planned to personally contact several famous people and use their names to bolster further appeals. As a busy person, she couldn't manage all of this herself, so I ended up typing the many letters that were sent to Leonard Bernstein, Jacqueline Onassis, and others. My "free time" became even more limited.

No matter how frustrated or exhausted I became, with working full time and usually out in the evenings, I always became newly motivated when a new piece of information was discovered. Patricia Barnes obtained a copy of Nureyev's official government file and showed me that Rudolf's many attempts through the U.S. State Department were all flatly refused. On one visa application form, it stated, "I, Rudolf Nureyev, a stateless person, guarantee to provide financial support for my mother when she is permitted to leave Russia." Copies of government letters and telegrams from various senators in Washington, many of them notarized by Henry Kissinger himself, were sent to the Soviet Embassy through the State Department. A heartbreakingly personal letter to President Ford in Rudolf's handwriting read, "I beg you to do something, as my mother is now in total despair." The saddest document was an airline ticket, in his mother's name, which was returned after the visa was again rejected, with a note from an Embassy official stating, "Hopefully you can use this next year."

In May, Barnes was largely instrumental in helping Nureyev with his next big step: testifying before the U.S. Congress. On May 13, 1977, an extremely nervous Rudolf Nureyev appeared in Washington to plead his case before a special commission on Security and Cooperation in Europe, set up to monitor compliance with the Helsinki Accords. *The New York Times* reported that Nureyev "spoke in low, hesitant tones, his voice nearly inaudible at times." Later, through a friend, I obtained a copy of the taped testimony, and could barely hear Rudolf speak. He said that he had not complained in such a public forum before, because "I found my family problems rather distasteful to be in the press." He was now speaking openly as a "last resort" and because he had become "desperate." He also acknowledged in his testimony that "I have friends who are rooting for me and they went to those Embassies and were refused." He continued, "My mother went to an office in Ufa and they tried to say why she could not go to the West. They say 'you are old, too tired, you are ill,' and they tried to force her to sign some kind of document saying that she doesn't want to come out to see me."

The following day, a newspaper article quoted Nureyev as saying, "I last talked to my mother by telephone two months ago. She told me 'I'm too old now. I probably will never see you.'" Undaunted, Nureyev added, "Nothing will happen unless you make it happen."

The May 1977 *Dance and Dancers* Magazine published a brief item explaining the petition and invited readers to contact the Committee. The response was encouraging, because the National Theatre wrote requesting more petitions, as did the Bank of England.

During the following month's *Nureyev Festival*, we had a ready-made population each night as patrons entered the theatre. We were positioned at both the main entrance and the balcony entrance, on the side of the London Coliseum. The theatre staff condoned our efforts, but insisted we do the petitioning outside and not in the auditorium. Most people willingly signed, agreeing that it was absurd that Rudolf's mother wasn't allowed an exit visa. We collected hundreds of signatures nightly.

During the intervals, we gathered in the lobby to compare notes and see if any famous people had signed. One evening, the well renowned actor Peter O'Toole came to see Nureyev dance and when approached, explained that he never signed petitions, but would make an exception in this instance. He said that it seemed like such an ordinary request for an international star of Nureyev's caliber, to get to see his aging mother. A wealthy Japanese socialite attended Rudolf's performances regularly, arriving in her Rolls Royce. Although she barely spoke English, we asked her to sign the petition. "Nureyev? Mama? West? Sign? Yes." And she signed it.

One of the friendly ushers at the London Coliseum often had "Stage Door Duty," and mid-way through the seven-week marathon season with guests Natalia Makarova, Margot Fonteyn and Lynn Seymour, Rudolf seemed unbelievably tired. Despite his fatigue, he graciously signed autographs for over an hour. When he stood up to leave, he accidentally kicked over the chair. His coat was draped on the back and it fell to the floor. The usher attempted to retrieve it for him, saying, "I'll get it," but Nureyev insisted on picking it up himself. He did so very slowly and when he stood up, gave a slight groan admitting, "God, I'm SO tired." As he passed to exit the theatre, the usher fondly patted his shoulder and reminded him, "They loved you tonight, Rudi." Rudolf managed a smile and nodded. We were chatting with Luigi outside who related how proud Rudolf was of that season, when the dancer suddenly got very sad. When Luigi asked him why, Nureyev replied, "Because my mother never saw me dance and probably never will."

As the Committee's International Secretary, I prepared an information package for Rudolf. All the publicity ended up in a rather large binder that also contained a list of the famous people who signed the petition, the total signature count to date, a list of all sixty represented countries and other useful information. I had to carry this by hand when I flew to London. When it was presented to Rudolf at the Stage Door after a performance, he motioned how heavy it was and as soon as he got in his car, began leafing through it.

The very next day, June 17, 1977, with the help of his agent, Sandor Gorlinsky, a Letter to the Editor appeared in the *London Times* signed by Nureyev. The last paragraph read:

"Although I left Russia for the sake of my career, I think I have brought some credit to the country where I was born and to the great school in Leningrad where I studied. I am grateful for the help that has already been given by many people to my efforts to persuade the Soviet authorities to let my mother, sister and niece visit me after a separation of sixteen years. "

As the pressure mounted to present Nureyev's case at the Belgrade Conference to ratify the Helsinki Accords, the press coverage intensified. The *London Sunday Telegraph* ran a story on June 19, 1977 entitled, *Nureyev's Mother Refused Exit Visa*. In it, Rudolf stated, "It is my mother's greatest wish to see me again before she dies." Following his Congressional testimony in Washington, his mother was yet again refused an exit visa after making another application with the Soviet authorities. "My mother was thrown out of the office. She has been told that she is too old, that she doesn't really want to go. They put words into her mouth, and tried to force her to sign documents stating that she doesn't want to come out. She has refused."

We stepped up our efforts by organizing a demonstration outside the London office of Aeroflot Airlines, carrying signs demanding that Nureyev's family be allowed to see him. Leaflets were handed out with a photo of a forlorn-looking Rudolf Nureyev sitting at a table, captioned, "What if your mother was alive and you were not allowed to see her?" The demonstration was publicly embarrassing for the Soviets, especially on such a busy London street as Piccadilly, but nothing ever came of it, except for several suspicious KGB agents driving by to take notice.

Following his 1977 *Nureyev Festival*, Nureyev took his production of *Romeo and Juliet* on tour to Australia. One of his New York fans flew there to speak to him about the timing to present the petition. When she arrived backstage after the performance, Rudolf was so surprised to see her that he merely declared, "You're crazy!" She replied, "Yes, I realized that when we flew over Fiji – it's such a long flight!" He joked with her and asked if she was returning the next day. "No, I'm not as bad as you are. If I'm flying to the other side of the world, I'm at least going to stay for a week!" Because she worked for the airlines, he asked her how long it would take to fly to Manila from Los Angeles, because he had a five-day gap in his schedule. Apparently he was "stopping off" in Manila after Australia, to perform at a gala for the President of the Philippines. When she admitted she didn't' know, Rudolf exclaimed, "But you know everything!" She spent forty-five minutes discussing petition details with him. Everyone was getting concerned about when the petition paperwork would be presented and Rudolf's involvement in the presentation. He agreed to hold a press conference or make a personal appearance when the time came. "Am I allowed to give money?" he asked. "You most certainly are," came the reply. "How much and when do you want it?" he inquired, adding, "You know, I did offer once before." "The fans tried doing it on their own," she explained, "but they've nearly dried up." "You shouldn't have to," Rudolf assured her.

I was extremely relieved when I heard this, because I was spending so much money on international phone calls, that I was afraid I couldn't pay my phone bill. At times I was ready to give up completely, because I didn't want my frustration over the petition to spoil my enjoyment of seeing Nureyev dance. My mood fluctuated between "I don't care any more" to "we've got to get at least 100,000 signatures or more before we present it." Some of the committee members became disenchanted, but a few diehards joined me by petitioning at the annual Shakespeare in the Park performances. Since the free tickets were distributed prior to the performance, people lined up in Central Park at the crack of dawn, picnic baskets in hand, to make a day of it. With such a "captive audience," we obtained a few thousand more signatures.

One weekend, discouraged that no others were available to petition, I single-handedly went to the half-price ticket line again and circulated two or three clipboards. I could barely keep up with the people who wanted to sign, because they had read about Nureyev's case. I spent the entire day until about six o'clock in the scorching August heat, until I was asked to leave, because the petitioning was slowing up the line for distributing tickets to that evening's Broadway shows. I managed to get over 3,000 signatures each day and the ultimate irony was when a friend commented, "Gee, if you only had more people to help, we could have obtained a lot more."

One day in New York I spotted a chalk drawing on the sidewalk by a street artist. It appeared to be a kind of stained-glass window with a figure inside and was titled "Sacred Dancer – dedicated to Rudi's mother in Russia." I thought it amazing that an artist made such a touching public statement about Nureyev's situation. Luckily a friend and photographer captured the image before the rain washed it away.

As the petition effort swelled to more than 108,000 signatures, the time came for a coordinated effort to present the petition and plead for Nureyev's cause. Nigel Gosling, supportive as ever, exclaimed, "I think you have done wonders!"

Rudolf danced in Montreal and some of us needed fresh inspiration, so we attended his performances there. While in Canada, Patricia Barnes sat down with Rudolf to discuss the final presentation plans. Meanwhile, I had prepared another binder of updated information for Rudolf, since he requested, "I want to see ALL the material about the petition."

We originally settled on September 30th, as the date for the presentation, the day the representatives left for the Belgrade Conference. Rudolf agreed to make himself available for the presentation and a press conference. Our efforts to gather all the petitions were handled by those flying to London or Paris to collect them. The others mailed their petitions to the New York committee for photocopying, but somewhere along the line, some of them went astray. My 4 a.m. phone calls to Europe were met with angry frustration, trying to rectify the situation. Our Paris representative even cancelled her holiday plans thinking someone would collect the petitions, but it was obvious our latest letters crossed in the mail.

When Nureyev was in New York, he taped a TV interview with Dick Cavett, who asked him about the petition and what people could do. "The same, only more," he replied. It was rather like pulling teeth to get Rudolf to speak openly about it, until he finally stated, "If people want to help, they can contact the Committee." When the program was broaD.C.ast later, the Committee's contact information appeared on the screen.

A preview screening of the *Valentino* film took place at the Library for the Performing Arts in New York. Many of the fans gathered around the glass doors outside the auditorium, hoping to catch a glimpse of Rudolf. He finally arrived with Maria Tallchief, Lee Radziwill, Andy Warhol, Martha Graham and Francois Truffaut among others. Some of the fans arrived in long gowns and were obviously invited as guests. I wasn't expecting to go inside, but just wanted to show my support for Rudolf.

After some time, I noticed someone at the entrance trying to get my attention. I was distracted and busy while chatting with friends. Suddenly one of Rudolf's friends came outside in her evening gown and asked, "May I talk to you for a moment?" I was truly puzzled as she continued, "Rudolf has set aside a few seats for the members of the petition committee, and since you've been working so hard on it, he'd like very much if you'd come inside." I looked at her in amazement and without thinking replied, "You must be joking." She seemed surprised by my response. I told her I didn't come with the intention of getting in, as was obvious by my attire. "Don't worry about that," she said, "but please hurry, the film is starting and I know Rudolf would want you to see it." She pulled me inside the completely full theatre just as the film had started. I wasn't about to wander down the aisles looking for an empty seat, so I stood at the back for about twenty minutes, until an usher found a folding chair for me and I sat in the aisle – right next to Martha Graham! I had the best seat in the house.

The official premiere of the *Valentino* film in New York was held on October 3rd, with the London premiere two days later. Nureyev flew back and forth for both premieres as well as for the anticipated petition presentation. He didn't think it was wise to present the petition at the same time as the film premiere, so once again the presentation got postponed.

Meanwhile, our petition efforts continued. The Swiss committee, working in Zurich, Geneva and Bern, had responses from the delegates to the Belgrade Conference who seemed to take a real interest in Nureyev's case. However, because the Conference was being held so close to our intended presentation date, they were advised to present the Swiss petition directly to the Federal Chancellery, the official way to present any petition. After many trans-Atlantic phone calls, they went ahead and presented their portion of the petition on October 11, 1977.

Rudolf continued his hectic schedule, but whenever he was interviewed, he managed to mention the campaign to help his mother secure an exit visa. In one television interview, he passionately stated that bringing his mother for a visit "is my greatest dream right now."

Still without a fixed presentation date, we continued to push forward. Patricia Barnes met with the Ambassador to the United Nations, Allard Lowenstein, who provided all the file copies of Rudolf's case, as well as the letters the Committee members wrote to various members of Congress. They gathered as much information as possible and sent it via diplomatic pouch to the Belgrade Conference. Through the interest of the Ambassador, we began narrowing down a date to present the petition in order to ensure the most publicity.

At last the date was set for Thursday, November 10th at 11 a.m. in the offices of the United Nations. Thankfully Patricia was able to elicit the participation of the playwright Edward Albee, along with other prominent people, who were present. We originally contacted Secretary General Kurt Waldheim requesting that he receive the petition, but technically the UN wasn't permitted to do anything, unless requested by the participating countries. We then had to contact the missions of the United States, United Kingdom, France, Australia, Canada and Austria, asking them to request that Waldheim accept the petition on behalf of the United Nations.

It was all rather complicated and Lowenstein's office was most helpful, reminding us that this sort of thing had never been done before and there were no guidelines, so we were setting a precedent. We were advised that once the presentation was made, the actual petitions would be sent via diplomatic channels to the Human Rights League in Geneva. Ambassador Lowenstein even cancelled an appointment at President Carter's office in the White House, in order to be available on the day of the presentation on behalf of the U.S. Mission. Patricia Barnes, several political representatives and others, offered to attend the presentation in Washington, D.C..

Now that we had a deadline, the Committee swung into high gear. There was a massive coordination effort to gather and photocopy all the petitions from the various countries. At that time, I was working all day until 7 p.m. and then dashed to the office of one of our Committee members, dubbed "Petition Central," There, our work continued all night while copying, collating, indexing, cross-referencing the petitions, preparing fact sheets and press releases. The next morning, at 7 a.m., I'd finally rush home, shower, change, and then show up for my day job. I slept a grand total of six hours that entire week. I think I got through it on sheer adrenalin. A vivid memory that remains is the 4 a.m. wall clock over a huge table stacked high with petitions, while one of the fans stretched out under the table to grab a catnap.

Some of the biggest names in the performing and visual arts signed the petition, among them: Lauren Bacall, Alan Bates, Ingrid Bergman, Cecil Beaton, Leonard Bernstein, Claire Bloom, Karl Bohm, Sir Adrian Boult, Richard Burton, John Curry, Margot Fonteyn, Douglas Fairbanks, Jr., Carla Fracci, Sir Peter Hall, Katherine Hepburn, Sir Robert Helpmann, David Hockney, Trevor Howard, Eugene Ionesco, Glenda Jackson, Eartha Kitt, Christa Ludwig, Ian McKellan, Siobhan McKenna, Kenneth MacMillan, Sarah Miles, Kyra Nijinsky, Peter O'Toole, Cyril Ritchard, Ken Russell, Sir George Solti, Twyla Tharp, Liv Ullmann, Andy Warhol, and Oskar Werner.

For the presentation in New York on November 10, 1977, we elicited the help of Martha Graham and dancers from her company, as well as John Butler, set designer Rouben Ter-Arutunian, Murray Louis, James Wyeth, Edward Albee and of course, Patricia Barnes.

There were some zero hour snafus, when the various missions to the UN cancelled being at the presentation, because it was being held on the property of the American Embassy and they were concerned it might have political repercussions with their own governments. We emphasized to the American embassy officials, that even though the other missions had agreed to accept the petitions, it was a matter of bureaucratic red tape that those representatives couldn't attend and we had to personally deliver the petitions to the Canadian, French and Austrian missions. The petition was finally presented to Ambassador Allard Lowenstein of the United Nations Mission. The petitions were sorted in separate bundles by country and neatly tied with black ribbons. Spread out over a long table, they made an impressive sight. The various representatives accepted copies of petitions, signed by their respective countries. Photographer Bill Reilly documented the rare occasion. Because the presentation was behind closed doors and through diplomatic channels, the press coverage was rather disappointing. Even though the story ran in the daily papers, none of the media outlets covered it. I didn't get a chance to attend the presentation, because I had to make up for lost hours at work.

Up until the presentation date, in addition to getting so little sleep, we were in touch with the London Committee and with the help of Nigel Gosling, managed to turn the presentation there into a true "media event." The British Committee argued that they wouldn't be ready in time, while we insisted it had to be done on the same date for maximum effect. That morning outside the Soviet Embassy, most of the Royal Ballet dancers turned up, including its top ballerinas Dame Margot Fonteyn, Antoinette Sibley, Merle Park, Lynn Seymour, and others, each carrying sections of the petition. Two of Nureyev's partners, Patricia Ruanne of London Festival Ballet and Elaine MacDonald of the Scottish Ballet, arrived from their company tours to show their support. Groups of supporters carried signs reading, "Let the Nureyevs be Reunited" or "Sixteen Years is a Long Time," while members of the London Committee wore "Help Reunite the Nureyevs" T-shirts.

Margot Fonteyn was about to make a trip to the Soviet Union to begin filming her *Magic of Dance* television series. Hence, she was rather apprehensive to "trouble the waters" with the Russians, but could not refuse to support Nureyev in his efforts to see his mother. On the arm of a London petition organizer, they both carried an enormous bundle of petitions to the front entrance of the Soviet Embassy and rang the doorbell. It was not a surprise that nobody answered the door, so the petitions were left on the embassy steps. However, the resulting publicity drew plenty of attention to Nureyev's cause. It appeared in all the London papers and the media.

Within days of the presentation, a thankful telegram arrived at both the London and New York committees:

DEEPLY TOUCHED BY YOUR MAGNIFICENT AND GENEROUS SUPPORT * STOP * PLEASE CONVEY MY HEARTFELT THANKS TO ALL CONCERNED

RUDOLF NUREYEV

Even before the formal presentation, we began a letter-writing campaign, with letters to and replies from Senator Edward Kennedy and other prominent members of Congress, as well as Members of Parliament in Canada and Great Britain. Some fifty-two United States Senators and numerous members of the Canadian Parliament also organized and signed their own appeals.

I learned through a Geneva newspaper, that the Soviets threatened to leave the Belgrade Conference on Human Rights, if the West "continued to interfere in their internal affairs." Yet it was also reported, that three dissidents had been allowed to leave Russia and had moved to Vienna.

After devoting eighteen months to the petition effort without any results, I was suffering from total exhaustion and in need of a long break. I wanted to go to Vienna, because Nureyev danced several performances of his *Swan Lake* in addition to *Don Quixote* and a mixed program. I was able to stay there with friends. Exploring Vienna by day and watching Rudolf at night was just the tonic I needed. Rudolf seemed invigorated, relaxed, and injury-free. An Austrian journalist asked Nureyev about his mother and he mentioned the petition, "but nothing happened despite so many people working so hard. I'm not prepared to give up," he added, "but it's very, very tiring fighting all this bureaucracy." Whatever his personal difficulties, it never showed on stage.

A Paris *Nureyev Festival* beckoned with London Festival Ballet in his production of *Romeo and Juliet*. This time we could concentrate on the performances, recalling our previous season with all that petitioning. I took advantage of being "in between jobs" by heading to London, where I was lucky to secure a three-month assignment, while someone was on maternity leave. This ensured that I could take advantage of London's theatre, dance and music scene in the evenings. Working also enabled me to send money to New York and pay my rent. My British friends and I made a weekend trip to Amsterdam to see Rudolf perform. Many of those who worked on the petition were also there, so we had a reunion. As we joked, "Follow Nureyev and see the world."

After three months away, I returned to New York and began working six days a week to catch up on finances, after a roommate moved out. However, about the same time my Zurich friend received a work visa to move to New York. The timing was perfect and she moved in with me, until we could both get back on our feet financially.

Nureyev, meanwhile, continued his hectic performance schedule while pursuing his own visa attempts through private channels. In May of 1978, he performed in Germany, when Soviet Premier Leonid Brezhnev was there. Taking advantage of the situation, Rudolf wrote the following open letter that appeared on the front page of the *Frankfurter Abendblatt*:

Dear Mr. Brezhnev,

I write to ask if you would intervene in the case of my mother, who has been trying to visit me ever since I left Russia sixteen years ago. She is a widow of 74 years of age. She has applied again and again for a visa but it has always been refused, for no definite reason. I would be completely responsible for all expenses incurred by her visit, which could be either to America, France or England.

Knowing that the Soviet constitution claims to be based on high humanitarian principles and the respect for love between parents and children, I believe you will not be opposed to this simple family visit. I therefore earnestly request you to make it possible for my mother to see me again, before it is too late.

(Signed) Rudolf Nureyev

Since the escalation of publicity, things became difficult for Nureyev's relatives. Funds that Rudolf formerly sent to his mother were cut off, their phone calls stopped, and his sister, Rosa, was harassed after talking to a British journalist.

While in Washington in the summer of 1978, Nureyev met privately with President Carter. There were talks of doing an "exchange" between a Soviet chess player and a human rights activist, for several so-called spies being held in the United States. Rudolf kept a low profile during this period, not wanting to jeopardize any negotiations. There weren't any interviews about his mother in the press, because publicity could hurt rather than help the situation.

The London committee members kept in touch with Nigel Gosling about further developments with Nureyev's case. One member personally applied to invite Rudolf's mother for a visit. Someone "official" arrived on the doorstep and asked many questions. "Where would Nureyev's mother stay?" "With mutual friends." This "official" said they were going to contact Rudolf's friends, Nigel and Maude Gosling, to verify the information. As one of those on the committee remarked, "it seems as if the KGB extends into Great Britain, when you apply to have a Russian citizen visit you."

We read reports on the trial and sentencing of Yuri Orlov, the so-called "dissident" who formed a group to help monitor compliance with the Helsinki Accords and the outraged groups that sent protests to Brezhnev. We wrote letters to Amnesty International and other human rights organizations, reminding them that the Soviet Union was violating the Helsinki Accords.

"Because of my constant pleas to government officials, they aren't making things too pleasant," Rudolf was quoted in a London *Daily Telegraph* article in March of 1979. The article stated that, "The Russians have been unmoved by criticism that they have breached the Helsinki agreement on human rights."

Back in New York, Patricia Barnes championed a letter-writing campaign and letters by prominent artists, supporting Nureyev's appeal. The letters were printed in the *New York Times* and the *London Daily Telegraph* in March of 1979. Constance Cummings, Anne Jackson, Eli Wallach, Zubin Mehta, Richard Rodgers, Yul Brynner and Tennessee Williams signed the New York letter. The London signatories were Alan Ayckbourn, Sir John Gielgud, Beryl Grey, Yehudi Menuhin, Andre Previn, Dame Marie Rambert, Sir Ralph Richardson, Ken Russell, Paul Scofield and Tom Stoppard. It was a great show of support but shortly after, we learned that Rudolf's sister Rosa was dismissed from her job as a teacher without a pension.

By the spring of 1980, Rudolf was less guarded about his statements. When asked in an interview if it was painful not to see his family in Russia, he replied, "Of course it's painful, but dancers learn to live with all kinds of pain." He elaborated further, "Politicians only do deeds when it profits them. A visit by my family will not help any politicians, so it will not happen."

We continued our efforts directly through Nigel Gosling, who, because of failing health, was in continuous contact with Rudolf. Nureyev visited the Goslings whenever he had a free day, but was contracted to do an American tour with the Boston Ballet. Maude Gosling was coping as best as she could, but when husband Nigel was hospitalized, Rudolf's daily calls as well as calls from the London committee members, bolstered her spirits. Rudolf also arranged for a good friend to be with Maude while Nigel was hospitalized. When Gosling was near death, Nureyev actually cancelled part of his American tour, in order to fly to London. Gosling was like a father to Rudolf and his early death at age 73 in May of 1982 was a blow, not just for Rudolf, but also for Nigel's wife, and for many of the fans that cherished Gosling's friendship and advice. When the 1982 *Nureyev Festival* opened at the London Coliseum just days after Gosling's death, a program note indicated that Rudolf had dedicated the season to Gosling.

It was largely through Gosling's efforts that Rudolf was once again reunited with the Royal Ballet in October of 1982. Nureyev premiered his new creation, *The Tempest,* in December of 1982. Several of his fans gathered at Covent Garden's Stage Door, excited to see Nureyev back in London again. Before the performance began, Luigi pulled one committee member aside and said, "Come inside. There's someone I'd like you to meet." That "someone" was Nureyev's sister, Rosa, along with his niece, Gusell. How or when they obtained Russian exit visas was unknown and Luigi cautioned not to tell too many, since the news hadn't been made public and they were still "sorting things out." When the rest of us heard this, the committee member remarked, "You'll definitely recognize Rosa. She has Rudolf's cheekbones."

From my amphitheatre seat at the Royal Opera House, I was able to see Rudolf's sister and niece for the very first time. They sat in the company box on stage left. During the first ballet, danced by Anthony Dowell, Rosa kept a low profile, sitting at the back of the stage box. When *Raymonda Act III* started, which Rudolf danced, she sat right up front next to her daughter and leaned over the railing. She seemed to be commenting to Gusell, probably about how this English company was dancing this very Russian ballet. They had never seen their famous relative dance. My heartfelt wish was granted that night. I've always said that if they ever got out, I wanted to be present when they were in the audience, watching Rudolf dance.

When Rosa came out of the stage door, she looked a bit apprehensive by the enormous crowds waiting for her brother and looked relieved when she spotted Luigi. She didn't speak a word of English, but Luigi told us that Gusell was enrolled in an English course in London. While Rudolf patiently signed autographs for the masses, Luigi shepherded Rosa and Gusell into a waiting car. Rudolf stopped signing briefly to speak to them, explaining when and where he would meet them for dinner.

We always joked that if his relatives ever got out, we would be the last to know. Very little was said about this sudden turn of events and the press never picked up on it until much later, when Rudolf had settled his sister into his Monte Carlo villa, while Gusell continued her studies in Paris. Nureyev's mother, however, was still unable to secure an exit visa. She was the Soviet Union's trump card.

Rudolf resumed his hectic performing schedule and that winter after performing a *Friends* tour around France, a fan remarked to him how wonderful it was that his sister and niece were out of Russia. "Keep it to yourself," he discreetly advised. "Something's cooking and mother can come if she can get a passport."

After years of collecting signatures, letter-writing campaigns and numerous meetings, the Committee had exhausted all ideas and quietly disbanded. Rudolf continued to elicit help privately and in 1983 took a very bold step of becoming an Austrian citizen. Since Austria was a neutral country, he thought governments could assist him if he was no longer a "stateless" person and stated in the press, "I believe the human spirit will win eventually." I immediately sent him a telegram: "Congratulations to Austria's newest citizen."

Finally in November of 1987, twenty-six years after his defection, Rudolf Nureyev was granted a 48-hour visa to return to Russia. By this time, he was the Director of the Paris Opera and 49 years old. At the Moscow Airport waiting for a connecting flight to his mother's home in Ufa, about 700 miles east of Moscow, he was besieged by autograph seekers, friends, and a barrage of press. He obligingly made a snowball and tossed it for the cameras. He also acknowledged that the Soviet leader, Mikhail Gorbachev, "very possibly" was instrumental in permitting his return. When he finally arrived in Ufa, his mother was very frail and on her deathbed. She apparently didn't recognize her own son. It was a very difficult trip for Nureyev. He later revealed "It was too late." She died shortly thereafter.

In 1989, the Berlin Wall fell and Rudolf was invited to return to the Kirov to dance. Again, it was "too late." Injured during the dress rehearsal, he nevertheless danced the difficult Bournonville ballet *La Sylphide*, not wanting to let down the Russian public that was so devoted to him. Many were disappointed that the 51-year-old dancer couldn't execute the steps as precisely or jump as high as they remembered. Technique had changed a great deal since he left in 1961. However, Russian critic Galina Dobrovolskaya later recalling this performance spoke of Nureyev, the actor and said, "I saw a miracle onstage; a character emotionally and morally rich enough to communicate with sylphs."

While in Leningrad, Nureyev visited the Hermitage as well as the studio where he used to take class. At the Museum of the Vaganova School, he saw photographs of himself alongside other famous dancers from the Kirov. He became overwhelmed with emotion and had to leave the room. In 1961 following Nureyev's defection, his photos were removed as if he had never existed, despite his fame at the Kirov. Speaking to television reporters who covered this historic return to his homeland, Rudolf declared that even though the return to Russia was late in his career, "I feel vindicated."

"All the arts interest me. It's a daily diet you have to applaud."
~ Rudolf Nureyev, Atlanta Journal, April 4, 1982~

OTHER PERFORMANCES

Nureyev singing Mad Dogs and Englishmen at Covent Garden Christmas Party, London, December, 1974. Photo: Melissa McQuillan

Rudolf Nureyev often spoke of his "destiny" to dance and remained faithful to dance throughout his life. However, because he was so curious about all art forms, he seldom missed an opportunity to be on stage, as illustrated by some rather unusual performing appearances.

Living in London meant that I saw Nureyev's only performance with Anthony Dowell in Bejart's *Songs of a Wayfarer* at a Royal Ballet Gala. Other roles Nureyev seldom performed outside of London were Robbins' *Dances at a Gathering,* Balanchine's *Agon* and *Prodigal Son,* and MacMillan's *Song of the Earth.*

I also had the pleasure of attending the annual Friends of Covent Garden Christmas Parties. These events were great fun when members of the Royal Opera shared the stage with the Royal Ballet performing in various skits or vaudeville numbers, showing another side of their talents.

In December of 1974, Rudolf consented to appear as a singer, or as the papers reported, "Rudolf burst into song…sort of." He strode onto the stage, clad in his ankle-length fur coat, hat, and snakeskin boots. In one hand he clutched a yellow paper with the words to *Mad Dogs and Englishmen* written on it. In his other hand was the microphone – his speaking voice was very quiet – and he half sang, half spoke the lyrics to the Noel Coward tune.

His fans teased him at the Stage Door, calling out "Bravo, Caruso," and when asked when his album would be released, he humorously responded, "When I get more songs!" But the fans also agreed that Nureyev "shouldn't quit his day job."

At the following year's Christmas party, Rudolf outdid himself. Clad in a tux, tails and top hat, and sporting a cane, he half danced and half strode onto the Covent Garden stage. This time, without written notes, he sang Cole Porter's witty *I'm A Gigolo*, and broke into a tap dance, even joking to the audience, "You weren't expecting that, were you?"

Except for occasional television interviews, many people never heard Nureyev speak. That suddenly ended in 1975, when he agreed to make a recording of Stravinsky's *Soldier's Tale* with Glenda Jackson as the Narrator. Rudolf took on the role of The Soldier, but his self-consciousness at reading lines was evident, especially next to the experienced British voice of Glenda Jackson. Rudolf never hesitated to take risks.

He was originally going to narrate the *Soldier's Tale* for a ballet created by Eliot Feld, objecting that "my voice is too soft," but was assured it would record well. There was also talk of a filmed version, with Nureyev dancing the role of the Soldier and Marcel Marceau as the Devil, but the project never materialized. After reports that Rudolf would provide the narration for Maurice Bejart's *Notre Faust* ballet, the press made it sound like Nureyev was about to retire, by stating that he was "trying to find alternative careers for this aging dancer with creaky knees." Nureyev was only 37 years old at the time.

Always fascinated with cinema, Nureyev directed his own production of *Don Quixote*. Shot in an airplane hanger in Australia, the film has been hailed as one of the best dance films on record. Technology has changed dramatically since then, but for its 1973 premiere it was quite a breakthrough for filming dance. Nureyev was responsible for all the camera angles and shots and did his own dancing late at night, after the company's sections were finished.

Many of us got all dressed up for the gala premiere in London. Nureyev arrived wearing beige thigh-high boots over slacks and a beige jacket, as he escorted Princess Margaret down the steps to the cinema, which was in the lower level of an apartment complex. Both sat a few rows ahead of us and occasionally Rudolf turned to Princess Margaret and explained something about the filmed sequence. After the screening, the audience gave him a standing ovation. Everyone filed out into the lobby and Rudolf glanced at us in our finery as he stood at the top of the staircase. He paused occasionally to chat with well-wishers before joining Princess Margaret in a receiving line. When he spotted a young man dressed in a T-shirt and jeans, he asked, "Aren't you cold?" The man replied, "Naw, I only live upstairs and just had to come down!"

A friend asked Rudolf to sign his souvenir program and Rudolf playfully bopped him over the head with it. "Get out of here!" he joked, "I'll be ready in one minute." Precisely sixty seconds later, he stopped signing autographs and said, "That's all, bye-bye" and went off to a private party. The papers mentioned that Rudolf's gala attire upstaged Princess Margaret's. The Princess was very interested in the ballet and at one point Nureyev even gave her private lessons.

Throughout Nureyev's career, there were reports of various film projects with famous directors. Rudolf was supposed to play the life of Vaslav Nijinsky on several occasions, but his performing schedule prohibited those projects. In 1976, the press announced that Rudolf would portray the Moor to the Iago of Mick Jagger, who was called "The Nureyev of the pop world." In another film, that was to be directed by Roman Polanski, Rudolf would have possibly teamed up with pop star Michael Jackson, but none of these came to fruition.

The filming of Ken Russell's *Valentino* was a major risk for Nureyev, because it required several months off from his dancing. After suffering from a bout of pneumonia, Rudolf accepted the offer, thinking it would give him some time to regain his strength. Ever disciplined, he did a daily ballet class while on the set, and took tango lessons from none other than Sir Frederick Ashton. There was a scene in the film in which Valentino danced with Nijinsky, played by Royal Ballet dancer Anthony Dowell. He had a dialect coach for the rather clipped Italian accent required in the film, despite speaking beautiful Italian through his long association with Luigi Pignotti. He also took boxing lessons for a key scene in the film.

During any "down time" while filming, he kept up with the latest news and studied the text of *Romeo and Juliet* for his upcoming ballet version. In the evenings, he began working with the London Festival Ballet dancers in translating Shakespeare's text to movement. At Glen Tetley's insistence, the tireless worker also spent six weeks working with the choreographer on his ballet *Pierrot Lunaire* for future *Friends* programs. Nureyev managed to stick to his film schedule, napping anywhere from three to sixty minutes daily. As Luigi once told us, "Rudolf may not need sleep, but I do!"

There was a lot of publicity for the film, including a storefront window display at a Fifth Avenue New York department store, prominently featuring a large photo of Nureyev as The Sheik. The window had a desert setting with sand, palm trees and camels, as well as jeweled "Sheik" merchandise.

Valentino received mixed reviews, probably due to Russell's unique interpretation of his leading characters. Shortly after, the diaries of Lincoln Kirstein were published which revealed Kirstein's thoughts on dance as a religious ritual and why dance seemed impossible to translate for film or television. However, one of his quotes was: "The best filmed sequence I have ever seen was in Ken Russell's *Valentino* which... not only revealed a great dancer as an equally great actor, but in the climatic boxing match, it photographed one of the most astonishing pas de deux ever filmed, virtual perfection in setting, speech, music and dancing."

There was talk of several dancers making a record for Cynthia Gregory's husband who was in the music business. Rudolf asked Gregory after the *Valentino* screening, "Did you like my singing of *O Sole Mio*?" When she said she did, he quipped, "Tell your husband if I'm to sing on his record, I want to do *Save the Last Dance for Me*." This never came about, mainly because of Rudolf's first priority – his dance schedule.

Having tap danced in Ken Russell's *Valentino* film, Nureyev repeated a similar routine, this time with *Putting on My Top Hat*, on *The Muppets Show*. He also displayed his great sense of humor while dancing *Swine Lake* with Miss Piggy. In a later sequence on the show, he was clad in a towel and sang *Baby It's Cold Outside* while in a steam room with "The Lady Pig." Nigel Gosling told me that the script was not entirely to Rudolf's liking, so he made some suggested changes and wrote much of the Steam Bath scene himself. In London prior to the show's airing, a TV "teaser" had this narration: "Stay tuned as the bravest man in the world faces the Muppets."

On March 8, 1977, Fonteyn and Nureyev participated in an evening of conversation with moderator John Gruen at New York's Town Hall. The auditorium was packed to the rafters with fans in the audience "wired" to their cassette recorders so that they could tape this historic evening. The effusive Gruen gave a lengthy introduction that went on for at least a quarter of an hour, causing titters from the audience. Sensing that this would be a long evening, Rudolf jokingly interrupted, "As I was saying…" The restless and amused audience applauded. When asked to comment on the Fonteyn and Nureyev partnership, Rudolf stated, "We walk around the same goal – do we have to discuss it?" Gruen continued to probe, implying there was something more to their partnership, to which Fonteyn said glibly, "That's YOUR fantasy!"

Both dancers seemed more animated when it was time for questions from the audience. One person asked Nureyev whether he read any of the books upon which several ballets were based. "Oh, you have to, you have to!" he repeated. Margot sheepishly chimed in, "Shall I admit that I don't?" Rudolf looked out to the audience, pointed to Fonteyn and said impishly, "Generation gap!" During the applause and laughter that followed, Rudolf turned bright red, covered his face, and looked apologetically at Margot, who brushed off his remark as if it was a joke between two friends, but shared by the entire audience.

Later when asked what had happened to his production of *Nutcracker* that was announced for that December at American Ballet Theatre, he replied diplomatically, "I was supposed to do it this year, but something happened along the way – ahem – and we did all those galas to raise money but apparently it wasn't enough…at least for my version." Baryshnikov's version was mounted instead.

During the summer of 1980, the Berlin Ballet appeared at the Metropolitan Opera House performing Nureyev's production of *Nutcracker*.

Also that season was Valery Panov's production of *The Idiot* and a program featuring Nureyev with Galina Panov in *Miss Julie* and Nureyev in *Five Tangos*. That was the season of The Phantom of the Opera, and no, not the musical.

The incident involved a violinist in the orchestra who was murdered en route to meeting Valery Panov backstage, after a performance. The morning papers heralded *Murder at the Met*, and left all who worked in the theatre on edge. The police investigated everyone backstage. Luckily Nureyev had departed to tape a television variety program hosted by Julie Andrews in an outdoor theatre near Washington, D.C.. He and Berlin Ballet co-star Eva Evdokimova performed *Sleeping Beauty* and Rudolf did a jazzy song and dance "I've Got Your Number," from *Little Me*. He also demonstrated the five basic ballet positions for the many enraptured children in the audience. Had he been in New York during the murder investigation, he would have been extremely nervous because he always feared there would be a KGB plot against him. There had been many "accidents" that year involving Soviet dissidents and some even thought the murder was a ploy to somehow implicate the Panovs. The ongoing investigation revealed that the murderer was a Met stagehand, which cast a dark cloud over the remaining season.

In an appearance with Barry Humphries on the *Dame Edna Show*, Rudolf again performed a tap dance and the Dame joined him in a romp around the stage, ending in a deep backbend. The disparity in their sizes, Rudolf at his 5'8" and the much taller, stockier Dame Edna, made it all the more comical. The TV crew even staged a mock flower throw, which finished with the cast unceremoniously tossing the flowers back to the audience as well as at the cameras.

Nureyev's next film, *Exposed*, was directed by James Toback. Rudolf spared some time from his dancing to make the film with co-star Nastassia Kinski. The film was not a success, although Nureyev dedicatedly took musical lessons, so he would look believable as a concert violinist in the film. He joked that it was a good thing the sound was turned off during his concert scenes, because the "music" coming from his violin while he "played" it, was simply dreadful.

Nureyev made two subsequent films never released in America. *Carnival in Venice* was filmed for Italian television and served as a fund-raiser to help rebuild Venice after devastating floods. Rudolf portrayed a university professor and his co-star was the Italian ballerina Carla Fracci. Another film, without much dialogue, was *Coupe de Foudre*, with music by Frenchman Michel Legrand. This was not much more than Nureyev running through the darkened streets of Paris, in pursuit of a woman.

When Nureyev sustained a serious injury cancelling the Boston Ballet season's *Don Quixote* performances, he spent some of his time off in New York. He always loved to see the latest films, often telling us what he saw and recommending them to us. He especially loved the films of Ingmar Berman and was spotted in a cinema at a screening of *Fanny and Alexander*. He sat with his feet elevated on the back of the seat in front of him. An usher approached and told him to put his feet down. When the usher disappeared, Rudolf removed his boots and continued elevating his feet.

Having been fascinated by films all his life, it was no surprise that once he became the Director of the Paris Opera, he also played a film director in his Hollywood-style version of *Cinderella*. Nureyev had a minor part in which he donned a Groucho Marx disguise and had one solo in the entire production. *Cinderella* was primarily a showcase for his latest star dancer and lead, Sylvie Guillem and his long-time protégé, Charles Jude, as the Prince. The production, however, used everything from Nureyev's vast knowledge of cinema, including an Astaire-based dance for Guillem with a hat rack, a Keystone Cops section, an appearance by King Kong, and giant pin-ups of Betty Grable, as part of the set.

Nureyev's directorial skills were considerable and he was approached several times to direct other productions. In the late 1970s, the Metropolitan Opera planned to stage a new production of Mussorgsky's *Khovanchina*, with Nureyev as director. This production never came to fruition.

In the early 80s, the Met announced a triple bill program featuring Erik Satie's *Parade*, originally choreographed by Leonid Massine. Nureyev wanted to do something different; creating a psychological drama between Satie, Picasso and Ravel, but producer John Dexter disagreed with him. When Dexter demanded that Nureyev rehearse for six months – despite Rudolf having created most of his full-length original ballets in five weeks or less – he withdrew, stating "artistic differences." Subscription tickets were already sold, so the commission went instead to David Hockney, who haughtily stated in the press, "Nureyev has green brocade curtains in front of his eyes and can see no further." The resulting triple bill was given few performances.

One thing Nureyev hadn't tried was a musical and when the chance came following his departure from the Paris Opera, he co-starred with Liz Robertson in *The King and I*. Rudolf stated that he never saw the stage or film version with Yul Brynner, and he didn't want to shave his head, preferring to do his own interpretation. He prepared for his King of Siam role with a vocal coach to "turn my growls into something resembling singing," as he explained on several TV interviews. He had difficulty "wrapping my tongue around the dialogue," in a clipped Siamese accent, no less. Nureyev's regular speaking voice was soft and he wore a microphone to be heard in large theatres. His presence was incredibly strong, but his voice was rather gruff and forced. I gave him tremendous credit for memorizing all the dialogue and his "muscle memory" way of learning was, "I take so many steps here and then I say this; then I move here and say that."

A singer he wasn't, but he had a powerful presence as the King and a real rapport with the children in the play. Nureyev struck a majestic pose, hands on his hips, as each child marched out and bowed to him. He frequently broke character by smiling at the smallest of these urchins, before resuming his "stern" pose. Naturally he had great fun with the "Shall We Dance?" number despite having to pretend he didn't know how to dance, since "the King has to be kind of dumb-footed." He created real tension in the build-up approaching Liz Robertson when they began dancing together. Since she had a large hooped skirt, Rudolf took great relish in jumping over it every time they swirled around the stage, to the delight of the audience. His death scene was also always very moving.

The King and I premiered in Canada and toured extensively throughout North America. It was planned as a three-year tour prior to a Broadway run in 1991. Since Rudolf was still performing in various *Friends* programs, the tour schedule depended on Nureyev's dancing commitments, as well as theatre availability.

About twenty-five of us arrived for a Sunday matinee in Hartford, Connecticut. A line in the play has the King say to Anna, "Dinner is served" and he takes her arm and escorts her offstage. Normally the line garnered a laugh the way he said it, but at this particular performance, it did not. Outside the Stage Door after the matinee, Nureyev emerged to overhear us discussing where we wanted to go for dinner. He turned to us and joked, "If that line doesn't get a laugh tonight, you're all fired as fans!"

What was so endearing is how Nureyev interacted with the many children who waited for his autograph. One little girl with big blue eyes and blonde hair, probably no more than three years old, held up the program and looked at Rudolf in as awestruck a way as many of the adults did. He gently took her program and bent down to speak to her, meticulously turning the page to the cast sheet, rather than an advertisement. He signed it slowly and deliberately, in his "best" writing. When he handed it back to the child, her eyes filled with tears as she held up a pen and said, "But my mommy told me to use THIS pen." Rudolf chuckled and tried returning the program to her, but she refused to take it, clearly upset. Rudolf looked around for "mommy," who explained to her that Rudolf's pen was "better" than mommy's and the child was satisfied.

During a New York television appearance on *The David Letterman Show*, Nureyev discussed his role in the musical. Because of the constant touring, he never had time to eat properly, so he joked that in many of the towns where they played, the only food he could get after the performance was a cheeseburger. Letterman quipped that it was a forty-six-cheeseburger tour. After seeing Rudolf perform the King in Hartford, I gave him a card depicting him in a regal pose from one of his ballet curtain calls. The greeting inside said, "Good luck on your forty-six-cheeseburger tour." If you looked closely, Nureyev was holding a cheeseburger that I sketched into his extended hand – there was no Photoshop then!

At a gala performance in New York saluting Lerner and Lowe, Rudolf appeared with his *King and I* co-star, Liz Robertson, in a rendition of "The Rain in Spain" from *My Fair Lady*. Liz took on the role of Cockney Eliza Doolittle while Nureyev was Professor Higgins, exclaiming emphatically, "By Jove, she's got it!" when Eliza enunciated properly.

Nureyev was also heading to Paris for further negotiations of his contract as Director of the Paris Opera. Baryshnikov had recently resigned as Director of American Ballet Theatre and Jane Hermann had been appointed as acting director. She too, had been in negotiations with Rudolf about taking over ABT. Many orchestra conductors hold duel positions. We speculated on

Nureyev directing both ABT and the Paris Opera simultaneously, while continuing to perform in a Broadway musical. In the end, neither position was offered.

While Nureyev continued with the extensive *King and I* tour and his numerous *Friends* programs, he used his free time playing Bach on his keyboard. Seeing his options for performing dwindling, he began the next and most courageous phase of his career…as a conductor.

*"If I had another life, I might explore some other art for a change,
such as music, become a pianist, perhaps."*
~Rudolf Nureyev, Washington Post, August 6, 1978~

CONDUCTORS AND CONDUCTING

*Nureyev outside Metropolitan Opera House, NYC,
May 4, 1980. Photo: William J. Reilly*

Despite his impoverished childhood, Rudolf Nureyev discovered music before he discovered the dance. As a child, he listened intently to music on the radio. He wanted to learn to play the piano, but extreme poverty prevented him from doing so. When he began his formal dance studies in his late teens in Leningrad, he became familiar with all kinds of music. He was an avid record collector, and once in the West, he never traveled anywhere without his music. He listened to music while in the car, when alone and relaxing, waiting for planes at airports, and while unwinding to pop music, evidenced by the numerous times he was photographed disco dancing in various places around the world. In an 1978 interview with critic Walter Terry in the *Saturday*

Review, Nureyev spoke of music as "The friend, the companion, the pest, because it is ever-present. It talks to me. I talk back. There is no intermediate person between us. It's a very jealous person."

Nureyev had his own ideas about how he wanted the music played. At a young age when setting his production of *Swan Lake* on the Vienna Opera dancers, he took the baton from the Vienna Philharmonic conductor to illustrate the tempo he wanted. Probably more than anything else that goes into making a performance, the conductor can make or break the ballet. Without the right tempo, the dancers cannot dance their best. Much of Nureyev's career was spent dealing with conductors, which is probably one of the reasons, why he took up conducting late in his life.

Whenever Rudolf danced, we always knew when he was pleased with the conductor at curtain calls. He shook the conductor's hand and gestured toward the musicians in the orchestra pit. If displeased, he dropped the conductor's hand and seldom looked at him. He genuinely admired some conductors, but sometimes the orchestra pained him.

Unfortunately, many ballet companies use "pick-up" orchestras, consisting of musicians who are employed for a particular season. They obligingly follow the conductor, but sometimes there are dreadful blips and squeaks coming from the orchestra pit. During one *Nureyev and Friends* season in Paris, the violinist's string broke and what resulted was such unpleasant screeching, that Rudolf looked into the pit with a most pained expression. There were occasions when he actually stared into the pit as if trying to find the offensive noises. At other times, he pursed his lips and raised one eyebrow disdainfully, while trying to keep a straight face.

Prokofiev's *Romeo and Juliet* was particularly challenging for most orchestras, but especially for the seasonal musicians. Since Nureyev performed this ballet frequently, there were numerous difficulties with the music. At one London performance, Prokofiev's score was being "slaughtered" in the orchestra pit, when suddenly three horns blasted off key and well ahead of their cue. The horns fizzled out when they realized their mistake, but they sounded rather like elephants trumpeting. Rudolf and Rick Werner, portraying Tybalt, had to hide their faces into each other's shoulders to keep from laughing out loud.

Even when he wasn't dancing, Nureyev could tell if the music wasn't right. At another *Romeo* performance, he kept looking into the pit during the flag-waving dance, while sitting on the side with Benvolio and Mercutio. Rudolf began beating out a faster tempo by thumping his knee. After repeated attempts to get the conductor's attention failed, he audaciously crawled forward on all fours and looked into the pit to see if the conductor was there. He crawled back into position to his astonished friends and said audibly, "A bit slow, eh?"

At other performances, one half of the orchestra got a few bars ahead of the other, making a dreadful noise. Nureyev stared at the conductor in disbelief, but thankfully the orchestra rectified itself and brought on a smile from Rudolf.

It wasn't always the conductor at fault. A brief power failure at the beginning of the balcony scene caused the organ to malfunction, so the piano took over. Later, some of the instruments fizzled out, completely forcing other interesting musical replacements.

During another *Romeo and Juliet* in 1977 after a pause in the ballroom dances, the company returned to the stage to finish the dance and waited for the conductor to begin. The conductor, in turn, waited for the dancers to start again. There followed a long silence, until Nureyev glared into the pit and yelled "Shit!" The music returned, but the dancers couldn't conceal their laughter.

Nureyev wasn't the only one frustrated by undanceable tempi. During the *Flower Festival* pas de deux on Broadway, Eva Evdokimova began yelling "faster, faster!" through her clenched-teeth smile to the conductor. Rudolf looked amused, knowing he wasn't the only one who had tempi difficulties. At the following performance, Eva yelled out, "Come on, faster," and then finally "Shit" when nothing happened. After the third performance, the tempo was to everyone's liking and even the conductor led the applause for the dancers.

Evdokimova's performance in *Don Quixote* with Nureyev was completely ruined by the conductor's funeral dirge tempo. In the middle of her third act fouettes, she screamed "Faster," since those steps are easier to perform with a brisk tempo and she could barely manage with the snail-paced music. By the time Rudolf joined her in the finger-snapping dancing finale, he showed his displeasure with the progressively reduced musical speed by doing a wobbly-kneed step like an old man.

Sometimes the conducting was fine, but it seemed like the musicians were deliberately sabotaging the performance. Once in *Petrushka* with music by Igor Stravinsky, the players were audibly laughing at all the wrong notes they were playing. A police siren passed the theatre echoing the same note the trumpets were trying to play, causing laughter from the audience. At the conclusion of the ballet when Petrushka thumbs his nose at the Magician, the trumpet player hit every wrong note imaginable, making it appear, as if Nureyev was thumbing his nose at the lousy orchestral playing.

Nureyev was in a rage over the slow tempo that spoiled another London performance and the conductor was booed at the curtain calls. The tension was broken when the curtain went up for another call and Luigi, Nureyev's masseur, was seen scurrying like mad out the back door of the set. Rudolf couldn't help but laugh. Exiting the Stage Door, Nureyev said to the fans, "Cheer up the orchestra; they need encouragement."

Nureyev was again unhappy with one conductor and in a fit of frustration, made a rude gesture. Later Luigi told us that Rudolf apologized, saying, "His temper is stronger than he is."

During a performance of *Songs of a Wayfarer* with Johnny Eliasen, Rudolf was so dissatisfied with the slow tempo that he snapped his fingers and glared at the conductor to get his attention. He actually shouted, "Faster, come on, faster." Conductor Stanley Sussman finally looked up while Nureyev continued, "Hey, Stanley come ON!" Rudolf clapped his hands signaling the orchestra to stop, went to the edge of the stage, shaded his eyes from the spotlight, and said, "Stanley, we can't dance to this." We couldn't believe our eyes. His professionalism usually carried him through, but on this particular occasion, Nureyev simply couldn't tolerate the sluggish tempo another minute. He resumed his position; pouting, glaring and somewhat embarrassed, but instructed, "We start at two." Sussman asked, "The whole thing?" Rudolf insisted, "From the beginning – from two." All the musicians fumbled for the right music and Rudolf repeated the entire song. Later we overheard him say to Eliasen, "Sounds like same tempo, no?" Johnny tried his best not to laugh. Joffrey Ballet dancer Gary Christ was in the audience and later confided that he always wanted to stop the orchestra due to bad tempos, but Robert Joffrey told him it was "unprofessional."

During those moments in his own productions when he wasn't on stage, he still felt responsible for everything, including the music. We frequently heard him in the wings, snapping or clapping out the tempo to the conductor, so that his dancers could be seen to their best advantage. Sometimes this helped, but all too often it was to no avail, if the conductor never looked up and watched the dancers.

If anything, Rudolf preferred a brisk tempo to a slower one. This was an absolute must in the coda or those dancing finales that sent everyone home very happy. Watching a rehearsal of Rudolf's *Sleeping Beauty* production with London Festival Ballet, Patrice Bart as the Prince and Eva Evdokimova as Aurora, were practicing the finale. The tempo was taken at breakneck speed and Bart, new to the role, couldn't keep up. He paused to rest while Eva humored him, "But Rudolf likes it fast!"

There were difficulties with the ABT conductor when Nureyev's production of *Raymonda* was presented in 1975. On most nights the tempos were simply too sluggish. During one rehearsal, a couple of the fans decided to set up a "walkie-talkie" system with one in Nureyev's dressing room calling out "faster, faster" and the other seated behind the conductor. When Rudolf learned of this idea, he began laughing hysterically, but admonished them, "Go play with your machine."

We witnessed many finales when Rudolf snapped his fingers at the conductor while shouting "Faster." We used to break into giggles just watching him lead the dancers out in the finale of *Raymonda*. Grinning madly, he was heard above the music saying, "Faster, faster, that's it!" and even an occasional "yippee!" The audience exploded in excited applause even before the finale finished.

At one performance, the usual announcement was made about "photography not permitted during the performance," but for some reason the microphone was left on. When the curtain went up, the dancers heard only a loud buzzing and static, but couldn't hear the orchestra. The audience began shouting, "Fix the sound!" The dancers left the stage and the curtain was lowered briefly, until the offending microphone was turned off. Rudolf was amused.

At the enormous Palais des Sports in Paris, the orchestra is amplified, but the delay from the speakers often threw the sound off. Sometimes it sounded like one half of the orchestra was playing something different than the other. *Apollo* was the opening piece on one program and the orchestra was a disaster. Nureyev was so annoyed, he often stopped dancing to stare incredulously at the conductor. By the end, he waved his hands, conducting the tempo he needed. When it finished, he shook his fists at the conductor. The last work on that program was *Moor's Pavane*. By this time Rudolf had given up on the conductor, who was roundly booed. Nureyev's partner, Merle Park, began giggling when Rudolf made an obscene gesture under his Moor's robe to show his displeasure. That night he called the orchestra "scrambled eggs."

At still another *Apollo* performance, Nureyev counted out, "One, two, three, let's get going." Later in the program, he smirked at the conductor as if to say, "I'm going to dance in spite of you!" And who could forget some of those *Apollo* performances when Rudolf led his muses up the steps to Mount Olympus, stomping out the tempo? He even snapped his fingers for the tempo he wanted. One fan quipped, "It's *Apollo* in ragtime!"

At his first Broadway *Friends* program, those who were at the rehearsal heard Rudolf ask the conductor, "Isn't the music too slow here?" "I don't know, is it?" the conductor replied. Annoyed, Rudolf explained, "I'm a dancer. You have the music in front of you. LOOK at it." His pleadings for a faster tempo were to no avail. And when Apollo "faints" in the hands of his three muses, the conductor failed to pause. Losing patience, Rudolf walked towards the orchestra pit and asked the conductor, "When are you going to stop here for mother-fucking shit's sake?"

During *Flower Festival*, Rudolf shouted, "Could you play the music faster, please?" "Faster?" the conductor asked. When the orchestra and dancers whizzed through it, Rudolf said to the conductor, "See? It's a different matter now." He later asked the conductor not to hold the music too long at the final pose. "Otherwise it's much ado about nothing." At another pose when his partner, Merle Park, leans in arabesque on Nureyev's shoulder, Rudolf explained again not to hold the music too long. The conductor, who was French, asked, "You mean when she's lying on you?" With twinkling eyes, Rudolf replied, "Exactement, coucher sur moi."

When he first mounted his production of *Sleeping Beauty* for London Festival Ballet, some of the tempi sounded quite slow, especially for the Garland Dance. Some critics remarked that the orchestra sounded "stuck in molasses" and had ruined the performance. This was because the dancers had just learned the complex choreography and Rudolf wanted to make sure the dancing was "clear and clean." The following season, the production was encored and Rudolf was overheard at the rehearsal telling the conductor to speed it up, because "the dancers know it already."

It took some time for Rudolf to be satisfied with his conductors. When Terence Kern conducted *The Sleeping Beauty* in London, he listened to Nureyev's suggestions but sometimes objected, "That won't work musically." Rudolf replied, "OK, let's try it your way." At one performance, the ballet was conducted so fast, that it finished a full fifteen minutes earlier than when alternate conductors were in the pit.

During long seasons conductors sometimes alternate performances. In the balcony scene of *Romeo and Juliet*, the tempos were so inconsistent that Rudolf had an "I submit to my Fate!" expression on his face. The pas de deux was so unbearably slow, that the dancers had to squeeze every ounce of phrasing to fill the music. When it came to doing double assembles, the music suddenly became so fast, that Nureyev could barely keep up.

During the tomb scene, the music nearly stopped, it was so sluggish. Rudolf began fondling Juliet's hand and kissing her and still had more music to fill. Finally in exasperation, he glared into the orchestra pit and said, "Who's in the pit?" and collapsed in a heap for his death scene. When Patricia Ruanne as Juliet woke up, she had an amused expression on her face. She, too, had to stretch, yawn, and devise all sorts of things to fill the dawdling playing during her own death scene. Rudolf once called Prokofiev's score "spaghetti music by the yard," because there was so much of it. Many a death scene had been ruined by sluggish playing or dancers new to the roles that simply "died" far too soon, with yards of music left over, while the audience stared at the lifeless bodies.

One of Nureyev's favorite conductors was John Lanchbery, who conducted ballets for several companies as well as arranged music for choreographers, including Sir Frederick Ashton's production of *La Fille Mal Gardee*. He collaborated with Rudolf on the music for his productions of *Don Quixote* and *Nutcracker* and was a frequent conductor for many of Nureyev's performances. Lanchbery was a conductor who loved the ballet and always attentively watched the dancers, making sure that the orchestra finished when the dancers did. Otherwise it makes the dancer look unmusical.

We sat through several seasons of performances with spoiled variations, because the conductors had their heads buried in the score rather than watching the dancers. A brilliant variation could be ruined when the music finished earlier or later than the dancer. The "finish" of a solo is the last thing an audience sees and even if what came before was thrilling, they remember the final pose as "not in time with the music."

Sometimes Rudolf merely instructed the conductor to "just play it; we'll keep up." Above all, he wanted the music to sound good and the dancers to look good while dancing to it. If a conductor didn't grasp what was needed, Rudolf frequently hummed or counted the tempo for him.

In the dress rehearsals, Rudolf often sat behind the conductor "conducting" the tempo he wanted. He instructed the conductor to slow down in certain places, "because I have to do pirouette here" or speed up in another place, because a particular sequence required a brisk tempo. Taking the size of the dancer into account was also important. Taller dancers with longer legs need slightly more time to wrap their legs around certain steps. Since Nureyev was of average height – 5'8" – he generally liked the faster tempi.

Sometimes there was miscommunication between the conductor and the dancers. After performing a stunning *Sleeping Beauty* pas de deux in London in 1976, Nureyev and his Aurora, Eva Evdokimova, acknowledged the audience applause while the conductor rested. The finale music hadn't started and Rudolf usually signaled the conductor to begin, before he and his partner left the stage. Unable to get the conductor's attention, Rudolf extended one hand and said audibly, "What are you waiting for?" and stalked off. When he returned to join the dancers in the finale, he snapped his fingers at the conductor to pick up the tempo.

At another *Beauty* performance that same week, Rudolf made his entrance while waving his arms, so the conductor could see what tempo was required. Later, when the Prince's aide removed Rudolf's boots prior to his variation, the music had speeded up so fast that Rudolf mimed "hang the conductor!"

During his solo entrance in *Le Corsaire*, the harpist didn't begin the musical introduction right away, so Rudolf merely held a long arabesque until the music caught up with him.

At one *Swan Lake* rehearsal, Rudolf was working for the first time with the Boston Ballet's conductor, giving instructions on how he sets the tempo for his third act solo. "Well, I glower at you, you glower at me, and we take it from here." Halfway through, Nureyev stopped and asked if the music could be played "more butch."

At a rehearsal of *Don Quixote*, Rudolf argued with the conductor that the Minkus music sounded "too flat." He wanted it accented differently and added, "Take some cymbals or drums out or something." This conductor flatly refused, arguing, "That's the way it's orchestrated and I'll conduct it like that." However, on another occasion even members of the audience remarked, "The orchestra is assassinating the composer!" Music is so vital to the ballet, but can be problematic for both the dancers as well as sensitive music lovers in the audience.

Another conductor Nureyev respected was Andre Presser who conducted Tchaikovsky's *Manfred* Symphony, when the Zurich Ballet performed his production. At the dress rehearsal in London for the 1982 *Nureyev Festival*, Presser never watched the dancers and just conducted his own tempo. Rudolf wanted to go over a few things and after one scene, knelt down at the front of the stage, and tried getting Presser's attention. The conductor was absorbed in the score repeating certain passages with the orchestra, while the scenery was being changed. Rudolf managed to get the attention of one of the musicians, instructing, "Tell him to look UP – I want to talk to him." When he finally had Presser's attention he said, "The reprise, the bit…" and then hummed "la de da dum – is too fast. Can you do a pause there? Maybe make a note of it so you don't forget?" He spoke so meekly, like a schoolboy asking the professor something and doing so half-heartedly for fear of being reprimanded.

Seymour Lipkin conducted the Joffrey's Diaghilev Program at the New York State Theatre in July 1979, using several musicians from the recent Soviet Émigré Concert that had played earlier. Nureyev liked the conductor and bowed to him every night during the curtain calls, even though Lipkin never quite knew when to leave the stage. Rudolf always exited ahead of Lipkin into the wings, still in character as the puppet Petrushka, his gloved hands flapping while taking tiny running steps.

Often there was mutual respect between the conductor and Nureyev, and the musicians remained in the pit to applaud the dancers. At one *Sleeping Beauty* performance, some orchestra players actually stood up in the pit to watch Nureyev's long slow solo.

Nureyev was also instrumental in discovering musical talent. During a Broadway season with the Murray Louis Company in May of 1978, he performed an original work created by Louis, called *Vivace*. The music was Bach's *Toccata and Fugue* and played onstage by Andrew Litton, a 17-year-old pianist from the Juilliard School. We could tell that Rudolf admired Litton's playing very much just by the way he presented the young man at the curtain calls. He shook his hand warmly, gently pushed him forward to receive the applause, and insisted he take another bow. Litton was not used to this kind of protocol, but Rudolf insisted. That young man went on to make his Carnegie Hall Debut at age 20, took the Russians by storm with his playing of Gershwin at the Moscow Conservatory, and become a widely respected pianist and conductor.

Esteemed conductors Karl Bohm, Leonard Bernstein and Herbert van Karijan had encouraged Nureyev to take up conducting, the latter even offering to give private lessons. They admired his musicality as a dancer and told him that conductors generally live long lives. The Juilliard School offered Nureyev a scholarship to pursue further study. Rudolf gave it serious consideration, but when he ended his contract as Director of the Paris Opera in 1989, he switched to musical comedy by performing the lead in the Rogers and Hammerstein musical, *The King and I*. It provided him with a way of prolonging his time on stage.

During this multi-city five-month tour of the musical, Nureyev studied and practiced on a piano when available, or on his portable keyboard that he took with him everywhere. When *The King and I* finished, he returned to dancing by touring with his *Nureyev and Friends* programs. Rudolf traveled with his keyboard, and his fellow cast members heard him playing Bach late into the night. Music was his constant companion. He said it was the "perfect person to have a dialogue with."

Whenever he was in Vienna, Nureyev attended concerts and made the acquaintance of Wilhelm "Papa" Hubner, former president of the Vienna Philharmonic, and a professor at the Vienna Academy of Music. Rudolf began to study conducting with him, learned to read scores, and was provided with the Residenz Orchestra, founded by Hubner, consisting of a group of talented young musicians.

While Rudolf was familiar with much of the music he conducted, he kept the score in front of him for his own reassurance. Some critics dismissed Rudolf as being a dilettante, but "Papa" Hubner found it astonishing at how quickly Nureyev learned and absorbed music. As with his studies in Leningrad at age 17, when he completed the normal eight-year course of study in three years through his sheer determination and hard work, Nureyev was ready for his conducting debut in just seven months.

On June 25, 1991 in Vienna's magnificent Auersperg Palace, a tuxedo-clad Rudolf Nureyev stepped to the podium, gave the orchestra a strong downbeat with his baton, and the music seemed to pour out of him and back again. The evening began with Haydn's *La Chasse*, followed by Mozart's *Violin Concerto K 218* featuring guest concertmaster of the Vienna Philharmonic, Rainer Kuchl. It concluded with Tchaikovsky's *Serenade for Strings*, with the first movement of Mozart's *Jupiter Symphony* as an encore. Nureyev was visibly nervous and unsure of what to do "in between" movements, but once in command, he relaxed and brought enormous vigor and freshness to the music. My Viennese friend who played the piano commented to me later, "The way Nureyev showed the structure of the Haydn was beautiful. The phrasing became clear and the tempi were fantastic. I've heard others conduct it, but it seemed as if Nureyev's brought more 'life' to it."

Following the concert was a dinner for the three hundred invited guests. Rudolf arrived later, having changed to more casual attire, and wasn't able to eat because he was bombarded with autograph seekers and people wanting to say hello. He eventually disappeared into the kitchen for a while in order to get some food.

On the program of his second concert a few nights later was Stravinsky's *Apollo*. The faster sections were conducted at a brisk pace and he brought out the humor, serenity, transparency and majesty of the score. In that night's audience sat Ully Wuhrer, who danced with Rudolf in his very first

Apollo in 1967. When Rudolf finished, she jumped to her feet and shouted "Bravo maestro!" It was probably the first time she heard the score played the way they had both wanted.

Rudolf was especially fond of the first violinist's playing and presented her with bouquets following each concert. At a rehearsal, another violinist frequently tried to lead the string section, until Rudolf became irritated and said firmly "No, don't lead." Hubner backed him up, instructing the violinist sharply, "Nureyev is your conductor now and you must follow him, not the other way around."

Nureyev's conducting style was one of economy. His arms and hands were beautiful and, of course, there was still much "dance" movement in his torso. He had a serious, no-nonsense approach to the music. But it was interesting to watch the interaction between Nureyev and the musicians, as both seemed so eager to please.

In a German television interview shortly after his conducting debut, Nureyev said of his orchestra, "You have to control them and make a dynamic tempo." In defending his career choice of conducting, he stated, "I'm 53 and want to study. You should be proud of me. I should try, before I die, everything I'm capable of." In another interview, he admitted, "Now I know how those bastard conductors feel. You have this fantastic struggle with the orchestra to keep the tempi up; the brass is heavy…to keep them together with the violins, you have to goose them."

Up until this time, only my friends in Vienna, well versed in music, had seen Nureyev conduct. I decided I simply must go and see for myself, and so made the long journey to Vienna when Nureyev conducted a very special New Year's Eve concert, again at the Vienna Palais Auersperg. The program consisted of many Strauss waltzes, Tchaikovsky's *Serenade for Strings*, and finished with the *Radetsky March*, as is the custom with the New Year's Day concerts. Following the concert several dancers from the Vienna Opera Ballet waltzed around the palace in tuxedos and long white gowns and the entire evening was capped with fireworks in the garden.

We noticed that at the start of the concert, Rudolf had difficulty mounting the step to the podium and later learned that he wore a catheter that had bothered him. Once the concert started, however, he seemed transported to another world. His dancer's body took over and while he never made huge, dramatic gestures, the economy of his movements mingled with the music and the music itself energized him.

At a rehearsal earlier in the week, which was recorded for Austrian television, we saw Rudolf arrive at the Palais swathed in scarves, hat, coat, gloves, and looking deathly pale. A chill went through me when I saw his face, with his eyes looking rather sunken. It was then that I realized how ill he actually was. A few moments later when we were seated in the ballroom where the musicians had assembled for the rehearsal, a completely transformed Rudolf Nureyev strode confidently to the podium. He wore one of his multi-colored sweaters and casual slacks and looked very refreshed. A television monitor was close by and as I glanced between Rudolf conducting his musicians to the close-up of his face on the monitor, I thought to myself how much "the cameras loved that face." He looked younger, stronger, happier, and healthier than he did in the corridor just minutes before. As with his dancing, the music revitalized him.

Following the rehearsal, we waited in the corridor and once more he was completely wrapped up from head to toe while prepared for the cold weather outside. As he headed straight for me, I instinctively extended my hand and said, "Congratulations, Rudolf, on your new career." He took both hands and grasped mine – his hands were warm – and smiled sincerely, thanking me for coming. We made small talk on the way downstairs and I wished him a Happy New Year. It was the first time I really spoke to him in a longer conversation. I had a flash of "it's now or never." And that was the last time I saw him up close. He admitted that "my dancing days are over," but that conducting kept him going.

At further concerts throughout Europe, he frequently invited his fans to rehearsals. During one such rehearsal in Vienna, Nureyev nearly collapsed and had to lie down momentarily. After a concerned fan asked if he was all right, he resumed the rehearsal. By the end of 1991, he had a bladder operation.

As his health continued to deteriorate, Nureyev seemed more driven than ever. He continued to study and conduct other orchestras, mostly in Eastern Europe, enlarging his repertoire. He conducted the ballets *Swan Lake* and *Sleeping Beauty* in America and abroad. In March of 1992, he even managed to perform the role of Carabosse in his production of *Sleeping Beauty* for the Berlin Ballet.

All those frustrating years of dancing to sluggish tempos seemed to pour out of him, when he conducted *Romeo and Juliet* for American Ballet Theatre on May 6, 1992. I had a box seat at the Met for that performance, so I could watch both the conductor and dancers. The minute Rudolf Nureyev entered the orchestra pit, an explosion of applause greeted him. He looked a bit sheepish, waving his hand in an arc and it looked like he was saying, "I haven't done anything yet!" Even the musicians in the orchestra applauded him. Then he turned to the orchestra, and the music began.

I remember vividly his clear, strong downbeat for Sylvie Guillem's Juliet solo in the ballroom scene and how different the Prokofiev score sounded under his baton. He had a definite idea of how he wanted the music performed. It was both lyrical and majestic and he approached it like concert music, without the bombast that had crept into it over the years from varying ballet orchestras. Everyone in the dance world turned out for Nureyev's conducting debut at the Metropolitan Opera House. Jackie Onassis was there and was photographed with Rudolf after the performance.

What most people didn't realize was the incredible will it took for Nureyev to get through the evening. Charles Barker, ABT's principal conductor, sat on a stool next to the maestro in case he was unable to finish. Hidden from the audience's view, he was not noticed except by those in the side boxes. Rudolf was incredibly weak from AIDS, but somehow mustered up the strength to conduct the three-hour ballet. Only when his Paris Opera Ballet protégés, guest artists Sylvie Guillem and Laurent Hilaire, brought him on stage for a bow, did the audience realize how sick he was. He seemed to be shuffling across the stage rather than striding and appeared quite frail. Members of the orchestra stood in the pit and applauded him.

There was a party for Nureyev at his Dakota apartment following the performance, to which many of his friends and some fans were invited. Rudolf was understandably drained and wanted to rest, but he had the satisfaction of conducting a very acceptable performance at the Met. Most of the reviews were favorable, with critic Clive Barnes writing, "He performed wonders" and noted the more majestic Russian manner that reflected Prokofiev's debt to Tchaikovsky. Barnes concluded that Rudolf's conducting of ABT's orchestra "elicited perhaps the best performance of *Romeo and Juliet* I have ever heard from it."

In a 1992 TV interview in Vienna, Nureyev was asked if he'd like to conduct the Vienna Philharmonic. "That would be the greatest," he enthusiastically replied.

Rudolf's health continued to fluctuate. First he would rally and then a new problem would develop, but he adhered to his conducting schedule as faithfully as he did when he danced. In September of 1992, one of his fans telephoned him in Vienna. He sounded very bad, informing her that he had just had a kidney stone removed. In true Nureyev form, he nevertheless conducted a performance in Berlin of *Songs of a Wayfarer*, danced by Peter Schaufuss and Patrick Dupond.

In October it took every ounce of his strength to oversee his production of *La Bayadere* for the Paris Opera. The dancers and staff were eager to please, but for the premiere, Nureyev watched from a stage box while reclining. He was helped to the stage and when the audience saw how fragile he looked, they jumped to their feet and gave him a much-deserved ovation.

After a brief visit to St. Bart's, he returned to Paris and began planning a new production of *Coppelia*. When he was hospitalized, he was still reading the score and planning steps.

It was a terrible time for the fans. We claimed "Nureyev was our passport to friendship" and that he was "the one constant in our lives" for decades. We sent him cards and letters, but it seemed inadequate for all the years of joy he brought to our lives.

Over the years I had recorded many performances, including the applause, on my mini cassette recorder to help me remember the ballets. I decided to loop all the applause and bravos together into one hour-long tape and sent it to Nureyev. Whether he listened to it or not, I wanted him to leave us with our never-ending applause.

January 6, 1993 was the day we all dreaded when Nureyev died. My phone was jammed with all kinds of messages, but the first call from my friend Bob Gable was the most poignant. In his raspy voice, all he said was, "It's over."

Nureyev's death made front-page news around the world. His funeral service, held on the Paris Opera's grand staircase, was lined with dancers and friends. He was buried in St. Genevieve du Bois Cemetery outside of Paris, while his grieving dancers tossed their ballet shoes on top of the coffin.

As with the dance, he gave everything he had to his music. His passion, dedication and keen intelligence never left him. He accomplished more in his fifty-four years than most people could in a few lifetimes. But there was still the nagging question: how much more could he have done had he lived longer?

After Nureyev's death in 1993, I had a very vivid dream. He appeared and instructed, "Remember me." He then added, "Stay together." We have. The fans are still in contact and we toast his birthday or anniversary. Not only do we remember, but we'll never forget him. In Dido's Lament from Purcell's opera, *Dido & Anaeus*, she sings, ""Remember me, remember me…oh, but forget my fate."

"If culture is to survive, find not only the power of reminiscence but of renewal."
~Rudolf Nureyev, PBS "Dancing" TV series, May, 1983~

REFLECTIONS

Nureyev outside Uris Theatre, NYC, 1975
Photo: William J. Reilly

After nearly three decades of watching Rudolf Nureyev dance, it's difficult to choose a favorite role or the most memorable performance. Speaking from experience, those marathon seasons when Nureyev danced eight performances a week for several consecutive weeks, were probably as challenging for us as for Rudolf. As one fan recalled, "The impressions from single performances lasted longer. The marathon seasons tended to blur together; it took incredible mental stamina to digest them all."

Whenever Nureyev was dancing, it was hard NOT to see him. You felt you might miss something exclusive, because every performance was unique.

Supporting casts or conductors alternated. Nureyev's mood changed each time he performed, so we never knew what to expect. The audiences' energy varied and often altered the performance. No matter what happened, Nureyev always said that he danced better when he was tired. He performed a dynamic and breathtaking matinee that would exhaust a mere mortal, only to outdance himself in the evening performance. After a Saturday matinee, we wouldn't think of missing the evening performance because Rudolf was thoroughly warmed up. We expected fireworks and he seldom disappointed.

His partnership with Margot Fonteyn was truly magical. They had the same vision and sense of professionalism. This was exemplified by the way Fonteyn danced during the WWII London bombings or when Nureyev danced while injured. I was grateful to have seen them in most of the classical ballets. They moved as one, from the angle of their heads to the mirror-like placement of arms and feet. Even as they matured, they created magic on stage.

Early film clips of *Giselle* with Fonteyn make Nureyev appear overly self-conscious at Giselle's grave when he fondled the flowers, knowing the camera had zoomed in on him. As he matured in the role, he found different approaches and his later interpretation became his signature piece. He knelt at Giselle's grave; hands clasped to his mouth in grief, and slowly let his arms float to his sides as the curtain fell.

This didn't mean he couldn't be boldly animated. In the first act when hiding behind Giselle's cottage, Albrecht blew kisses to her. Nureyev's were so audible that the audience laughed. When Giselle sat on the bench, this Albrecht was practically on top of her and stopped abruptly, because she spread her skirt out and left no room for him to sit beside her. The mischievous way he turned from her to the audience and plucked one extra petal from the daisy to show Giselle that he loved her, always garnered titters.

When Giselle introduced him to her friends, he nodded to each one, grabbed a grape or two from their harvest baskets, popped them into his mouth and mimed, "Umm…very good!" Pretending he didn't know how to dance when Giselle asked him to join her, he performed the first steps haltingly, carefully watching Giselle's feet, until he succeeded.

In Peter Wright's production of *Giselle*, both Giselle and Albrecht remained on stage to watch the peasant dancers. Once while seated on opposite sides of the stage, Rudolf stared at Giselle and slowly began to roll up his sleeves. He had been rehearsing the psychotic dance teacher in *The Lesson*, and repeated this gesture, which rather unnerved his Giselle.

His entrance in the second act mesmerized me throughout the years. With his long cape draped around him, cradling the flowers in his arm, he walked slowly and extended one arm in search of Giselle's grave. His cape billowed out behind him when he ran the circumference of the stage, then engulfed him once he stopped. He visibly shuddered at the grave when he sensed Giselle was behind him, drawing his cape around him like a security blanket. I remember the way he "embraced" the empty air when he thought he saw Giselle.

A 1977 performance of *Marguerite and Armand* with Fonteyn was truly unforgettable. Both were so involved with the characters they portrayed, that they appeared unaware of the audience. Nureyev entered, executed solid and beautifully elongated arabesques, as if "announcing" himself to Marguerite, who in turn, was both coy and flirtatious. After he kissed her hand, he gently brushed it against his cheek, as though it was the center of his universe. In the country scene, Nureyev dropped to his knees while clasping her hands in his. She responded in kind and chucked him under the chin in a playful manner. One fan sitting next to me was fixated on both dancers' hands because they were so magnificently expressive.

Thinking Marguerite betrayed him when she returned to the Duke, Armand publicly insulted her by tossing money at her feet. As he backed into the wings with an outstretched and accusing finger, he turned toward her again with a look of doubt as if to say, "But I did love you!" Then Fonteyn, broken with grief, exited with her "crying feet," as we referred to her halting steps on point.

In the final scene, Armand rushed across the upstage, cape flying behind him, tossed it off with a flourish, and spun Marguerite around in his arms. Weakened from her illness, she fought desperately for life by clawing the very air. Armand, truly shocked, couldn't react when she collapsed to the floor. He cradled her hand as huge tears welled up in his eyes. In resignation, he let her lifeless hand fall to the floor.

During his 1979 Nureyev Festival, Rudolf coaxed Fonteyn into dancing with him in a reprise of his Diaghilev program. Fonteyn danced two performances of Nijinsky's *L'apres Midi d'une Faune* with Rudolf that week. The frieze-like movement required more walking and posing than actual dancing. We learned that Rudolf taught her the role one afternoon in the living room of Maude and Nigel Gosling's flat, where he stayed during his London seasons.

Just before that week's Saturday matinee on June 23rd, a staff member walked out in front of the curtain and announced, "Ladies and gentlemen, at this afternoon's performance of *Le Spectre de la Rose*, the role of the Young Girl will be performed by Margot Fonteyn." The curtain opened and Margot stood by the window, dreamily smelling the rose. Fonteyn had officially retired from the stage, but despite her age at 60, she truly embodied the spirit of that young girl dreaming of a rose, presented to her at her first ball. She made so much of those opening moments, especially the way she gently placed the rose on her lap before letting her hand drop, as she fell asleep in the chair. When Nureyev stood behind her armchair, encircling his arms over his head, it was a picture for posterity: their "debut" together in this ballet at the ages of 60 and 41! Fonteyn didn't wear point shoes, but it didn't matter. She and Rudolf transported everyone in the theatre.

We found out that Fonteyn would dance again that evening, so it took a lot of phone calls to other fans to make sure they didn't miss it. Tickets were sold out and people in the street waved wads of pound notes in desperate attempts to obtain a ticket. My friends and I were in standing room and once I secured my spot, I dashed downstairs and opened a side door, letting in dozens of fans that would have been heartbroken, if they couldn't see this performance. Within minutes, the standing room was three rows deep, with fans jostling for places with the press. The ushers turned a blind eye, realizing that there wasn't much they could do without starting a riot. With her confidence boosted from the matinee, Fonteyn appeared at the evening performance wearing her point shoes. She seemed to skim across the stage floor and once again Fonteyn and Nureyev worked their magic.

There were moments of such tenderness, as when he gently raised her from the chair to dance with him, barely touching her. When she "awoke," she opened her eyes wide, blinked several times, and ran after him as fleet-footed as the young girl she portrayed. Once she returned to her chair, Nureyev kissed her on the forehead, a luminous smile on his face. He then pulled himself up, so his entire body seemed to float upward before the famous leap out the window. The house erupted into rhythmic clapping, showered them with flowers, and both dancers seemed temporarily overcome with emotion about their dancing reunion. The applause lasted longer than the ten-minute ballet, while the press recorded their curtain calls for posterity.

There were other memorable performances when Nureyev no longer performed with Fonteyn. By his own admission, Rudolf insisted there was no such thing as a "perfect" performance. It was the striving for perfection that motivated him. Nureyev brought his production of *Don Quixote* with the Australian Ballet to the London Coliseum in the fall of 1973. On that October 6th closing night, Nureyev surprised even himself at how well he danced. The company knew they were watching "one to remember," because they had looks of disbelief on their faces at just about every step Nureyev danced.

At the curtain calls, the audience would not stop applauding and went on for more than forty-five minutes. The cheering public called the dancers out again and again. Nureyev was flanked by Sir Robert Helpmann as Don Quixote and Lucette Aldous as Kitri, and at one of the final calls, he smiled at both as if to say, "How about this reception?" Robert Helpmann, the former partner of Dame Margot Fonteyn long before Rudolf Nureyev came on the scene, joined in and paid Rudolf the ultimate compliment. He knelt before Rudolf, bowing in submission, hand over his heart, as if to say, "This evening belongs to you."

The euphoric elation after that performance is impossible to describe. I remember waiting with friends for the subway, totally oblivious to the late hour or the crowded platform. We were all smiles and talked so animatedly that I didn't notice a fellow co-worker on the platform trying to get my attention. Finally she approached me and said, "Nancy, are you ON something?" She was probably expecting me to admit to being tipsy, but I simply said, "No, a Nureyev high." There was no point in trying to explain it. Unlike champagne, this high lasted for weeks.

Another date I'll never forget was on August 8, 1976 at the Metropolitan Opera House in New York. Rudolf had danced a series of performances with the Canadians after performing all over the globe, following a bout of pneumonia earlier in the year. As his way of "resting," Nureyev had accepted a contract with Ken Russell to make the *Valentino* film, and the closing night *Sleeping Beauty* was his temporary farewell to the stage for several weeks.

We knew from the moment he made his entrance, that this would be "one for the history books." If ever he danced a perfect performance, this was it. His turns in the Vision Scene were absolutely seamless and slowed down to a perfect finish with the back foot "kissing the floor," as several fans described it. His landings were soft and controlled; his footwork was fast and light -- movement just flowed from him. For his big variation in the last act, he was flawless. After executing beautifully finished double turns, he tore around the stage like a dancer possessed, meriting applause well before his "stop on a dime" finish in his tight fifth position.

I was in standing room and couldn't believe the noise level emanating from all parts of the Opera House. It sounded like fans cheering at a winning sports event. Suddenly I saw the entire Met audience standing as one, applauding, cheering, and screaming. A person nearby exclaimed, "I have never seen a standing ovation following a variation – at the end of the evening, yes, but not in the middle of the ballet." Nureyev once remarked in an interview, "Sure you can dance, but can you raise them off their seats?" That night he certainly did. As he stood in his tight fifth position, arms extended as if embracing the audience, his eyes welled up with tears. He wanted to relish the moment as long as possible, before walking off and saluting the King and Queen.

It was hard to watch the finale after the excitement he generated. At the curtain calls, despite enthusiastic cheering that went on for over forty minutes, many people were exhausted from applauding and began rushing up the aisles for their homeward journey. The magic of that performance, however, lingers to this day.

Another performance seared in my mind was during the 1982 *Nureyev Festival*, featuring his revised production of *Manfred* with the Zurich Ballet. That season was dedicated to the memory of Dame Marie Rambert, who had died that week, at age 94. The publicity for *Manfred* was minimal; an article appeared in the Saturday press, which got little attention. As a result of this "new" work, the house was not sold out. Nevertheless, fans and admirers arrived from the U.S. and Europe to see the production.

A hush fell over the crowd as the curtain went up to reveal Nureyev, center stage, his back to the audience, expressing Lord Byron's agony. The audience seemed to lean forward as one, as he drew us in. For the next hour Rudolf Nureyev completely captivated his audience. After the public had journeyed through the life of Byron/Manfred, there was a stunned silence, causing concern on Rudolf's face at that first curtain call. As if having a delayed reaction at what they had seen, the audience erupted into cheers. People stood in the boxes, cheering madly. The audience stomped its feet and clapped rhythmically. Rudolf attentively acknowledged those in the gallery, then the entire auditorium. He then bowed to the dancers and blew them a kiss. They, in turn, applauded him.

Ever since I saw the premiere in Paris in 1979, fans begged me to tell them about *Manfred*. I refused, not wanting to spoil it for them, because I wanted them to experience it for themselves. Those who were seeing it for the first time rushed up to me and said, "Now I know why you never wanted to tell me about it. That work is so powerful, my heart is still pounding." It was definitely a "solar plexus" reaction.

That night in London, Rudolf signed autographs for nearly another hour, no doubt pleased to hear comments from the public. After he left, we remained behind and the policeman who was waiting by the Stage Door remarked, "I hear there was a disturbance at the Coliseum tonight." "Yes," we replied, "the audience nearly raised the roof cheering!"

In August of 1984, a last-minute *Nureyev and Friends* season replaced a previously scheduled Broadway engagement. Producers contacted Rudolf to do a *Friends* season and he was eager to leave his directorial duties with the Paris Opera and return to Broadway. Nureyev was originally going to present *Bach Suite*, but didn't think it would be suitable for "summer tourists." Despite $100,000 worth of tickets sold in the first hours, performances were sparsely attended, since New Yorkers escaped the summer heat by heading to the beaches. Rudolf, however, was in excellent form thanks to the summer heat that kept his muscles warm and free from injury.

Despite having seen the program numerous times, these performances left us mesmerized. Nureyev infused every movement with meaning, especially in Songs of a Wayfarer. In the Lindenbaum section, it was as if the wind was blowing through his body. He became transparent; no flesh and bones; just pure dance.

When the lights came on at the end, Nureyev appeared stunned. Yet he didn't look tired or strained. If anything, he looked calm, peaceful and self-contained as if he had just purged himself. The applause seemed an unnecessary intrusion. His partner, Jean Guizerix, stared at him in disbelief. I wondered what it must be like to be on stage when something transcendent like that takes place. At the interval, none of us could speak until we came out of our daze. We couldn't quite comprehend what we had just experienced.

But Rudolf Nureyev wasn't finished with his public that night. He gave a *Moor's Pavane* that was completely different; sharp, majestic, proud yet dignified. Even when standing still with his back to the audience, Desdemona at his side, you could feel his conflicting emotions, doubting her fidelity and yet remaining exquisitely tender with her. In his final scene, a convulsive sob went through his entire body as he gave her one last embrace. It was a moment of such intense personal sorrow, that it seemed the audience was trespassing onto the "sacred space" of the stage. Rudolf often referred to the stage as his religion and his salvation.

Whenever Nureyev was chasing an "ideal," especially in *La Sylphide* or *Swan Lake*, roles he performed throughout his entire career, his interpretation made you wonder if this "ideal" was real or imagined. In *La Sylphide*, Rudolf's reaction when the Sylph disappeared up the chimney always amused me, because of the double take he did. Practically standing in the fireplace, he looked up and was startled when fiancé Effie and friends arrived. Because of his early days in Ufa when he learned folk dancing, he relished the Scottish Reel and his eyes twinkled in anticipation, as he took his place among the other dancers waiting for it to begin. Yet when the Sylph appeared at the top of the staircase or even crossed the stage in front of him, you could "feel" his confusion as to whether he saw her or not.

The Sylph reappears near the end of the first act and steals the ring that James planned to present to Effie at their wedding. She pleads with James to follow her. Nureyev's reaction was clear as he first mimed "Absolutely not" and then hesitated, clasping his empty ring finger. Finally he cannot resist and follows her, his eyes lighting up like a child's. This decisive moment was performed exactly to the music. In the Sylph's wooded domain, he switched from absolute elation while waving the scarf in anticipation of capturing her, to total grief at causing her death.

In the early 60s, Nureyev inserted his melancholy solo in *Swan Lake*, and this has now become traditional. The particularly beautiful way he "unfolded" his leg from one step to another, turning his body inward and outward again, expressed the melancholy of Prince Siegfried. He created that solo at the age of 23 and two decades later affirmed, "the mood of it still possesses me."

In the ballroom act when the Queen Mother admonished him to choose a bride, he seemed almost afraid to disobey her and showed extreme sadness. When he pleaded with his mother that Odile was the one he wanted to wed, he transformed to boyish glee when she agreed. At one Royal Ballet performance when Gerd Larsen portrayed the Queen Mother, she took Rudolf's head in her hands and kissed him on the forehead, rumpling his hair, as a mother would to share in her son's happiness.

His debut in *Manon* took place at the Met in 1975, before he debuted the role in London. Most memorable was Nureyev's entrance as an awkward schoolboy, books in hand. After searching for somewhere to sit, he appeared very uncomfortable in the bustling town square. When a rat catcher passed by, he held his nose and fanned himself, which caused titters from the public. In the second act's brothel scene, his character, Des Grieux, stood to one side, extremely ill at ease. The way Nureyev conveyed his feelings caused people to watch him, rather than some of the dancers on center stage. When everyone vacated and he was alone with Manon, he danced for her, pleading to take him back. Merle Park as Manon mimed how she had changed since they parted, showing off her jewels while he could offer her nothing. As he was on the floor looking up at her with pleading eyes, she found it hard to resist and agreed to help him by cheating at a game of cards. Hoping he wouldn't get caught, Nureyev put extra cards into his waistcoat pocket for all the audience to see. When he won the first game, he truly did have a guilty smile that critic Richard Buckle described as looking "like a kid caught with his hand in the cookie jar."

On reflection, so many of these "memorable moments" were about Rudolf's stillness in addition to his dancing. He infused his characters with such meaning, that the dancing was almost secondary.

Because Nureyev was such a public figure, when he crossed over into modern dance, there was literally no place for him to fail. He didn't have the advantage of out-of-town tryouts like most Broadway performers have, but made his mistakes in full view of the paying public. When he first performed with the Martha Graham Company in 1975, Rudolf shared his own education with the audience. Yet one could see his progress almost daily. After a rather shaky start in *Night Journey* when he was loudly booed, he rehearsed nonstop especially with the complicated props, and showed a marked improvement by his second performance. At curtain calls, he appeared apprehensive. As the applause enveloped him, he beamed like a proud schoolboy who had done his homework.

Aaron Copland conducted his score for Nureyev's debut as the Preacher in *Appalachian Spring*. Nureyev's magnetic presence was captivating as he stood on his rock at the back, hands firmly clasped, eyes riveted on some invisible spiritual force. When he suddenly looked up just prior to the lead couple's wedding ceremony, it appeared both spontaneous and divinely inspired. It was this tranquility of expression that moved me. His mad dance was performed with fierce energy, seemingly exorcising the devil out of his very being. Once he gave the blessing to the marriage, he had a deliberate, almost comical way of following them offstage. He clasped both hands behind his back, unfolding and closing them in a very determined way confirming a job well done – or perhaps contemplating some mischief.

Always in character at curtain calls, Nureyev took enormous strides to center stage, hands folded in prayer, head down, bowing deeply from the waist. After several curtain calls, this Preacher suddenly turned classical, arms outstretched, head elegantly raised, beaming like a Cheshire cat.

As Nureyev matured, his energy and emotional intensity changed. When he first performed in *Moor's Pavane* in the early 70s, he wore a false nose, darkened his make-up, and was all bulging eyes, as he emphasized the jealous rage and fury that Othello experienced by Desdemona's betrayal. Just as there are different approaches to interpreting Shakespeare, Nureyev developed the role to emphasize the Moor's doubt and anguish. He later performed with minimal makeup and without the false nose.

Rudolf's comic side came through in roles such as Colas in *La Fille Mal Gardee*, Basilio in *Don Quixote*, or Franz in *Coppelia*. He continuously added new touches to his characters. Audiences particularly loved his mock death scene in *Don Quixote*. With twinkling eyes barely visible as he covered his face with an enormous cloak, he proceeded to mime how his beloved Kitri preferred Don Quixote to his own character of Basilio. He pulled out the enormous razor from beneath his cloak, opened it, revealed it to one and all, and stabbed himself. After looking at the hard floor beneath him, he deliberately circled his body in unwinding motions until his cloak loosened and he purposefully placed it "just so" on the floor before falling on it. Other dancers performed this role, but somehow the way Nureyev mastered the use of that cloak has seldom been duplicated.

Nureyev's sense of stagecraft was remarkable. His productions built and utilized various tricks to create illusions. I recall sitting next to a small child who was utterly enchanted at the beginning of the Vision Scene in *Don Quixote*. Kitri is transformed into Dulcinea and appeared to float across the stage, beckoning the Don to follow her. The child asked her mother, "How do they do that?" The man behind the ballerina wore black and because he remained out of the lights, you couldn't see him lifting and carrying her across the stage. Rudolf borrowed many ideas from his world travels and when the effects work, they create magic.

I loved the beginning of his *Sleeping Beauty* production when the dimmed stage began to glow from the lit candelabras as the courtiers descended the staircase. The stage lights grew brighter as each member of the court entered, followed by the King and Queen in full regalia. The scene builds to match that of the Tchaikovsky score. One moment I particularly relished was prior to the Vision Scene, when the Lilac Fairy appeared to the Prince. In mimed gestures, Rudolf, one hand on his heart, waved with the other hand, "No love have I" and stepped back, foot perfectly pointed behind him. When he woke the sleeping princess with a kiss, he stepped back with a mixture of pride and wonder as if to say, "Look what I did!" While Aurora jumped off the bed to wake her friends and parents, Rudolf mimed his story of how he, the prince, came from afar, found the beautiful Sleeping Beauty, kissed her, and just in time to take her hand, indicated, "Here she is." Then he gave a regal bow before the King and Queen and mimed "I want her hand in marriage" while the court gathered around and showered them with flowers.

On April 15, 1977, prior to the London premiere of Nureyev's original *Romeo and Juliet* production, Nureyev gave an in-depth interview to Sydney Edwards of the London *Evening Standard*. Nureyev explained, "It might be that certain things strike me in a different way...I want to concentrate on what happened to Romeo and Juliet and all those forces, which influenced them on the way – all those barriers to overcome before the final union. It was a race towards death." He described Prokofiev's score as "music by the yard" and very padded due to the script. At first Rudolf wanted to use 13th and 14th century music, but admitted, "I got cold feet. Two hours of that in the theatre might be very tiresome." He did endless research, including studying texts on which Shakespeare based his play, claiming, "It will be as close to Shakespeare as I can make it."

Nureyev also told critic Walter Terry in the November 11, 1978 issue of *Saturday Review*: "I read the words of Shakespeare. Because I asked questions about the words, about some that were stumbling blocks for me…many of the words are angular, very strong and powerful, but I think today's readers have forgotten what they originally meant."

Nureyev's production is packed with details and symbols. The ominous mood begins when the curtain rises. Dice players representing Fate and the black cloth of death tumble onto a cart of plague victims. En route to the Capulet's ball, Romeo is momentarily stopped by a street beggar. He reaches into his pocket and hands a coin to the unfortunate soul who then collapses. When Romeo starts to depart, he gives the beggar a long second glance and stares upwards as the lights dim. In just a few seconds, the scene foreshadows the sense of Fate and makes visible Shakespeare's words, "Some consequence, yet hanging in the stars…"

The production follows the text closely, bringing the words to life through the movement. In the balcony scene, Romeo runs to the back, holding up his hand to the moon to swear his love for Juliet. She, in turn, grabs his arms and admonishes him: "Swear not by the moon, the inconstant moon, that monthly changes in her circled orb." Looking quizzically at her, Romeo opens his arms to inquire, "What shall I swear by?" Juliet responds by folding his arms to his chest, indicating, "Swear by thy gracious self." Romeo bursts into a jump of joy, as if "newly baptized." I overheard Trevor Nunn, then Director of the Royal Shakespeare Company, remark in the lobby: "Nureyev is the only choreographer who has really read the play."

In the pivotal scene in which Tybalt slays Mercutio, the text has Romeo say to Mercutio, "The hurt cannot be much." Meanwhile Mercutio's life is ebbing away while Romeo and the others mock him. Nureyev's initial reaction, laughing and joking, tapping Mercutio's chest as if to say, "Quit the clowning," suddenly changes to a chilling shudder when he realizes his friend is dead. In a daze and urged by his fellow Montagues to avenge Mercutio's death by killing Tybalt, this Romeo shook his head violently, wanting no part of it. With Tybalt provoking him, Romeo begins the fight on his knees, at first backing away and tossing his own sword to one side, still too stunned to react. This slow reaction gradually builds and when Tybalt continues to taunt him, Romeo lashes out with astonishing fury before striking the final blow.

Another favorite moment in Nureyev's production is Romeo's dream in Mantua, just before learning of Juliet's death. In the text, Romeo says "An unaccustomed spirit lifts me above the ground with cheerful thoughts." Rudolf used six "spirits" to lift Romeo, who dreams that Juliet "breathed such life with kisses in my lips, that I revived and was an emperor." As they rock Romeo back and forth, more and more forcefully, the "spirits" disappear to reveal Benvolio pulling on his arm to wake him. When told of Juliet's supposed death, Shakespeare's text, "Then I defy you stars!" becomes a dance of despair, as Romeo hurls himself forcefully in a backbend into Benvolio's arms. The frantic running around the stage further emphasizes Romeo's agitation.

Nureyev's professionalism transferred to other dancers, as exemplified by Nicholas Johnson who performed the role of Mercutio in New York, during a 1978 season at the Met. Back in London, Johnson's wife, Laura Connor, gave birth to a son. Complications occurred and Johnson received the sad news that their baby had died. Johnson bravely performed, but it was obvious he was not his usual mischievous self in the role. He managed to get through the performance, but when he took a solo curtain call, he began to sob uncontrollably and ran offstage. On closing night, Rudolf brought company director Beryl Grey to center stage and she gave a deep curtsy to Rudolf. After Nureyev acknowledged the company, he bowed to Nicholas, took his head in both hands and kissed him affectionately on both cheeks. Nicholas held on, blinking back tears. Rudolf patted his back as they walked off stage together, showing compassion and gratitude for Johnson's professionalism. Nicholas had to go on – there was no second cast for the role of Mercutio.

Nureyev gave less than a dozen performances in the role of Prince Myshkin, the innocent, saint-like figure in Dostoyevsky's *The Idiot*. Here was a case of Nureyev's performance outshining the ballet, choreographed by Valery Panov. The characters were difficult to develop and without extensive program notes, most American audiences had trouble following the plot. The ambitious three-act extravaganza had fifteen cumbersome set changes, along with beautiful backdrop projections of St. Petersburg, and gorgeous costumes for the large cast. Unfortunately Nureyev wore boots throughout the entire ballet, which somewhat hampered his footwork. The production contained more theatrics than dancing in order to develop the various characters. Panov portrayed his character rather like Rasputin. The second act contained an endless chase scene with much bravura dancing amidst a carnival-like atmosphere. Confetti and streamers cluttered the stage floor, making many of us concerned about the dancers slipping. During the end of the second act, Panov and Nureyev danced together holding two lighted candles and during a tricky moment, Panov's candle flared up dangerously close to Rudolf's face.

At a pivotal moment when one of the male characters was infuriated with Myshkin, he shouted aloud to him, "Idiot!" The startled look of disbelief and hurt on Nureyev's face was visible clear to the balcony. The third act contained the most dancing. Set in a park with strolling townspeople, nannies pushing baby carriages, and children playing, they eventually joined Nureyev. The charming dance concluded with a little girl perched on Rudolf's shoulder posing for the park photographer. He clearly loved this dance and so did the children. The finale's bell-ringing scene, had Myshkin, dressed in a loincloth, tolling a gigantic bell. This was hoisted high above the stage, with Rudolf holding on and spinning like an aerial artist. It brought down the house.

One of the last ballets Nureyev performed, also adapted from a Russian novel, was Gogol's *The Overcoat*. Flemming Flindt choreographed it for Rudolf, but gave him surprisingly little dancing. When Akaki, Nureyev's character is mugged and his beloved overcoat is stolen, the drama is disrupted when "ladies in black veils" rush in and dance around Akaki. Every time Nureyev tried to build his character, the ensemble dancers interrupted him. Rudolf was so adept at conveying inner thoughts and feelings through movement, that I wondered why he wasn't given a solo to express himself.

One of the most haunting scenes was when Akaki's stolen coat appears to him in a dream. Akaki waltzed with this long white overcoat in a bright spotlight. As this vision began to build, the dramatic flow was disrupted by a ballroom scene in which Akaki ran in and out of the ensemble, rather than standing in their midst showing his discomfort as an outcast.

The final portion of this forty-minute ballet was so muddled, it left the audience perplexed as to when Akaki died. There was a striking image of Nureyev in a hospital bed and then dancing a solo, but was this the spirit of

Akaki or had he gone mad? Another scene was unclear whether Akaki planned his revenge or if it actually happened. The audience referred several times to their programs, asking, "Is it over or is this another scene?" At the Stage Door, even the fans who had gone to Cleveland for four performances, asked Rudolf, "Just WHEN are you supposed to die?" His reply was priceless: "I don't know!" If the star doesn't know because the scenario is poorly developed, how could the public comprehend it? We had several suggestions on how to improve the ballet, but Nureyev was at the mercy of the choreographer.

I have watched numerous renowned dancers over the years. Many have been more-technically proficient, but none have captivated me as completely as Rudolf Nureyev. When dancers are young, they are eager to show off their technical tricks and only when a dancer matures, does the artistry develop. Nureyev was a complete performer. He committed himself thoroughly to his art, bringing mind, body and spirit to each role. He remarked that some of the best dancers who were immensely talented simply didn't give a "generous" performance. With passing years, he stated in various interviews that some dancers looked like "clones" and that "their art is strangely empty," adding, "Individuality of character has disappeared."

In 1985, Rudolf admitted that those who saw him twenty years earlier might be disappointed in him. "But if a spectator sees me for the first time today, I can still offer him something that comes from deep inside me, an idealization of gesture he won't find in a younger dancer, even if he leaps higher than I do." He continued, "There's no need to try and shine by taking shortcuts." Nureyev never took shortcuts. His commitment to dance never wavered. "I hang my survival on work. It is my only country, my only lover. My only passport is my work."

Nureyev began performing character roles very late in his career. I've always thought he would be a most majestic King or even a fierce Madge the Witch. I never saw his only performance as Carabosse or his role as Dr. Coppelius, both performed abroad. When the choreographer, Dennis Nahat, wanted Nureyev to take four days to learn the role of Dr. Coppelius, Rudolf laughed, "With four days I could learn to dance the whole Bible."

Rudolf Nureyev believed that an artist is a leader, enhancing the public's demands and refining their taste. "I am glad they are there; it's ultimately the public for whom you dance." He continued, "I thank the audience for the staunch support through my career, through many adversities. Only they keep me sane and able to go on."

Part Two

Don Quixote with American Ballet Theatre, Metropolitan Opera House, NYC, 1978. Photo: William J. Reilly

~ A lot of work goes into it. . . It is not just cash and carry. ~
Rudolf Nureyev, London Daily Mail, June 6, 1977

ANECDOTES

INTRODUCTION

There are many components that must come together to make a dance performance, starting with the dancer. After years of training, a dancer polishes their art with daily classes and rehearsals. With talent and luck, a dancer might join a company as an apprentice or part of a touring company. In other cases, they can enter the company's corps de ballet, the "body" of the company. From there they work their way through the ranks to principal dancer. Many dancers never make it to a professional level, realizing the total commitment required to achieve their dream. Some dancers love dance so much, that it doesn't matter if they spend their entire careers at the corps level. Others go through years of training just for the discipline and health benefits, without ever hoping to make it a career.

It's not enough to be a good dancer. That dancer must be seen in a proper setting, usually in a theatre. The supporting cast must be well rehearsed, not just knowing the steps, but their ever-changing placement on stage in relation to the other dancers. The ensemble must be in character, depending on the ballet being performed. There are vast differences in deportment, stance, and characterization from everyone on stage, whether they are portraying a member of a Royal Court or a village peasant. Even the way a dancer walks, runs, or stands is important. Nureyev used to get annoyed with dancers in the background standing around or sitting "like they were waiting for a bus." The dancer must have a thorough understanding of the period and character portrayed, or the roles won't be believable.

How a dancer enters or exits the stage sets the mood of the piece. I've seen many beautifully gifted dancers perform astounding solos and then ruin it when exiting the stage, by trotting or slumping into the wings, completely breaking character, as if the audience couldn't see them. When Nureyev entered the stage, he literally transformed the energy of the performance. His entrances, particularly in his production of *The Sleeping Beauty*, made a statement: "Here I am!" His walk was majestic when he exited, first saluting the King and Queen, before disappearing into the wings. The exits in his productions were often "dancing exits," that required the dancers to maintain their characterizations until they were completely off stage.

The costumes for everyone from the principal dancers to the extras or "supers" filling the stage must be properly fitted, cleaned and pressed and still look fresh after numerous performances and shared by many dancers. Most of the costume glitches are worked out during the rehearsal process, but occasional malfunctions do occur and it's important that the costume mistress or someone backstage is on standby, to make speedy repairs.

Lighting is crucial to all performances. If the lighting cues go awry or someone in the lighting booth decides not to place a follow spot properly, the performance suffers. Sometimes overly bright lighting can wash out a dancer's features. The trend for backlighting or extremely dim lighting can be difficult for the audience to discern who is dancing. If lights are not set or aimed properly, the dancer can reach a momentary "blind spot" and is in danger of falling off the stage – another reason why flash photography is prohibited.

Sets play an important part in any production, particularly the full-length classical pieces. When something goes wrong with a set, particularly in tricky scenic changes, the evening is spoiled. Backdrops must be changed quickly and if something malfunctions, a dancer can be seriously hurt.

Numerous backstage personnel are equally important. If they are in the wrong place at the wrong time, a dancer doing a fast running or leaping exit can crash into someone. A rapport is generally built between the stagehands and the performers. But they too, can spoil a performance by leaving part of the scenery or a prop in the wrong place or lowering the curtain too soon or too late, at the ballet's conclusion.

Most large companies based in world-class theatres are lucky to have an in-house orchestra with its own conductor. In Vienna, the Vienna Philharmonic plays for the ballet performances. In many theatres, pick-up orchestras assemble, play together for the season's duration, and then seek work elsewhere. Unfortunately, some companies must use recorded music, because the costs of employing a real orchestra become prohibitive.

Orchestra conductors can make or break a ballet performance. Because the music is such a vital component to any dance performance, the dancer should not only be musical, but needs to modify each performance depending on the conductor. Because no two conductors are alike, the dancer must match their variations in time with the music at each performance. This presents a greater problem when the conductor doesn't watch the dancer or is a late substitute and hasn't seen the dancer in rehearsal, to know how fast or slow the dancer will manage certain musical passages. Tall, long-limbed dancers naturally take more time to get their feet around certain steps while smaller dancers generally move faster. If Conductor "A" suddenly fills in for Conductor "B," the different tempi used can wreak havoc, causing the dancer to adjust their dancing accordingly. Otherwise, the dancer will appear unmusical.

All of these components must come together to make a complete performance. Sometimes the dancer will give the performance of a lifetime, but the orchestra may have played dreadfully. Other times a dancer may have missed an entrance on time, because of some mishap going on backstage. A truly "perfect performance," therefore, is rare indeed.

By its very nature, ballet is ephemeral and exists in time only during the performance. The number of hours spent rehearsing for that performance or a new production takes its toll on the dancer's body, particularly if they perform long seasons with varied repertories. The dancer cast in their first leading role may go on stage under-rehearsed or face a different partner than the one they had in rehearsal. Injuries happen and different partners affect the outcome of each performance. Cast changes are inevitable and often someone's injury is another dancer's opportunity.

Over the course of watching Nureyev, there have been some remarkable performances and some when everything seemed to go wrong. Nureyev cared deeply about performing and wanted the audience to enjoy it. He became upset when things weren't to his liking. His annoyance was difficult to hide at times, particularly with bad playing in the pit. With his own productions, he was a perfectionist. His temper revealed itself over a mishap that was preventable, if the stage crew were more attentive. He set the highest standards for himself and expected everyone else to live up to those standards. He could forgive the mistakes of fellow dancers, because he knew how hard they tried to give their best, but he was often less forgiving if he didn't live up to his own expectations.

I remember a very vivid dream I had in the 70s. Nureyev was taking a curtain call following a performance of *The Sleeping Beauty* and I was watching him through my opera glasses. He was going through the motions of taking his bows, but kept turning to his right and appeared to be in a fury with his partner or whoever was next to him, audibly mumbling a few obscenities. I couldn't figure out why he was so angry and put down my opera glasses to get the fuller picture. The person he was screaming at was another Rudolf Nureyev, standing next to him. He was very upset with the way he performed that evening, despite acknowledging the applause from the audience.

Rudolf Nureyev had such passion for dance that he claimed he wanted to die on stage. On occasion he nearly did. A number of memorable performances were those when things went wrong. It was interesting to see how Nureyev reacted. The following are some of those anecdotes that may prove enlightening or amusing.

"I have to be on stage like a fish in the water."
~Rudolf Nureyev, London Sunday Times, March 12, 1983~

THE SHOW MUST GO ON...

Nureyev exits Metropolitan Opera House, NYC, July 19, 1986
Photo: Susanne Richelle Whitehead

Nureyev gave thousands of performances during his career and seldom cancelled. However, there were occasions when performances were interrupted due to reasons beyond anyone's control. Whether the curtain was held due to traffic jams, last-minute tickets being sold or other snafus, Rudolf Nureyev experienced them all. In every instance, all he wanted was to dance, even at the risk of his own life. He stated that he had a right to die on stage and one night he very nearly did.

I was in Paris for the 1977 *Nureyev Festival* to see Nureyev and Natalia Makarova perform in Bournonville's *La Sylphide* with the Scottish Ballet. A favorite ballet of Nureyev's, he portrayed the Scotsman James who abruptly leaves his fiancé in pursuit of the elusive sylph, which represents his ideal. Prior to this ballet, Rudolf danced in Hans van Manen's *Four Schumann Pieces*. From my seat toward the side of the stage in the Palais des Sports, I looked into the wings and noticed how little space there was to exit between the lights.

After the interval, I found an empty seat toward the back of the orchestra level, but more central for watching *Sylphide*. The ballet was delightful and things were going well, until midway into the last act. As the sylphs exited on Stage Right - which is the audience's left - I heard a crash and knew that a light had been knocked over. The rest of the exiting sylphs clutched their tulle skirts to their sides in order to pass between the narrow wing space and the lights.

Suddenly people in the theatre began shouting "Fire, fire!" and pointed to flames shooting up some fifteen feet above the curtain. In just seconds the painted backdrops caught fire. When the flames began reaching alarming heights and smoke billowed onto the stage, some of the sylphs panicked and dashed off stage as quickly as possible. Some of them even jumped into the shallow orchestra pit. Stagehands rushed across the upstage area with fire extinguishers. This was clearly not part of the ballet and by now the spectators realized it. Audience members got up and raced for the exits. Most of the orchestra also began to flee as they realized what was happening.

And where was Rudolf? He was eagerly awaiting his big variation and as the music began, he burst into his wonderful beating steps despite the chaos around him. I had one eye on Nureyev and one eye on the flames shooting higher and higher overhead. People screamed, "Fire! Get off!" We were afraid that scenery would come crashing down on him.

Theatre personnel began herding the audience outside as more and more musicians, realizing the danger, put down their instruments and headed for the exit doors, jostling with escaping sylphs en route. But Rudolf danced on, apparently oblivious to what we observed from out front. As long as one note of music could be heard or one person remained in the theatre, he was determined to keep going. Rudolf was annoyed, casually looked over his shoulder at the fire and then glanced back to the audience. He noticed some people were remaining in their seats, so he kept dancing. While in mid-turn Nureyev spotted the escalating flames and momentarily slowed down, when witnessing his audience leaving en masse. One of his fans near the stage screamed, "Rudi, it's a REAL fire!"

In sheer desperation, someone backstage closed the curtain on him, forcing him to leave the stage. Gendarmes arrived and ordered everyone to evacuate. I overheard an American teenager complain, "Gee, just as he was about to do his big solo" while others wondered if Rudolf was safe. As I made my way out, I spotted the dancer portraying Madge the Witch, leading two dazed sylphs toward the exit.

The fans bolted to the Stage Door just as fire trucks arrived, sirens blaring. The blaze was contained, but the theatre was filled with blinding smoke. Fire Marshalls tried clearing the Stage Door area, but the large crowd refused to leave until they knew Rudolf Nureyev was safe. After several anxious minutes, he emerged wrapped in his fur coat and sable hat with tails, that we called his "Davy Crockett" hat. As people flocked around him, he instructed, "Keep cool, don't burn me." Then, ignoring all questions about whether there would be an evening performance, his only other remark about the aborted performance was, "They ruined my variation!"

After Nureyev left, his most loyal fans went across the street to a café for a drink and dinner. Most of the dancers were at adjacent tables, all babbling excitedly about the fire and how nobody could find the fire extinguishers earlier. They told us that Makarova had narrowly missed being hit by a piece of falling scenery, as she tried getting Nureyev to leave the stage. Assuming that Rudolf would leave, Luigi had dashed to the dressing room to save the costumes. The company members remarked that Nureyev was like the captain of a sinking ship, refusing to abandon the stage.

There was indeed an evening performance despite the lingering smell of smoke and a later start time, which caused the audience to applaud impatiently. When we returned, we saw stagehands outside the Stage Door removing burned scenic backdrops. They asked us if we wanted them as souvenirs before dumping them into the dustbin. The second act backdrop was considerably darker, because the firemen soaked it when putting out the fire. The new lighting was replaced in just two hours.

Nureyev was determined to make up for the aborted matinee. His first solo merited three curtain calls. Just before the Scottish Reel, he got into position, arms folded, and just about giggled aloud to Andrea Durant as Effie, in anticipation of dancing. Despite all his classical roles, he still loved the folk dance steps.

Another incident occurred – again with *La Sylphide* – this time during his 1976 *Nureyev Festival* in London. He was making his debut in Flemming Flindt's *The Lesson,* a ballet loosely based on the Ionesco play about a psychotic teacher who murders his pupils. The work was on the same program as Bournonville's *La Sylphide* with the Scottish Ballet.

On that warm July evening, an announcement was made that "Mr. Nureyev has sustained an injury prior to curtain time, but will perform anyway and begs your understanding." We couldn't imagine what had happened, since we saw Rudolf enter the theatre in good spirits and fine physical shape. "Probably during the warm-up," we remarked, knowing that he always prepared by dancing his part in the ballet on stage, while waiting for the curtain to go up. When the curtain opened to reveal Nureyev as James, asleep in the chair, we recognized a support bandage beneath his Scottish stockings. As the ballet progressed, we noticed that he had difficulty with the intricate choreography, particularly in the jumps, and favored one foot over the other. The characterization was not changed, but the dancing was less than his best.

At the interval, we speculated on what may have happened, and feared the worst when the length of the intermission dragged on and on. The British public is an enthusiastic one, but if kept waiting, they can be close to the point of anarchy. Finally a staff person came on stage to make another announcement. "Ladies and gentlemen, Mr. Rudolf Nureyev regrets that his injury will prevent him from dancing in the second act. Replacing him in Act Two will be Graham Bart." Collective "oh no's" and shouts of disappointment emanated from the capacity crowd to the point of drowning out the rest of the announcement: "He will, however, be performing in *The Lesson* this evening." Some members of the audience cheered at the news that Nureyev was injured and we wondered why they were there in the first place. The audience became verbally abusive while the announcer tried to continue. Only with the arrival of the conductor to begin the second act, did they finally settle down. Graham Bart, the leading dancer with the Scottish Ballet at that time, performed valiantly with his sylph, Sally Collard-Gentle. Under the circumstances, it was a very good performance.

Then something strange happened after the interval. The curtain went up for *The Lesson* to reveal the ballet studio and a very agitated pianist straightening up chairs. It was Vivi Flindt of the Danish Ballet, who was also the choreographer's wife. Suddenly a white-haired figure entered the room to help her clean up. I looked through my opera glasses to see the transformed face of Rudolf Nureyev portraying the mad ballet teacher. He was barely recognizable under the whitened make-up and wig. After I realized he was indeed making his debut after all, I became so involved in the ballet that I quite forgot who I was watching. I was not aware that this was the same dancer who performed the first half of La *Sylphide* earlier in the evening, nor was I aware that he was injured. Since it was the first time that Nureyev performed the role, and the first time that I was seeing the ballet, I had no idea if he favored one foot over the other. Later I was told he did all the jumps on the uninjured foot, but during the performance, I was so transfixed that I never thought about the actual dancing. To me, his portrayal was all one, where the acting and dancing blended seamlessly.

The trauma of being injured while debuting in a new work caused Nureyev's adrenalin to work overtime, for he was quite manic in the role. At the ballet's conclusion, the demonic teacher strangles his "pupil," Andrea Durant. The force with which Nureyev shoved her around caused audible gasps and a few stifled screams, when he performed the deadly deed.

When the curtain came down, I forgot that I was in a darkened theatre with hundreds of other people, and the sounds of applause jarred me back to reality. Nureyev came out to receive the applause, taking his curtain calls in character, but being gentlemanly enough to "present" his supporting cast ballerinas. When Andrea Durant came out, he grasped both her hands in his and gave her the longest, strongest kiss imaginable, almost as if apologizing for the way he was throwing her around, while so deeply involved with the role. It seemed the only way to snap out of his characterization.

He was pleased that the evening turned from tragedy to triumph and stayed to sign autographs at the Stage Door, scoffing at the fan's concern over his injury. We later learned what had happened. Minutes before curtain-up, Luigi was helping Rudolf pull off his legwarmers when they got snagged on his foot, twisting it badly. Luigi felt terrible, but even a last-minute massage didn't help. Sustaining the intricate footwork in the Bournonville ballet was only making it worse and Nureyev didn't want to jeopardize the premiere of a new work. Perhaps the greatest "compliment" paid to Nureyev that night was from an elderly British woman who queued for his autograph at the Stage Door. "Oh, I was so sorry not to see you dance tonight," she told him. "But I DID dance in *The Lesson*," he replied. She stared at his radiant face, looked puzzled, and then asked, "Was that YOU?"

During that same summer, London experienced an unusual heat wave, with temperatures in the 90s. Nureyev performed an unprecedented seven-week-season at the London Coliseum, dancing at every performance. He seemed to dance better than ever, because the hot weather kept his muscles warm. London theatres were not air-conditioned at that time and the balcony felt like a sauna. It was difficult to concentrate on the performance, when we had to mop our faces periodically just so we could see the stage. The cold drinks concession did a booming business.

One Saturday matinee when the temperature was almost unbearable, we had an unusually long interval between ballets. The last work on the program was Jose Limon's *The Moor's Pavane* with Lynn Seymour as Desdemona, Monica Mason as Amelia and Limon dancer Fred Matthews as Iago. The costumes in that piece are heavy, with the women in long gowns and the Moor, played by Nureyev, in a long red velvet robe over tights. We were uncomfortable enough sitting in the sweltering theatre, but could not imagine how the dancers performed in those heavy costumes under the hot lights.

The interval seemed to go on and on until finally an announcement was made over the loud speaker. "Ladies and Gentleman, Fred Matthews has taken ill and is unable to perform in this afternoon's performance of *Moor's Pavane*. Instead, Lynn Seymour and Rudolf Nureyev will dance the pas de deux from *Flower Festival*."

The two dancers had rehearsed it, but not with the orchestra. The musicians in the orchestra pit scrambled to get the right music. Since it was a chamber group expecting to play the *Moor's Pavane*, complete with harpsichord, the music for *Flower Festival* sounded very "thin" because the rest of the orchestra had already left. The curtain went up to reveal Lynn Seymour wearing her blonde Desdemona wig and Rudolf, a bit red-faced from having to yank off his Moor's mustache and beard, poised and ready. They were scheduled to dance *Flower Festival* the following week and had obviously rehearsed it, but certainly didn't expect to dance the ballet during that afternoon's performance.

Later in the week I happened to be riding home on the Underground, when Lynn Seymour took a seat near me. I spoke to her about the terrible heat wave and she replied, "Oh, Rudolf and I love it. There's nothing like working up into a good lather. Our muscles stay warm that way and we can dance better." One critic wrote, "When we last left our champion, he was still on his feet and I'm happy to say he's thriving"

Sometimes backstage issues could delay a performance. During one season, the unions gave Nureyev trouble for wanting to use taped music in part of the program. The unions prevented this and the original program was cancelled just four days before it opened. Then Rudolf wanted to rehearse for a new program on a Sunday, but that too, was refused. This resulted in the cancellation of the regularly scheduled Monday performance, because the dancers needed Monday for the dress rehearsal. Consequently opening night was moved from Monday to Tuesday, and the Box Office refused to sell standing room until 7:30 p.m., delaying the performance start time. Of course Rudolf Nureyev and not the unions got blamed for this.

As Director of the Paris Opera, Nureyev brought his *Swan Lake* production to the Kennedy Center in July of 1986, introducing his company to the Washington public. Just before the White Act pas de deux, the curtain came crashing down and an announcement was made, "Ladies and gentlemen, please evacuate the theatre immediately." Apparently, there was a bomb scare.

The entire audience filed out to the grounds adjacent to the theatre while police with dogs searched the complex. It was an unbearably hot and sticky night and everyone was squished together, fanning themselves with their programs. As we wandered around the grounds, we saw dancers still dressed as swans, sitting on the edge of the fountain trying to keep cool without getting their tutus wet. Another bevy of swans sat on the grass smoking cigarettes. Still another was draped over a "No Parking" sign while a fellow dancer took her picture. Patrice Bart, dancing Rothbart at that performance, wore jogging pants over his costume. Soon the TV news crew arrived and the girls began clowning around, lying on the grass and criss-crossing their legs doing entrechats in the air. Another bent over to stomp out a cigarette and gave everyone a view of what the underside of a tutu looks like.

We were somewhat on edge, wondering if the performance would ever continue, when suddenly we spotted Nureyev sitting under a tree. He was sipping tea and his bathrobe was draped around his shoulders. He appeared calm, but his eyes showed his irritation at the disruption. Ushers tried to keep people from bothering him. We found out from one of them that when the order came to evacuate the theatre, Rudolf had locked himself in his dressing room. The usher banged on his door saying, "Mr. Nureyev, you have to leave the theatre!" Nureyev shouted back, "I'm not afraid of oblivion!" The usher replied, "Well I am!" Nureyev finally emerged and parked himself under the tree.

A few of his loyal fans surrounded him and because of his annoyance over the disrupted performance, he muttered, "Tight-assed hysterical Americans!" One who heard him slapped him playfully on the knee with a bouquet she intended to toss at curtain calls and reasoned, "Wouldn't you rather be safe out here than be blown up?" Then, realizing she hit him with her flowers, she said, "Oh, you're not supposed to see that, are you?" and he laughed. Finally he got up and wandered around the grounds, chatting with some of his dancers and the general public. He was doing his best to be sociable, but also trying to find out if the performance would continue.

After ninety long minutes, an announcement was made over a loudspeaker, "Swans and orchestra may go back in. All others remain behind." What followed looked like something out of a Fellini film, with a tuba player followed by a cygnet; a bassoon player surrounded by a bevy of swans; a musician carrying a large drum, all being filmed by the late night news. Rudolf followed this unlikely parade and just as he got to the Stage Door, we all yelled "Bravo!" and he turned and waved, in considerably better spirits.

The audience was allowed back in and there was a full intermission, giving everyone time to have a drink or use the restrooms, and after another twenty-minute wait, an announcement was made that due to the late hour – it was now 11 p.m. – the White Act would be eliminated. Cries of protest and disappointment rang out at having missed this beautiful act, but the dancers' adrenalin was so strong that they danced an amazing Act Three. Nureyev and his Swan Queen, Florence Clerc, seemed slightly "off" because of the long disruption, although the mood was very strong.

When the final act began, we noticed the swans had left the stage. Nureyev looked at conductor Andre Presser, who tapped the podium while musicians frantically fumbled with their sheet music and the "eliminated" White Act pas de deux we missed, was inserted into the last act. It worked perfectly well. The rest of the ballet proceeded as normal and the audience went home about one o'clock in the morning – late but happy.

Sometimes technical problems delayed or altered the performance. A rather amusing incident occurred at a performance of *Marguerite and Armand* at Covent Garden in the early 70s. The beautiful red Opera House curtain emblazoned with the Royal initials E.R. refused to open. Apparently the mechanical apparatus failed and an embarrassed staff member announced that there would be a delay of at least thirty minutes, while the stage crew attempted to fix it. The bemused audience filed out to meet friends or have a drink and returned to the auditorium to discover the curtain had been opened – by hand – and the lighter red one used as a backdrop when the front curtain parted for curtain calls, now filled the entire space. When Fonteyn and Nureyev finished the ballet, they had to enter from the side of the stage to acknowledge the applause.

A similar incident occurred at the London Coliseum in the early 80s. When *Petrushka* started, the orchestra played for about two minutes and then suddenly stopped. The curtain refused to open. Someone came on stage to explain that the hydraulic mechanism had broken and the curtain would have to be manually lifted. Again, the audience filed out for fifteen minutes or so, until the crew could raise the curtain.

Dancers from American Ballet Theatre joined Nureyev in a *Friends* program in 1988. The evening opened with *Apollo*, and as Nureyev sat on his stool to watch his muses dance, there was a long pause. His first muse waited for her musical cue, but nothing happened. The music tape had broken. Nureyev began gesturing discreetly into the wings and finally, in desperation, said loudly, "Curtain!" and it was lowered at once. Most of the audience thought it was an interval and began to head up the aisles. When the technical difficulties were resolved after five minutes, the public rushed back to their seats, not making the dancers very happy with their noisy re-entry.

A 1979 winter storm in Vienna caused a blackout in mid-performance when Nureyev performed in *Ulysses*, a new work by Rudi van Dantzig, with a taped score by Stockhausen. Rudolf continued in total silence until the emergency power came on.

At a *Sleeping Beauty* in Vienna, Nureyev began his slow solo in the Vision Scene when something appeared to cause him pain. He bent down, fiddled with his shoe, uttered something out loud and left the stage. The music continued, the corps de ballet entered, as did his Aurora that evening, Gisela Cech, while Rudolf remained in the wings. Finally the curtain was bought down and an announcement was made that "Mr. Nureyev has injured himself slightly and will continue after a brief pause."

It turned out that he had several splinters in his foot from the old stage floor. He removed most of them himself, dismissing the doctor, and after receiving a tetanus injection, continued the performance exactly where he left off. He was cheered warmly upon his return to the stage and after a somewhat tentative start, looking slightly worried, he finished the performance. He omitted nothing; executing double assembles, and strong assured jumps, and partnered his Aurora like a dream.

On many occasions it was other dancers who caused program changes. In 1978, at a Sunday matinee of a mixed program with London Festival Ballet in Washington, Rudolf arrived at the Kennedy Center to discover that Elisabetta Terabust, portraying the Young Girl in *Le Spectre de la Rose*, had suddenly taken ill with flu. Vivien Loeber promptly replaced her, but it meant several cast changes for the rest of the program. Marion St. Claire went on in *Conservatoire* and she had never danced the role before, let alone danced with Nureyev. They held a quick stage rehearsal while the audience, assembled for a two o'clock matinee, grew restless when the performance didn't start until nearly half-past.

When the curtain finally went up, Rudolf was wringing wet – water even dripped off his shoes – from rehearsing two different ballerinas in two ballets. St. Claire was so nervous she could barely dance and Rudolf was very tender with her, realizing the difficult circumstances. Since *Conservatoire* is set in a ballet studio, whenever Nureyev wasn't dancing, he chatted with members of the company and gave reassuring smiles to the ones who so valiantly "filled in" for the original cast.

At the final week of one of his Paris *Festival*s, Danish dancers Vivi Flindt, and Johnny Eliassen joined Nureyev to dance in Glen Tetley's *Pierrot*

Lunaire. The French audience didn't take to this modern work with music by Schonberg and the piece was booed on several occasions, to Rudolf's great disappointment.

On the closing Sunday matinee, the curtain was held for some time, because Nureyev learned that Vivi Flindt awoke with a scratched cornea and couldn't open her eye. There was no understudy for her and Rudolf was concerned, telling management, "No doctor, no performance." It was difficult finding a doctor on a Sunday, but when one was finally located, Vivi was given a painkiller and some salve so she could open her eye, although she could barely see. During one section in the ballet, Vivi had to lie on her back. Rudolf gently placed his arm over her face, shielding her eyes from the bright overhead lights. The show went on and Vivi recovered in time to repeat the role for the Broadway *Nureyev and Friends* season the following week.

It was a real case of "the show must go on" during a 1982 performance of *Don Quixote* with the Boston Ballet. Near the end of Act One, Marie-Christine Mouis as Kitri executed a supported pirouette with Nureyev, and dislocated her shoulder. As she was clearly unable to go on, Rudolf carried her offstage, totally in character, while the music continued. He returned to the stage, improvised a dance and directed the rest of the company to keep going. They rose to the challenge, shaking their tambourines and moving about the stage with one eye on Rudolf.

The music for the big one-arm lifts was fast approaching and, right on cue, Laura Young, who alternated in the role of Kitri, came dashing out from the wings in toe shoes and costume, but no tights, wig, or make-up. Without having warmed up, she went right into the one-arm lifts with Nureyev. Young finished the entire performance, while many in the audience probably didn't even realize this sudden change of cast.

In 1980, Rudolf's newest protégé, Evelyne DeSutter, debuted in his production of *Romeo and Juliet*. In one of the tricky lifts halfway through the balcony pas de deux, she appeared to have twisted her arm and her face contorted in pain. She immediately stopped, unable to continue. Rudolf held her and turned her toward him to see her face. He started to kiss her, but she couldn't move. She looked momentarily stunned, perhaps due to a muscle spasm. My friends sitting in the stalls said they heard Rudolf ask her, "Can you dance?" He tenderly and protectively walked her to the center of the stage, almost as if it was part of the choreography. Whatever it was, she gingerly stretched her arms out. At exactly the right musical cue, they both continued dancing; she very tentatively at first, but all seemed well.

The rest of the performance was a revelation and her debut was an enormous success. A beaming Nureyev brought her forward to receive the audience's enthusiastic ovation. Evelyne was presented with flowers and when Rudolf kissed her hand, she joyously and in total abandon threw both arms around Nureyev's shoulders and gave him a huge hug. He hugged her in return and the audience loved it. Evelyne was nearly crying with joy – and relief – while Rudolf was bursting with pride for her. Someone tossed a bouquet of roses that Rudolf retrieved and presented to her. She cradled them to her cheeks and Rudolf couldn't resist giving her a kiss.

A week later, they were paired again and little things were irritating Rudolf throughout the sold-out performance, along with the thousands of camera flashes at the curtain calls. Evelyne, once again breaking protocol, threw both arms around his shoulders and gave him a big kiss. He looked surprised, but then just beamed from ear to ear.

Nureyev loved discovering new talent and at the Stage Door, I couldn't help but remark, "Rudolf, I love your new Juliet. I understand she is coming to New York to dance *Nutcracker* with you." He gave me the biggest smile and said proudly but fondly, "Yes…she IS!" Unfortunately Evelyne suffered a serious hip injury prior to the New York engagement and Evdokimova replaced her, so many of the New Yorkers never got to see her.

During another series of *Romeo and Juliet* performances, Rudolf became irritated over a mounting list of things going wrong. Between sets that got stuck, lighting cues mucked up, and some of his most reliable dancers flubbing steps or even falling, after performing these roles numerous times, his temper got the better of him. Anyone who knew him felt that he just wanted to throw in the towel, but he had to finish the performance.

The final blow resulted in one of the most comical death scenes he ever performed. He hauled his Juliet, Patricia Ruanne, onto the bier and reached for his vial of poison. He simply couldn't get it out of its pouch and his musical cue was swiftly approaching. Suddenly he just let Juliet's "dead" body slump to the bier, while he used both hands to retrieve the poison. He merely gulped it down mechanically and plopped over.

Ruanne finished the performance, but there was a noticeable "gap" in the company curtain call line-up. Rudolf refused to take a curtain call. The company members kept looking at each other, half in amusement and half in bewilderment, while Ruanne, ever the professional, took extra long bows when she realized Rudolf was not coming back.

"Get out of my way," was all he could say to the enormous Stage Door throngs, and stormed through the crowd towards his "getaway car" with Luigi driving. As the car reached the nearby corner, one of his fans shouted, "Keep smiling" and Rudolf turned around, managed a half smile and waved.

*"Seven days a week I dance and only now do I feel
that I'm starting to recognize my right foot from my left."*
~Rudolf Nureyev, Australian Telegraph, June 9, 1975~

MISSTEPS

*Nureyev in Canarsie Venus by Murray Louis, NYC, 1978
Photo: William J. Reilly*

I never saw Nureyev fall on stage, although there have been some close calls and amazing recoveries. His training and numerous performances gave him the necessary experience to deal with mistakes. If you didn't know the choreography or happened to blink at the wrong time, you might not have noticed a misstep. One such recovery occurred in 1974, at a performance in Paris, when Rudolf performed the pas de trois in Balanchine's *Agon*. At the beginning of his solo, he took one jumped step forward, lost his footing on the slippery stage, and ended up in a sitting position. Instantly he put both hands to his sides and pushed himself up so quickly, that you wondered if it was part of the choreography.

In his strive for that unattainable "perfect performance," Nureyev was often mad at himself if something went wrong. In the late 60s, during a performance of *Nutcracker* with the Royal Ballet, he accidentally kicked Merle Park during the finale of the Grand Pas de deux. He became so upset that he stalked off the stage, leaving Park to finish on her own. With the music continuing, she improvised bravely, calling to him in the wings whenever she was at the side of the stage. He returned to finish the ballet, but was visibly embarrassed. Yet after the performance, he emerged from the Stage Door and was "meek as a lamb," to quote one fan. Much later, Park told us that Rudolf presented her with some jewelry, to which she added, "He always gives me pearls when he's sorry – I have quite a collection!"

Sir Frederick Ashton's *La Fille Mal Gardee* is probably one of the trickiest ballets to perform, not just because of the choreography, but also because of all the props.

The lovers' solos are difficult enough, but the Coda or finale to their Harvest Scene pas de deux is extremely fast, culminating in a "sit lift" when Colas holds Lise aloft with one hand. Lesley Collier and Nureyev shared an unforgettable performance of *Fille* during the Royal Ballet's 1976 New York season. It was the first time they danced in the ballet together. Rudolf was tired from rehearsing *Auerole* and *Corsaire* for an upcoming season, while Collier was understandably nervous dancing with him in New York for the first time. During the harrowing one-handed sit-lift, we noticed that Nureyev whispered something to Collier. Instead of getting into position for the lift, he somehow grabbed her knees and got her into a shoulder lift. It appeared that he would attempt to get her into a sit lift from that position, but the next thing we knew, Collier was toppling head first to the floor. Rudolf swiftly caught her in a fishdive, telling Lesley to arrange her arms in a pose to try covering the rather awkward moment.

The audience gasped, but that wasn't the end of it. Somehow in helping Collier to her feet, she got tangled in his legs and the beautiful pas de deux ended in an embarrassing fumbling mess of intertwined limbs. There was no way to get out of it gracefully. Collier kissed him while he wrapped both arms around her in a big hug, but both were visibly upset and didn't take a bow. They finished the rest of the scene, but Collier remained extremely shaken and Rudolf kept kissing her apologetically.

By curtain calls, both were professional enough to smile and acknowledge the audience applause. Collier presented her bouquet to Rudolf, but he refused to take it. Even more embarrassing was the fact that Martha Graham came to see that performance.

When Collier emerged from the Stage Door, anxious fans asked how she was. "I'm okay, but wobbly," she admitted, no doubt preferring to forget the whole thing. Meanwhile, Nicholas Gunn, a Paul Taylor dancer who performed in the 1975 *Nureyev and Friends* Broadway season, had gone backstage to see Rudolf. Gunn later related how upset Nureyev was, describing how he put his head down, nearly in tears, and said, "But I DROPPED her!" At subsequent performances with Collier, he wisely omitted the sit lift and put her directly into a fish dive.

Fille has always been a wonderfully comic ballet, made even more so by the antics of the dancers. Rudolf took special delight with the four dancing chickens and the rooster, who inserts himself into the harvest scene, before the rainstorm ruins everyone's fun. Graham Fletcher was inside the rooster suit at a 1977 performance of *Fille*. Incidentally, he also portrayed Miss Piggy in *Swine Lake* on the Muppets show that same year. When as the Rooster, he got in the way at one point, Rudolf goosed him and blew the loose tail feathers from Fletcher's costume into the air. At the second performance two nights later when Rudolf tried to goose the Rooster, Fletcher turned on him and chased him instead. Rudolf looked surprised and did a comic run, trying to escape.

The antics and missteps continued during the second act when Rudolf tried to hide from Widow Simone. He pretended to conceal himself in the fireplace, but went too far inside and nearly kicked the back of the set in. Collier pointed to the dresser drawer and tried lifting Rudolf's leg to fit inside the drawer, causing Rudolf to fall flat on his backside. He looked quite surprised, but got up and ran upstairs to Lise's room to hide, forgetting to take the pink scarf he had given her earlier in the scene. Collier quickly tossed it in the fireplace to "hide the evidence" that they had been alone together while her mother was out. Even the curtain calls became a game. Every time Nureyev kissed Collier, the audience applauded even louder. Someone tossed a bouquet from the audience, but it landed in the orchestra pit. Another person rummaged around in the pit until the bouquet was retrieved and tossed on to the stage, causing Nureyev to break up, probably wondering "What next?"

Songs of a Wayfarer created for Nureyev and Paulo Bortoluzzi by Maurice Bejart in 1971, was often performed at numerous *Nureyev and Friends* programs. The work suited Rudolf like a second skin and showed off his technical and dramatic abilities during the two decades that he performed it. The Mahler songs were generally performed "live" by a singer in the pit. On later tours, a taped rendition by Dietrich Fisher Diskau was used.

One night, during a 1977 performance in New York, something happened with the baritone William Metcalf's microphone and it shorted, causing a terrifically explosive noise. One woman seated near me screamed, because it sounded like a gunshot. Nureyev must have thought so too, because he stopped, patted himself across his chest, arms, and thighs. Then, realizing he was still intact, he ran upstage to catch up with the music and executed the most brilliant double turn imaginable. His partner, Johnny Eliasen, could barely conceal his surprise and amusement. The momentary shock from that shattering noise no doubt raised Nureyev's adrenalin and he covered it beautifully.

Ann-Marie Vessel joined her fellow Danish dancers in *The Lesson*, when it was performed at the 1977 Paris *Nureyev Festival*. Nureyev portrayed the ballet master and Vessel his pupil. In the first scene at the ballet barre, Rudolf stood next to his pupil gesturing for her to place one foot onto the barre. Vessel quickly raised her leg and accidentally kicked Nureyev right in the jaw. The audience gasped. Rudolf drew his head back momentarily, but continued right on as if it was meant to happen.

Later that year in London, Natalia Makarova portrayed his pupil. Nureyev became quite demonic in this role, especially near the end of the ballet when he was threateningly chasing her around the room. Makarova, then about three months pregnant, fell to the floor, missing a musical cue. Nureyev improvised momentarily and ran upstage, getting his foot tangled in the curtain. For a brief moment it looked like the entire studio "wall" would fall on him, before he managed to get untangled. Fortunately after that misstep and mindful of Makarova's condition, he was rather gentle with her at the end of the ballet.

The role of James in *La Sylphide* was one of Nureyev's favorites. He performed it in various productions and in two completely different versions: the more frequently performed interpretation by Danish choreographer August Bournonville, and the original Taglioni rendition, reconstructed by Pierre LaCotte.

My first exposure to seeing the LaCotte production was with the Paris Opera at the Palais Garnier. In an elaborate staging, the second act opens with several sylphs flying high overhead, magically suspended by wires. Unfortunately, this effect couldn't be duplicated when the production was brought to Broadway with the Boston Ballet at the smaller Uris Theatre, but they did manage to "fly" the sylphs for the finale.

In November 1980, Nureyev danced a three-week *Friends* season with the Boston Ballet on Broadway, dancing the role of James in *La Sylphide* at all performances. Paris Opera Etoile Ghislaine Thesmar, wife of choreographer Pierre LaCotte, guested as the Sylph, alternating with the Boston Ballet's Elaine Bauer.

Nureyev was so "up" from these performances that some nights he was nearly out of control. There was a bit of a traffic jam in the second act. At one point Nureyev got carried away doing a series of entrechats and Elaine Bauer as the Sylph, came behind him to begin her diagonal of brisés, little jumped steps across the stage. Rudolf started to back up for her and nearly crashed into her, gesturing "Your turn." It looked like one of those embarrassing, "After you; no please, after you" moments. The audience burst out laughing and Nureyev stood there, red-faced, because of his gaffe. We joked later that this particular version needed a traffic cop. One of the fans even suggested making a sign saying, "Danger, sylphs crossing."

It nearly happened again during a matinee performance, when Rudolf scurried to get out of center stage and hopped over the corps girls' feet when they were kneeling. He continued doing little hippity-hop steps into the wings, almost imitating the lead sylph's brisés. The audience began to titter, because Rudolf was so light footed in trying to avoid stepping on anyone while exiting.

During this same Broadway season, a sylph took a belly flop due to a slippery spot in center stage and had a hard time righting herself again. The most disconcerting slip was at the end of the ballet after James tries to capture the Sylph – danced by Ghislaine Thesmar – and causes her death as a result of a poisoned scarf that he's wrapped around her. She collapses into the arms of the other sylphs and they carry her off. When the last of the four sylphs came forward, she slipped on Thesmar's fallen wing and nearly caused the other three sylphs that were carrying Thesmar, to drop her. Rudolf momentarily broke character while starting toward the fallen sylph, not sure if he should help her or not, but she quickly recovered and helped carry the "dead" Thesmar into the wings. This caused the audience to "buzz" and rather spoiled the poetic ending, when the Sylph and her entourage are seen upstage while flying slowly upward, as if ascending.

For the 1976 *Nureyev Festival* at the Palais des Sports in Paris, Nureyev performed the Bournonville version of *La Sylphide* with Natalia Makarova and the Scottish Ballet. A large stage was erected at one end of the sports palace and the audience filled the seats on the three remaining sides. At one performance in the second act, Nureyev, as James, finished his variation and was supposed to make a quick exit before the corps de ballet returned for the finale. Rudolf was enjoying the moment so much that before he headed for the wings, the incoming white-tulled sylphs instantly surrounded him. It was too late to exit, so he stood in a perfect fifth position in center stage as though he belonged there. The stage was resilient to adjust for the many jumped movements, and the buoyancy isn't that noticeable when everyone is jumping. But because Nureyev was merely standing there, he was bouncing up and down like a rubber ball while the sylphs jumped all around him. At first he looked annoyed, then embarrassed, but when the audience began to chuckle, he broke into a huge grin at this rather amusing predicament. Once Makarova returned to the stage, he instantly resumed character, and joined her in the rousing finale.

Four Schumann Pieces was a work created by Hans van Manen for Anthony Dowell and the Royal Ballet. In 1978, Rudolf performed it in Amsterdam with Alexandra Radius of the Dutch National Ballet. There was a misstep on Rudolf's part, when Radius was walking around Rudolf and his timing was off. As a result, he bumped into her rather hard. He gently touched her to make sure she was okay, paused momentarily and said "Sorry." She carried on without batting an eyelash, but Rudolf made a face of disgust and stopped momentarily, upset because it was obviously his fault.

Nureyev mounted the production of *Sleeping Beauty* for the National Ballet of Canada in September of 1972. It was billed as "the most expensive production ever" at a cost of $500,000. This production toured America for over four months, opening at the Met in New York in April of 1973. The Canadian dancer portraying the Lilac Fairy in *Sleeping Beauty* was new to the role, when the company returned for the 1976 Met season. The Lilac Fairy is a non-dancing role in Nureyev's production and wears a long dress. She skims across the floor in the style of Georgian folk dancers. During the ballet's Vision Scene, the corps dancers form two diagonal lines and the Prince follows the Lilac Fairy in and out between the dancers, to eventually see Princess Aurora. This Lilac Fairy stopped each time she passed between the corps dancers, causing Nureyev, who followed her, to call out "Move!" because he kept stepping on her long skirt. This same Lilac Fairy tripped coming down the staircase, causing one of the fans to remark, "It's not a good day for fairies!"

In a performance with his first cast Aurora, danced by Veronica Tennant, a comical misstep occurred in the Grand Pas de Deux. Tennant had pirouetted across the stage and got into an arabesque. Nureyev, on the opposite side of the stage, ran to catch her. He grabbed her extended foot and nearly burst out laughing. She had managed to hold the position until he reached her. She told us afterwards, that when she asked Rudolf what happened, he merely replied, "I was too confident in you!"

When the Festival Ballet took the production of *Sleeping Beauty* to Paris, one memorable misstep occurred in the Grand Pas of the last act. Rudolf must have had a memory lapse, since he alternated nightly with long-limbed Eva Evdokimova and the smaller Patricia Ruanne. He performed the traditional fishdives with Ruanne, but with Evdokimova, he placed her in a sidebend after her pirouettes. This time, he placed Eva facedown instead of into the sidebend and while "righting" her, had an amused expression as if to say, "How did THAT happen?"

During a 1976 *Romeo and Juliet* performance with the Royal Ballet in New York, everything that could go wrong did, but somehow it was still a good performance.

The dancer portraying Lady Capulet was new at that performance and her timing and spacing was not what it should have been. When she angrily tossed the sword toward Romeo for killing Tybalt, it went flying dangerously close to Rudolf's face and into the wings. Romeo is supposed to cling to Lady Capulet's skirts to beg forgiveness, but this Lady Capulet kept moving away from him, causing Rudolf to crawl on his hands and knees to reach her. The more she pulled away, the faster he had to crawl.

In the final tomb scene after Romeo consumed the poison and fell to the floor, Juliet's final backbend over the tomb was so precariously close to falling off, that Rudolf very discreetly raised a supposedly "dead" arm to prop her up.

When Nureyev created his own version of *Romeo and Juliet* for London Festival Ballet, he did much of the choreography in the evenings after a full day's filming on the *Valentino* set. One of my friends was able to watch a studio rehearsal. She related how Rudolf was running out of inspiration to choreograph a difficult piece. Since it was very late, he stretched out on the floor for a few minutes and said half joking, half serious, "Please, help me!" He suddenly jumped up, newly inspired, and plunged into activity.

To make the fight scenes more realistic, he relied on the expertise of J.H. Barrie, who staged productions for the Royal Shakespeare Company as well as numerous other productions. Barrie commented in an interview that Nureyev had a remarkable sense of space onstage and once advised Barrie while staging a production, "Don't unwrap all your Christmas presents at once – save some for the climax."

Since the ballet's London premiere on June 2nd 1977, we observed how the production evolved over the course of the twenty-five performance run. Juliet's costume changed several times until Rudolf was satisfied with it. One evening near the end of the balcony scene, Rudolf as Romeo, was on his knees facing the audience while Patricia Ruanne as his Juliet, ran up behind him and gently pulled his head back to kiss him. Rudolf loved this spontaneous addition and it remained in the production for subsequent performances.

After one especially good performance, Nureyev and Ruanne performed a touching bedroom pas de deux. He kissed his Juliet tenderly upon leaving and hopped over the window ledge only to land on a stage-light, uttering an extremely loud "SHIT!" Ruanne had to stifle her laughter when the entire audience began to laugh.

The second act marketplace scene contains trios danced by Romeo, Mercutio and Benvolio. After what seemed like endless pirouettes, Nureyev trustingly leaned back to be caught by his two friends. Unfortunately, they missed the timing and Rudolf fell to the floor on his backside. At first he looked annoyed, then embarrassed, and finally his eyes twinkled in amusement, which sent the audience into laughter. Both dancers pulled him to the sidelines, still laughing, to watch the marketplace flag dancers.

At the end of the scene, Romeo is banished from Verona for killing Tybalt. Benvolio, performed by Kenneth McCombie, backed up into the wings supporting Nureyev, and tripped on a sword that was left on stage. Both dancers fell and made their exit by crawling on all fours into the wings.

A dancer that was new to the role of Paris was so nervous being on stage with Nureyev, that he mucked up the tomb scene. Realizing Nureyev's performance intensity, this Paris stabbed himself for fear Nureyev would hurt him. However, he fell "dead" on the wrong side of the stage. During the pas de deux with the supposedly dead Juliet, Rudolf informed her that Paris was in the wrong spot, to make sure she wouldn't trip over him when she woke from her sleeping potion.

Nureyev staged his *Romeo and Juliet* at LaScala and when it was presented at the Met, Carla Fracci danced the title role with Dame Margot Fonteyn as Lady Capulet. During the marketplace scene, Rudolf bumped into two supers who were in his way; he just kept walking until they finally moved. He remarked to us one night about the rather "tame" marketplace scenes compared to those that the British cast had given, and asked, "Why can't these Italians act more like Italians?"

The Berlin Ballet brought Nureyev's production of *Nutcracker* to New York in 1980, this time with Eva Evdokimova. At the end of the grand pas de deux, Evdokimova had to make a quick change back into her costume as the young Clara, but she missed her cue. Rudolf had already donned his white wig and coat as Drosselmeyer, who is supposed to discover Clara asleep in her chair. Instead, Rudolf literally carried her from wings and put the "sleeping" Clara into the chair, but first waved at her "naughty, naughty" for missing her entrance cue.

During the 1976 *Nureyev Festival* at the London Coliseum, Rudolf alternated *Le Corsaire* performances with his Royal Ballet colleagues Lynn Seymour and Monica Mason. An amusing misstep occurred the first night he switched from partnering Seymour to dancing with Mason. At a moment in the pas de deux, Rudolf lifts his ballerina and she arches into a lovely pose, before being returned to the floor. Mason, a very strong dancer and a different size than Seymour, jumped off the floor and nearly out of Rudolf's grasp. Instead of having a firm grip around her, he was barely holding her by her calf muscles. Mason leaned precariously forward, arms beautifully arched over her head. In order to provide counterbalance so he wouldn't drop her, Nureyev had to run several steps toward the wings. The whole thing somewhat resembled the Scottish Highlands game of "tossing the caber," where athletes lift long poles from the bottom and after taking several steps with the pole precariously balanced, they toss it into the air and are scored by the distance tossed. Rudolf began laughing and put Mason down immediately when he realized he was nearly in the wings and spent the rest of the pas de deux trying not to laugh.

At another *Corsaire* performance, this time with Natalia Makarova, Nureyev danced with a bandaged ankle. The tempo from the conductor was clearly inconsistent. He finished his tours a la seconde with his back to the audience, but instead of bothering to turn himself around, he did the next step facing upstage, so the audience could see his back for a while. He did it with such panache that it seemed it was choreographed that way.

In a performance of *Giselle* with the La Scala Ballet at the Met in 1981, the dancer playing Albrecht's squire, either had stage fright or a memory lapse. He simply forgot to do the mime scene indicating to Albrecht that the royal hunting party was approaching. So Rudolf did it for him, miming that someone was approaching and they should hide.

Carla Fracci seemed to have a mental block and missed an important entrance cue in the second act of *Giselle*. Rudolf ran around the stage in character "calling" audibly, "Carla, Carla, come here!" causing laughter from the audience. She had been dancing the role of Giselle for twenty years, but it was just "one of those nights."

When Nureyev performed in Mikhail Baryshnikov's production of *Don Quixote* in 1978 at American Ballet Theatre, he was scheduled to dance with Gelsey Kirkland. She cancelled at the last minute and a young soloist named Yoko Ichino, who knew the role, replaced Kirkland. Rudolf was very pleased with Ichino during the performance. She made eye contact with him, flirted with him, and together they had a marvelous chemistry.

One of the fans happened to know Yoko and the dancer confided, "I never knew from night to night what to expect from Rudolf," reflecting on his in-the-moment response to his partners. "One night I did something and he said to me, 'oh, that's good; do it again!' But when I'd do it the next night, he had changed it to something different. You really had to keep up with him." Yoko even managed to outwit him on a Sunday night performance. During the gypsy dancing in Act Two's Windmill Scene, Don Quixote, played at that time by Alexander Minz, sat next to Yoko as Kitri. She offered her hand to the Don in a flirtatious way. Rudolf pretended to be jealous, bodily picked her up and deposited her on the other side of him, thus sitting in the middle between Don Quixote and Kitri. Unfazed, Yoko merely continued flirting, reaching across Rudolf to give her hand to Quixote. Nureyev pulled her hand away and offered the foolish old man his own hand to kiss. Their antics continued until audible laughter from the audience made them realize they were taking attention away from the gypsy dance.

In Nureyev's production of *Don Quixote* for the Paris Opera in the early 1980s, one of the soloists took a very nasty fall just before Nureyev's big solo in the last act. He always set up the audience for this solo by walking the circumference of the stage with one hand placed on his hip and the other extended forward, rather like a bullfighter entering the ring. At that particular performance, the audience was audibly upset over the soloist's fall. When Nureyev came out doing his grand walk around the stage, it was as if his outstretched hand was indicating, "Calm down, it will be okay. I'm here and I'm going to dance for you." His dancing soothed the audience, and thankfully the soloist recovered in time to appear during the finale.

The Zurich Ballet performed Nureyev's production of *Don Quixote* in London in the summer of 1980. The role of Kitri was alternated between long-limbed Eva Evdokimoa and petite Zurich ballerina Elise Flagg. In the tavern scene, Kitri hurls herself at Basilio from quite a distance and when dancing with Evdokimova, Rudolf miscalculated her size. Eva overbalanced and had to put her hands on the floor, looking embarrassed. Later when they were at the side, Nureyev kissed her and said audibly, "Sorry!" At the curtain calls, Eva wanted to present a flower from her bouquet to Rudolf, but it fell apart in her hands so she handed him her entire bouquet. Rudolf just laughed.

At another *Don Quixote* performance, Nureyev hit a slippery spot on the stage and nearly went over. In the windmill scene, Elise Flagg as Kitri ran toward Rudolf while he spread the shawl on the floor, slipped, and went right down on her bum. As the two rolled on the floor, both were audibly laughing.

Because Rudolf was so relaxed, he executed a letter-perfect solo in the third act's wedding scene. The triumph was short-lived, however. In the very last pose when Kitri is tossed into the air before the final kneeling pose, Elise Flagg's arm bashed Rudolf in the face, momentarily stunning him.

Nureyev's production of *The Tempest* premiered at the Royal Ballet in London in December of 1982. An open pit at the back of the Covent Garden's darkened stage was used for some of the production's special effects, such as Prospero conjuring up the storm for the shipwreck scene. For the storm sequence, Nureyev as Prospero, knelt at the edge of this open pit, facing the audience, while a stagehand in the pit draped an enormous cape over his shoulders and handed him his magic staff. At one performance, Nureyev got far too close to the opened pit and nearly toppled backwards, until a stagehand steadied him. Two years later when the production transferred to the Paris Opera, the cape and staff were lowered from the flies while Nureyev stood center stage, thus eliminating any potential mishaps.

While on tour in 1974 with the National Ballet of Canada, Rudolf performed the lead role in John Neumeier's *Don Juan*. When alone on stage, he heard a commotion and the audience began reacting strangely. He turned and saw a streaker rush across the stage. As Rudolf later recalled in a television interview, "There I was, acting away and suddenly I thought, 'Should I compete with him or pretend nothing happened?'" When asked by the interviewer, Dick Cavett, if the man showed signs of talent, Nureyev humorously commented, "He had the right to be naked."

*"Basically you have a sense of responsibility and vitality...
If you capture the audience, you've won."*
~Rudolf Nureyev, Women's Wear Daily, April 11, 1973~

STRIKES

Public turned away due to strike, Paris, March, 1989
Photo: Nancy Sifton

Rudolf Nureyev rarely cancelled. As ticket-buyers, we were accustomed to seeing him dance unless something very serious happened. Occasionally strikes took place that had nothing to do with him, but the public ended up being cheated out of the performance.

Shortly after I returned from London to New York in 1975, a musician's strike on Broadway played havoc. Nureyev's *Raymonda* production for American Ballet Theatre was being performed at the Uris Theatre, to be followed by a *Nureyev and Friends* program.

The fans knew the dates for *Raymonda*, so we submitted our checks well in advance, even prior to the newspaper announcement. None of us received a response from the Box Office, which had been forced to close because of the month-long musician's strike. No orchestra, no Broadway musicals, no Nureyev tickets.

When the strike finally ended, the staff at the Uris had over 30,000 orders to process. They were so overworked, that they returned everyone's check without explanation or tickets. A few received notes with their refunds explaining, "All performances for dates requested are sold out." Since we had sent our ticket orders in weeks before tickets went on sale, we were perplexed. Apparently, not enough time had been allowed between postal and personal bookings. Until the mail orders could be sorted out, a "Sold Out" sign was displayed on the Box Office window.

Since many people never received a notice, either about getting a refund or their tickets, they went to the Box Office the first day tickets went on sale to the general public. Needless to say, total chaos ensued. People who arrived at 8 a.m. didn't get their tickets until 3:30 that afternoon. Lines doubled around the theatre because nobody knew where to go. There was one window for purchasing tickets to ABT's entire season, another for the *Friends* program and still another for performances of Raymonda. An additional line was for *Treemonisha*, the musical then playing at the Uris Theatre.

I tried going on my lunch hour on that Monday, but it was hopeless to wait because of the long lines. People got more and more impatient and the stressed Uris Box Office staff grew ruder and ruder. Meanwhile, the lines kept getting longer and longer. About three people per hour were being served, because everyone was buying so many tickets. One Box Office staff person said desperately, "I don't know anything about *Raymonda*. I'm selling *Nureyev & Friends* tickets. I've never experienced anything like this. People are desperate to get those tickets and I'm working myself to death." People were told that performances were sold out. Yet, when we went a few days later, tickets were readily available.

ABT was concerned that, because of the strike, patrons and subscribers wouldn't get their promised seats, so a notice was sent giving them the chance to obtain their tickets on the first day of booking, which resulted in total chaos. Tickets for the five-week *Friends* program in all parts of the theatre cost $13, an unprecedented amount at that time. If tickets were purchased for every *Friends* performance, it would cost over $400. Fans also had ABT tickets and an upcoming Martha Graham season to pay for. As Nureyev's friend Nigel Gosling told us, we certainly did have to "pay for our pleasures."

In the spring my roommate arranged a trip to Paris. When she arrived, it was "National Strike Day." Performances went on without a full orchestra; dancers performed to a single piano. When she returned, the New York City Ballet Orchestra went on strike. It was a bad year for audiences!

Many fans went to London for the annual *Nureyev Festivals* held each summer. During one season, the Musician's Union announced they would strike if recorded music were used. A seldom-performed work by Maurice Bejart called *Sonate a Trois* was cancelled completely because of this, and Nureyev performed *Songs of a Wayfarer* to live music instead.

Over the Christmas holidays in 1978, I was lucky to get a standby plane ticket to Paris, where Nureyev performed *Swan Lake* with Natalia Makarova. I had booked for four performances, including one on New Year's Eve. For the first performance, Rudolf arrived at the Paris Opera well before curtain time, only to learn that the stagehands were on strike. The performance was cancelled. The following night he phoned in to determine whether or not the show would go on. It didn't.

Luckily, the Kirov Ballet was in Paris at the same time, so a friend and I got a last-minute 40-franc ticket to sit on the steps inside the mammoth Palais des Congress. It was totally against fire regulations. The ushers wouldn't give us cast lists, unless we bought an expensive souvenir program. It was a lovely performance consisting of classic ballets. We noticed that Nureyev and Makarova were in the audience. They were chatting at the intermission and we overheard him say, "How I love this company!" Quite understandable, since it was both his and Makarova's alma mater. Crowds asking for autographs soon surrounded Rudolf, and he obliged by signing the Kirov program. He tried going backstage to say hello to some of his former colleagues, but wasn't permitted.

For New Year's Eve, the Paris Opera stagehands "allowed" the performance to go ahead, but without scenery. Rudolf was so frustrated, he offered to put the sets up himself or dance without them, which is exactly what happened. The dancers simply performed *Swan Lake* on an empty stage, forcing the audience members to use their imaginations. Makarova made her entrance in the White Act through the back door of the Opera's mammoth stage. The swans framed the stage nicely, so that when Nureyev or Makarova ran to what should have been the offstage wings, they went behind the line of swans and remained in the shadows until their next entrance. A chair was retrieved for the throne in Act Three, but other than that, the dancers and the lights created the magic.

Most of Nureyev's difficulties seemed to occur at the Paris Opera, both early in his career and especially later, when he became Director. When he mounted the Shades scene from his production of *La Bayadere* for the company in 1974, Nureyev expressed his frustration with the dancers, who didn't want to work as hard as Nureyev asked them to and wouldn't dance on point. He later told us, "It was difficult. They refused to go on fucking point."

In November of 1979, he mounted his original *Manfred* production on the Paris Opera. Instead of premiering in the majestic Palais Garnier, it opened at the cavernous Palais des Sports, with Nureyev sitting in the audience, sidelined by a broken toe. The theatre was booked for an entire month. By mid-December, Rudolf was back on stage, dancing in *Manfred* and George Balanchine's *Le Bourgeois Gentilhomme*.

Nureyev very much wanted *Manfred* to be seen elsewhere. In 1980 he began negotiations to bring it to the Met. Anthony Bliss, then the general director, had seen *Manfred* in Paris and loved it. But the Paris Opera hadn't been to America in decades and the general public was unfamiliar with either the dancers or with *Manfred*. The plan was for the company to showcase the ballet with a six-week tour. The dancers balked. They insisted on bringing six different full-length ballets, leaving just two New York performances of *Manfred*. The Met said that would be unfeasible. Then the dancers began protesting about working conditions and insisted they would not be a "backup" for what they saw as another *Nureyev Festival*.

What they didn't take into account was the huge size of the Met. Without Nureyev, this company – rather unknown to most American audiences – couldn't sell enough tickets to make it viable. Consequently, the Met dropped any further negotiations and cancelled the entire tour.

I sent an "open letter" to the Paris Opera dancers, accusing them of being unprofessional. I also wrote to the Met. Anthony Bliss responded that he felt disappointed the Paris Opera couldn't "see the light," but added, "There have been new developments and the situation may reverse itself." The solution would have been to bring only the lead dancers that were in the *Manfred* premiere and use another company as the corps. Unfortunately, this never materialized.

Undaunted, Nureyev later contacted the Zurich Ballet, then under the direction of former New York City Ballet dancer Patricia Neary. Funding was found and a newly designed *Manfred* was created in 1981. It was this version that was finally presented at the 1982 *Nureyev Festival* in London.

A strike of a different kind occurred during that year's *Nureyev Festival*, when the London Transport went on strike, causing havoc for the entire city. Traffic was snarled. Some city buses ran only once an hour, causing long waits and overcrowding. This greatly hampered everyone's ability to get around. We had to leave extra early for performances. On occasion, we walked from our friend's place in South Kensington to the London Coliseum near Leicester Square, a distance of more than two miles.

Nureyev's tenure with the Paris Opera was troublesome even before it started. According to information received from one of my French friends, his contract to direct the Paris Opera had been signed some time before the announcement, but his dance commitments prevented him from taking over immediately. So Rosella Hightower was named Interim Director. Nureyev's contract was filled with clauses that permitted him to continue dancing, while directing the company. He was to be paid for directing and receive a separate salary for choreographing. There were other stipulations, including a fee for other companies to use the rights to stage his productions, as well as any broaD.C.ast rights. All together, he would earn a hefty sum, but not as much as Daniel Barenboim who was then Music Director.

The announcement wasn't immediately released to the press. The Paris Opera administration wanted to wait for the Kirov Ballet, then performing in Paris, to return to St. Petersburg, before releasing the news. When the Kirov administration was told that Rudolf Nureyev would be the next Director of the Paris Opera Ballet, they were angry, stating that as long as "that traitor" Nureyev was in command, there would be few artistic exchanges between the French and Russian companies.

Nureyev galvanized the Paris Opera Ballet during his tenure. His first production was a new full-length version of *Raymonda* that premiered in November of 1983. He brought in new choreographers, expanded the repertory, and the company performed in the newly opened Opera Bastille, which provided a larger theatre capacity and backstage facilities. He revamped the way the dancers worked, moving daily class from noon to ten in the morning. He also provided his dancers with the opportunity to be "exchange artists" with the Royal Ballet and other companies, giving them further stage experience.

When Nureyev planned to showcase his production of *Raymonda* at the 1984 *Nureyev Festival*, the dancers balked. They refused to dance if Rudolf did, which didn't make much sense, as it was billed as a *Nureyev Festival*. Negotiations went on for some time, but in the end the entire season was cancelled – the only year out of a decade that his annual London *Nureyev Festival* did not occur. Instead, Rudolf joined up with the Berlin Ballet at the San Antonio Festival in Texas, to perform in Bournonville's *La Sylphide* and in Birgit Cullberg's *Miss Julie*.

In early August of 1984, the Paris Opera performed *Raymonda* in the Herod Atticus in Athens. The audiences loved the company, the production, and especially Nureyev. At the closing performance on August 12th, Nureyev danced with Florence Clerc, the wife of Charles Jude. The company appeared to sabotage the performance. Only half of the corps de ballet showed up. In the opening scene, when Raymonda's friends were supposed to be admiring her wedding dress displayed on a mannequin, they were on the floor as though searching for a contact lens. When they were supposed to admire the bridal veil, they disrobed the mannequin and tied the clothes on the dummy's head. Furthermore, some dancers decided not to wear costumes for the first scene.

A diagonal of roses are placed on the floor by the friends, which are picked up one at a time in Raymonda's entrance variation. However, the dancers plucked them up for her and applauded the flowers instead. At this point, Rudolf came on stage and glared at them in disbelief.

The dancers behaved themselves for a while, but during a large corps de ballet waltz, the men appeared in their underwear. During the waltz, several dancers just disappeared into the wings. Rudolf, as Jean deBrienne, walked out onto the stage, clapping and gesturing for them to return. When they did, the men danced with each other while the women watched.

They also spoiled Jean Guizerix's entrance as the Saracen, by cavorting and applauding. Nureyev was furious the way his production was being sabotaged, and held up his hand to the conductor to stop the performance, feeling the audience was being cheated out of truly seeing his production. The Greek audience couldn't understand what was going on. Some began to boo Rudolf for wanting to stop the performance. The orchestra kept going, since they were so close to the end of Act One.

Whatever ensued backstage during intermission, the company behaved themselves for the rest of the performance. Pranks were one thing, but spoiling the performance for the paying public was another. When the dancers emerged after the performance, some fans told them how unprofessional they were, to which they sarcastically replied, "Merci" and continued on their way.

Rudolf took the Concorde to New York the very next day, to negotiate a last-minute Broadway *Friends* season. Except for Paris Opera dancer Jean Guizerix, who had danced the lead in Nureyev's 1979 *Manfred* production, the rest of the Friends were dancers he respected, had worked with before and were quite professional. After dancing thirteen consecutive performances in a stifling New York heat wave, he was refreshed and energized again.

He toured South Korea and Japan dancing his production of *Sleeping Beauty* with the Vienna Opera Ballet, then returned in Paris to mount his *Romeo and Juliet* on the Paris dancers. This time he danced the secondary role of Mercutio.

Rudolf returned to New York again, trying to get financial backing to bring the Paris Opera to the Met. The French government told him, in effect, "You want to take the company to New York, then YOU raise the money." Returning to Paris, another battle ensued, when he premiered his new version of *Swan Lake* in December of 1984. The dancers complained the choreography was too difficult and preferred the former production by Vladimir Bourmeister.

Many of us planned to be in Paris during the Christmas break. One friend from Caracas contacted me to arrange her ticket order and hotel, because a postal strike in Venezuela prevented her from doing it herself. After flying to Paris, we approached the Opera House only to find a *Relache* sign on the door, indicating the performance had been cancelled. Some of the very dancers we came to see were on the steps of the Opera, handing out leaflets explaining their strike to the arriving public. We were extremely disappointed, which we told the dancers, but they dismissed us matter-of-factly.

Rudolf was philosophical about it – he went to see something else that evening. Fortunately, the Bolshoi Ballet was performing in another theatre and we managed to get tickets at the last minute. Sure enough, Nureyev was there in the front row. If he couldn't dance in *Swan Lake*, at least he could watch it.

After the one performance of *Swan Lake* that we did see with Nureyev, we waited for him at the Paris Opera's Stage Door. Some fans gave him gifts and he grinned and said, "NOW it seems like Christmas." He confided that the dancers missed fifteen days of *Swan Lake* rehearsals, because they felt the choreography was "too difficult." In order to be ready for the premiere, Rudolf rehearsed them until 3 a.m. the night before it opened.

After the strikes ended, I attended the Saturday matinee, December 29, 1984 when Nureyev came on stage, microphone in hand, and promoted 19-year-old Sylvie Guillem to the rank of *Etoile*. She not only bypassed the usual Paris Opera hierarchy, she became the youngest dancer to be promoted to the highest level.

Making a stop at a performance in London before returning to New York, I ran into Maude Gosling. She confided that Rudolf was "most upset" about the décor and especially the color of the costumes for his *Swan Lake* production. "They're not what they're supposed to be." She was of the opinion that the Costumers' Union tried to sabotage the production, mixing the purples with oranges and so on. "Rudolf wants them all redone, but they're expensive, so they'll have to stick with them for awhile."

She also explained that Nureyev wanted the sterile white floorcloth removed or sprayed, but designer Ezio Frigerio said the dancers wouldn't be able to dance otherwise. She told me that Rudolf complained to Jack Lang, the Minister of Culture, who told him he should spend more time in Paris to supervise his productions.

"If I dance opening nights," Rudolf told us, "they will strike." The dancers even demanded that Rudolf stop dancing in Paris, or they would refuse to do any more of his productions. The various claques booed both Rudolf and the new *Swan Lake,* because the dancers preferred the old Bourmeister version and wanted it returned to the repertoire.

Despite his troubles with the Paris Opera, he still believed in his dancers, striking or not. But he was also busy with his own career. In a Scottish press interview, Rudolf remarked, "I get forty performances per year in Paris... Do they expect me to sit there and rot?"

His persistent attempts to showcase the company in America finally paid off. It was announced, that Nureyev and the Paris Opera would be the primary attraction at the 1985 San Antonio Festival. We ordered our tickets, made our plane reservations and even planned to go to Chicago, where the company would appear afterwards. When we called to inquire about our tickets, we were notified that the San Antonio season with the Paris Opera was cancelled "for budgetary reasons." We suspected it was because the dancers threatened to strike again, particularly because they were scheduled to perform in Nureyev's *Swan Lake*. Rudolf bargained with the dancers, saying they could bring back the Bourmeister production, but only if they danced his version in Texas. Unfortunately, the compromise was not accepted, so the entire engagement was cancelled. When we called the Chicago Box Office about a ticket refund, they knew nothing about the sudden cancellation.

Nureyev's production of *Washington Square,* based on the Henry James novel with music by Charles Ives, premiered in Paris just prior to his 1985 Nureyev Festival. I managed to see one performance. While it was overly ambitious, I thought it contained some of his most original choreography. We heard that the dancers and the stagehands were not happy with the production. The stage crew was disgruntled with the cumbersome sets, part of which blocked the view of many people on one side of the house. The Met's presenter of productions, Jane Hermann, was in the audience and thought the production would work at the Met, so negotiations to present the company in New York began.

Nureyev performed at that summer's Edinburgh Festival, dancing *Bach Suite*, accompanied by Yehudi Menuhin. He returned to Paris to begin rehearsals for his production of *Nutcracker*. He worked intensely before flying off to New York again "on urgent business," where it was rumored that a planned Met season was in doubt. After his brief visit, he was back in Paris, but left again to rehearse *Miss Julie* in London. He was spotted that night at the Royal Ballet's performance of the *Sleeping Beauty*. Then he dashed at intermission to catch Northern Ballet Theatre's new *Othello* production at a nearby theatre. He never wanted to miss anything. He returned to Paris on November 2, 1985, to promote Isabel Guerin and Laurent Hilaire to the rank of Etoile after their performance of *Swan Lake*.

When *Nutcracker* premiered in December, many of us traveled to Paris over the Christmas break to see it. *Nutcracker* was not the holiday moneymaker as it is elsewhere, because it is not a French tradition. The entire production seemed to be sabotaged. We couldn't believe this was the same company we saw in *Swan Lake*. The dancers didn't take the production seriously. At the five performances I saw, there was always one missing corps member in the Snowflakes scene. The stagehands also neglected to remove the Christmas tree along with one-half of the wall from the party scene. The dancers giggled and talked their way all through it. On the nights I saw it, careless partners dropped girls in the Waltz of the Flowers. Nureyev was so incensed, that when one fan later asked him what his next production would be, he snapped, "*Nutcracker* here, now. Enjoy it!"

Backstage, Rudolf was busy going over budgets and signing documents with Marie-Susanne, his assistant. "Such chaos!" he mumbled. Then he remarked he had to "lock up shop because there are people waiting outside." He chatted briefly with dancers Laurent Hilaire and Monique Loudieres, who had danced that evening. He wished them "Bon Anee, banana," a favorite play on words at New Year's.

1986 brought more problems for Rudolf. Maurice Bejart was invited to choreograph *Arepo* – which means Opera spelled backwards – for Sylvie Guillem and Eric VuAun. Following the performance, Bejart was presented to the public to acknowledge the applause. He made an announcement that he was promoting a promising young dancer VuAun to the rank of *Etoile*. However, the Director of the Paris Opera is solely the one who promotes dancers. Bejart, who had always wanted to direct the company, caused a scandal. In a press interview, Bejart stated that Nureyev had ruined both the school and the company. Naturally, Rudolf was furious. His only public remark was, that Bejart was "going through a difficult time."

Nureyev made a guest appearance with London Festival Ballet in *Coppelia*. The warm reception he received from the dancers and the public energized him. He sent a message to the fans waiting after the performance, that he was "too tired to sign." En route to his car, he confessed that the Paris

Opera "eats me." In April of 1986, Rudolf was also emotionally drained by the death of dancer Erik Bruhn, having flown to Toronto to be at his bedside.

Later that month, Nureyev took a select group of his dancers, including Guillem, in a newly formed troupe named *Ballet de Louvre de Paris*, and danced *Giselle* in the Seychelles. Both Rudolf and Sylvie posed for photographs on the beach, with Sylvie on top of a gigantic tortoise.

Nureyev's persistence in trying to get the Paris Opera seen in New York finally came to fruition on July 8, 1986, when the company did a joint gala with American Ballet Theatre. He arranged selections from his full-length *Raymonda*, showcasing many of his dancers in various solos, pas de deux, and the complete Act Three. After the vision pas de deux, danced by Sylvie Guillem and Manuel Legris, the Met audience exploded with applause, which was so overwhelming, that the dancers actually took two steps backwards from the roar of the cheering public.

The following evening, Nureyev's own version of *Swan Lake* was finally seen in New York, but he played the secondary role of Rothbart, dancing the Prince only on closing night. He also danced just one performance of *Washington Square* at the Met.

Many of us traveled to Washington, D.C. for the final portion of the tour, where Rudolf danced two performances as Prince Siegfried. The company wowed the American audiences. Thankfully, no strike erupted at the last minute. After touring briefly with a loyal group of Paris Opera dancers in more *Friends* programs, he was back in Paris, preparing for another new production.

Nureyev created a reimagined version of *Cinderella* for Sylvie Guillem and Charles Jude, which included a salute to Hollywood and the glamour of the era. For his own part, Nureyev was the "Director," who gave himself a brief solo after donning a Groucho Marx disguise and cigar.

Cinderella was showcased at the Met in the summer of 1987 to mixed reviews. While he was in New York, he met with one of his fans, who had just begun a new job. She told him that some of the workers had gone on strike. Rudolf retorted, "Oh good, we have something in common!" At that time he showed off his new "toy" – a mobile phone. It allowed him to conduct Paris Opera business while still performing around the world.

In 1988, he brought his *Swan Lake* and *Nutcracker* productions to New York and Washington, D.C. Rudolf danced the role of the Prince with Sylvie

Guillem in *Swan Lake* and *Nutcracker* with his latest protégé, Elisabeth Maurin. It was also an occasion for a gala to honor Nureyev's 50th birthday.

As Nureyev's roles became more limited, he wanted to bring the Paris Opera to New York once more, where the entire company could be seen to its best advantage. For months he negotiated to present his dancers at Radio City Music Hall, a historic landmark theatre. The world-famous Rockettes had performed there for years, but the theatre was having trouble booking acts that could fill the 6,000-seat venue. In recent years, rock concerts managed to fill the house. The Rockettes were forced to take their act on tour.

Rudolf flew via the Concorde to do a TV interview, promoting the idea of a season at the Music Hall. He stated that for more than twenty years he had wanted to dance there and it would be the only time in his career, to perform on that great stage. Rudolf proposed several works, including *Les Sylphides, Pressage, Petrushka, Spectre de la Rose*, and Nijinsky's *Faune*. These would require huge casts, sets and costumes, but Rudolf said much could be borrowed from either ABT or the Joffrey Ballet, to help offset the expense.

Later in 1988, an announcement appeared about the Paris Opera coming to Radio City. We excitedly bought our tickets. It had long been a fantasy of mine to have Rudolf Nureyev sell out that magnificent theatre with an all-ballet program. For once, the large productions wouldn't look cramped, when performed on the Music Hall's enormous stage.

Despite his best efforts, the engagement never happened. The dancers threatened to strike if Rudolf danced. They understandably wanted to be seen for their own merit, but without Nureyev's name to sell tickets, the presenters felt it was too risky.

We were notified by Radio City Music Hall to claim our refunds. It broke my heart to take my fistful of tickets back to the Box Office. I asked how the tickets had been selling and they replied "well enough." Not only did the constant strikes jeopardize bringing *Sleeping Beauty* to the Met, but a fascinating program to Radio City Music Hall never happened.

By this time the fans realized, that the only way to see the company was to go to Paris. However, we grew tired of flying there to see new productions, only to find another *Relache* notice on the closed doors of the Palais Garnier.

Nureyev's production of *Sleeping Beauty* for the Paris Opera was scheduled to premiere on March 17, 1989 with a fund-raising gala. The dancers once again refused to dance. A gala birthday dinner for him was planned to follow the performance. Since the gala was a fundraiser, those with tickets just for the performance were turned away; those with gala dinner tickets were escorted to the foyer for an earlier-than-expected meal. Rudolf duly celebrated his birthday with friends and patrons.

Nureyev had faced his biggest frustration in 1989. His prized protégé Sylvie Guillem left the Paris Opera for the Royal Ballet. Later that year, his contract was to be renewed. Until it was sorted out, Nureyev embarked on a new phase of his career: musical theatre. He accepted the role of the King of Siam in *The King and I* and toured in multiple U.S. cities. When the administration in Paris gave Nureyev an ultimatum to return to Paris "or else," Rudolf ignored them. Thus ended his tenure as Director. He adored the company he revitalized, but was worn down by the endless battles. He declared, "Maybe it's time to leave. One cannot just sit in the office and wrestle with 150 egos." He wanted to do as much as he could elsewhere. Trying something new would keep him on stage a bit longer.

"If an artist doesn't have temperament, then nobody goes to see him."
~Rudolf Nureyev, The Record, July 19, 1980~

PRANKS

*Nureyev as Petrushka after stagehands dumped snow,
Mark Hellinger Theatre, NYC, March 17, 1979
Photo: William J. Reilly*

Closing night performances were great fun, because many companies that Nureyev danced with were notorious for playing pranks. While Rudolf had a great sense of humor, he didn't encourage these antics, because he felt it interfered with the performance, especially if it was his own production. Since we knew the productions so thoroughly from repeated viewings, the company jokes greatly amused us.

When Carabosse entered in Nureyev's production of *Sleeping Beauty*, her entourage of "Nasty Boys" as we called them, clambered down the grand staircase, held Carabosse aloft, and paraded her around. When she took possession of the King's throne, the boys climbed on it, forming a human pyramid. They then raided the trays and drinking cups from the banquet table and danced around Carabosse, while loudly jingling the props. Upon exiting, some of the Nasty Boys tried taking the fairies with them, and one started a fake punch-up fight with another dancer, who was taken by surprise at these improvised antics. Of course, this was without the watchful eye of Nureyev, who doesn't appear until Act Two.

After the Prince's variation in the Hunting Scene, Rudolf reached for his goblet and someone else grabbed it out of the valet's hand, before Nureyev got it. He simply stared at them in disbelief. In the last act, the cats reversed their roles; the male cat raised his leg while the female cat stroked it, and upon exiting, both of them hissed and meowed audibly at each other. At one point Nureyev mimed "Naughty, naughty" to the company, for pulling so many pranks.

During one stifling summer at the Coliseum, before the theatre acquired air-conditioning, we all suffered from the heat except Rudolf, who thrived on it. Once again in the Hunting Scene, Rudolf reached to the dancer portraying his valet, for a drink. Whether this goblet contained real water or not is beside the point; it was all part of the Prince's routine. As he raised the goblet to his lips, he reeled back in horror at whatever was inside the cup. Obviously the company was trying to make him laugh, but he gave a disdained, "We are not amused" look to them, even though his eyes were twinkling.

At other performances, the valet handed the Prince a white handkerchief, for Nureyev to mop his brow. This was done very much in character and somewhat surreptitiously, especially when Rudolf had a cold. But on this occasion the valet unfolded a gigantic white dinner napkin and shook it like a matador for the entire audience to see, before handing it to the Prince. Rudolf's eyes grew wide in mock surprise as he grabbed it and folded it down to a more manageable size before returning it to the amused valet.

Sometimes the tables were turned on the dancers. In *Sleeping Beauty*, Nureyev - as the Prince - made his entrance in a fur-trimmed blue waistcoat and plumed hat, which were removed by his valet along with his boots, before he performed his big variation. Sometimes when Rudolf was in a devilish mood, he gave the valet a difficult time by clenching his fists and keeping his arms clamped to his side, while the boy struggled to remove his jacket. Then he would look at him quizzically as if to say, "Having trouble?"

The company's biggest prank was during *Sleeping Beauty's* rousing dancing finale. The corps deliberately halted at one point, making it look like the Prince and Aurora were out of step, as they performed their pas de chats. Rudolf was not amused.

During the many *Nureyev Festivals*, Rudolf's production of *Romeo and Juliet* kept evolving and so did the pranks. Company dancer Rick Werner was cast in the role of Tybalt. Following the duel in Act Two, Romeo stabs Tybalt, who falls to the floor. At each performance, Rudolf was so involved in his characterization that he lunged on top of Tybalt, until the other Montagues pulled him away. During one of these performances, we learned that Rick sustained a cracked rib from the impact of Rudolf falling on him. On closing night when Romeo pounced on Tybalt's chest, a theatrical blood pouch that Werner had concealed under his tunic burst, spewing red fake blood everywhere. Rudolf's eyes widened in shock – this time he wasn't acting – and looked horrified, as they pulled him offstage to be "exiled." We noticed that Tybalt "died" with a satisfied smile on his face.

As Mercutio, Nicholas Johnson was also a prankster. During the marketplace scene, aside from those choreographic inventions of Nureyev's, the crowd scenes often became very rowdy. Some nights the rude gestures in the marketplace scene caused gasps from the audiences. Other nights, the fight scenes seemed overly realistic, with some of the guys spinning each other around and seemingly hurling each other into the wings. As we scanned the panorama, we often found Nicky wearing several huge floppy hats, borrowed from the various marketplace stalls and clowning around with members of the corps.

At one performance, the Nurse handed Romeo the letter asking him to meet Juliet at the church. There must have been something amusing written on it, because when Rudolf opened it, he looked to the audience and said, "I know it, I know it." The first few rows in the audience burst out laughing, but none of us ever knew what the message said.

On the final night of the company's tour in Washington, D.C., the marketplace antics took on a Keystone Cops quality. When one of the Montague boys was taken aback by a Capulet's rude gesture, he jumped into his friend's arms and began chewing his fingernails in mock fright. Another of the Montagues always fought with an imaginary enemy in the offstage wings, somersaulting back onto the stage and then returning for more. At this performance, he rubbed his hands together, pretended to roll up his sleeves, before leaping into the wings to pursue his enemy. He emerged at one point wiping his hands together gleefully, when suddenly a Capulet pulled him by the collar back into the wings with the Montague boy's feet flying in the air.

When the production went to Paris in 1978, Nicky Johnson as Mercutio was even more outrageous with his pranks. In the marketplace scene, he snatched the nurse's veil, wrapped it around his waist, and stuffed a vendor's pumpkin under his shirt. When Romeo entered looking for the nurse, Nicky opened his legs as though giving birth and out popped the pumpkin, which he tossed at Romeo. Rudolf laughed and tossed it into the wings. After several such antics, I heard Rudolf say, "That's enough now!"

At a later performance, Johnson found a basket of grapes from a marketplace vendor and offered them to Benvolio and Romeo. Nicky then balanced the basket on his head. Rudolf took it and dumped it upside down over Johnson's head, causing Nicky to pick up all the loose bits of artificial grapes, before he could continue his scene.

In Flemming Flindt's *The Lesson*, Nureyev, as the ballet master, instructs his pupil at the barre. Whether a prank or not, the ballet barre wasn't secured properly. Rudolf wiggled it for all to see that it was unstable. At the end of the ballet when he went to strangle his pupil, the barre began to tip over, so he grabbed it and let his pupil slip to the floor.

During the curtain calls of *La Fille Mal Gardee* with the Royal Ballet in New York, Brian Shaw as Widow Simone was presented with a bouquet consisting of turnips and carrots. Alexander Grant as Alain was presented with a brand new red umbrella with a carnation on top and red, white and blue streamers dangling from it. His other umbrella, a key prop for his character, had broken during the previous performance.

Nureyev's *Swan Lake* production for the Paris Opera came to New York in 1986. Rudolf alternated in the roles of Rothbart and Prince Siegfried. Since Nureyev's productions were always sumptuous with large casts, there was a call for supers to "fill in" the crowd scenes in Acts One and Three. Some of these supers were dance enthusiasts who were "extras" in numerous opera and ballet productions at the Met. During Act Three of *Swan Lake*, Nureyev sat on the throne, when one of the ladies-in-waiting crossed in front of him to say hello. He did a double take when he recognized her and a most amused expression crossed his face.

When the Joffrey Ballet joined forces with Nureyev in their Diaghilev Program, the first piece on that program was Leonid Massine's *Parade*, in which various circus characters appear. One of them was a horse designed by Picasso. After four weeks of nightly performances, the two dancers in the horse costume decided to kick up their heels on closing night and made the choreography quite comical. Later in the program toward the end of *Petrushka*, the Devil tossed snow at the crowd and danced with the Nursemaids, which was not part of the ballet. On closing night, Robert Joffrey was the Head Coachman, barely recognizable under his Russian garb and beard. The stagehands dumped all the snow during curtain calls, while Joffrey removed his beard so the public could recognize him. Later at the Stage Door, someone had a green balloon in the shape of a frog with the words "Kiss Me" on it. This was given to Rudolf as he got in his waiting car. Holding the frog balloon on his lap, he laughed as the car disappeared into the night.

At the closing night of *Scheherazade* with Festival Ballet in London, Rudolf portrayed an absolutely wild Golden Slave, another role created by Nijinsky. The company outdid themselves in the bacchanal scene near the end of the ballet. The female odalisques dipped themselves in sequins and some of the women ran off into the wings, chased by the slaves who were set free. One of the male principal dancers of London Festival Ballet came out dressed in harem garb, complete with veil and a jewel in his navel. As frenzied dancers whirled in the bacchanal scene, we noticed this one odalisque trying to catch Nureyev's eye. Rudolf lifted the veil to discover who it was, then gave him a big kiss on the cheek and kept right on dancing.

(Because I work hard) "I'm never taken by surprise during a performance, never taken aback by something going wrong."
~Rudolf Nureyev, London Sunday Times, March 12, 1983~

PRODUCTION BLOOPERS

Curtain call after Don Quixote, Boston Ballet, Boston, 1982
Photo: Judy Bellaragione

LIGHTS

Botched lighting cues can ruin a performance and Nureyev was particularly adamant that the cues be accurate, to present his productions in the best possible way. It wasn't a rule just for his productions, but ALL productions in which he danced. He respected the lighting cues of other choreographer's works. On occasion he would have heated discussions with the technicians, if the lighting was incorrect.

In 1980, Nureyev's *Nutcracker* opened at the Metropolitan Opera House with the Berlin Ballet. The complicated lighting cues and set changes didn't work at the key moment when the Nutcracker was transformed into the Prince.

When Rudolf entered as the Prince, he stood in center stage, snapping his fingers to signal that the spotlight should come up. Instead, the music began and he was standing in total darkness. After much fruitless finger snapping, he screamed out loud, "Assholes!" A friend said in amazement, "Did he just say what I thought he did?" The entire audience burst out laughing, but the spotlight came on immediately.

Lighting cues in the Awakening Scene of his *Sleeping Beauty* production were equally troublesome. Standing at the top of the palace staircase, Nureyev waited until the lights came up, before making his entrance to awaken his sleeping princess. More often than not, however, Rudolf stood at the top of the stairs snapping his fingers or stomping his feet like a flamenco dancer, so the overhead spot could find him. These missed lighting cues were especially irritating, because if he waited, he would miss the musical cues leading up to the Awakening. But descending the staircase in the dark could be dangerous.

The production seemed to be cursed when it came to the Awakening Scene. At another performance, the lighting technicians decided not to bother finding the Prince with the spotlight, as he descended the staircase. After much finger-snapping and foot-stomping, the elegant Florimund plopped himself forlornly on the staircase, head in hand just waiting patiently for the follow spot to come on. When it finally appeared, Nureyev performed a most Chaplinesque mime sequence, hurriedly rushing through the entire section in order to kiss Aurora on time with the music.

At the Stage Door, someone remarked what a beautiful production it was, adding, "But why is it so dark?" Nureyev shrugged and replied, "Maybe they don't want to see me." One fan blurted out, "Honey, nobody could be THAT stupid!" Nureyev gazed at her, laughing, and she flushed and muttered, "Did I say that??"

During one matinee at the Met, Nureyev once more began the Awakening Scene in total darkness at the top of the grand staircase. Suddenly a bright shaft of REAL sunlight streaked through the darkened theatre, caused by some patrons leaving early. The light coming in from outside provided enough lighting for the stage and Rudolf could successfully and safely descend the staircase to awaken his Princess.

Lighting difficulties abounded when Nureyev mounted his *Sleeping Beauty* for The London Festival Ballet. After a long rehearsal, Rudolf was so upset about the lights he began yelling obscenities to the lighting technicians, such as, "Make the lighting fucking darker; it's too bright here." After several attempts, the lighting tech retorted, "I'm fed up with your fuckin' lighting. How many more fuckin' changes do you want?" At this point, Dame Beryl Grey, then the Artistic Director, piped up in her inimitable sweet voice, "Don't speak like that to Mr. Nureyev!"

Sometimes Rudolf had no choice but to "submit to his fate." On a Sunday matinee of *Spectre de la Rose* in Paris, the follow spots got "stuck" and remained that way throughout the ballet. For half of the ballet, the audience couldn't see Rudolf properly, unless he was dancing in center stage. Instead of having a temper tantrum, Nureyev merely danced, giving one of his most beautiful performances in the role.

During the many times Nureyev performed *Songs of a Wayfarer* throughout his career, there was always a battle over the lighting cues. The lights set the mood of the piece, but quite frequently, the cues didn't match the dance sequences. Many times when Rudolf walked upstage in between "songs," he would glare into the wings and snap, "More light, NOW!" At one performance he was irate that the cues were wrong, so he turned to the wings and yelled "Silly buggers! May we have the lights NOW?"

When Nureyev's *Romeo and Juliet* premiered at the London Coliseum on June 2, 1977, the performance went well, except for some mistimed cues. The very next night during the scene change for the wedding, the lights suddenly came up, revealing the stagehands dashing behind the church set they had just wheeled out. Rudolf was plodding his way towards the church with his Juliet, Patricia Ruanne, when they realized the lights had come up too soon. They immediately dropped to their knees, pretending to plead with Friar Laurence to marry them, from the far side of the stage.

During another performance of *Romeo*, at the time of a record heat wave, the technician working the follow spot must have fallen asleep or gone outside for a breath of air. At one point in the ballroom scene, Nureyev broke character, looked up past the Coliseum balcony to the lighting booth, and pointed an accusing finger at the technician. Nothing happened, so he raised and lowered his eyebrows to the amusement of the audience. Soon Nicky Johnson as Mercutio and Jay Jolley as Benvolio joined him and they, too, pointed to the lighting booth, even shading their eyes to see if anyone was there. The audience turned around in their seats to see what they were pointing at. At that point, Ballet Mistress Betty Anderton, who was portraying the Nurse, came over to "scold" the cast and they all resumed character.

The acoustics at the Kennedy Center in Washington allowed us to hear Rudolf backstage. His production of *Romeo and Juliet* was being filmed that night but, in the scene when Tybalt and Mercutio returned to haunt Juliet, the lights didn't come up. We heard Rudolf's voice in the wings shouting, "Lights up, NOW! Shit, they worked okay before, put them on NOW!" One of the ushers headed toward the front of the auditorium to see who was causing such a disturbance. A fan whispered, "It's Nureyev. He's in the wings and you can't do a thing about it." The usher was dumbfounded.

Near the end of the first act of the Boston Ballet's production of *La Sylphide*, the sylph's "double" is supposed to appear in the fireplace, but the lights didn't come on. Rudolf, as James, gestured and pointed to the fireplace's brick wall to signal the lighting cues, but nothing happened. In desperation, he walked to the fireplace and banged on it with both hands, as if to "shake" the lights on. Finally one of the technicians got the message and the sylph's "double" appeared. However, by this time, Ghislaine Thesmar as the sylph that James was pursuing reappeared, so we had two sylphs on stage at the same time. This gaff caused one fan near me to giggle and remark, "Tonight Rudolf is in love with a brick wall!"

SETS

Sets convey the mood of the ballet, whether depicting a wooded glen, a sumptuous palace, a lakeside scene, country village, or a marketplace. Even the more abstract ballets often have a backcloth to suggest the atmosphere of the piece.

Nureyev's productions were elaborate, with draperies, colorful backcloths, and sumptuous costumes. Sets, whether fixed or mobile, gave the scene added realism. His *Sleeping Beauty* production was rich in décor and costumes by designer Nicholas Georgiadis, and evoked the court of Louis the Sun King.

Insulted at not being invited to Princess Aurora's christening, Carabosse put a curse on the baby, warning that she would prick her finger on her 16th birthday and die. The Lilac Fairy glides down the staircase to reverse the curse, pronouncing that Aurora will not die, but sleep until a Prince wakes her with a kiss.

During a set change, Carabosse gave three underlings knitting needles and their dance steps mimicked knitting movements. The furious king locked the trio in the stockades, commanding "off with their heads" for disobeying his ban on needles. During one performance, the scrim suddenly went up, revealing the Garland Dance couples warming up for Aurora's birthday scene. It was quickly lowered.

When Princess Aurora pricked her finger from a needle hidden in a bouquet, her lifeless body was borne on the shoulders of four men from the Garland Dace. The entire court followed in procession around the stage and up the castle steps. The Lilac Fairy cast her spell by putting everyone to sleep as vines grew magically, transforming the courtyard into a tangled forest.

The Vision Scene, set one hundred years later, introduced the Countess, who arrived in a huge carriage, followed shortly after by the Prince. At a few performances, her carriage was left upstage. When Nureyev prepared for his big solo, he went to the corner where the carriage was "parked" and tried to push it offstage. "They're impinging on my variation," he remarked audibly. At another performance, he merely pushed it back into the wings.

The transformation scene proved the most magical. The Lilac Fairy reappeared and the Prince joined her, as her magical boat glided back and forth across the stage in a mist of dry ice. To emphasize their journey, tree-painted curtains crossed the stage while the boat artfully dodged between them and made its way into the wings.

A darkened scrim was lowered as Carabosse and her entourage entered, attempting to thwart the Prince from reaching Aurora and wake her with a kiss. Carabosse stretched out a long thread from a spindle, just when the Lilac Fairy entered with a burst of bright light. The thread or spell was broken and Carabosse was defeated.

A massive set change occurred behind the scrim, as the stage was transformed back into the sleeping palace for the Awakening scene. The Prince descended the staircase, acknowledged the sleeping King and Queen with a deep bow, awakened the Sleeping Beauty with a kiss, and the kingdom rejoiced.

When the production was new, these effects usually caused a lot of difficulties. The boat frequently got tangled in the trees and the Prince matter-of-factly exited the boat to untangle them. On other occasions, Nureyev straightened them when passing by, because they weren't hanging properly. Often while traveling with the Lilac Fairy, he did a complete revolution in the boat, supervising all the trees and scrims. One group of trees got stuck half way as they crossed the stage and the stagehands reversed them. The rest of the trees were mistimed and crossed the stage too fast, leaving a lot of empty space, so Rudolf kept turning around in the boat, gesturing, and trying not to laugh. By the final performance of the season, everything worked perfectly and Rudolf looked around in total amazement.

One set of trees got caught on the Lilac Fairy's boat. Rudolf tried lifting the tangled trees loose, but they remained firmly stuck. Someone backstage then lifted the entire scrim of trees. Nureyev did a lovely mime gesture, lifting his arms in amazement as if trees were rising upward by magic. The Lilac Fairy turned her back to the audience, trying hard not to laugh.

At one performance, the boat seemed to be in a race with a tree and the tree collided right into Nureyev. He just grabbed the irksome tree with both hands and yelled loudly, "Stop!" while the audience laughed out loud. Not only did the tree stop, but the boat and the dry ice did as well. Once he got untangled, all Rudolf could do was chuckle.

Nureyev's production of *Romeo and Juliet* for the London Festival Ballet had designs by Ezio Frigerio. The production utilized walled sets which were wheeled in or out for different scenes. On opening night, June 2, 1977, Dice Players symbolizing Fate made their entry, but the walls immediately got stuck when the Players tried to part them. A cartful of plague victims was swerved dramatically to avoid a collision, as frantic stagehands pushed and pulled the walls into the wings, with much creaking and squeaking.

Nureyev's entrance immediately followed, but he had to enter from a different spot, while the stagehands struggled to remove the wall. During his dance when trying to attract Rosaline's attention, he momentarily turned to the wings and mumbled, "get the bloody wall OFF the stage!"

A huge black cloth symbolizing the plague was supposed to billow down to the floor, immediately following the cartful of plague victims. On several occasions it either came down too late or too soon. Once it even got stuck and Rudolf's voice could be heard in the wings shouting, "Pull it down!" to the last person following the cart.

The sense of Fate occurs in many of Nureyev's productions. The sets caused havoc when *Romeo and Juliet* debuted at the Met on July 18, 1978. The black cloth representing death came billowing down in the middle of the fight scenes between the Capulets and Montagues, rather than at the very beginning. At a later performance that same week, the walls didn't separate during the marketplace scene and were absent for the scene prior to the ballroom, revealing several stagehands setting up the banquet table upstage. These walls stuck several times in the ballroom scene, which caused the guests to walk around them to get to center stage. Juliet nearly collided with Mercutio and friends, who had just dodged the wall to get offstage. Rudolf acted as a stagehand by pushing the wall offstage.

The church wasn't on stage in time for the wedding scene. Rudolf was heard shouting, "NOW – push! Oh, shit!" When the lights came up for the wedding scene, Rudolf was actually pulling the church. It simply wouldn't budge, so he and Juliet got married in "the open air."

Despite the difficulties, Frigerio managed to convey Renaissance Italy with a magnificent backdrop of a village square, as well as a panorama of Verona. During the last act, at a key moment in the choreography, Romeo hurls back the dark, heavy curtains of Juliet's room. It reveals the dawn breaking over

Verona's rooftops, which makes his inevitable departure all the more tragic. However, at one performance, the heavy draperies wouldn't open, nor did the lights come up. Rudolf tugged on the curtains and looked into the wings, and the draperies finally parted.

During one performance, Nureyev had trouble finding the opening to the bedroom curtains, to make his entrance into Juliet's room. There was much shaking of the curtains, almost like in the *Petrushka* puppet theatre, until Rudolf just ducked under them. Clearly this was not a very romantic entrance.

When the production was shown at the Palais des Sports in Paris, a few of us changed seats, because a black curtain forming a "wing" in the sports stadium had temporarily blocked our view. By moving to the side, we could see Rudolf sitting in the makeshift offstage "wings," sipping tea, and watching the performance. At one of his moments off stage, he suddenly looked up and saw us staring. He did not look happy and glared at us, until he realized that the black curtain blowing outwards had blocked our view of the stage. He immediately spoke to a technician and was gesturing wildly about how that obstructing curtain needed to be fixed. Almost at once, a technician came to our side of the house, and saw that the billowing curtain was blocking the view. Soon the cooling fans were cut down, so that the curtain returned in place and we enjoyed an unobstructed view of the stage.

Since Nureyev was a Pisces, he loved the water and this was used as a significant stage effect in two of his original productions. In his *Swan Lake* at the Vienna Opera, the Prince and Odette are not reunited in some eternal afterlife as in most Western productions, nor did his production have the happy ending so prevalent during the Soviet era. Instead, because of Siegfried's betrayal, Odette is condemned to remain a swan forever and the evil Rothbart causes the lake to flood, drowning the Prince.

I had the opportunity of seeing this production on several occasions at the magnificent Vienna Opera House and the stage effect was truly magical. Near the end of the last act, the floor cloth suddenly rises from the stage floor, billows upward higher and higher, engulfing the Prince. Nureyev always did this scene beautifully, raising his expressive arms toward Odette and falling beneath the waves, rolling over and over until the curtain fell. On one occasion, however, the floor cloth didn't come up so easily and Rudolf pulled and tugged at it until the stubborn "waves" could rise up to engulf him.

Billowing fabrics and floor cloths proved very effective, when they worked. In his production of *Manfred*, the Byronic hero was engulfed in waves during the final moments of Tchaikovsky's score. The corps de ballet ran upstage and picked up the ends of an enormous volume of white parachute silk. Then they slowly moved forward beneath them until these "waves" filled the stage. Nureyev as the Byron and Manfred character, fought against drowning, pulled himself up onto a broken cart and collapsed, while his beloved Astarte walked toward him. This was a powerful image, but occasionally the "waves" were rather uncooperative and once got stuck on the cart. Rudolf simply ripped it apart, until he could "get to the surface" again.

Problems with the sets frequently spoiled the performance, whether in Nureyev's productions or someone else's. When Balanchine's *Le Bourgeois Gentilhomme* transferred to the Zurich Ballet as part of the 1980 *Nureyev Festival* in London, we learned from a dancer that the sets hadn't arrived in time for the first night. They improvised by using the front curtain from Nureyev's *Romeo and Juliet* production, that was just staged at the Palais des Sports. For the drawing room, they borrowed the Royal Ballet's set from *The Rake's Progress*, until the proper scenery arrived the following evening.

Another comical mishap occurred during the run of *La Sylphide* with the Boston Ballet on Broadway in 1980. At one moment in the first act, the Sylph makes an appearance at the window and is lowered to the floor on a very small elevator platform. Normally it's a magical effect, but midway through the two-week run, the elevator either jerked its way down or sped too fast, all the while squeaking, ruining the Sylph's ethereal effect of floating into the room. Both James and the Sylph had to use every bit of control to keep from laughing.

At a *Giselle* performance, the cottage door where Albrecht hides his sword couldn't open. The dancer portraying Albrecht's squire, Wilfred, gestured to Nureyev to give it a try. The door wouldn't budge. Rudolf merely gestured that they would take a stroll into the "woods," and exited the stage no doubt trying to discern the trouble.

When Nureyev appeared in Roland Petit's *Hunchback of Notre Dame* at the Met, the sets consisted of a series of moveable platforms, maneuvered to suggest different locations. At one point, the platforms began moving from both sides, while Nureyev stood in the middle of the stage. He would have been squashed between them, had a dancer not pulled him out of the way at the last moment.

At the end of Valery Panov's production of *The Idiot* at the Met, an enormous bell was lowered from above the stage lights, with a long rope dangling from it. Rudolf grabbed hold of the rope and literally became the bell ringer. He was raised high above the Met's stage and began spinning rapidly like some aerial artist, as the curtain descended. At subsequent performances, he discreetly donned a thick glove, to get a better grip on the rope and avoid rope burn. Jane Hermann, then presenting the engagement, said that Nureyev's safety was of utmost importance. The speed and height at which Rudolf was spinning caused the entire audience to gasp and applaud, before the curtain descended.

Petrushka got off to a comical start at a matinee with the Joffrey Ballet in 1979. In the opening scene, the scrim came back down instead of going up, as if wanting to end the performance early. Luckily one of the Joffrey dancers portraying a Coachman had the presence of mind to dart in front of it, improvising a brief dance to distract the audience. The scrim was raised quickly while the audience convulsed in laughter.

In the bedroom scene of Nureyev's *Romeo and Juliet*, which Rudolf jokingly called the "consummate the marriage" scene, the curtains surrounding Juliet's bed got in the way, during a complex over-the-back lift. Holding on to Juliet with one arm, he shoved the offending curtain out of the way with his other hand, causing laughter from many parts of the house.

In a performance of *Marguerite and Armand*, a set of white curtains from the first scene was suddenly lowered during the Country Scene. Fonteyn merely clutched the curtains to one side during Nureyev's solo. Both then had to dance around the curtains for their pas de deux. We later learned that the man who works the curtains had to go to the bathroom and simply forgot about them. Fonteyn and Nureyev heartily laughed when they heard about this.

COSTUMES

Costume malfunctions could certainly spoil a performance. One of the more amusing glitches occurred in the country scene of *Marguerite and Armand* when Fonteyn's bodice broach got stuck on Nureyev's shirt. Momentarily stuck together, Margot tried to untangle it while Rudolf put his head down to "cover" the situation. The choreography called for them to be interrupted by the Duke. When both dancers, still grappling to get untangled, finally pulled the offensive broach free, they didn't need to act to show their embarrassment at being caught in such a compromising situation.

In the "insult" scene in the same ballet, Rudolf's character of Armand is incensed to find that Marguerite has returned to the Duke. The choreography calls for him to snatch her necklace, a gift from the Duke, and hurl it to the floor. At one performance, the necklace wouldn't come off when he grabbed at it and Fonteyn lurched forward a couple of steps from the sheer force of Rudolf's gesture. He tried a second time and the necklace finally broke free.

In a *Giselle* performance, the top of Nureyev's tunic came undone. While waiting to do his big variation in the second act, he pushed it closed again. Thank God for Velcro! We always wondered how his costumes fit so well with no visible zippers, hooks, or snaps.

At a performance of *Scheherazade*, his ballerina's sequined costume got caught onto Rudolf's when he executed a wrap-around-the-body lift. There was no graceful way to get untangled. Nureyev held her upside-down by her legs, making it appear they were playing a game of "wheelbarrow," until they broke free. Since there is a lot of grappling in the orgy scene, it almost appeared to be part of the choreography.

At a crucial moment performing Jose Limon's *Moor's Pavane* in 1984, Jean Guizerix as Iago jumped on the hem of Nureyev's robe that he wore over red tights. Rudolf's eyes widened as he heard a very loud rip while Guizerix tried not to laugh. The entire back seam of Nureyev's robe was ripped at the waist and was dangling loosely. After "killing" Desdemona, Rudolf rolled his costume up at the back before turning around.

Rudolf's costume for *L'Apres-midi d'un Faune* practically unraveled with each successive performance during a Broadway season. Based on the original design worn by Vaslav Nijinsky, the leotard was recreated by Rouben Ter Arutunian and had black spots on it to emulate a spotted faune. Early during the season, Rudolf's costume sported two holes at the knees, which eventually grew to the size of quarters. Soon his kneecaps were sticking out. It became a race to see if the costume would last until the final performance or he would simply paint his knees black to match the costume's other spots.

Whenever something falls on the stage floor, whether part of a costume, a tissue, a jewel or anything else, it needs to be removed so dancers won't slip on it or possibly injure themselves. One of the witches in *La Sylphide* left behind a scarf in the opening scene of Act Two, where it remained on the floor. Rudolf made his entrance chasing the Sylph into the wooded glen, and immediately noticed it. Still he character, he bent down on one knee, scooped up the scarf, and waved it overhead before tossing it into the wings.

During the Vision Scene of *Sleeping Beauty*, the bow the Prince wore at the nape of his neck flew off as he pirouetted. When the corps de ballet entered, Nureyev turned his back momentarily and gestured to the bow resting near the foot of one of the girls. She picked it up, handed it to him, and he shoved it inside his vest. At subsequent performances, we learned that the bow was sewn into his hair so it wouldn't come out.

Rudolf's sense of comic timing was unique, particularly in his mock death scene in *Don Quixote*. One memorable performance occurred in 1980 with the Zurich Ballet in London when Nureyev's cloak string got caught on his costume. He is supposed to meticulously spread the cloak on the floor before "dying." Unable to remove the cloak without struggling, conductor Andre Presser stretched out the music as long as possible while waiting for Rudolf's death scene and finally stopped the orchestra. There was an audible gasp from the audience while Rudolf struggled to untangle the cloak string. Once freed, he matter-of-factly spread his cloak on the floor, and plopped himself onto it to continue. The audience burst into applause as howls of laughter emanated from all parts of the house.

Washington Square, based on the Henry James novel, was performed in New York with the Paris Opera in 1986. Rudolf was eager to show off his many protegés in the company, including Elisabeth Maurin in the role of Catherine and Charles Jude as Morris Townsend. In a crucial scene when Morris visited the Sloper home, the Aunt, performed by Clothilde Vayet, ushered him into the parlor before fetching Catherine's father, Dr. Sloper, performed by Nureyev. A brief pas de deux between Morris and the Aunt preceded Nureyev's entrance. Suddenly, in the middle of an arabesque, Vayet's bustled skirt came undone and dropped to the floor. Embarrassed, she snatched it up and ran into the wings. Those sitting on the far side of the theatre saw Nureyev, watching from the wings, put his head in his hands. Charles Jude as Morris then performed a marvelous bit of improvisation, while Vayet's costume could be repaired. Jude admired the wall decorations, ran to the top of the staircase to see if anyone was there, and in the space of about sixty seconds, Vayet returned, skirt affixed to her bodice. Without breaking character, she gestured how apologetic she was for having kept him waiting and how mortified she was at what had happened. Indeed, a woman in the audience next to me asked, "Was that supposed to happen?" Shortly after Nureyev's entrance, he and Jude danced a kind of competition duet, up and down the staircase. Both Rudolf and Charles danced it with a fury, no doubt to relieve their frazzled nerves at Vayet's unexpected departure.

In the final scene of *Marguerite and Armand*, Rudolf made a dramatic run around the stage to reunite with the dying Marguerite. One night his cape refused to unfurl. He normally tossed it aside with great flourish and rushed into Marguerite's arms. Instead, he tugged it to the left and right and finally began shaking the stubborn cape like it was a piece of sticky flypaper while looking at Marguerite in total frustration.

In Nureyev's production of *Romeo and Juliet*, he choreographed Mercutio's Queen Mab speech. The cloak Mercutio sat on during this dance, suddenly ripped in half. Instead of imitating riding in a chariot being pulled along the floor by his companions, Mercutio was unceremoniously dumped on his backside with half the cloak dangling in the hands of his astonished friends. Rudolf, watching from the sidelines, laughed so hard his shoulders were shaking as he put a hand over his face to try to stop.

With Nureyev's insanely tight schedule, it was a miracle that he had the right costume for the right ballet wherever he performed. There were occasions when he left the theatre in full make-up and costume in order to get to the airport. During the 1977 Martha Graham season when he performed *Appalachian Spring*, more than likely he changed from his preacher's costume to street clothes in the back of the car.

At a couple of guest appearances with American Ballet Theatre, his own costumes hadn't arrived, so he wore his white tights and tunic from *La Bayadere* for the White Acts of *Swan Lake* and his black tights from a recent *Miss Julie* performance for the Black Act.

Rudolf made a "flying visit" to dance a *La Sylphide* performance with The London Festival Ballet and didn't arrive at the theatre until 6 p.m. without the right costume. He had to improvise by borrowing one from another dancer.

For his February 1977 *Nureyev Festival,* Nureyev brought Glen Tetley's *Pierrot Lunaire* with members of the Danish Ballet to Paris. His costume wasn't ready in time, so he wore the costume belonging to Danish dancer Nels Kehlet. It didn't fit him that well and critics wrote that the hat obscured his facial expressions. The next night Rudolf wore a smaller hat, which was later used for the Broadway season the following month.

His debut in Roland Petit's *Hunchback of Notre Dame* in New York, was delayed twenty-five minutes because he had just one rehearsal due to his hectic schedule. Additionally, his costume wasn't ready so he borrowed Richard Cragun's. There was a considerable difference in their proportions and height, and the tunic kept riding up at the waist. Nureyev's own costume was ready by the second performance.

In June of 1975, Martha Graham created *Lucifer* for a gala performance. When it was repeated in December of 1975, Nureyev was listed as a member of the Graham Company and not a "guest artist." Fonteyn's part was danced by Graham company member Janet Eilber. During one performance, Nureyev and Eilber were grappling on the floor when audience members in the front row heard a loud rip. Eilber's side seam of her costume had split. Both dancers were chuckling about this during the curtain calls until Graham came out, at which point Rudolf gave Martha a deep and humble bow.

Perhaps the most comical of costume mishaps occurred during American Ballet Theatre's *Swan Lake* when Lucia Chase as the Queen Mother, made a regal entrance with Rudolf Nureyev. As they entered upstage, suddenly Lucia lurched backward – her long train stuck on something. Rudolf looked surprised and when he saw she truly couldn't move, he bent down and ripped the train off the offensive nail. Giving Chase an amused grin, he regally offered his arm to escort her to center stage while trying not to laugh.

PROPS

Nureyev managed all types of choreography, but with the exception of handling capes – at which he had no equal – props often gave him difficulty.

To watch Rudolf Nureyev trying to tie a bow on a staff in Frederick Ashton's ballet *La Fille Mal Gardee* was quite charming. Like a small child, he bit his tongue in concentration and then looked surprised and proud of himself when it actually worked. More often than not, he dropped the ribbon before it could be tied and when it was secured, resembled a wadded chunk of ribbon rather than a bow. During a rehearsal with Merle Park, she saw he was having difficulty so she told him, "It's just like tying your shoes." Reflecting on his impoverished childhood, Nureyev explained, "Our shoes had buttons."

Also in *Fille*, Ashton devised a cat's cradle made out of ribbons. The two lovers started out with yards of pink ribbon and, through their intertwined choreography, ended up making a cat's cradle. This has tripped up many a dancer, but it always gave Rudolf problems. Often the finished product would be "presented" to the audience as the most lopsided and tangled cat's cradle imaginable. At one performance he dropped the ribbon and it stuck to his costume. Then he couldn't untie the ribbon's knot for the next sequence, so his ballerina had to help him.

These performances generally brought comic relief to the audience members who knew the ballets and enjoyed Nureyev's quick-witted improvisation when things went wrong. During a 1976 performance of Ashton's *La Fille Mal Gardee* with the Royal Ballet in Washington, we watched in amazement as a key prop failed and then witnessed the subsequent unnerving of Rudolf Nureyev.

In the second act, Rudolf's character, Colas, has smuggled himself into Lise's house to be alone with her. When Lise's mother returns unexpectedly, Lise hastily sends Colas to her room to hide. Nureyev bolted up the staircase, grabbed the doorknob to Lise's room, and it came off in his hands. At first he tried to get the door open with his fingernails but when that failed, he held the doorknob up for one and all to see and had just seconds to "hide" before the mother opened the front door. Quick-thinking Lesley Collier as Lise pointed to the room "down the hall" which was nearly in the wings. Just as the mother entered, Rudolf crouched to the floor behind the banister and crept along the floor leading to "the room down the hall."

There is an entire dance sequence with mother and daughter before Lise is sent to her room. But our eyes were on Rudolf wondering how he would get that bedroom door open, since it played a crucial part in the ballet. After creeping around on all fours behind the banister, he began banging on the door to Lise's room. Then we could hear him whispering "psst, psst" to get the stagehands' attention, holding up the doorknob to show his predicament. Finally, after what must have seemed an interminable time, a stagehand opened the door from behind the set. Nureyev crawled on his hands and knees toward the door, then stood up and gestured "sshhh" to the audience as he snuck into the bedroom. The audience burst into applause at his success.

Later in the scene when Widow Simone sent Lise to her room, Collier gingerly opened the door, hoping the door would, in fact, open. To everyone's great relief, at the crucial moment in the ballet when the lovers are discovered together, the door actually opened, and Lise and Colas looked out with very amused expressions on their faces. The critics stated, "It was a comedy of errors…that worked!"

At another performance, things began going wrong from the very first scene in the farmyard. A bowl and spoon are left on a bench in front of the barn. When Nureyev entered, instead of resting his staff on the bench beside him, he placed it between his knees. When he found the spoon inside the bowl to check its contents, he went to lick the spoon and the staff lurched forward and smacked him in the face. Stunned, he started to lick the staff and grab the spoon. He tossed both aside and ran to peek through the window of Lise's house just as the props on the bench crashed to the floor.

Later he accidentally wrapped his arm to the staff while tying the ribbon to it. The bow came untied and the ends of the ribbons dangled in his eyes during his variation. An annoyed Nureyev put the staff on the floor to do his turns.

As bad as props causing trouble, the lack of props at the wrong time could drive Rudolf up the wall and none more so than in his own production of *Don Quixote*. So many things went wrong during his 1980 production with the Zurich Ballet in London, that it seemed more like a rehearsal than a performance. In the mock death scene in the tavern, the cape used to "hide" Kitri from her father was missing. "Cape, bring me cape!" Rudolf barked repeatedly, hiding Kitri with his own body when the cape never emerged. The final blow was his mock suicide. His barber's razor was missing and he couldn't exactly kill himself with his finger. Searching quickly, he grabbed Gamache's sword and stabbed himself. Since it's such a comic scene, the audience applauded his ingenuity.

A whip that Rudolf loved to crack when introducing the gypsy dances was nowhere to be found, causing him to run into the wings to get it. When he went to crack it, the whip flew right out of his hand. He comically jumped up and down in irritation while retrieving it. When the whip failed to crack after several attempts, Rudolf began convulsing with laughter, along with the audience. The gypsy dancers carried on, but Rudolf was determined to get that whip to snap. When the whip finally made a loud cracking noise, the gypsy girls glared at him and he responded with a very sheepish grin.

When in January 1983 his *Don Quixote* production moved to Broadway with the Boston Ballet, Rudolf managed to crack the whip several times. He did a little jump and turn of delight whenever that happened.

In the moonlight pas de deux in the second act, he whirled Kitri overhead, while she swirled her shawl. When Marie-Christine Mouis as Kitri, swirled hers, the shawl became wedged between them when Rudolf placed her in a fishdive. Nothing could be done to get from this position to unfurl the fabric so they could lie down on it. Rudolf began to giggle, which caused the audience to giggle. They disentangled each other, spread the shawl onto the floor, and plopped down on it, still chuckling. At a performance later that week with Laura Young as Kitri, the same thing happened. Rudolf could not stop laughing and neither could the audience.

While performing *Don Quixote* in Vienna, Rudolf leaned against the windmill in the second act and it started to move. He seemed slightly embarrassed and walked away from it immediately. He seemed equally flustered when assembling the puppet theatre on the cart and the curtains were tangled up, taking much longer than usual to establish a theatrical setting for the children. When the "stage" was finally set, Rudolf peeked from behind the curtain in a mischievous way and signaled the children to begin their little pantomime. Some of the children had only performed their roles once, so when they went through the motions, "Uncle Rudolf" stood beside the cart doing the pantomime with them. When they finished, he swooped them up in his arms and gave them pats on their heads for doing a good job.

A missing prop during the opening party scene of *Nutcracker* proved very amusing. Disguised as Drosselmeyer, Nureyev began performing the magic tricks and realized his magic wand wasn't in his pocket. He merely stuck his hands out miming "hocus, pocus" and then looked surprised when the "dolls" came to life. He had fun with the moment, shaking his "magical hands" at all the party guests.

When Drosselmeyer presented Clara with the Nutcracker, the wooden toy wouldn't sit up while Clara danced for it. Nureyev as Drosselmeyer sat at the piano, pretending to accompany her solo. The stubborn Nutcracker doll still toppled over so Nureyev got up, magically shook his hands to make it behave and then kept it upright with his foot while proudly watching Clara dance. When the doll still fell over at the end, he "scolded" it and playfully kicked it, causing much laughter from the audience.

Rudolf had "sword trouble" at one performance after the death of Mercutio. Reluctant to fight Tybalt, Nureyev tossed aside Tybalt's sword with such force that it went skittering across the stage and flew into the pit, nicking a woodwind player in the arm. Rudolf followed its course with wide eyes and seemed upset, but had to continue the performance. At the interval, the musician who got nicked was animatedly describing how it happened to audience members sitting in the front row. Fortunately, he wasn't seriously hurt. At a later performance during the duel scene with Tybalt, both Rick Werner as Tybalt and Rudolf as Romeo fought with a vengeance. Suddenly, Werner whacked at Rudolf's sword with such fury that the sword flew out of Nureyev's hand and went flying into the orchestra pit, just missing one of the violin players. Breaking character momentarily, Rudolf watched as the terrified string player picked up the sword. Borrowing another sword from someone on stage, Rudolf and Rick finished the scene. For the rest of those performances, however, protective netting was strung across the Coliseum's orchestra pit.

Later in the last act after Juliet's potion scene, when she appears to be sleeping, mandolin players toss coins on the floor to symbolize good luck for Juliet's wedding to Paris. At one performance the coins rolled into the orchestra pit and onto the kettledrums and cymbals, making a loud crash during an otherwise quiet scene.

Nureyev first performed in Balanchine's *Prodigal Son* with the Royal Ballet in 1973. I was very fortunate to see him in this, because he did so few performances, either with the Paris Opera or the Royal Ballet Touring Company. One particular point I remember clearly occurred in the first scene. The rebellious son longed to see the world, but was beckoned to join his two sisters while their father blessed them. Nureyev sunk from his knees to a sitting position and broke away from the group, looking outwards longing for some distant place. This simple movement related well with the audience, chuckling in recognition. Later in his entwined pas de deux with the Siren, the locket around his neck broke. Nureyev momentarily felt his chest and realized it had fallen to the floor. At an appropriate time he stopped, made a point of looking for it and reacted for the audience, "Oh, it's not lost after all" and put it round his neck. This is a key prop later in the scene when he is robbed of everything, including the locket that the Siren greedily snatches for herself.

At the end of the first act of a *Giselle* performance, Hilarion accidentally dropped the sword he shows Giselle to expose Albrecht's true identity. Albrecht is supposed to seize the sword from Hilarion, but tosses it to the floor when the royal party enters. During Giselle's mad scene, she steps on this sword and attempts to stab herself with it. Quick-thinking Nureyev grabbed a sword from Wilfred, his valet, and pretended to "attack" Hilarion again. He managed to let the sword drop to center stage, so Giselle could successfully complete her mad scene.

One major prop malfunction occurred during Flemming Flindt's *The Lesson,* in which Nureyev portrayed a mad ballet master who murdered his pupils. As the young pupil, Danish dancer Anne Marie Vessel was supposed to be strangled to death near the end of the ballet. One night when Nureyev placed her into a backbend over the ballet barre to strangle her, the barre suddenly broke under the force and Vessel fell to the floor. Nureyev's eyes grew wide with surprise and, once realizing she was okay, nearly broke character with a half smile creeping to the side of his mouth. He then pretended to be angry at the barre for ruining the dramatic climax, and somehow this worked.

In Martha Graham's *Night Journey*, there is a moment near the end, when the characters of Jocasta and Oedipus are entwined in ropes by the Greek

Chorus, symbolizing their illegitimate union. At one performance, Rudolf got a rather nasty rope burn when the Seer separates the couple from their umbilical chord stance. He rubbed his thigh and stomach briefly before resuming the performance.

In the cell scene of *Petrushka,* the wallpaper covering the hole that the puppet character breaks through, came unstuck and one side began rolling up. When banging on the walls to express his frustration, Nureyev paused and pressed the wallpaper down – all in time with the music – and the audience applauded his cleverness. A few bars of music later, he crashed through. He did it with such a force, much like a karate chop, that the window frame shattered into several pieces!

Another puppet-like character Nureyev portrayed was in Glen Tetley's *Pierrot Lunaire,* a role he frequently performed in his many *Friends* programs. In one scene, long elastic bands are attached to Rudolf's limbs, making him appear like a marionette. On opening night in 1977, these elastic "puppet strings" broke, ruining an important effect.

At a 1976 performance of *Sleeping Beauty* with the National Ballet of Canada, the dancer portraying the Countess in the Hunting Scene is supposed to present the Prince with an arrow to hit the nearby target. She was a bit late in handing him this prop so Rudolf grabbed it from her hand, displayed it for the audience to see, and tossed it feather-tip first toward the target held by one of the huntsmen. It went whizzing past the poor fellow's head but yet the arrow "magically" appeared in the center of the target anyway, causing laughter and applause from the audience. His valet had trouble removing the Prince's jacket when the Countess mimed to him, "Shall we dance?" Rudolf mimed back, "I can't. I'm being undressed!"

Probably the most unforgettable prop failure occurred during his 1985 Nureyev Festival when the Matsuyama Company from Japan joined Rudolf in their production of *Swan Lake*. During the peasant pas de trois in the first act, Nureyev left the stage so he wouldn't have to, as he often joked, "sit on his ass" and let his muscles get cold before his melancholy solo that followed. Just before the pas de trois ended, Rudolf returned to the stage and walked around greeting all the corps members before resuming his place on his chair.

When he went to sit down, the chair made a loud "crrr…unch" noise and shattered beneath him like toothpicks. The look on Rudolf's face was one of absolute horror. He righted himself as quickly as possible and was so embarrassed, he immediately went to the corner table and poured a "drink" which he downed in one gulp and then had another. He walked around chatting with everyone, but was visibly shaken.

While attention was diverted to the peasant pas finale and the dancers taking their bows, the stagehands were busy whisking the broken chair backstage. In the time it took Nureyev to walk the circumference of the stage, they had his larger throne chair from the third act in its place. Rudolf returned and sat down without so much as a glance in the wings, just assuming it would be replaced. He was totally back in character, his embarrassment at landing on his Royal Backside all but forgotten.

"I believe that what has been done stays on the planet. That's all."
~Rudolf Nureyev, London Evening Standard, April 19, 1991~

THE AUCTION ~ FINAL SALE

The Ballet Shop, NYC, January 1993, Photo: William J. Reilly

The revolving door at Christie's main entrance just never stopped. It was January 8, 1995, the second day of viewing of the Rudolf Nureyev Collection. We had barely scratched the surface in looking at things the previous day, and simply had to see it all before it went on the auction block. The coat check attendant looked exhausted while two additional coat racks were brought in. The staff apologized that there was no more space for coats and we'd have to carry them throughout the viewing. Once we got into the main gallery, we felt like salmon swimming upstream. The crowds were so thick that nobody could move. I passed two friends going in the opposite direction seemingly carried along against their will and as they passed they said, "We saw your picture in the photograph boxes!"

Since two other friends joined me, I decided to show them the Back Stage area. I wanted to see what I missed the previous day and take a second look at the bag containing the hats. If enough of us bid on it, we could each have a hat. This time I really examined each one. When finished, I repacked them gently so they wouldn't get crushed and placed the sable hat on the top, giving it a little pat. The attendant remarked, "That's packed with a lot of love." I assumed some of the others were not as careful with them.

We passed a staff member frantically handing out the Nureyev shopping bags to the long lines of people who wanted them as souvenirs, knowing full well that they would not be bidding on any items at the auction. She looked like she was dealing cards, she was doling them out so quickly. A few minutes later she wasn't there. A senior staff person explained they had run out of bags, catalogs – everything. Photocopies of the catalog were available for $35 to those still wanting them, so I was very lucky to have obtained one.

We stayed again until closing and the following day one of my co-workers who had seen my catalog, coaxed me into going to Christie's on our lunch hour. Again the place was packed and I ran into at least half a dozen Nureyev fans I knew. "Can I see the hat you gave to Nureyev?" my colleague asked, so once again we made our way to the Back Stage area. There, looking at the hats, were two friends from London. I knew they had planned to attend the actual Auction, but to meet up with them this way was typical of the situations we shared when Nureyev was performing. "You see," one remarked in her delightful British accent, "Rudolf's brought us together again." By this time the attendant called two of her colleagues over. "These people know each other from New York and London," they exclaimed, not quite realizing the universality of Nureyev's career.

I noticed that Nureyev's personal wardrobe was displayed on coat hangers in the main hall and was getting mixed up with some of the shirts he wore in various productions. People were actually trying them on. The whole thing took on the look of a bargain basement sale. I heard remarks about how "ghoulish" it was to see Nureyev's clothing. I was rather glad it was time to return to work.

On Thursday, January 12, viewing at Christie's was open from 10a.m. until 2p.m., because they had to clear the space for the Auction that evening. Several more friends flew in from other parts of the country and we met at Christie's to register and bid on the hats and ballet slippers to share among the fans. *The Sunday New York Times* ran a feature article entitled "Giving Away

What Nureyev Never Would," about the numerous pairs of ballet shoes up for auction. We had a sinking feeling that the $40 starting bid for the shoes suddenly skyrocketed because of that publicity.

On this visit, we discovered shawls, sweaters, Obie awards, more textiles and personal memorabilia in the various Back Stage shopping bags. We noticed, however, that some items were missing or were put into a different shopping bag, so that if someone wanted a specific item in a certain lot, it may have been moved. We also noticed when returning to the photographs that some of them were missing and brought this to the attention of the Christie's staff.

Despite the sheer exhaustion of the staff, we had a strong connection with them. When the gallery closed at noon, they apologized for having to remove the boxes from us and wished us "good luck tonight." One of the attendants became emotional, her eyes filling with tears, as she said, "I saw him dance and wish they wouldn't sell all these things." All of us felt the finality of the situation.

After fortifying ourselves with lunch, we decided we'd better get in the line for the six o'clock Auction. We arrived back at Christie's at four o'clock and found our two British friends in the front of the queue. We barely got in the line when the press arrived. The BBC interviewed our British friends in line; other news organizations soon followed. Within an hour the line stretched around the block some 2,000 strong. Christie's staff kept coming out to look at the gathering crowds and shook their heads in disbelief.

The time passed quickly as strategies were finalized. Two young students needed a third to bid on a lot number containing shoes; a friend from out of town arranged to do a phone bid on a different bag of shoes that mutual friends would also bid on in the gallery; another fan was determined to obtain one of Rudolf's costumes. The excitement was palpable rather like queuing for a Nureyev performance. The doorman braved the cold to joke with those in the front of the line and wished us good luck.

When the doors opened at six o'clock, we raced up the stairs just like the standees did to claim their places for a performance. This time we saved seats for one another, while those intending to bid on items finished registering and picked up their paddle numbers. About 500 chairs were set up in the main hall. At the back was a platform absolutely crammed with TV cameras, sound equipment, wires, and dozens of reporters. The Auction was a news event.

To one side of the Auctioneer's podium was a lovely photograph of Nureyev in his Paris apartment. On the other side was a picture window stage with theatrical lighting to display the various items for sale. A man in a tuxedo wearing white gloves and holding a pillow displayed the hats and smaller items. To our right was the large board, rather like the arrival and departure boards in train stations, listing the lot numbers, opening bids, and prices, which were instantly converted into U.S. dollars, British pounds, French francs, Italian lire, and Japanese Yen. Along the sides of the hall were long tables with banks of telephones staffed by Christie's personnel, sometimes on two phones at once, accepting phone bids.

In the main gallery, now stripped of its contents except for the Venetian chandelier, a giant closed circuit television screen linked an additional 500 people into the proceedings. The auctioneer had to keep track not only of those in the main hall bidding, but the telephone bidders each holding up their corresponding paddles, plus those in the gallery linked in via closed circuit television.

At seven o'clock, Christopher Burge made the opening remarks as well as an announcement that certain lot numbers were withdrawn for the Royal Ballet Archives. He added, "Members of the Nureyev Foundation would be bidding on certain items for use in a proposed Nureyev Museum in Paris." Everyone gasped and applauded. At that, the auction began with a bang. The opening item, an R-shaped diamond-studded pin, estimated from $600 to $900, was sold within fifteen seconds for $5,200.

When Nureyev's Albrecht costume from *Giselle* began at $2,000, the excitement in the hall mounted as the price escalated to $45,000. "In the gallery" could be heard over the loud speaker and Burge paused to ask, "What was that?" while the associate said, "We're definitely out." When the auctioneer's hammer hit the block, the entire audience burst into applause, not so much because the costume was sold, but that it brought in so much money.

One of Rudolf's friends, Monique von Vooren, sat directly in front of us. Nureyev used to stay with her in New York prior to purchasing his own apartment at the Dakota. She tried bidding on a piece of jewelry she had given to Nureyev, but the prices were inflated out of her range. She was visibly upset when the costumes were being sold off and left the hall.

A fan sitting in the front row was determined to get the headpiece Nureyev wore in *Afternoon of a Faune,* a ballet made famous by the legendary dancer Vaslav Nijinsky. She was annoyed that a phone bidder tried to outbid her. We knew very well that these anonymous bidders were either art dealers or agents of wealthy celebrities like Madonna, who expressed in an interview that she wanted to bid on some of the items. The fan simply held her paddle up and refused to put it down and when the price went up to $3,000, we were afraid she was out of her league. Since there were no higher bids, she got the headpiece. Everyone burst into cheers. A bit later, another fan got his plumed hat from *Bach Suite*. Even Christopher Burge seemed pleased that the "ordinary people" were able to buy certain items. Later one of Nureyev's friends was overheard remarking, "I'm so glad the fans were here. Their enthusiasm was contagious."

At last the moment came to bid on the one thing most associated with Nureyev's career: his ballet shoes. The press leaned forward; the fans sat up in their seats, paddles ready. Mr. Burge said, "We have opening bids starting at . . . $1,500." Everyone in the hall gasped. "What happened to $40?" we exclaimed to each other. Our hopes of ever getting a pair of Nureyev's ballet shoes disappeared quickly as the prices skyrocketed, largely from an anonymous dealer over the phone. Four pairs of the shoes went for $10,000.

A kind of panic set in when some of Nureyev's shirts worn in various productions such as *Romeo and Juliet* went up for bid. The fans furiously competed with the phone bidders. Two fans managed to get the shirts; the two students we met in the queue that wanted shoes managed to get a shirt. The most expensive shirt from *Marguerite and Armand* sold for $16,500 but most of them sold for under $1,000. Burge really wanted the fans to get them and often stopped the frantic bidding to ask, "Are you sure you can't go any higher?" About half a dozen shirts finally went to the fans, always topped by a round of applause from those in attendance.

After the auction finished at 10 p.m. the press rushed forward to interview some of the people who purchased various items. "What do you think Nureyev would think of all of this?" a reporter asked one of my friends. "I think he's on some stage right now and laughing!"

We had to get home, because the final day of the auction would be a long one and we desperately needed to rest.

The next morning, Friday, we arrived at 9:30 a.m. to see another very long line snaking around the auction house. We overheard art dealers discussing bids on the larger items like the Venetian chandelier, the furniture, paintings, and so on. We certainly weren't bidding on those items, but wanted to be present to see what they were worth.

The trouble was there were so many items, that the morning session ran overtime by nearly two hours. It was supposed to finish by twelve so the galleries could be cleared to admit those waiting outside for the two o'clock session. We had planned to get a quick lunch and return, but if we left the building we knew we would never get in again. We decided to do what we had done many times throughout Nureyev's career: hide in the Ladies' Room until the house was open and then run to claim a seat.

Many of the paintings sold in the morning session went for over a million dollars each. The Venetian chandelier sold for $338,000. One of Nureyev's friends remarked, "But Rudolf only paid $25,000 for it!" It took absolutely hours to get through the lots of textiles, but by four o'clock the hats and other memorabilia were on the auction block. One of the fans held her paddle up for all of us who wanted a hat and luckily she was not outbid. Later we divided up the hats and I got the red cowboy hat that I wanted. I hoped to bid on his conductor's baton since I had seen Nureyev conduct a few times but at $500, it was over my budget and after all, it was just a stick. Just about all of the fans ended up with something – an antique map, a print or a textile, so we went home quite happy. All together, the auction brought in over $8 million for the Foundation. That was just the New York auction. Another sale at Christie's in London took place less than a year later.

When Rudolf Nureyev died on January 6, 1993, he made front-page news of every paper around the world. Page-long obituaries tried to sum up his life in dance. He was the first of the Russian defectors, the first to create his own original productions, the first to promote ballet through his numerous *Friends* and *Nureyev Festival* seasons, the first to bridge the gap between classical ballet and modern dance, and a dancer who was credited with popularizing the ballet. Describing his impact on the dance world were adjectives such as "Comet," "Lord of the Dance," "Electrifier," "Trailblazer" and "Gatecrasher." Reading through hundreds of tributes, I came across a cartoon that one of the British fans sent me. It depicted St. Peter guarding the Pearly Gates of Heaven while the "gatecrasher," Nureyev, was shown in a grand jeté, leaping over the gates. The caption read, "The gate's open, Mr. Nureyev…oh well, suit yourself." And he did.

Since Nureyev's death, exhibitions, and galas have been held. A ballet school bearing Nureyev's name has opened in his hometown of Ufa. Nureyev Ballet Competitions and scholarships have given opportunities to many young dancers. Streets have been named after him. His productions are still performed by companies around the world. Many of the protégés he nurtured now direct schools and dance companies. He truly was an international star.

Two international Nureyev Symposiums were held, the first in New York City in 1997 and the second in St. Petersburg, Russia in 1998. Many of Nureyev's colleagues gathered to discuss working with him, illustrated by video recordings provided by Nureyev's friend, Wallace Potts. I was assisting Wallace in compiling lists of Nureyev video recordings that eventually became the basis for the Nureyev Collection at the performing Arts library in New York and the Rudolf Nureyev Foundation, established after the dancer's death.

What happened to all the items sold at the Auction? Many of the fans bought them. Various dance companies as well as the Nureyev Foundation acquired costumes. A wing of the *Centre National du Costume de Scene* in Moulins, France, held a large display of Nureyev's personal items and costumes.

And what happened to that cowboy hat I bought? I kept it protected in an archival box for many years. When relocating back to Michigan in 2016, I decided a long-distance move meant I had to downsize. I gifted some items to younger fans. My extensive Nureyev Collection was donated to the Dance Library in New York. I realized from having worked there, that my collection had to be organized and cataloged and I did just that prior to donating it.

Many of the Nureyev fans continue to gather or stay in touch. We see as many dance performances as possible. Despite the advances in technical ability and the many dancers that were inspired by Nureyev, we still believe that he was truly unique in the way he captivated us, all those years ago. Our international group may have grown smaller, but we can't forget who it was that brought us together. The physical evidence of Nureyev's career has been disbursed all over the world, but his legacy lives on in the hearts and minds of those who witnessed him dance.

PHOTO ALBUM

Rudolf and George looking for taxi, NYC, December, 1975. Photo: William J. Reilly

Leaving Uris Theatre, NYC, July 15, 1979. Photo: William J. Reilly

Fonteyn & Nureyev, Spectre de la Rose, London,
June 23, 1979. Photo: Barbara Kosarska

Reception following Honorary Doctorate Award,
Philadelphia, April 25, 1980
Photo: Susanne Richelle Whitehead

Nureyev singing I'm a Gigolo at Covent Garden
Christmas Party, 1976. Photo: Barbara Kosarska

Rudolf and George leaving Uris Theatre,
January 18, 1983. Photo: William J. Reilly

Surprise street party outside London Coliseum, June 17, 1984. Photo: Beatriz Sanz

With children in The King and I, Hartford, CT, October, 1989. Photo: Gina Wexler

Surprise champagne party outside London Coliseum, June 17, 1984. Photo: Beatriz Sanz

Le Corsaire, The Minskoff Theatre, NYC, 1978. Photo: William J. Reilly

Receiving Lifetime Achievement Award, NYC, 1989. Photo: William J. Reilly

39th Birthday Balloons, Uris Theatre, NYC March 17, 1977. Photo: William J. Reilly

Closing Night, Nureyev Festival &Matsuyama Ballet, London, 1985. Photo: Beatriz Sanz

Leaving via taxi, Metropolitan Opera House, NYC, July, 1986. Photo: Judy Bellaragione

The house at Nureyev's Leesburg, Virginia farm, 1990. Photo: Katie Glaser

Nureyev promoting Manuel Legris to Etoile, Metropolitan Opera House, NYC, June 8, 1986. Photo: William J. Reilly

Leaving New York State Theatre, NYC, 1979. Photo: William J. Reilly

ABOUT THE AUTHOR

Nancy Sifton was born in Detroit, Michigan and attended the University of Detroit prior to moving to San Francisco. There she attended numerous arts-related classes in addition to writing performance reviews and weekly newsletters for friends. A lifelong diary writer, she kept journals from her extensive travels. After three years in London, she moved to New York City and received her Arts Administration certificate from New York University. A volunteer for both New York City Ballet and American Ballet Theatre, she began contributing performance reviews to *Ballethotline*, a dance website. She had articles published in *Ballet Review, Dance Magazine, Dance and Dancers,* and *Dance Now.* She has transcribed over 100 interviews for the Oral History Project at the Performing Arts Library, and archived photo collections there. Prior to returning to Michigan in 2016, she donated her extensive Nureyev Collection to the Dance Library in New York. She helped organize and provided reports for two international symposiums on Nureyev's career, first in New York in 1997 and the second in St. Petersburg, Russia in 1998.

Visit Author Website at:
www.NancySiftonAuthor.com